Published in the United States of America

This Bramcost Publications edition is an unabridged republication of the rare original work first published in 1956.

www.BramcostPublications.com

ISBN 10: 1-936049-31-7
ISBN 13: 978-1-936049-31-8

Library of Congress Control Number: 2009941963

WESTMORE BEAUTY BOOK

A COMPLETE 1950S GUIDE TO VINTAGE MAKEUP, HAIRSTYLING & BEAUTY TECHNIQUES

By

PERC WESTMORE
Internationally Renowned Beauty Authority and Consultant on Make-Up and Hair-Styling

WALLY WESTMORE
Director of Make-Up and Hair-Styling for Paramount Studios

BUD WESTMORE
Director of Make-Up and Hair-Styling for Universal-International Pictures

FRANK WESTMORE
Director of Make-Up for Independent Motion Pictures

MONT WESTMORE
Make-Up Artist for Universal-International Pictures

Contents

Hair-dressing Saloon,

82, HIGH STREET, NEWPORT, I.W.

(Next Door to the Baptist Chapel)

G. H. WESTMORE

Begs to inform the Inhabitants of Newport and neighbourhood, that he has opened the above premises as a FIRST-CLASS

Hair-dressing, Shaving & Shampooing

establishment, and hopes by careful and prompt attention to business, combined with moderate charges to merit a share of support.

CAREFUL ATTENTION GIVEN TO THE CUTTING OF CHILDREN'S HAIR.

HAIR WORK OF EVERY DESCRIPTION.

Ladies' Combings made up to any convenient design.

A STOCK OF TOILET REQUISITES.

82, HIGH STREET, next door to the Baptist Chapel.

opened 1901.

H. CRAY, PRINTER, NEWPORT.

CHAPTER ONE

Prologue to Beauty

by PERC WESTMORE
Internationally Renowned Beauty Authority and Consultant on Make-Up and Hair-Styling

During the many years we have worked in Hollywood, every member of the Westmore family has been asked repeatedly, "Why don't you write a book?"

Our answers, collectively and individually, have been many and varied.

"We're too busy."

"We still have a lot to learn."

"We will—some day."

Some day has arrived for us; and no single question we've been asked has ever been as challenging as the one we now ask ourselves.

"Why *do* we write this book?"

To this there can be only one answer. If there is one all-embracing fact our combined experience has taught us, it is this: "When a woman gives beauty to herself, she gives it to everyone she meets."

In our work for Hollywood's motion-picture studios, it has been our happy task to help the stars properly showcase their full loveliness. In our salon, in our lecture work and in our other contacts with the public, it has been our added privilege to help women from every walk of life discover and dramatize their full, and often unsuspected, beauty. Every time we have done this, whether it concerned a star or a homemaker, each woman has added to her personal happiness and automatically enriched the lives of those around her as well. And always, each one has reflected some of her new-found happiness back to us.

From serious, scientific, first-hand observation, we know there is no such thing as a woman without loveliness. There are only women without the courage and the beauty know-how needed to bring their loveliest self into being. Our book is written to share this bound-to-produce-beauty knowledge with you.

MY FATHER AND HIS SONS

Sometimes when I, personally, am asked, "How did this business of Hollywood glamour make-up begin?" I am tempted to answer, "It all began in a barber's lather cup, on the Isle of Wight—"

My father, the late George H. Westmore, started his career at the age of 13. He was an assistant to a barber, and it was his job to mix the lather in the mug while the shaving expert honed and stropped the razors. Perhaps it was this early preoccupation with soap and water that years later made my father, the first teacher of make-up in Hollywood, impress upon his sons this maxim: The beginning of facial loveliness is in a bar of pure, mild soap and a jar of cleansing cream.

Dad had established himself as one of the finest hairdressers and beauticians of his day by the time I was born. But it was not until I was 12 years old and we had moved to America that I, in the best Old-World tradition, prepared to follow in my father's footsteps, professionally speaking. One evening Dad, as we had long expected, called his sons together and asked, "Which one of you wants to become a wig-maker?"

I raised my hand and without further ado I took my place at the apprentice's bench early the next morning. There I toiled for many a year before my father considered me a true professional.

In those early years, our family was like a floating cork. My twin brother, Ernie, and I were born in Canterbury, England, as were our brothers Wally and Mont. Bud was born in New Orleans; Frank arrived after we had made our way to Los Angeles; Mont, Jr., the son of our late brother, Mont, is also Los Angeles-born.

WESTWARD HO, THE WESTMORES

When, after a long and circuitous route, we arrived in the then young motion-picture capital, it was Dad's artistry that opened the studio gates to all of us. We were still in our teens when he started training us in screen make-up and hair-styling. Ever the exacting taskmaster, he never ceased to emphasize that one of the abiding principles by which we should work was: "Make yourselves indispensable. Never let them shoot an important scene without you. Powder the star's nose—or snip a stray piece off her hair."

Dad always meant what he said and seldom failed to follow his own advice. I remember that when he worked with Nita Naldi and Rudolph Valentino on a picture, Miss Naldi started the film with hair to her waist. She ended the film with what was perhaps the first wind-blown bob on record. Certainly the first in movies, at any rate.

Basically speaking, however, Dad was completely right; and during the more than 30 years that I was Director of Make-Up and Hair-Styling for Warner Bros. Studios, I watched make-up artists become genuinely indispensable to pictures—and in exactly the degree and serious manner in which my father intended they should and would. The past four years that

I have spent as consultant to women in all professions and walks of life have additionally convinced me that the art of beauty has become indispensable to all women.

Many a fashion in beauty has flourished and faded since the Westmores first entered the field. Rest assured that these ever-changing fashions will always be with us. From our collective experience, however, we know that the timeless, basic requirements for lifetime beauty are individuality and naturalness. This is true beauty, as we see it. And it is exactly this kind of beauty that we will make possible for you in this book. Never forget, moreover, that this is the kind of beauty we have been privileged to bring to hundreds of Hollywood's most glamorous stars.

GLAMOUR IS A GOLDEN WORD

To begin with, we Westmores have had the happy advantage of being an integral part of an industry in which beauty bears a million-dollar price tag. Hollywood believes in the power, practical and personal, of the attractive female. As a consequence, motion-picture studios have spent large sums to help the screen actress to become and remain her most glamorous, influential self.

Thus, over the years we have personally had at our convenience the most fabulous make-up and hair-styling laboratories ever created. All of the facilities and equipment that money could buy were allotted to us by such far-sighted men as Joe Schenck and Darryl F. Zanuck of 20th Century-Fox; Jack Warner of Warner Bros.; Y. Frank Freeman of Paramount; and Edward Mull of Universal Pictures. We have had, and still have, permanent staffs of chemists, cosmetologists, hair-care researchers, sketch artists, and photographers. Nowhere else have so many man-hours of labor been spent to make certain that a nose didn't shine or a kiss smear. Make-up and hair-styling film tests have cost from $5,000 to $10,000 each. It is no exaggeration to say that often a star's golden blonde coiffure would have cost less had it been fashioned of 18-karat gold.

As the scientist used his microscope, we make-up artists used the camera. And, as a proving ground for our efforts, there was the screen itself—a great, merciless, public mirror which, even on the standard-size screen, magnifies the features more than 200 times.

Today, the results of Hollywood's elaborate expenditures all belong to you, the housewife, the business woman, the school-girl. Out of our early experiments have come inventions and innovations now packaged by dozens of manufacturers, to suit virtually every purse—however thin or plump.

All of the tools and ingredients with which to star your own good looks are now packaged for home use—with one exception. Your will-power is the beauty catalyst no one can package. There is no beauty product made, no theory printed that can work a miracle for you, unless *you* will it. Your will-power is yours, and yours alone, to command.

HERE'S TO A LOVELIER YOU!

It would be our greatest pleasure if it were possible to invite each one of you into our salon, or into our studio make-up departments: Since this is impossible, we have pursued a more practical course. On these pages we have set forth all the important facts and time-tested theories our combined Hollywood experience and family tradition in the beauty profession have taught all of us. These can be of direct value to you. Here in this book, as in our salon, we take the time to explore the psychology of beauty. Once we have you in the proper frame of mind, we then subject you to a soul- and mirror-searching questionnaire which puts down in black and white your individual beauty debits and credits. This will give you a real starting point for your beauty build-up. Armed with this knowledge, we can help you chart your face-type simply and graphically, determine your feature attraction, and make your hair play its proper role—a frame for your face. The how and why of make-up magic are set forth for you, and you, with our help, can adapt this knowledge and know-how to your individual make-up needs. Your skin and its care, cosmetics—their use, their value and what they are—all these facts and theories are related to you, the individual. Nor do we overlook beauty parlor tricks for special problems. Figure fascination is given its due, as are the elements—sun, wind and rain—and what they can do to you and for you.

YOUR QUESTIONS, OUR GUIDE

Whether your need be a custom home permanent, a home haircut, a new hair tint, or a more professional-looking manicure or pedicure, the answer to your beauty query is to be found in these pages. We even make it possible for you to set up periodic check-ups, thereby assuring yourself of a continuing beauty program. Beauty bonuses are the sections dealing with eyeglasses, the photographic make-up special, and the appendix devoted to questions selected from some of the thousands we have received. We consider these queries to be 50 of the most-asked beauty questions. In addition, we show you how to use this book long after you've completed the big over-all beauty plan that becomes yours when you turn this page.

In this book you will truly find a beauty program you can use at your convenience at home—today, tomorrow, and for years to come. It is our firm contention that if you can read, you can be more beautiful than you are today, provided, of course, that you add to our gift of beauty the magic catalyst which you alone command—will-power.

With that we say, begin your march to beauty. And never forget, we are with you every step of the way.

CHAPTER TWO

Beauty Is Its Own Psychology

by BUD WESTMORE
Director of Make-Up and Hair-Styling
for Universal-International Pictures

GIVE YOURSELF FULL MEASURE

Beauty begins in the heart.

You have only to look into the smiling face of a happy bride to know this. You have only to look at the face of a woman in love to see a beauty that transcends perfection of feature. This is the kind of beauty possible for you if you accept the fact that the greatest yardstick of your beauty is the love and warmth within you. Without an inner conviction as constructive and strong as this, all our beauty efforts are wasted on you. Without the firm belief that within you there is a potential expression of beauty, you will emerge no more desirable than the flawless of face and feature mannequin you see in a store window.

For the past 20 years, I have been associated with an industry constantly on the alert for a new attraction. It is an industry which actually exists in large measure on its ability to bring to you a never-ending parade of personalities, particularly feminine personalities.

All of these are women who came, just like you, from familiar walks of every-day life. Yet, there is something different and exciting about them when they come before you on the screen. They have had an eyebrow changed or a lip line corrected; a flattering new hair-style has been created to help glamourize them. All of them are wearing glamour, that precious, intangible something which, in my business, is recognized as a manufactured effect. Nonetheless, each one is a woman surprisingly like you. The big difference between these successful and totally glamourous women and you is that they have learned what you are now learning. They have worked to dramatize and demonstrate fully and beautifully the inner and outer loveliness that is theirs.

As an example of this sort of inner projection, you may remember the Academy Award performance of Jane Wyman in "Johnny Belinda." In her role of the deaf-mute girl, Jane had no spoken lines with which to express herself, still her emotions reached you as strongly as if she had put them into words. It's interesting to know that in preparation for this role, Miss Wyman lived for two weeks with her ears stuffed with cotton. For a while, she actually was a girl hearing nothing but the "voices" of her heart and mind.

ACT THE ROLE OF A BEAUTY

You, too, have these voices within you. They can be put to practical and helpful use, if you teach them the right things to say. Try it sometime —tell yourself, "I *am somebody.* I am lovely to look at. I am charming to know. I have beauty, both inner and outer." Keep telling yourself this—keep a beautiful picture of yourself in your mind, and react as a self-assured woman who knows she looks her best.

It's totally impossible to hold this mental attitude without feeling a physical uplift as well. Your head will raise itself, your eyes will gain awareness, your smile will come more easily, your walk will take on purpose and grace. Try it—and prove what I say.

Among your acquaintances, I am sure, there is some woman who, by harboring ill thoughts of herself, actually makes herself homely. She has an idea that her mouth is not a pretty one and she cannot smile for fear of calling attention to it. Or her nose is too large, she thinks, and she lives behind this nose instead of living with it. The eyes and the mouth, which could overrule the nose with their color and merriment, never get a chance. Perhaps she despairs because her years are showing, and she forgets that the only really aged countenance is the one fallen into dullness and monotony. In each case she is building a barrier for herself, using her "bad" feature as an obstruction to keep the real expression of beauty from coming through.

DO YOU KNOW YOUR FACE VALUE?

You are continually being photographed by the human eye, the fastest camera in the world. It takes your picture, the line and design of your appearance, and develops and prints it upon the observer's mind in sensitive detail. Yet, in spite of its magic, the eye cannot capture your personality unless you cooperate. The awareness you want to arouse in the beholder must be projected to him by you, and it must show—first of all—in your face.

Your face is more than a collection of features. Your face is *you.* A thousand others may duplicate your figure measurements. A relative may have your exact tone of voice. But should some other human being appear with more than a reasonable facsimile of your facial features, some expression—or lack of it—will still tell your friends they are looking at a stranger.

All the best you have to give must first be expressed through your face. All you hope to gain must be won by it. Your face is where a lover sees his first response; where your husband looks to find the understanding and inspiration he needs; where your child looks for love and comfort when unhappy or frightened. Your employer hires the intelligence and trustworthiness he sees there; your companions are drawn by the warmth and gaiety they find there.

Since all the world must first take you at face value, never under-value that face. There is almost no limit to what your face can do for you—or what you can do for your face.

For each of us there is a choice. It is up to you to determine which way you prefer to look at life. "One man looks into his cup and sees it half empty; another looks and sees it half full." You can see how much you lack, and let what you do possess go unused and unrealized. Or you can see how much is already there and take hope in the knowledge that it would be only half a job to fill the cup to the brim. This choice is emphatically yours when you look into your mirror and see your physical attributes or your lack of them. Your potential loveliness, it might be said, is the measure of the difference between what you have done and what you can do, beauty-wise.

CONFESSIONS—BEAUTY NEVER HAPPENS BY ACCIDENT

You spend 24 hours a day growing older. Why not spend 30 minutes a day staying young?

Beauty is a way of life and it can last all your life. It is a positive program of self-improvement. It is a program rich in rewards, and all that it asks of you is that you approach life from the "do" angle instead of from the "don't." Your very first, all-important "do" is—*do it today!*

The beauty bonus you can give yourself right now is an honest, soul- and mirror-searching check-up on the You the world sees. Do this by completing our beauty questionnaire.

Be honest—this is our only warning. If you hedge, you cheat yourself, no one else.

HOW TO COMPUTE YOUR BEAUTY I.Q.

It is our considered opinion that an *easy* test is a little like a half-hearted answer to a serious question. No one benefits. This test, therefore, is undoubtedly more demanding than any you have given yourself.

Unlike many tests, this questionnaire is designed to test your whole beauty I.Q. This takes you to account in terms of what you know, what you do, what you fail to do. It also approaches your problem in terms of you, the individual. Because we have little patience with the flawless-of-face-and-figure beauty who contributes nothing except her beauty, we have made this a test of your all-around beauty knowledge and know-how. The chances are that your score on this test may be lower than it has been on other such tests. This is as it should be. This test forces you to see yourself as you are today.

One last cheering note. Once you have mastered the information in this book, you will be able to answer every question in this test correctly—and effortlessly. You will also be more beautiful than ever.

YOUR BEAUTY QUESTIONNAIRE

1. Are you more attractive and more beautifully groomed today than you were five years ago? YES ☐ NO ☐
2. Have you "worked at" and succeeded in maintaining a normal weight for your height and age throughout the past five years? YES ☐ NO ☐
3. Do you set aside a specific amount of time each day for a rigidly adhered to beauty regime? YES ☐ NO ☐
4. Have you modified this regime during the past five years to take into account your varying beauty needs and your ever-on-the-increase beauty know-how? YES ☐ NO ☐
5. Do you understand and accept the relationship between diet and beauty and general good health and beauty? YES ☐ NO ☐
6. Will you give up certain foods if you find they make it impossible for you to keep your weight normal or if you find that, beauty-wise, you tend to react unfavorably to specific foods? YES ☐ NO ☐
7. Is your individual beauty plan in keeping with your personality and way of life? YES ☐ NO ☐
8. Are you mindful of the need for a regular beauty check-up and do you give yourself a thorough beauty check-up at least once every six months? YES ☐ NO ☐
9. When and if your beauty regime fails to produce the desired results, can you truthfully say it is because of your need for more beauty know-how and not because of lack of persistence or will-power? YES ☐ NO ☐
10. Have you acquired at least five beauty skills—such as the ability to give yourself a professional-looking home permanent, a beautiful set, hair cut, etc.? YES ☐ NO ☐
11. Do you accept the need to look, think, act and feel like a beauty if you wish to be accepted as a true beauty? YES ☐ NO ☐
12. Are you ever on the alert for new ways to help showcase your particular type of beauty? YES ☐ NO ☐
13. Are you willing to share your beauty knowledge with your friends? YES ☐ NO ☐

14. Do you realize that beauty today is often more a question of know-how than money? YES ☐ NO ☐

15. Have you set a beauty standard for yourself that is truly indicative of your real beauty potential? (This is no time to be modest, please note. This is an important question and should be answered thoughtfully.) YES ☐ NO ☐

16. Are you content in the knowledge that your beauty can be individual and rare and, as a result, as attention-getting as that of any woman, be she movie star or society beauty? YES ☐ NO ☐

17. Do you know how to make beauty work for you in every sphere of your life? YES ☐ NO ☐

18. Do you make a point of appearing at your best even when you are at home alone? YES ☐ NO ☐

19. Do you keep abreast of the developments in the world of beauty—as well as the world in which you live? YES ☐ NO ☐

20. Can you truthfully say that you are a more interesting (as well as better groomed) person today than you were five years ago? YES ☐ NO ☐

21. Do you know your own face-type—in terms of beauty? YES ☐ NO ☐

22. Do you know and follow the beauty and make-up principles applying to your face-type? YES ☐ NO ☐

23. Are you aware of the magic that make-up can work for you? YES ☐ NO ☐

24. Do you apply your make-up carefully and not rush through it just because you think you've mastered the basics of make-up? YES ☐ NO ☐

25. Do you vary your make-up to suit the occasion as well as the time of day? YES ☐ NO ☐

26. Do you know exactly what make-up can and cannot do for you? YES ☐ NO ☐

27. Do you know your good points and bad points? YES ☐ NO ☐

28. Do you (as a result of the knowledge of what make-up can and cannot do for you) take full advantage of its corrective powers to minimize your weak points and accentuate your good ones? YES ☐ NO ☐

29. Do you also understand and employ the principles of highlight and shadow in make-up to dramatize your beauty? YES ☐ NO ☐

30. Do you always make a point of applying make-up on a scrupulously clean face? YES ☐ NO ☐

31. Do you always remove all of your make-up before going to bed? YES ☐ NO ☐

32. Does your make-up last? YES ☐ NO ☐

33. Do you know the characteristics and purpose of each of the beauty products you use from face powder to creams and special preparations for particular beauty problems? YES ☐ NO ☐

34. Do you budget for beauty? Will you give up some luxuries, if necessary, to make a proper beauty budget possible? YES ☐ NO ☐

35. Do you try to buy as many products as possible from one line of cosmetics? YES ☐ NO ☐

36. Do you give every product you buy a real test and make certain that you follow the manufacturer's instructions to the letter? YES ☐ NO ☐

37. Do you know how to buy cosmetics and are you certain you are not soft-talked into buying something simply because it is new? YES ☐ NO ☐

38. Do you know your skin-type? YES ☐ NO ☐

39. Do you give new beauty procedures a fair and conscientious trial? YES ☐ NO ☐

40. Do you knowingly adapt your buying of cosmetics and creams to the particular requirements of your skin-type? YES ☐ NO ☐

41. Do you know how to enhance your skin color with the help of make-up? YES ☐ NO ☐

42. Do you know when a skin problem can be effectively corrected by you and when you should seek professional advice? YES ☐ NO ☐

43. When you have a skin problem, do you attempt to correct it immediately? YES ☐ NO ☐

44. Do you keep your hands off your face? YES ☐ NO ☐

45. Do you absolutely and finally refuse to squeeze pimples or blackheads? YES ☐ NO ☐

46. Do you know the causes of blackheads, whiteheads, enlarged pores? YES ☐ NO ☐

47. Do you faithfully cleanse, lubricate and stimulate your complexion each and every day? YES ☐ NO ☐

48. Have you also learned that no matter how tired you may be at night you must take the time to perform your needed, basic beauty routine? YES ☐ NO ☐

49. Do you accept the fact that homeliness is virtually nothing more than a bad habit? YES ☐ NO ☐

50. Do you know the right and wrong way to apply creams? YES ☐ NO ☐

51. Do you protect your complexion with protective cosmetics? YES ☐ NO ☐

52. Do you know the beauty value of eliminating mugging habits, and have you checked yours lately? YES ☐ NO ☐

53. Do you realize that a change of hair color can sometimes work beauty wonders? YES ☐ NO ☐

54. Do you realize that gray hair can be beautiful? YES ☐ NO ☐

55. Do you accept the fact that you can tint your hair at home successfully—provided that you follow the manufacturer's instructions carefully and apply the tint with some skill? YES ☐ NO ☐

56. Would you know how to pick a flattering color for yourself if you once decided to tint your hair? YES ☐ NO ☐

57. Would you (or do you if you already tint your hair) make the prescribed predisposition and patch tests? (You make them before you use the product for the first time and, for your own sake, at regular intervals even after you have used a product for a time.) YES ☐ NO ☐

58. Do you understand what is involved in terms of color and your hair if you decide to make a drastic change in color, particularly if you plan to switch from brunette to pale blonde? YES ☐ NO ☐

59. Do you know the difference between a tint, dye and rinse? YES ☐ NO ☐

60. Do you know whether or not it is advisable to use a tint over a henna pack? YES ☐ NO ☐

61. Do you know what information you should give a beauty salon operator if you have tinted your hair at home but want a professional touch-up, etc.? YES ☐ NO ☐

62. Do you know how to give yourself a home permanent? YES ☐ NO ☐

63. Do you know whether or not you are giving yourself the right kind of permanent wave? YES ☐ NO ☐

64. Do you know that there is a basic hair-style that is most flattering for your individual face-type? YES ☐ NO ☐

65. Do you know that you can cut your hair at home yourself and do it very successfully provided that you take the time, learn the basic procedure and use the proper tools? YES ☐ NO ☐

66. Do you shampoo your hair once a week (unless you have an unusually oily condition, naturally)? YES ☐ NO ☐

67. Do you brush your hair regularly and do you know the proper way to brush your hair? YES ☐ NO ☐

68. Do you know how to use hair-styling for feature correction? YES ☐ NO ☐

69. Is your posture a beauty and health asset? YES ☐ NO ☐

70. Do you exercise regularly to keep your body toned up? YES ☐ NO ☐

71. Do you know why it is considered advisable to wait a while after you have exercised before taking a hot tub or shower? YES ☐ NO ☐

72. Do you make certain to wait until two hours after eating before beginning your exercise period? YES ☐ NO ☐

73. Do you know that exercise can work wonders in terms of measurements while diet is primarily concerned with changing your weight and that the two together produce fine figure results? YES ☐ NO ☐

74. Is your personal daintiness score beyond reproach? YES ☐ NO ☐

75. Do you use a deodorant regularly? YES ☐ NO ☐

76. Do you bathe or shower daily? YES ☐ NO ☐

77. Do you keep your legs, underarms and face free from superfluous, unsightly hair? YES ☐ NO ☐

78. Do you have a series of beauty tricks and pick-ups to help you over emergency hurdles? YES ☐ NO ☐

79. Do you put a fresh puff in your compact daily and do you make certain your handbag always contains the beauty essentials needed for make-up pick-ups? YES ☐ NO ☐

80. Do you include facials in your beauty program? YES ☐ NO ☐

81. Do you realize that you can wear a denture without in any way detracting from your personal beauty? YES ☐ NO ☐

82. Do you know how to make eye-frames a beauty asset? (Same principles apply to sunglasses, so this question applies to everyone.) YES ☐ NO ☐

83. Do you keep your hands at their prettiest and wear gloves when working in the garden, doing housework, laundry, etc.? YES ☐ NO ☐

84. Do you have all the essential beauty aids you need at home and at the office? YES ☐ NO ☐

85. Do you know why eyebrows are considered the expression marks of the face? YES ☐ NO ☐

86. Do you give your feet their due—in terms of health and beauty? YES ☐ NO ☐

87. Have you worked out a series of safety valves, as it were, to keep you on an even keel emotionally, physically and mentally? YES ☐ NO ☐

88. Have you added beauty to your office, home and the world in which you live because of your own beauty and way of life? YES ☐ NO ☐

89. Have you done something truly generous for someone lately? YES ☐ NO ☐

90. Do you set aside a few minutes each day in which to relax? YES ☐ NO ☐

91. Do you give your eyes proper beauty care and do you conscientiously protect their health? YES ☐ NO ☐

92. Do you change your beauty with the season? (Fresh, suntanned in summer, clear-skinned for winter elegance, etc.) YES ☐ NO ☐

93. Do you make color work for you in every respect—fashion, cosmetics, nail polish, etc.? YES ☐ NO ☐

94. Do you study your mannerisms enough to know whether or not you need to eliminate awkward poses, talking with your hands or similar distracting habits? YES ☐ NO ☐

95. Do you know how to make up and pose for a flattering picture—even a seemingly candid one? YES ☐ NO ☐

96. Do you have a medical check-up once a year? YES ☐ NO ☐

97. Do you have a dental check-up once every six months? YES ☐ NO ☐

98. Do you know the beauty value of a smile and a pleasant disposition? YES ☐ NO ☐

99. Do you realize that there are several beauty stages in any woman's life and that every woman passes through all of these stages—whether or not she chooses to admit it? YES ☐ NO ☐

100. Do you have the good sense to act your age—and enjoy it? YES ☐ NO ☐

Each of the 100 questions counts 1. Add up your "yes" answers to find your rating.

Rating	*What It Means to You*
100	You should have written this book—or you studied it before taking this test!
90-99	Have you given yourself the benefit of the doubt all too often?
85-89	You must be the town's most beautiful woman.
80-84	You've improved on Nature—and you can do even better.
75-79	If you've learned this much, why stop here?
70-74	You are well on the right road to beauty, but you still need help.
60-69	You haven't even begun to realize your full potential, although you are probably considered an attractive woman.
50-59	You need to be more serious about the business of you and your beauty I.Q.
0-49	It's a good thing you bought this book!

PLOT YOUR OWN TIME CHART

With the results of your questionnaire at hand, you no longer have any doubt about the *why* of your beauty program or the direction it needs to take. Since this is true, we want you to take the next step on the road to improvement—start a time chart. This is important from two standpoints. First, you must make up your mind that from this day forward your beauty program is a daily program. A day missed is difficult if not impossible to reclaim. A do-or-die persistence in the execution of your daily beauty ritual is as important as the ritual itself. Even if you give yourself only 30 minutes a day to keep young, zealously claim those 30 minutes for yourself—come what may. Second, it is obvious that no less than once a week you must allow extra time for the specials: the facial, the shampoo, the complete manicure and pedicure, and the other beauty tricks that require extra care and time and should not or cannot be done daily. Consult the daily Beauty Progress Chart, Appendix C.

We repeat: The care and nourishment of a glowing complexion, a luxuriant and well-kept head of hair, and a trim and buoyant figure require constant, daily effort. You can have loveliness, if you want loveliness more than you want the things that are keeping you from it. Debits can become beauty credits, for homeliness is only a bad habit.

CHAPTER THREE

Your Face-Type— What Does It Mean to You?

by FRANK WESTMORE
Director of Make-Up for
Independent Motion Pictures

As the youngest of the Westmore brothers, and, therefore, the most recent to engage in make-up and hair-styling as a profession, I have had many rewarding experiences. Not the least of these has been going on tour with the motion pictures I have worked on, and meeting beauty-eager women all over the country. Especially gratifying has been the fact that one of the questions most often asked me by women everywhere is, "What is my face-type?" Another is, "Why is it so essential for me to know my face-type?"

Both are important questions. And if you are one of those rare individuals who has never asked yourself either of these questions before answering our questionnaire, we know you asked them once your beauty score was computed.

One of the basic reasons for knowing your face-type is that it automatically indicates to you the kind of make-up you need. This, in turn, indicates the type of hair-do most flattering to you and suggests how to adapt your new beauty knowledge to your particular needs.

The theory of the Seven Face-Types was created by my brothers in 1930. It was designed to serve as a basic guide for make-up and hair-styling artists.

In the early days of screen make-up there were, unbelievable as it may seem today, no known beauty frames of reference, no beauty charts, and no measurements for proportionate features. In real life, a slight irregularity can make a face individual and interesting. On the screen, where everything is magnified many times, irregularity usually becomes distortion.

Wrong make-up and incorrect hair-styling increase the distortion. Therefore, we are hypercritical of over-all balance and proportion. If there is any feature predominant over the others, it becomes a disturbing factor.

In the 'thirties, movies were still a rapidly growing industry. Since the Westmores founded the first Hollywood studio make-up departments, it was necessary to train others in this new art of make-up and hair-styling. For this purpose, there had to be some practical, time-tested procedure which would make it easy for a star who was lovely and natural-looking in one film to appear equally lovely and natural-looking in succeeding films.

THE "SEVEN FACES" THEORY

From my brothers' researches in physiognomy, they knew that the human face ordinarily falls into one of seven shapes: Oval, Oblong, Round, Square, Triangle, Inverted Triangle, or Diamond. (Occasionally, a face is a combination of two of these primary shapes.) With this as a basic means of classification, they worked out a series of make-up and hair-styling principles by which each type could be given its full proportion of symmetry and beauty.

Since then it has become accepted Hollywood procedure for an actress to be "face-charted" for her first film. Her face shape and the special treatment for her features are carefully recorded. Her hair-style may change from picture to picture, but the basic contour of her head—putting fullness where she needs it or creating the illusion of added length to disguise a long neck, etc.—remains the same. This basic chart becomes a kind of "frame of reference" for her particular beauty.

The things the actress learns about herself in all this scientific procedure, she uses to advantage in her personal make-up and off-screen appearance. Because it was felt that every woman could likewise profit by a proper appraisal of her own features, the first Face-Type Theory was published in the Hearst papers in 1935 by my brother, Perc Westmore. We still consider face-measurement one of the most important lessons we give you in this book or in a personal consultation.

THE OVAL IS THE IDEAL—WHY?

The oval has long been recognized as Nature's purest, most perfectly balanced design. Every one of us begins life in egg-shape, in the ovum. Our entire body—arms, torso, legs—is a series of elongated segments of ovoid curve. It is easy then, to understand why an oval face is accepted as the most desirable balance for the rest of the body. It also explains why an artist, when drawing a face, first sketches an oval. He then adds features that fit within it or join to it.

There is nothing un-beautiful about a face that is not oval. In fact, every type has its own personality. Loretta Young is an Oblong; Claudette Colbert is a Diamond. Surely no one would want to destroy the distinctiveness of either of these two stars. Typing faces, therefore, is not for the purpose of trying to make every face look alike. Neither is it done to try to make every woman a carbon copy of some movie star.

To know your face-type is to know how to compliment and harmonize your appearance rather than distort it. Once you are aware of where your facial contour deviates from the oval outline, you automatically become aware of what is needed to increase the attractiveness of your face.

For example, during the many years I have worked in Hollywood, I have had the pleasure of doing the make-up for Ann Sheridan on several pictures. She has a square-jawed contour, which is a distinctive characteristic of her beauty. For this very reason, surprisingly enough, I always avoided doing anything that would emphasize this characteristic when making her up. To overemphasize such a characteristic would have tended to give her a heavy-faced or masculine look. By mastering the Face-Type Theory, Ann learned to use make-up and hairlines to keep her facial outlines soft, curved and feminine looking.

OVER-ALL BALANCE AND HARMONY

If you want to build a house, you must first have a well-thought-out plan. You wouldn't start by just nailing one board to another, helter-skelter. The structure must have balance. Its various components have to be in proportion, one to the other. Established rules of straight-line, curve and angle must be followed to build your house so that it will create the harmonious effect you desire. To achieve this desired effect (and have a soundly built house as well) there is a very considerable amount of serious calculation and planning to be done before you even think of buying the first plank of wood.

It is every bit as necessary to "floor-plan" your own appearance when you are building toward beauty. Your features get their proportion one from the other. Your face has high planes and low planes. These must be considered for harmony or contrast to each other.

Whether you are building toward beauty, building a house or building toward the successful achievement of another goal, there are certain preliminary calculations which must be made ahead of time if you want to attain a happy, rewarding and harmonious result.

Once you have personally gone through the process of measuring your facial construction, you will have a new and revealing view of its possibilities.

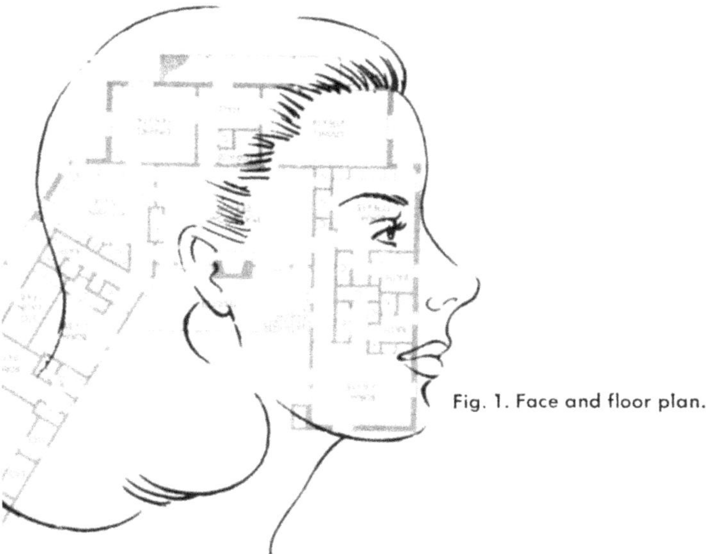

Fig. 1. Face and floor plan.

MEASURING YOUR FACE TO DETERMINE YOUR FACE-TYPE

For this analysis, you need a clear-cut outline of your face, unhampered by hair at the sides of the face or on top of the head. It takes only a minute to prepare a skull-cap from an old nylon stocking, as illustrated in Fig. 2. Be sure to cut the stocking top long enough to contain all your hair, and tie the end with a rubber-band or string. If your hair is heavy, piling it upward will elongate the face, so pull it straight back, pony-tail fashion, and secure it with a rubber-band or bobby pins before putting on the cap.

Remove all your make-up. Rouge and lipstick do illusionary things to your face. For the analysis, we want "the naked truth" as in Fig. 3.

Fig. 2. Nylon cap.

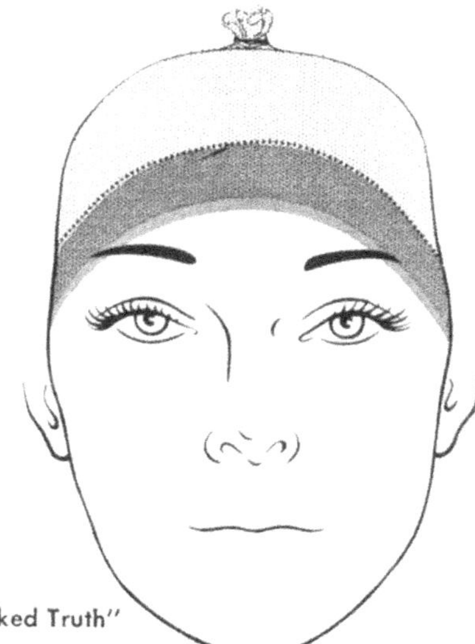

Fig. 3. Nylon cap—"The Naked Truth"

Prepare a sheet of paper so that you have an oblong 9 inches long and 7 inches wide. Draw vertical and horizontal lines as shown by ruler measurements in Figs. 5 and 6. Your measurement chart is now ready.

Trace the caliper from the page opposite and, using carbon paper, transfer the tracing to a piece of cardboard. Cut out the caliper. Fasten the two sections of the caliper together with a thumbtack. These two sections have to be movable in the center in order to use the caliper properly for measuring.

Now, use the caliper, a ruler, and the sheet of paper to record your face measurements in accordance with the following procedure:

(A) Place the two points of the caliper on each of your temples, right at the hairline. Take the caliper away from the face, measure the distance between its two points, and mark this on your ruled sheet of paper, as illustrated by the letter A. See Fig. 8.

(B) Now take your cheek measurement. Place the caliper at the high point of the cheekbone line; extend the points of the caliper all the way back to your ear. Chart this measurement at the letter B. See Fig. 9.

(C) Measure the widest point of your jawline (your jawbone) wherever it occurs. Chart it at the letter C. See Fig. 10.

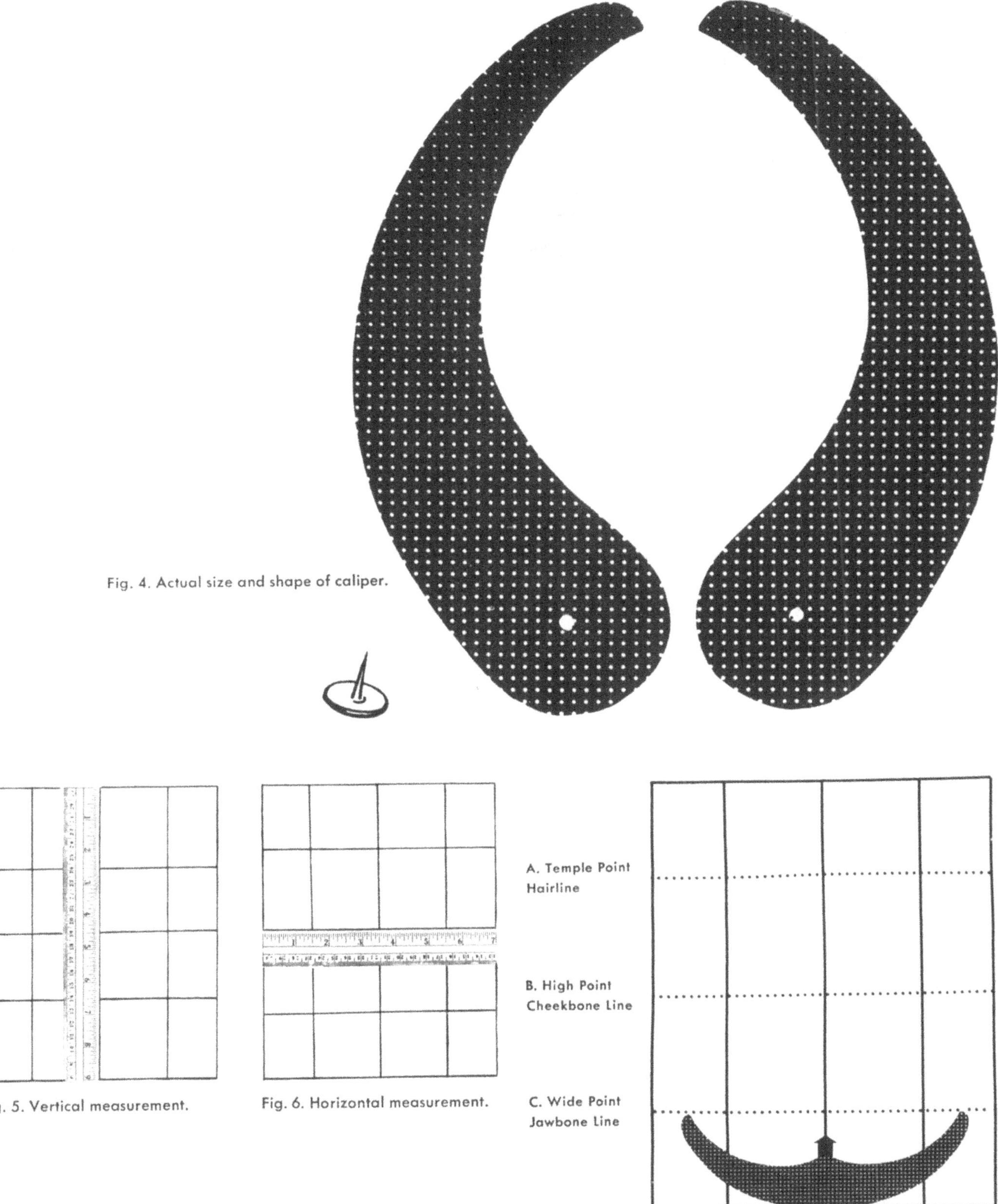

Fig. 4. Actual size and shape of caliper.

Fig. 5. Vertical measurement.

Fig. 6. Horizontal measurement.

Fig. 7. Caliper measurements.

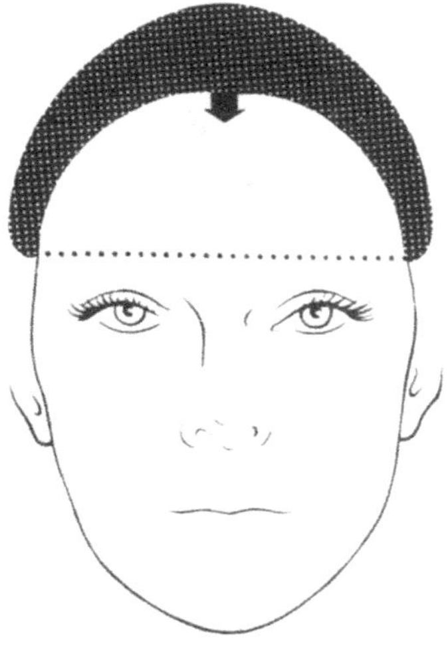

Fig. 8. Temple point hairline caliper measurement.

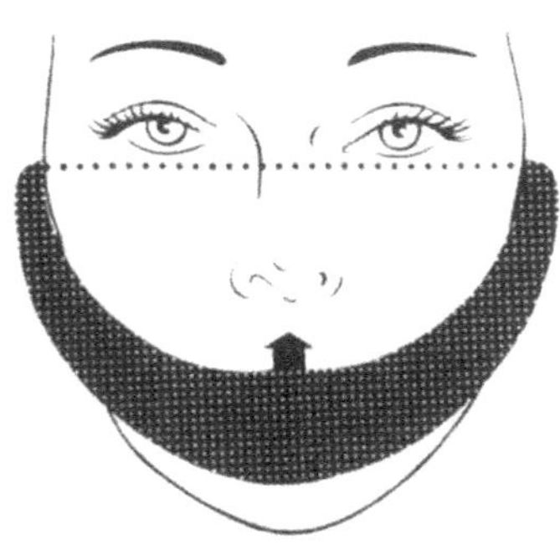

Fig. 9. High point cheekbone line caliper measurement.

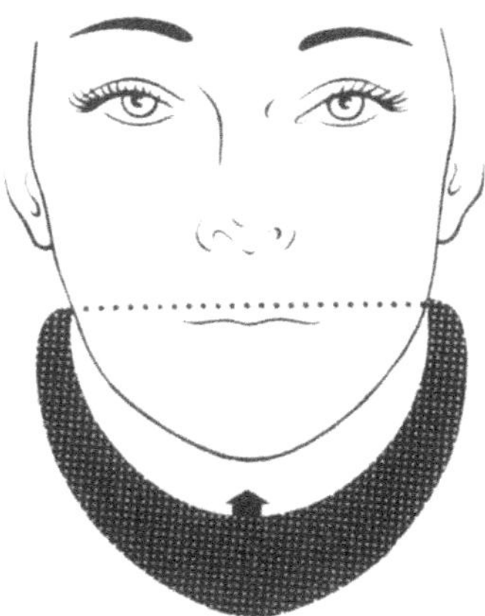

Fig. 10. Wide point jawbone line caliper measurement.

(D) Draw straight lines between the measurements on the paper, as illustrated, and you will have the geometrical figure which indicates your face-type. See Fig. 11.

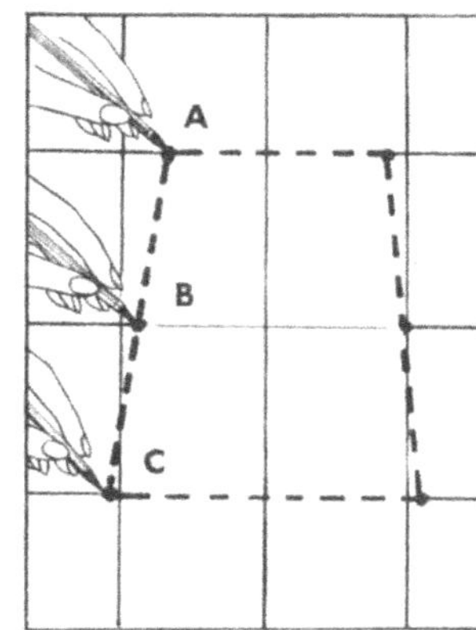

Fig. 11. Caliper example—composite type.

YOUR OWN FACE-TYPE—ITS GENERAL OUTLINE FOR ATTRACTIVENESS

Through this close self-study and measurement, you have discovered details that tell you what corrective methods you need. You can easily see where flatness could stand more curve. This is fine, but don't get ahead of your beauty plan by trying to correct these problems right this minute. You'll learn later how to make these corrections with step-by-step instruction in make-up and hair-styling.

What you need to do most right now is to identify your own face-type beyond a doubt. For this reason, consider and carefully check the characteristics of the geometrical forms after which they are named.

OVAL. Lucky egg-head, you're the "ideal" if: Your forehead is slightly wider than your chin. Your cheekbone width is approximately two-thirds the length of your face (from hairline to chin). Your cheeks and jawline taper gently off to a curved chin. It's possible for you to make mistakes in make-up or hair-style—but it's not easy! Chances are that the rest of your features and figure are correspondingly symmetrical. You have no strict "don'ts" in line or style. Just refuse to push your luck, and make good taste your guide.

Fig. 12. OVAL. Forehead is slightly wider than chin.

OBLONG. Your face is a long and narrow one. Oblongs do not vary too much from perfect-oval measurements in width and length of face—the difference comes in the long, thin side-planes of your cheeks, the angular jaw, and the straight or possibly pointed chin. There is a lack of curve from top to bottom. A high forehead and thinly padded facial bones are your characteristics. Curve, fullness and foreshortening will be your aims in

Fig. 13. OBLONG. Long narrow face with hollow cheeks.

make-up and hair-style. You can wear a sophisticated hair-style if you leave the side-planes of the face exposed. Don't cover and narrow the cheeks with dips and curls. White stand-up or softening collar effects will shorten your long, thin neck. Avoid long, pendulous earrings. The Oblong sometimes gets added height in a high forehead and a long chin. Concentrate on giving a foreshortened effect to overlong features.

ROUND. Consider the form of a circle—large or small. Yours is a face not too much longer than it is broad. You have a rounded hairline. Your greatest width is at your cheeks, which sustain their fullness right down to the jawbone, where your face rounds off into a short, full chin. This might be the result of being overweight. Curve is lovely, but it's our objective to make sure that it's not overdone. Nature, who generally does a pretty good follow-up on whatever she's started, has no doubt repeated the rounded pattern in your eyebrows and mouth, and given you a short, full neck. In hair-frame and make-up, you must always avoid circular patterns such as small, round curls, circular rouge application, etc. In dress, you'll eliminate round earrings, high, rounded collars, and so on. Straightened lines, an illusion of height and length—these are your objectives.

SQUARE. A square is a circle with corners. Yours, too, is a face almost as broad as it is long. Your face widths (although slightly wider at the cheekbone) differ very little from each other. You are distinguished from the Round type by a straight hairline and the fact that your generous jawbones have an angular form rather than a rounded one, jutting rather decidedly to a square-bottomed chin. Squareness is generally associated with strong character and individuality. You no doubt have very definite eyebrows, nose, and other features. For feminine purposes, we will soften these angular outlines, diminish any heavy-jawed look. Never do small things with a square face. Small mouth, small curls, small earrings, or small frilly collars are not for you since they increase the size of your face. Gentle curves are your fashion helps. Softly rounded shoulders and deep necklines give needed length to your neck.

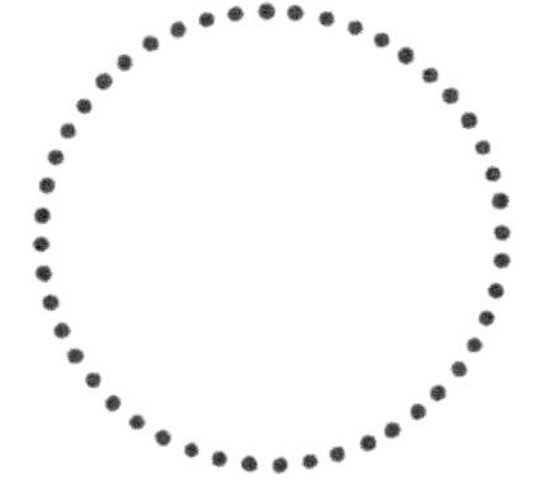

Fig. 14. ROUND. Round hairline; round chinline.

Fig. 15. SQUARE. Square hairline; square jawline.

Fig. 18. DIAMOND. Narrow forehead; broad jawline; narrow chin.

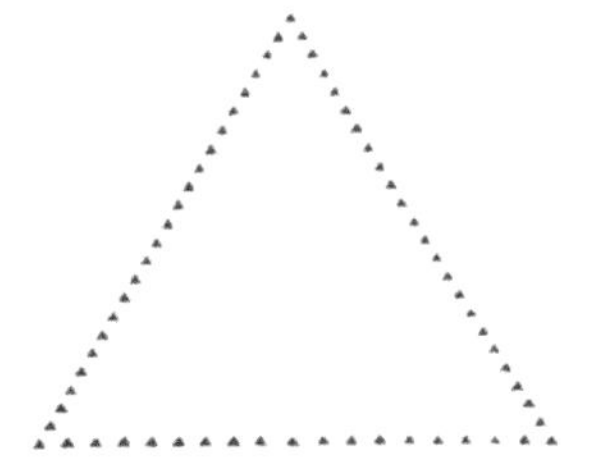

Fig. 16. TRIANGLE. Narrow forehead; wide jaw and chinline.

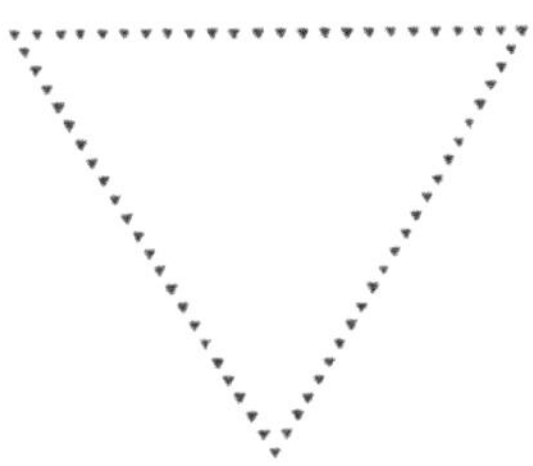

Fig. 17. INVERTED TRIANGLE. Wide forehead; narrow chinline.

TRIANGLE. In a full face, the Triangle is sometimes called pear-shaped. Your greatest width come in the lower section of the face. You taper upward, slightly narrower at the cheek, narrowest at the forehead. You may have a low and close hairline, which narrows the brow even more. For you, avoid hair-styling or accessories that crowd the temple. You can wear large, off-the-face, or wide-brimmed hats. Long V-necklines will draw emphasis away from the heaviness of your lower face. Never wear choker necklaces; try pendants on a chain.

INVERTED TRIANGLE. This means just what it says; you taper downwards. Your greatest width is at the forehead. The jawline is narrow and the chin is small. In hairdress and make-up, add fullness to your small lower face. Avoid anything top-heavy looking in hats and hair-dos. Large earrings and frilly, full collars to frame your neck are good.

DIAMOND. The diamond is sometimes a girl's best friend. There are small piquant Diamonds, and large, broad ones, both diamonds in the rough! The characteristic of each is extra width at the cheekbones (more than two-thirds the length of the face). Forehead and chin narrow off; hairline and jaw measurements are approximately the same. The extra-wide cheekbones may be definitely pointed in appearance, or may extend into a broad, full-fleshed cheek. For both large and small Diamonds, stay away from straight horizontal lines in hats, collars, anything running parallel to the width of the cheeks. For a small, thin Diamond, also avoid anything that will give a point to the narrow forehead or chin. Gentle curves are needed; have rounded lines everywhere, especially in the upper and lower parts of the face.

CHAPTER FOUR

Your Feature Attraction

At this point in your face analysis, it is a comfort to know that one of the world's acknowledged rarities is a human being perfect in every feature. It is told that when a famous artist painted his Galatea he could find no model who, all by herself, could fulfill his idea of the female divine. He searched the streets, then finally took the components of his portrait out of his own mind: A mouth he had seen and could not forget; a pair of eyes he had met in the market place; the proudly held head of one woman; the "hair softly curling at the nape" of another.

The significance of this story to us is that each one of the women the artist had seen had at least one feature she had used to such advantage as to make herself unforgettable to this searcher for beauty. If she failed to meet absolute perfection, it is obvious that she either didn't know or didn't let herself care. Where she walked, she went with color and spirit, a specialist in her own type of fascination. You can do the same.

Whether a specific feature is perfect or problem-type, there is a make-up trick to "accentuate the positive and eliminate the negative" qualities of each. We measure the features for the same reason we measured the contours of the face. What we want to know now is the specific relationship the features have to each other.

For this purpose, use a straight-on photograph of yourself. It has to be a picture in which you look straight at the camera. If your head is either tilted or bent forward, the proportions will be distorted. If you don't have such a photo, use a mirror and a ruler. It sometimes helps you to get the measurements more accurately if you close one eye as you hold the ruler straight in front of you as you stand before the mirror.

RULE OF THREE

In Fig. 19, we have divided the face into three horizontal bands. One runs across the forehead, one across the nose area, and one across the mouth and chin area.

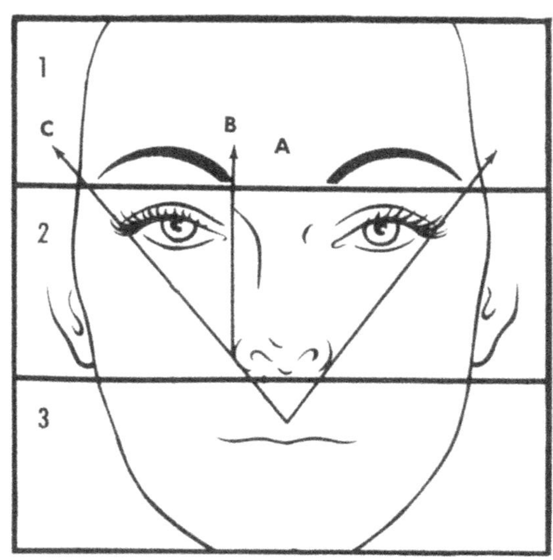

Fig. 19. Use of photograph in checking measurements.

In the proportionate face, the following distances are equal to each other: (1) The distance from the hairline down to the eyebrow line. (2) The distance from the eyebrow line to the end of the nose. (3) The distance from under the nose to the tip of the chin. This should settle once and for all the question of the height of your forehead, the length of your nose, or the shortness of your chin.

EYES

Take your ruler and measure from the top of your head to the tip of your chin. Your eyes should be at the half-point of this distance—in the center of your face.

The width between the eyes (across the top of the nose) should be equal to the length of the eyes themselves. To state this another way, the distance between the eyes should be the equivalent of the width of one eye. If you're working with a photograph, you'll note that the face, at eye-height, is about five eye-lengths across.

EYEBROWS

The perfect eyebrow follows the same basic contour as that of the eyelid. The distance between the eyebrow and the eye should be the same as the size of the eye when fully opened.

The eyebrow should start on a line even with the outside wall of the nostril (B), and it should extend just slightly past the outer corner of the eye so that if you drew a line down from the end of the brow to the end of the eye and down to the nostril (C), it would form about a 45-degree angle, as in Fig. 19.

Hint: Eyebrows are great beautifiers. Widening them, or pencilling them to make them appear closer, effectively minimizes the attention a faulty nose usually attracts. For other hints and added details, see Eyebrows for Feature Correction, as well as studying Fig. 20.

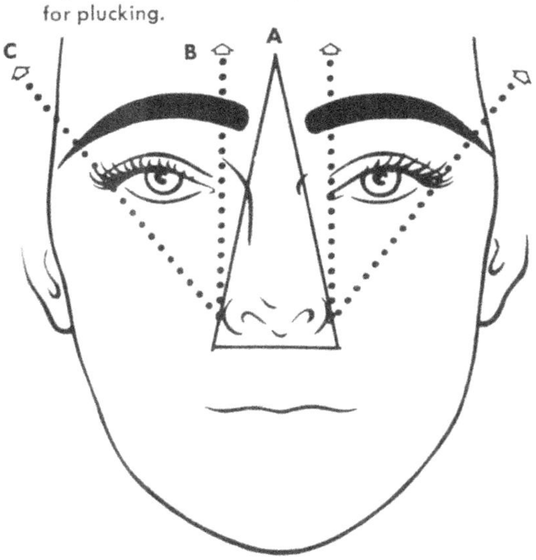

Fig. 20. How to measure eyebrows for plucking.

C B A

Fig. 21. Corrected eyebrow.

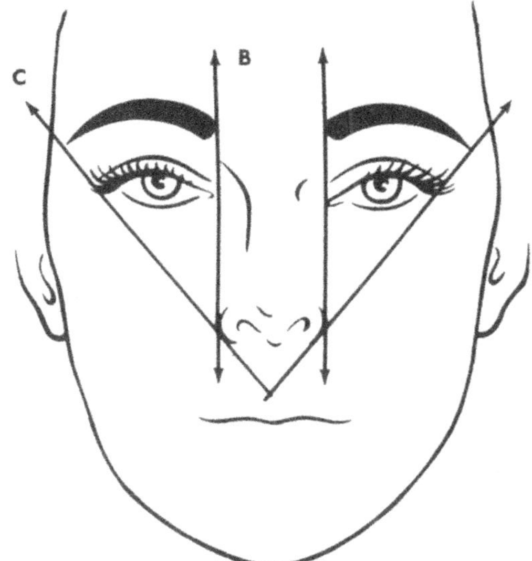

NOSE

Certainly you already know whether or not you have a large or small nose. The length of it (from where it joins the forehead close to the arch of the upper eyebone to its base, A) should be equal to the height of the forehead. The absolutely perfect nose has the nostrils running horizontally back to the base. Some noses have a tilted tip with the nostrils running downward. This increases the over-all length. If the base of the nose is halfway between your eyebrows and the end of your chin, you're still in good proportion.

The Grecian nose, running straight down in a perpendicular line from forehead to chin, was perfect only to the Greeks. The physically perfect nose should have a slight hollow where it joins the forehead and it should stand out at an angle to the face. In profile, the under part of the nose is allowed to be a third of the nose length.

The outside edges of the nose at the bottom should line up in a straight line with the inside corners of the eyes, as in Fig. 21.

MOUTH

The corners of the mouth, when smiling, should be in a straight line with the center of the pupils of your eyes. The lips should be of equal curve and fullness.

TWO-SIDED PEOPLE

All of us are two-sided people because there are no faces exactly the same on the right and left sides. In conception, we are formed in halves. This accounts for many facial irregularities. Folklore says that the right side possesses the characteristics of the father, or is male; the left side supposedly takes its characteristics from the mother, or is female. But be this as it may, it is true that all of us have two sides, physically and mentally.

Although all of us would like to be in perfect physical proportion, small facial irregularities can be very interesting. In make-up, if one brow is higher than the other, we don't try to change it; this irregularity often adds character to a face. Only when there is such a marked deviation as to result in distortion, do we try to bring the two features into line. To increase or achieve needed balance in a face, minimize a bad feature and accentuate a good feature.

EYEBROWS ARE YOUR EXPRESSION MARKS

A full, naturally arched eyebrow is a mark of beauty. Never at any time should the eyebrow be plucked or shaved into a thin and artificial line. There are several impossible-to-ignore reasons for this.

The eyebrows are the expression marks of the face. They play a vital part in accentuating or correcting the other features. The woman who plucks hers into a thin and pained expression is apt to find they will not grow back and that she has deprived herself of a natural asset.

In addition, although some scientists have said that they are unable to find a use for the human eyebrows, Nature did put them there for a purpose. This is a truth Hollywood learned by trial and error. In the early days of silent movies, when pencil-line brows were the fashion, many actresses suffered from weak eyes unable to meet strong daylight.

The fact is, eyebrows are meant to protect the eyes. The small hairs screen out much of the dust from the air that otherwise would fall into the eyes. Too, the brows are a natural shade intended to intercept strong light from overhead, rather than allow it to drain directly into the unprotected eye, as you will see in Figs. 22 and 23. It is interesting to note that ball players and other athletes often circle their eyes with smudges of black to keep the sunlight's glare from affecting their vision.

Fig. 22. Normal eyebrow accepting overhead light.

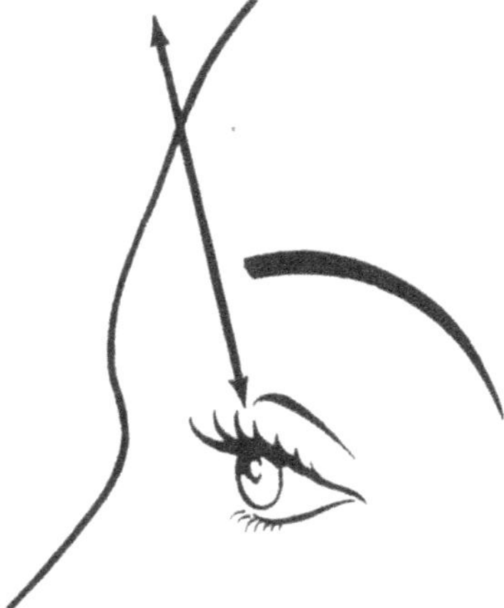

Fig. 23. Overhead light draining into eye.

USING EYEBROWS FOR FEATURE CORRECTION

It is best to tweeze the eyebrows only as much as is needed for shaping, for keeping the growth in hand, and for correcting feature proportion as is shown in the illustrations.

Instructions for tweezing the eyebrows will be found under Eyes and Eyebrows.

To raise an eyebrow for the purpose of feature correction, tweeze only the lower edge of hairs. Use the eyebrow pencil along the top of the eyebrow to give it the appearance of growing higher on the forehead.

To lower an eyebrow, tweeze only the top hairs. Fill in on the lower side of the brow with an eyebrow pencil to give emphasis. This will bring the eyebrow closer to the eye and achieve the lowering effect you desire.

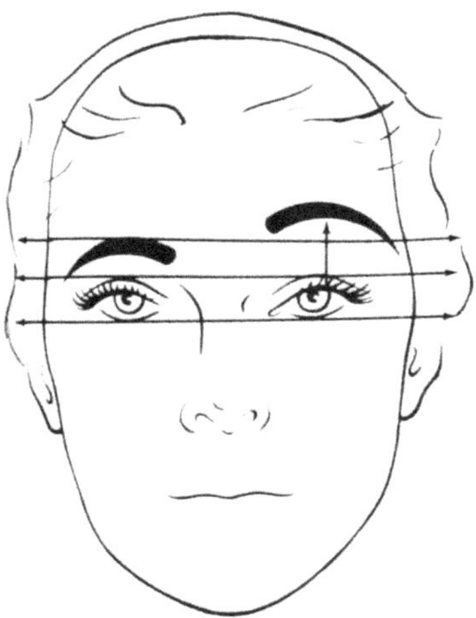

Fig. 24. The eyebrows can diminish or enlarge the apparent size of the eye.

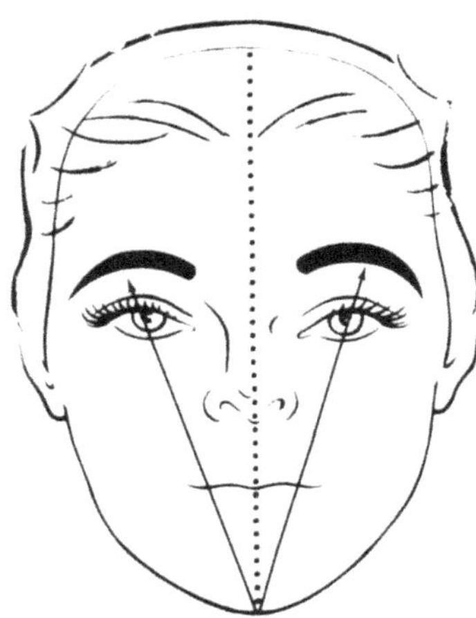

Fig. 25. Raise the eyebrows to give an illusion of length to a short nose.

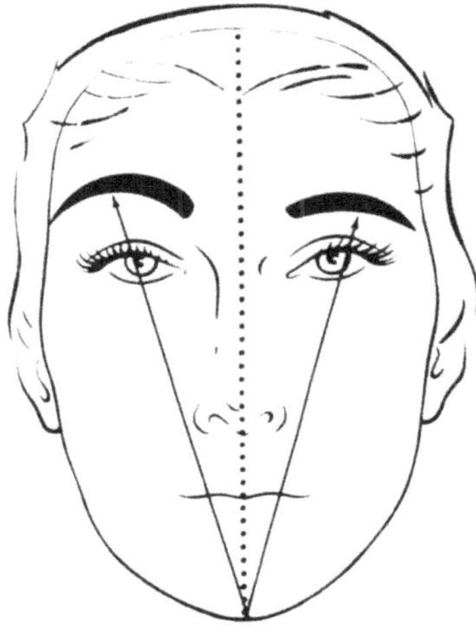

Fig. 26. Bring the eyebrows closer together to cut down the length of a long nose.

CHAPTER FIVE

Hollywood and You

by WALLY WESTMORE
Director of Make-Up and Hair-Styling
for Paramount Studios

One of the most obvious devices the star has used to increase her visual appeal is make-up magic. You have now reached the stage in your program of self-development as outlined in this book where it is appropriate for you to learn about corrective make-up—the make-up of illusion. When you have finished with this section of the book, you literally won't recognize yourself: you'll look so much better. Make-up magic can work for you if you follow these instructions as diligently as our Hollywood stars have done.

And it is easy to prove that the screen beauties have learned their lessons well. Pick any one of today's stars and compare a photo of her present-day self with a photo of the same woman at the time she made her first film appearance. You will feel as though you are looking at two different personalities. In the 28 years I have headed the Make-Up Department at Paramount Studios, I have never failed to be impressed by the fact that the stars continually seek self-improvement. The star of today walks differently, talks differently and thinks differently from the way she did in her ingenue, struggling-to-get-a-foothold days. A knowledge of good grooming has not only increased and refined her physical loveliness, but her constant search for self-improvement has also made her a woman of increased character and distinctive beauty. There is no Hollywood star you can name who hasn't had to work to find her most fascinating self. All of these stars are merely exalted examples of what any woman can do when she is intent on making the most of what she has.

THE "SECRET MAGIC" OF HOLLYWOOD'S ENDURINGLY YOUTHFUL COMPLEXIONS

No complexions are more constantly under make-up than those of the screen stars, and no other faces are so noted for keeping the smoothness of youth.

This, we believe, is a practical answer to both of the questions we are most often asked: "Can cosmetics really *improve* the skin?" or, "Is it true that a complexion is healthier without cosmetics?"

An actress, when she is making a film, reports to the make-up department at six in the morning. She is wearing cosmetics throughout a long working day until six in the evening, and sometimes much later when there is night shooting. Her social and public appearances are more numerous than those of the average woman, calling for additional hours spent in make-up. Nonetheless, the beauty of these stars is such that there is scarcely a housewife who hasn't looked at the satiny close-up of some star and wondered, "How does she do it? Not a line in her face—and at her age!"

We can assure you there is no secret magic here—no potions nor lotions available to the screen queens that are not yours as well. Hollywood's perennially lovely complexions are the result of simple, basic skin "sense" that can, and should, be adapted to your own procedure at home. The actress "does it" in four ways.

THE BIG FOUR

Thorough cleansing: Although she may be fresh from her soap-and-water ablutions at home, every studio make-up begins with a generous application of cleansing cream. The cream, taking away with it every bit of street make-up and every invisible particle of dust, is removed with tissues. Skin-freshener is then patted on with cotton, acting as a further solvent for the cleansing cream. After filming, the day's make-up is always removed by the same thorough cleansing cream and skin-freshener process before street make-up is put on.

Make it your own rule always to give your face a thorough cleansing before applying any cosmetics. Putting on new make-up over a previous coating of cosmetics is a sure way to clog and coarsen the pores. At night, make it a habit to use cleansing cream to dissolve the day's accumulation of dust and oil-caked cosmetics. Follow with a thorough soap and water cleansing.

Plenty of lubrication: Anytime you are inclined to doubt the necessity of lubrication for your skin, here's a simple experiment that should convince you. Take two small pieces of leather—one coated with oil, vaseline or cold-cream—the other one dry—and place them outside. After a few days of wind and sunning, compare the two pieces. You'll find that the coated piece has absorbed the oil, and stayed soft and supple. The untreated leather has become shrivelled, stiff, and wrinkled. This is a good visual example of what gradually happens to any unlubricated skin.

An actress, complexion-conscientious as she must be, knows the importance of night-creaming. As your second "must" for a non-aging complexion, select a good moisturizing skin-cream and use it regularly at night.

Protection with the powder-base habit: For filming, a skin must be well protected against the drying-out effects of the hot lights; therefore, an essential ingredient of every professional make-up is an oil or a cream base. Any actress who has once learned the benefits of combining protective cosmetics with the decorative cosmetics makes powder-foundation a rule for street make-up also. For your own facial beauty, acquire the powder-base habit.

Steady stimulation: Any face regularly treated to the first three of these Hollywood complexion rules has automatically found the fourth reason for the screen stars' habitually youthful skins. The steady, daily process of creaming, cleansing, toning and lubricating is a circulation stimulant and muscle-toner that cannot help but result in a skin that is healthier and more glowing than the face that receives only occasional care.

With a conviction born of experience, we say that the average skin cannot fail to be refined and beautified by the proper use of cosmetics. (The un-average skin is the allergic one or the face subject to eruptions. This face requires a dermatologist's care and advice.) Year after year we have applied the same basic treatment, the same ingredients to the same faces. From this first-hand observance we can honestly tell you that many of the screen actresses in the 30- to 45-year brackets have healthier and lovelier skins than in their younger years.

At a party recently, we met a former starlet who has been in retirement, a happy housewife, for the past ten years. "You don't look a bit different," an admirer exclaimed. "Where've you been keeping yourself—in a deep freeze?" You, too, have been astonished at the enviable freshness of some actress who makes a comeback looking as if she'd never been away. The truth, as we've urged you to learn for yourself, is that once any woman has made beauty care a part of her daily life, she never again wants to be "away" from loveliness!

MAKE-UP IS ILLUSION

The word illusion is described in the dictionary as meaning "to deceive." Optically speaking, we do deceive the eye by creative use of light, color, and line. It follows, therefore, that there are two principles so important to the over-all illusion of make-up that you should know and remember them as you do your own name and address. They are: (1) the importance of round, straight and angular lines; and (2) the principle of light and shadow.

HOLD THAT UP-CURVE! YOUR FACIAL CURVES

In any phase of make-up, the up-curve is the line of youth and beauty. Never, never forget this. In applying make-up to your own features, avoid the downward line. Even a very young face can be made petulant and hard-looking by eyebrows ending in a black, downward, pencilled line; by rouge placed too low on the face, and by lipstick drawn into a sulky, downward curve.

The older woman can best avoid these mistakes by taking an understanding view of what happens to a face as the years go by. To begin with, the human face is composed of some 39 curves. In youth, these curves of eyebrow, eyes, cheekline, lips, and so on, are definitely up-tilted. With added years, the fat under the skin of the face starts to break down, with the result that the curves of the face straighten out, disappear, or fall into a downward droop.

To keep a youthful appearance, middle-aged women should strive, through deft application of cosmetics, to maintain the upward curve of the eyebrow and the lips. If you are in the middle-aged bracket, your best help is a photograph taken when you were between 20 and 25 years of age. Use this earlier photograph to copy the curve of the eyebrows, mouth and other features of your more youthful face.

At any age, we repeat: Keep your face on the up-and-up. Never let your make-up show the "downs" in your life or disposition. Keep in mind the two masks of Comedy and Tragedy. This will help you to get the most out of a successful make-up.

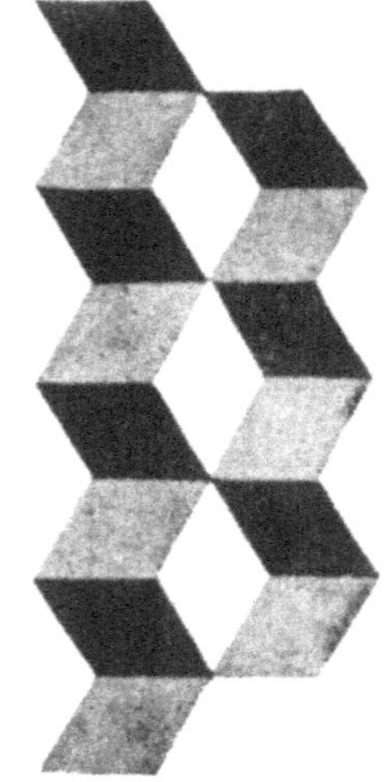

LIGHT AND SHADOW—FOR CONTOUR MAGIC

As a child, perhaps you were amused by examples of optical illusions such as you see in the illustrations here. As an adult seeking loveliness, the theories they demonstrate can help you to work make-up magic in your face.

A person distinguishes contour or shape by whatever highlights and shadows there are on the object he sees. Even a flat surface can seem to gain curve and depth by the contrast of light and dark color. Thus, on this flat piece of paper, the series of light, shaded and dark squares take on the appearance of three-dimensional cubes. The circle with a highlight at its center appears as a rounded bulge. The same circle with a shadow at its center seems to be a depression. Similarly, several wavy alternations of light and shadow create the illusion of ridges and depressions. In stage characterization, this is how we create the appearance of fullness or thinness in the face.

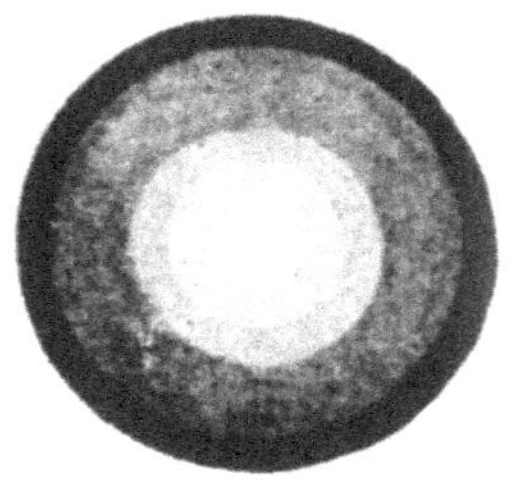

Corrective make-up is based on the use of light- and dark-toned cosmetics to highlight and shadow a face. By this method the contour of a face can be refined and faulty features can be given the illusion of perfect proportion.

Specific instructions in corrective make-up will be found in the pages devoted to each separate feature. Even if you possess features pretty as a picture, they can be distorted to the point of caricature by a misuse of highlight and shadow.

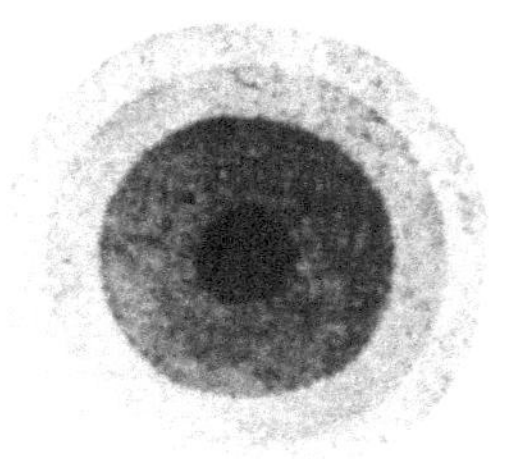

Fig. 27. Illusions.

Light *reflects* light. Any surface or feature of your face that is treated with a light cosmetic seemingly gains size and prominence. Highlighting is used to fill in a hollow, or to "clean up" deep lines wherever they occur. Also, any oily surface left unpowdered will create a highlight as contrasted with a powdered surface. Always, in any make-up, be careful *not* to give the highlighting treatment to any part of the face which may already be too large or too rounded.

Shadow *absorbs* light. Any dark-toned cosmetic seemingly cuts down size and width. For instance, a too-wide jaw is reduced in width by shadowing with a darker cosmetic on the outside edge of the jaw. By the same method, an angular jawbone can be given the illusion of softness and curve. In addition to dark-toned base make-up, rouge is an important cosmetic for contouring. Rouge also absorbs light. This is discussed in detail on the pages devoted to cosmetics, Chapter Eight.

TURN OFF THAT WHITE COLLAR

This may come as a blow to some of the women who believe that white worn close to the face is always youthful and flattering. The light reflected by white clothing puts an unkind emphasis on a too-wide jaw or a heavy chin.

To prove this, try a simple experiment on yourself or someone else. Take a sheet of white paper and hold it under the chin, as in Fig. 28. Stand directly under an overhead light or in the strong sunlight. Notice that the glare is reflected upward, and see how it spotlights the double-chin line. Hold the piece of paper on the shoulder (Fig. 29) and watch the reflected light emphasize the size or droop of the jawline. If you have a heavier face, pastel or dark clothing will be more becoming to you. If you must wear white, put plenty of skin area—preferably a V-line—between the glare the white creates and your lower face. You'll note that many men appear to have a double chin when actually it is only the unkind glare created by the white collar worn so close to the face.

By reverse, white collars and blouses are a definite help to the thin neck and the hollow or flat cheek. The reflected light serves to fill in the sunken areas and to give the illusion of fullness to the entire countenance. See Fig. 30.

FOR EVENING, WATCH YOUR LIGHTING EFFECTS

Lamplight also has a trick or two worth your learning. A knowing woman, out for an evening, will try to sit beside a table-lamp—never under the lights. The lighting from a lamp on her eye-level will wash out lines. Overhead lighting emphasizes them.

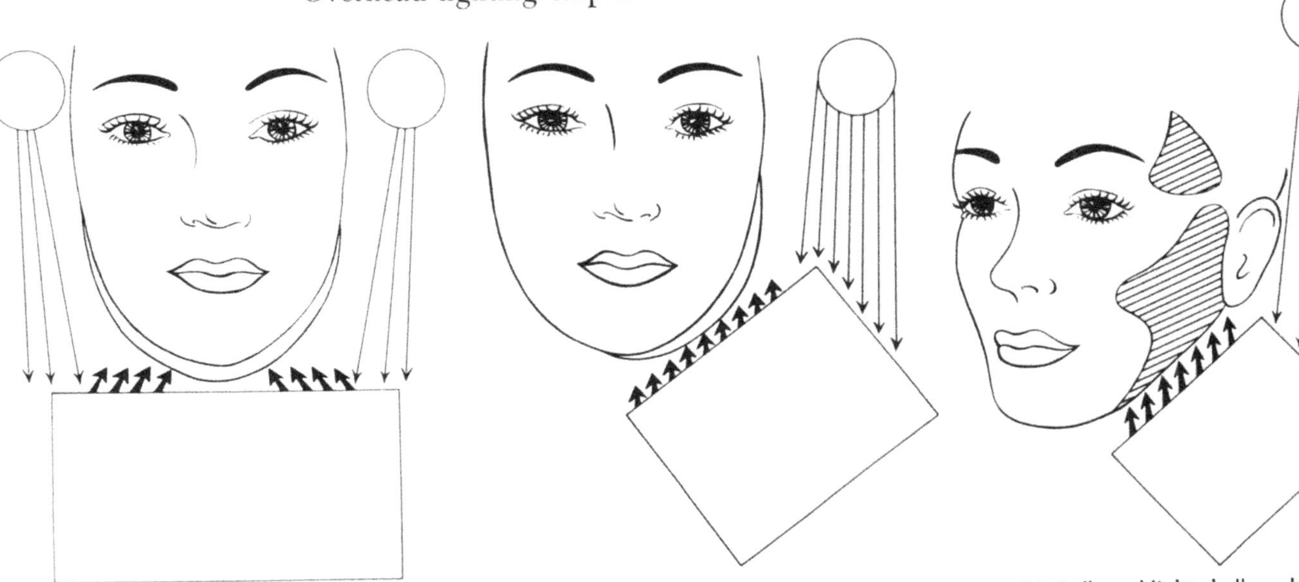

Fig. 28. Reflected light below chin.

Fig. 29. Reflected light—full cheek.

Fig. 30. Reflected light—hollow cheek.

CHAPTER SIX

Please, Be Subtle!

by MONT WESTMORE
Make-Up Artist for Universal-International Pictures

While we're on the subject of make-up and make-up tricks, I've always been proud of the fact that my father, Mont Westmore, Sr., the oldest of the Westmore brothers, did what still stands as one of the finest film make-up jobs in the history of the profession. I'm sure you remember the picture—"Gone With the Wind." Shortly after he had completed this major and exacting job, my Dad passed away and I went into the armed forces.

As a youngster, I had heard so much on the subject of make-up that I was far from enthused about the family profession. In the service, I had a lot of time to think, and I came to realize that the creation of beauty is a human, understanding, and worthwhile profession. I made up my mind that when I returned to civilian life I would place myself under the tutelage of my uncles, Perc, Wally, Bud, and Frank.

With this in mind, and being on the young side myself, I began to be extremely critical of the appearance of the young girls I met and saw on the streets. I felt then, and know now because of my work in Hollywood, that the day a girl learns the importance of refined and natural-looking cosmetics is the day she gives herself a beautiful start in life.

If, in speaking to any girl or woman, all of us Westmores were limited to just one piece of advice concerning the application of make-up, we would pick the one with which we know the entire male population would agree: Above all else, please—be subtle!

Make-up, like any other device, defeats itself when it becomes obvious. Very young and unmarried women especially are prone to think that if a little make-up is alluring, twice as much must be doubly so. The truth is, a man finds nothing kissable in a mouth made up to look like hot flypaper. He mistrusts the artificial look that comes his way through lashes gummed into hard black spikes. Rather than encouraging romance, the face that comes off on his shirt-front offends his sensibilities.

The successful make-up is the one the beholder doesn't realize is there.

COLOR CHART FOR MAKE-UP

	TINTED BASE	EYE SHADOW			ROUGE			TOUCH-UP CAKE	POWDER	PENCIL	MASCARA	LIPSTICK
		Blue eyes	*Gray eyes*	*Brown or Hazel eyes*	*Cream*	*Liquid*	*Dry*					
BLONDE												
White skin	Natural	Blue	Gray	Brown	Pink Pastel	Light	Pink Pastel	Natural	Colorless	Light Brown	Brown or Midnight Blue	Pale Pink
Fair skin	Flesh Natural	Blue	Gray	Brown	Pale Pink	Light	Pale Pink	Flesh Natural	Colorless	Light Brown	Brown or Midnight Blue	Pink Orange
Light Olive skin	Light Pink Beige	Blue	Gray	Brown	Pale Pink	Light	Pale Pink	Light Pink Beige	Colorless	Light Brown	Brown or Midnight Blue	Real Orange
Olive skin	Pink Beige	Blue	Gray	Brown	Pepper Red	Light	Pepper Red	Pink Beige	Colorless	Brown	Brown or Midnight Blue	Pepper Red
REDHEAD												
White skin	Natural	Blue	Gray	Brown	Pink Red	Medium	Pink Red	Natural	Colorless	Light Auburn	Brown or Midnight Blue	Pale Pink
Fair skin	Flesh Natural	Blue	Gray	Brown	True Red	Medium	True Red	Flesh Natural	Colorless	Light Auburn or Brown	Brown or Midnight Blue	Orange Pink
Florid skin	Flat Beige or Copper	Blue	Gray	Brown	Pepper Red	Medium	Pepper Red	Flat Tan Beige	Light Tan	Brown	Brown or Midnight Blue	Pepper Red
BROWNETTE												
Fair skin	Rose Flesh	Blue	Gray	Brown	True Red	Medium	True Red	Rose Flesh	Colorless	Brown	Brown or Midnight Blue	Pepper Red
Light Olive skin	Rose Beige	Blue	Gray	Brown	Pepper Red	Medium	Pepper Red	Rose Beige	Colorless	Brown	Brown or Midnight Blue	Rose Red
Olive skin	Peach Beige	Blue	Gray	Brown	True Red	Medium	True Red	Peach Beige	Colorless	Brown	Midnight Blue or Black	True Red
Dark Olive skin	Deep Peach Buff or Copper	Blue	Gray	Brown	Garnet	Dark	Garnet	Deep Peach Buff or Copper	Colorless	Black or Brown	Midnight Blue or Black	True Red
BRUNETTE												
White skin	Rose Flesh	Blue	Gray	Brown	True Red	Medium	True Red	Rose Flesh	Colorless	Black or Brown	Midnight Blue or Black	Pepper Red
Light Olive skin	Rose Beige	Blue	Gray	Brown	Pepper Red	Medium	Pepper Red	Rose Beige	Colorless	Black or Brown	Midnight Blue or Black	Pepper Red
Olive skin	Peach Buff	Blue	Gray	Brown	Garnet	Dark	Garnet	Peach Buff or Copper	Colorless	Black or Brown	Black	True Red
Dark Olive skin	Copper	Blue	Gray	Brown	Garnet	Dark	Garnet	Copper	Colorless	Black or Brown	Black	Garnet or True Red

With the exception of lipstick, artistically and cleanly applied, cosmetics are not meant to be seen. When a woman says, "I like that powder-base you're wearing," or "When did you switch to that green eye shadow, dear?" she could be giving you a friendly tip. One thing is certain—you've been far from subtle in the application of cosmetics.

Which make-up details tend to make a face look common—and which make-up gives a woman that delicate "perfect" look? The answers to the first part of this question are listed here for you.

THE SEVEN SINS OF MAKE-UP

1. *Too heavy application.* In applying any cosmetic, it's the minimum amount that gives maximum loveliness. In the use of all cosmetics that come without instructions, make this your guide: too little won't show—too much certainly will!

2. *Harsh or badly matched colors.* Cosmetics are intended to assist Nature, not to fight her. Help by choosing the right tints to complement your own natural color-scheme. Use your color chart, found on page 50, to learn your natural coloration. In general, avoid bizarre and artificial shades. They are both cheapening and aging. Harmonize your hues. A face should never be the battleground for colors that clash.

3. *Improper blending.* There is nothing more betraying to your cause than a line marking the beginning of one cosmetic or the ending of another. Harsh, round circles of rouge, eyebrow pencilling showing up in a hard, black line, a line of demarcation between the powder-base on your face and that of your throat—these are unsightly giveaways that sometimes escape your notice in a poorly lit mirror. Always check your make-up in good, strong daylight or its equivalent.

4. *Over-powdering.* The flour-barrel look hasn't been good since the day of powdered wigs. Powder caked in the crevices alongside the nose, around the eyes, and in the eyebrows and hairline—not to mention powder-stains on the neckline of your dress—are unsightly and a sign of carelessness and poor grooming. You may not be conscious of these things, but others certainly will be. There is a correct way to apply powder so that it will be a *finish* for loveliness—rather than an end to daintiness!

5. *Patchwork make-up.* This is the blotchy effect that develops from all-day dabbing—adding new rouge on top of old rouge, patting powder on powder until your nose is shades darker than the rest of your face, and so on. Learn to "set" your make-up properly when you first apply it, and you'll avoid this spotty repair work.

6. *The messy mouth habit.* Smeared lipstick, chewed-off lipstick, lipstick "bleeding" into the fine lines around the mouth, added-on lipstick partially covering the old application—these are the most noticeable and the most common offenses to beauty and grooming. Read the instructions for lip make-up, beginning on page 93, and stop being ol' messy-mouth.

7. *Incongruities of make-up and occasion.* Young or old, a woman has to "be herself" in make-up as well as in dress and deportment. Colored eye

shadow, heavily applied, is not for daytime wear. False eyelashes may be permissible for a chorus girl or dancer engaged in her occupation, but this theatrical make-up has no place in an office. Dark or purplish-toned rouges and lipsticks are not for the older woman. Many other make-up incongruities will spring to your mind as you read this, but a simple principle can insure you against them: *Good taste means good looks!*

When you are without any of the seven deadly sins listed above, you have already achieved the two most important requisites of delicacy—cleanliness and naturalness. The "perfect" look—that soft glow of color coming from beneath a translucent, rather than masklike finish—results from attention to the details of application which are set forth, step by step, on the following pages.

CHAPTER SEVEN

Make-Up Magic, Step by Step

ON YOUR FEATURES, NOT ON YOUR MIND

A beautiful make-up is one that has been put on with a knowing hand and an appreciative eye. Without these two factors, beauty knowledge and all the marvels of modern cosmetics are wasted. Take the time, then, to learn the how and the why of the order of make-up steps. Practice doing your everyday make-up according to these time- and Westmore-tested steps and you will truly be proceeding in the direction of a more beautiful you. Only when you have followed these steps so carefully and so often that you literally know them from memory, can you put this book aside as you make up. An added daily reminder might be a little white card on which you have copied the order of the make-up steps listed here. This could be put on the inside of your bathroom mirror or on the back of your office hand mirror. Never be without this guide until you are letter perfect in the art of beautiful make-up.

THE STEPS OF MAKE-UP—IN ORDER OF APPLICATION

The steps of make-up dictated here are the details as we have learned and practiced them to give the greatest amount of attractiveness to the greatest number of women. Your own face, however, is a highly personal property and anything that makes you feel artificial or uncomfortable is not for you. Cosmetics should be on your features, not on your mind.

Don't, however, decide against this make-up procedure or any beauty procedure without having first given it a fair and wholehearted trial. Something new often feels uncomfortable simply because it is new. Don't bypass the added beauty that can be yours simply because you haven't taken the time to become accustomed to a new and exacting beauty procedure.

We know from experience that once you have learned for yourself that you can literally add beauty to your face with the help of make-up skillfully applied, you will never again slip back into the old, careless ways.

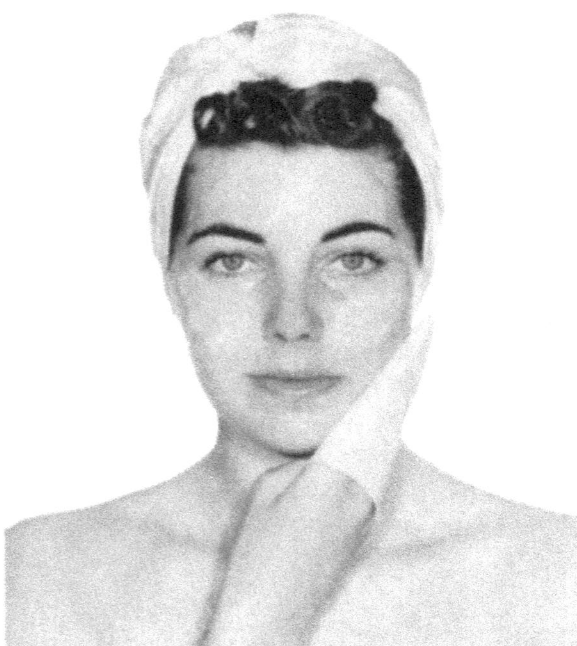

Fig. 31. Cleansing cream: Apply generously over face and remove with tissue. Be certain that every time you use a cream on your face—be it a cleansing cream or nourishing cream—that you follow the facial manipulations outlined in Chapter Nine.

Fig. 32. Skin-freshener: Apply with cotton square to remove all traces of oil, secretion and cream.

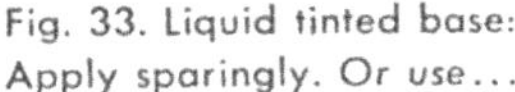

Fig. 33. Liquid tinted base: Apply sparingly. Or use...

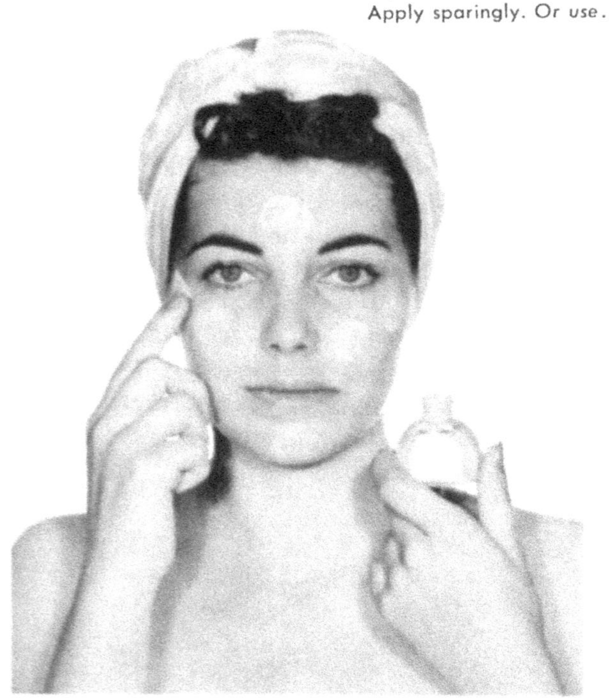

Fig. 34. Cake or cream tinted base: Apply sparingly.

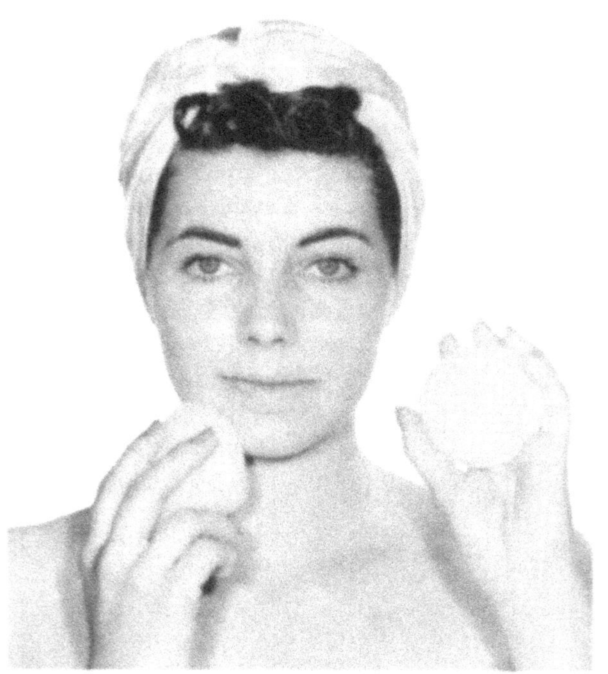

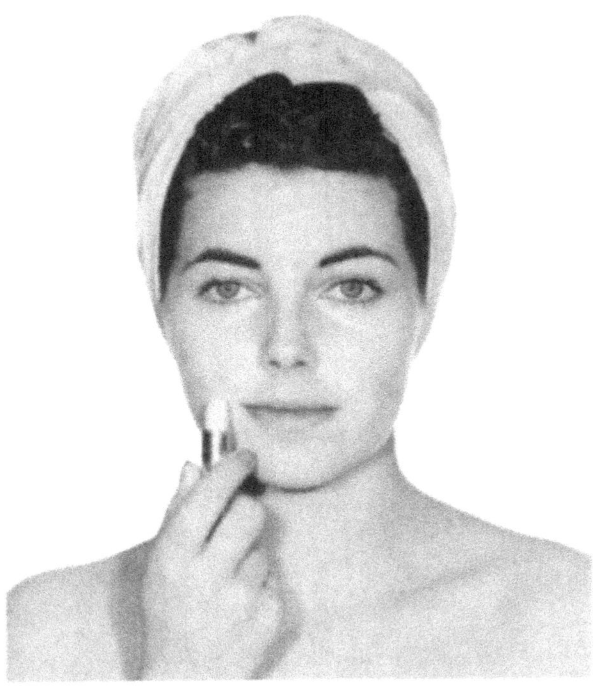

Fig. 35. Beauty-stick: Cover blemishes, freckles, etc.

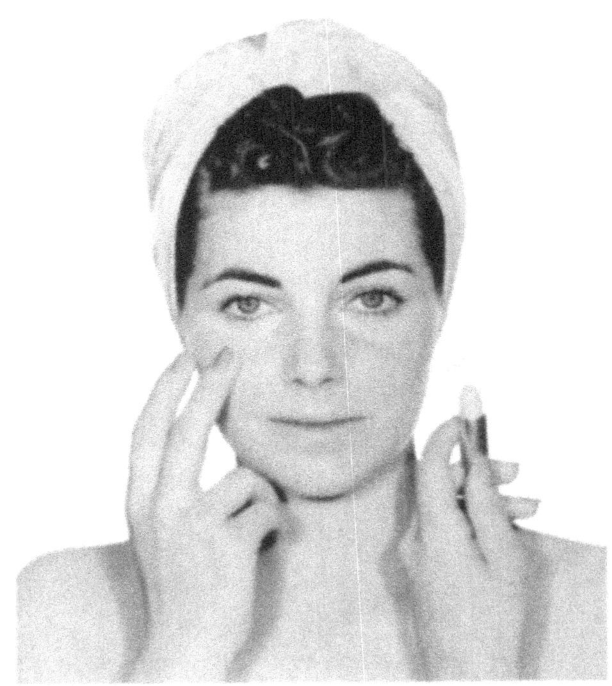

Fig. 36. Highlight or beauty-stick: Use for eye hollows or discolorations, down "laugh lines," for forehead or neck creases.

Fig. 37. Cream rouge: Pat on, do not rub, and blend. Or *use . . .*

Fig. 38. Liquid rouge: Dot on and blend.

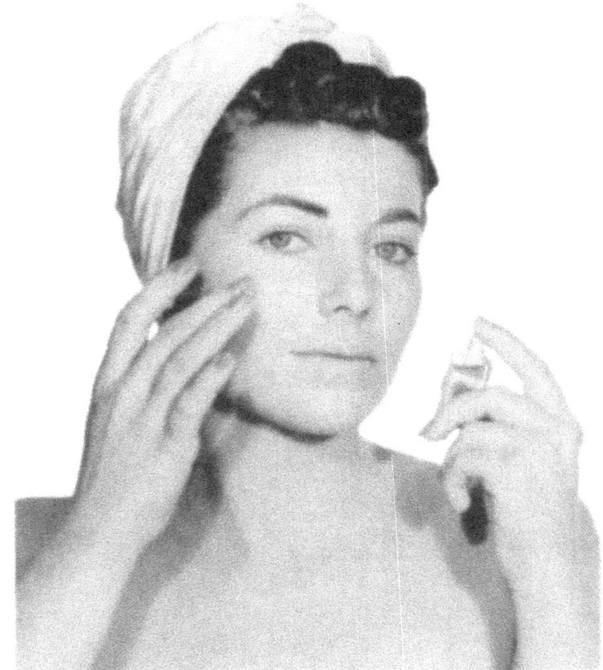

Fig. 39. Eye shadow: Apply heaviest at lash-line; fade to minimum at eyebrow.

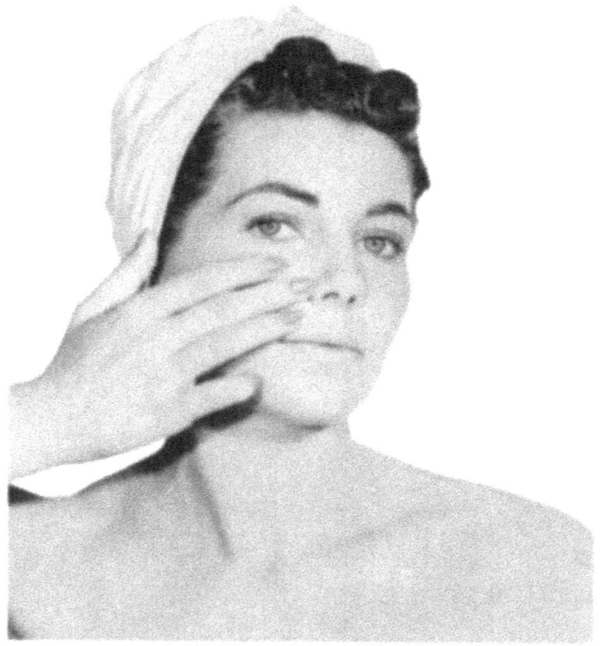

Fig. 40. Highlight: Retrace laugh lines (which may have become creased through facial movements) before powdering.

Fig. 41. Retrace under eyes before powdering.

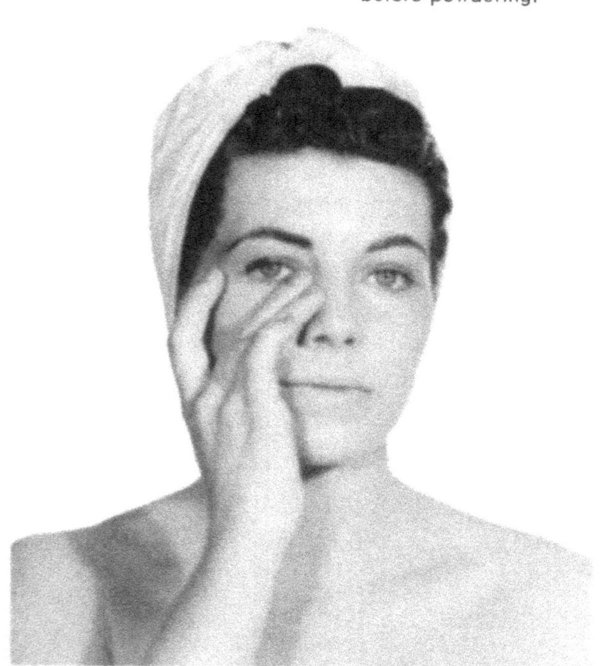

Fig. 42. Retrace forehead lines before powdering.

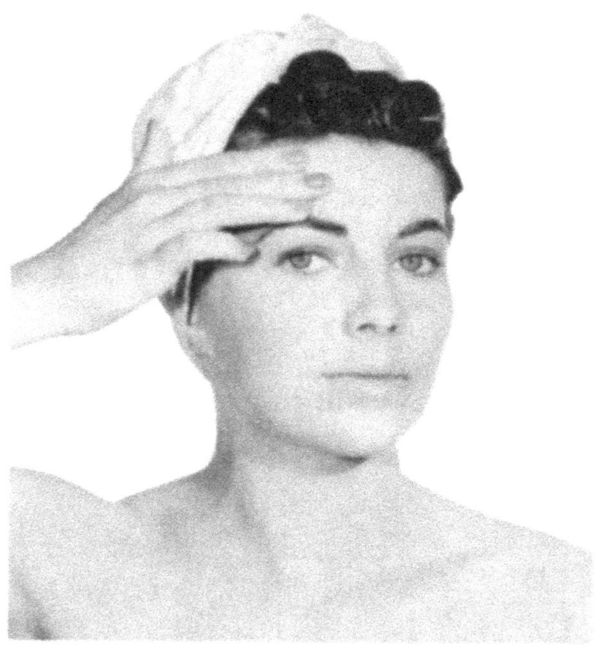

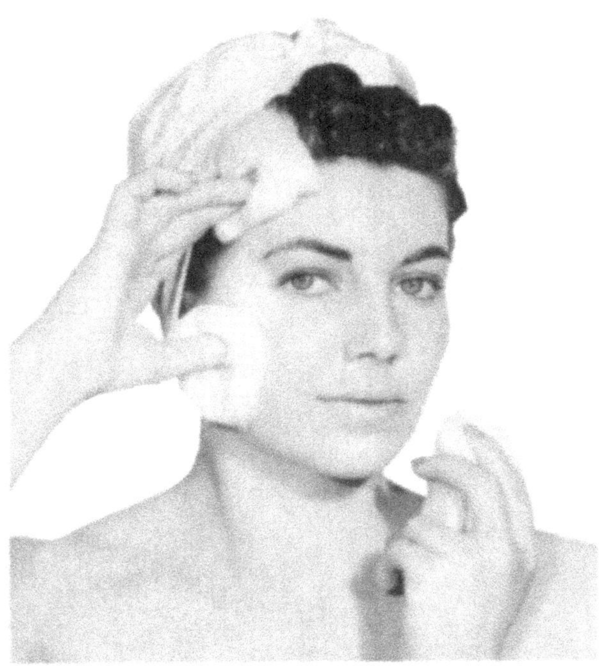

Fig. 43. Powder: Apply under eyes first, gently pulling apart squint lines or crevices to avoid creases.

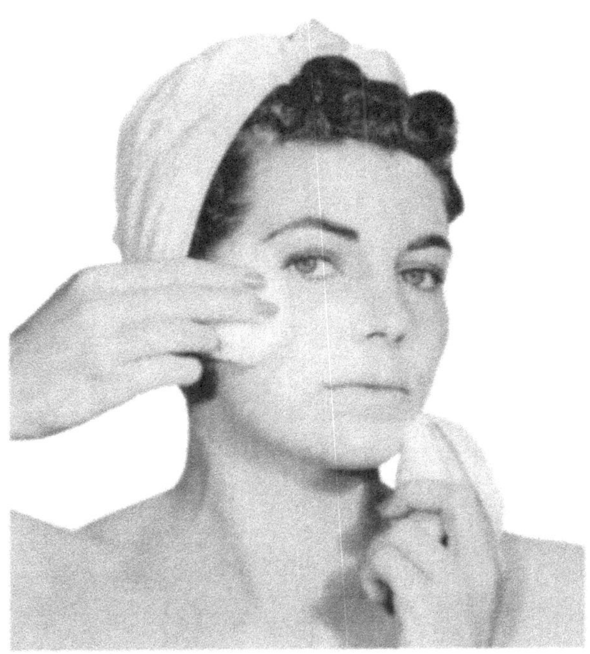

Fig. 44. Pull laugh lines apart ever so gently and powder.

Fig. 45. Powder face thoroughly; pat, do not rub, over tinted base. Pull apart and powder lines in neck.

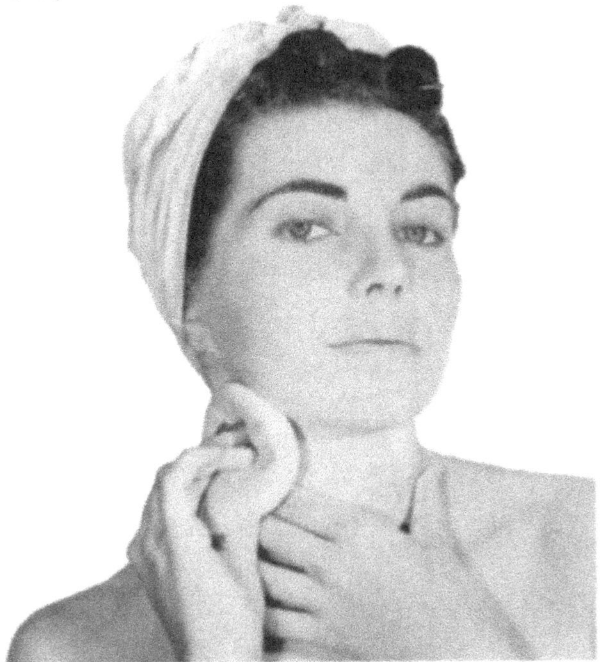

Fig. 46. Brush off excess powder with powder-brush or soft cotton.

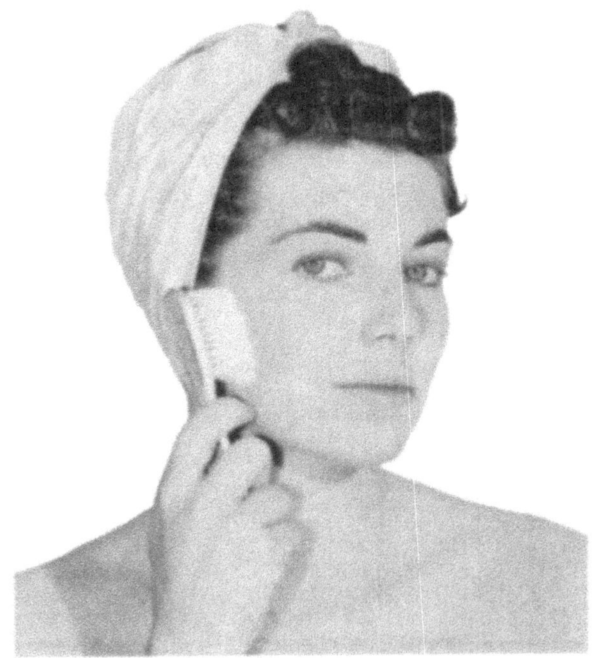

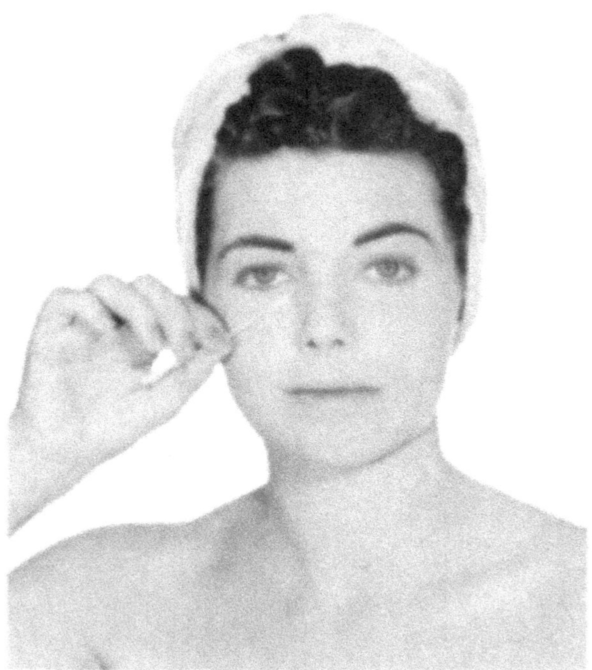

Fig. 47. Brush excess powder from under eyes with pipe-cleaner or swab.

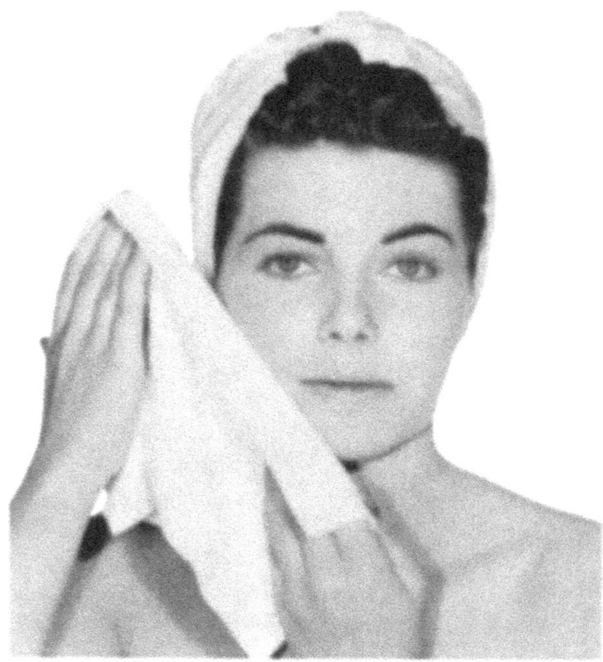

Fig. 48. Gently press towel, moistened in iced or cold water, to face to give smooth, natural-looking sheen to make-up. Cotton squares dampened in iced or cold water can be used instead of towel.

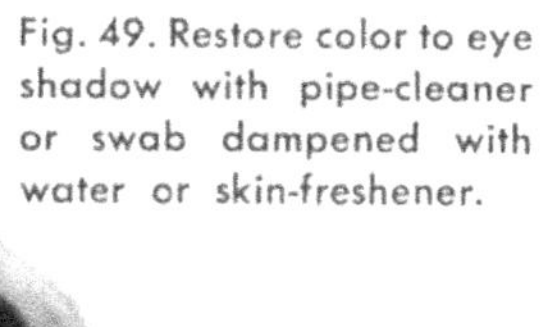

Fig. 49. Restore color to eye shadow with pipe-cleaner or swab dampened with water or skin-freshener.

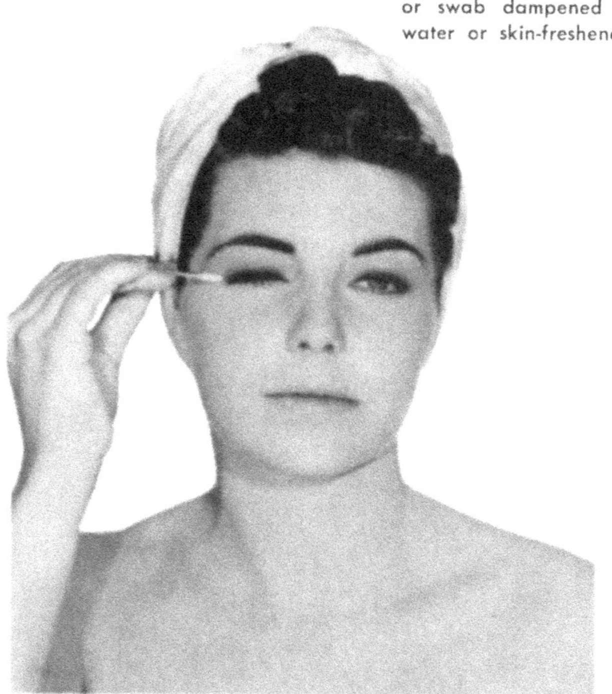

Fig. 50. Eyebrow pencil: Outline lash-line of upper lid (softly, not obviously) with pencil. Or *use . . .*

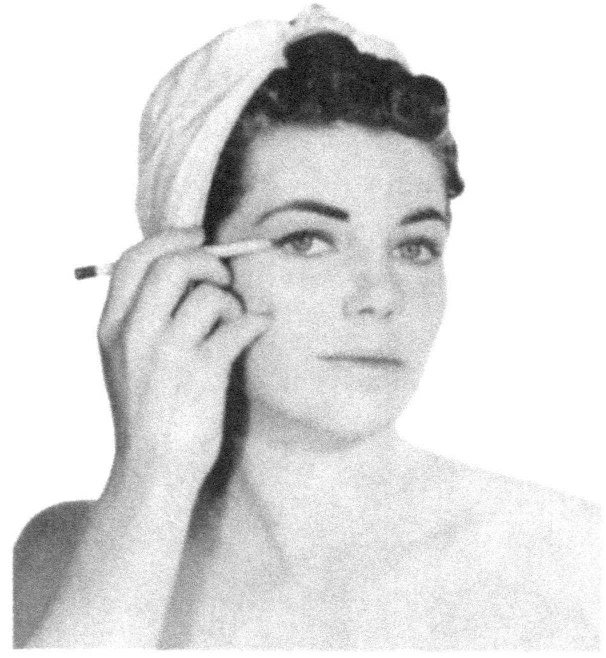

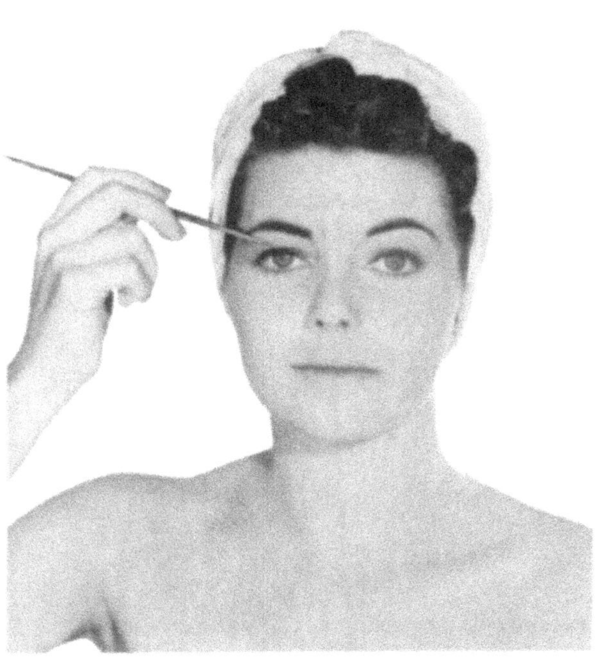

Fig. 51. Liner brush: Line upper and lower lids.

Fig. 52. Shape eyebrow with pencil (sharpened to flat, chisel point), using short, feathery strokes.

Fig. 53. Mascara: Apply heaviest on upper lashes. Use little or none on lower lashes for daytime wear.

Fig. 54. Lipstick: Apply with lip brush for clear, definite outlines.

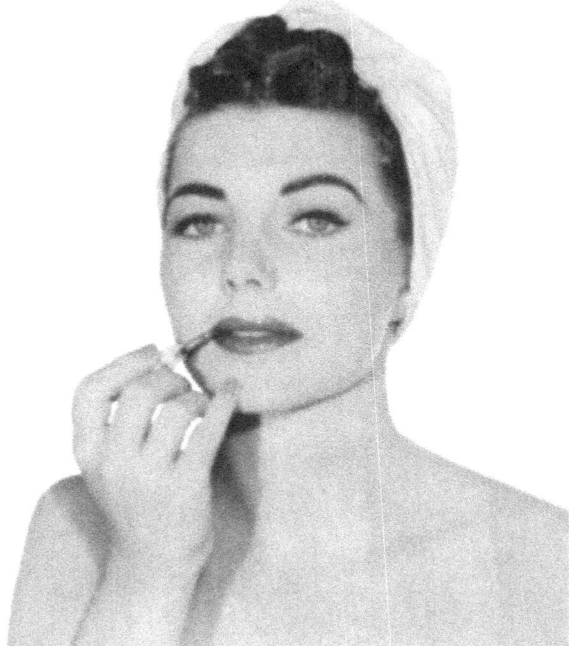

Fig. 55. Check on the shape of the mouth and your skill with the lip brush: Imprint your mouth shape on back of hand.

Fig. 56. Lift lip corners (with lip brush) for youthful, smiling appearance.

Fig. 57. Blot lips with tissue to remove excess lipstick. Check evenness of pattern on tissue imprint.

Fig. 58. Dry rouge: Apply with or without rouge brush. Apply as dusting finish on high-point of cheek.

Fig. 59. COMPLETED MAKE-UP.

COSMETICS—MAKING THE MOST OF YOUR MAKE-UP BUDGET

Almost any brand of cosmetics you can buy today is a good one, whether you choose it for name, price, or because the jars match the color-scheme of your dressing table. Huge sums are now spent by every manufacturer on scientific research and rigid drug laws guarantee the ingredients to be safe and pure.

The important thing *not* to do is to stock up on a hodge-podge of different brands, one article from each line. How many times have you rushed home with a new "wonder" rouge or powder, and found that although the advertising spoke of silken-smooth results, on you it gave nothing but streaks? In all probability you were applying this new cosmetic over other make-up products with which it was never meant to blend. This is unfair to the product—and unfair to your beauty budget.

Generally speaking, most of the various preparations that make up any one brand of cosmetics have a planned and specific relationship to each other in purpose and formula. For instance, a cream rouge in any particular brand is usually especially formulated by the manufacturer to blend most smoothly with the ingredients of his make-up base; the cleansing cream of that same line will contain the chemical qualities most effective in dissolving and removing its related cosmetics.

If you want to make the most of your cosmetic budget, find that certain powder-base, or the rouge, or the powder that gives you the happiest results. Then pick as many of your other make-up necessities as you can from the same brand. Regardless of whether you choose an expensive or an inexpensive line, this is economical buying—each preparation will go farther, and cooperate for smoother make-up.

BE CONSTANT—LIKE CLEOPATRA!

Next in importance: When you've found the right cosmetic treatment for your face, stick with it! It's foolish to dash out and buy a preparation merely because it has a new name, or makes brighter promises of "effortless, magical beauty," or just because you haven't tried it before. You'll end up trying everything and being helped by nothing.

The history of cosmetics goes back to centuries B.C., and although modern cosmetologists are constantly bringing you improvements in blends, tints, combinations of two- and three-purpose products and so on, the basic ingredients for beauty have changed very little since Cleopatra's day.

The Egyptian siren lubricated her face and body with oils made from lion, crocodile and hippopotamus fat—indelicate substances which required a liberal cover-up of aromatics and spices before she could submit her enticing smoothness to the close embrace of Anthony or Caesar. Today, the skin men love to touch preserves its softness with goose grease and the sheep fat known as lanolin. For you, these precious emollients come in dozens of forms of beauty preparations, refined and delicately scented.

In some parts of the world, geranium petals and berry juices are still used by women to tint cheeks, lips, the soles of their sandaled feet—and sometimes to draw a scarlet line down the center part of their hair to warn would-be lovers they have a husband. Vegetable dyes add the color of romance to your cheeks and lips also, but you have your choice of varied tints in blended rouges and creamy lipsticks.

Still, this abundance of cosmetic riches has confused the modern woman's beauty care far beyond what it used to be. Cleopatra had no temptation to be fickle to her dyes and unguents because they were the only ones she had. Like all beauties of ancient times, she used the materials at hand—constantly, artistically, and knowingly. History proves she got results.

If you've been flitting from jar to jar and bottle to bottle, stop wasting your money and your hopes. It's not so much which cosmetics you use as it is how you use them!

MAKE-UP ILLUSION FOR YOUR FACE SHAPE

On the following pages are given make-up pointers which will help you to achieve the beauty which is a distinctive part of your face-type, be it Oval, Oblong, Round, Square, Triangle, Inverted Triangle, or Diamond. The illustrations show the wrong and the correct make-up for each type.

MAKE-UP ILLUSION FOR YOUR FACE SHAPE

OVAL—Forehead slightly wider than chin

The Oval type is recognized as the ideal, and the purpose of your make-up is to create the illusion of as perfect an Oval as possible. Bear in mind that the incorrect application of cosmetics can actually distort the enviable symmetry of this type of face.

Fig. 60. Oval shape minus all make-up. Face looks expressionless and plain.

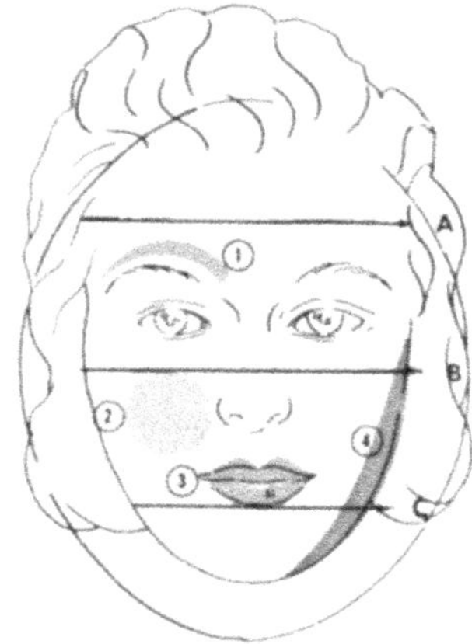

Fig. 61. WRONG MAKE-UP
A, B and C are your caliper measurements. (1) Do not tweeze the eyebrow too thin, or pencil it too heavily. The eyebrow should not be too high, too straight, too angular, or too round. (2) Do not place rouge in an obviously circular pattern in the center of the cheek. (3) Avoid a high Cupid's bow in the upper lip and a drooping lower lip line. (4) Do not use two tones of make-up on the jawline.

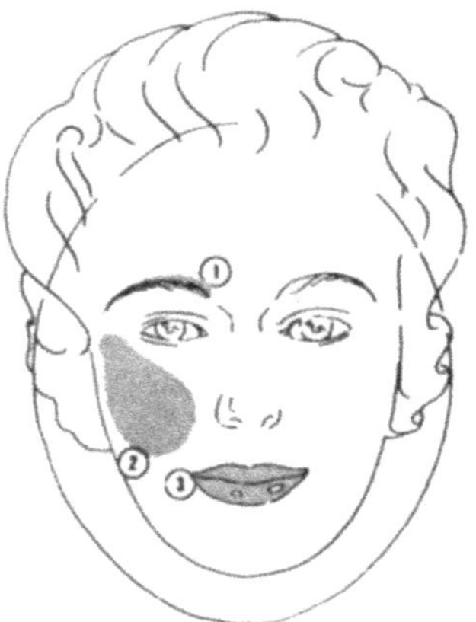

Fig. 62. CORRECT MAKE-UP
(1) Keep the eyebrow natural. The curve should come at the high point of the frontal bone. (2) Apply cheek rouge on the high point of the full smile; blend back and up, tapering into the base make-up. (3) Apply your lipstick to the natural lip line unless the mouth is overly large or small.

Fig. 63. All of the characteristics of the Oval face-type have been retained, defined, and accentuated.

MAKE-UP ILLUSION FOR YOUR FACE SHAPE

OBLONG—Long, narrow face with hollow cheeks

The Oblong face-type appears long, thin, and narrow. It is all too easy to give such a face a cold, hard look. Every attempt should be made to create a foreshortening effect. Never do anything that tends to emphasize the length of the face and the features. Concentrate on minimizing the hollow-cheeked effect which is so often found in this type.

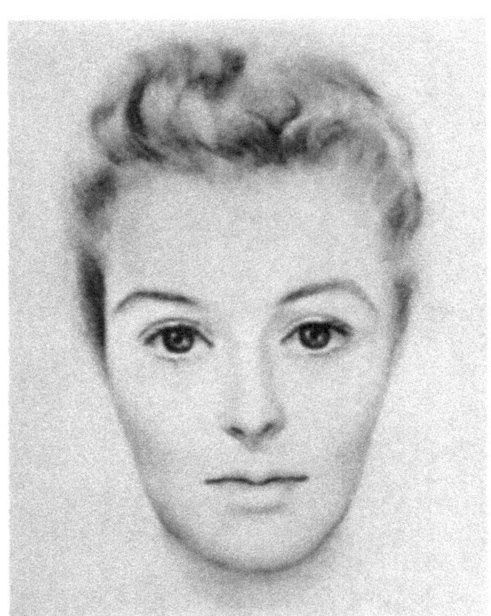

Fig. 64. Oblong shape minus all make-up.

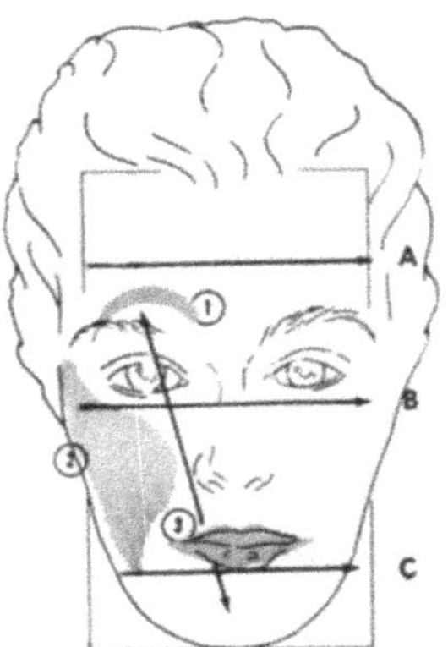

Fig. 65. WRONG MAKE-UP
A, B and C are your caliper measurements. (1) Do not arch or pencil the eyebrows too high. This will give your face an elongated look from the point of the chin to the top of the brow. (2) Avoid an elongated field of cheek rouge, especially if you have hollows in the cheek. (3) Do not make the mouth up too highly pointed or too wide. Too much width here will reduce the width of the lower part of the face.

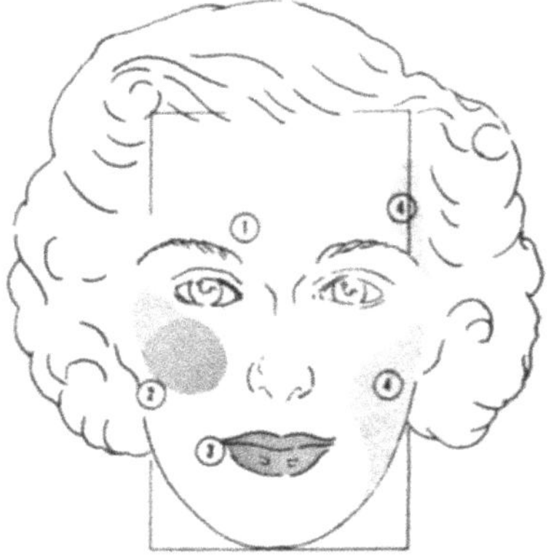

Fig. 66. CORRECT MAKE-UP
Create as much width as possible through the center of the face to de-emphasize the long, narrow look characteristic of the Oblong face. (1) Keep eyebrow perfectly natural; do not extend it. To do so is to tend to overemphasize the width of the forehead. (2) Apply cheek rouge (moist or dry) on the high point of the smile in a circular fashion; blend backwards and upwards, over the high point of the cheekbones. (3) Apply lipstick to the natural lip line unless there are feature problems such as a large nose, small teeth, or overly large teeth. (4) Highlight hollow cheeks and temples.

Fig. 67. Deft foreshortening, as shown here, gives the Oblong face-type desired width plus the illusion of an Oval contour.

MAKE-UP ILLUSION FOR YOUR FACE SHAPE

ROUND—Round hairline, round chinline

The Round face-type has great charm and youth; such women are usually generous and spirited. Make-up, properly applied, pays great glamour dividends for this type.

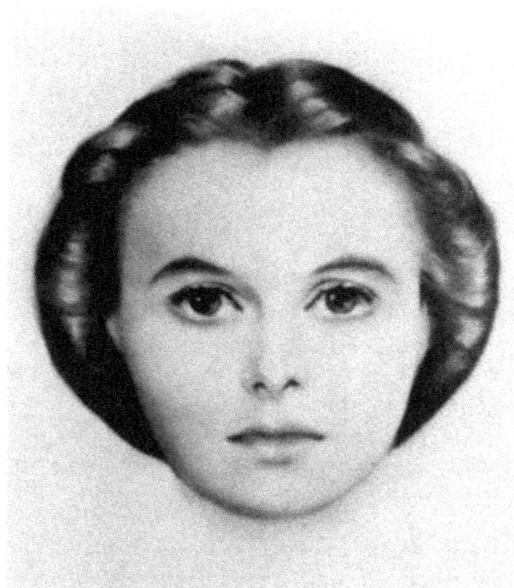

Fig. 68. Round shape minus all make-up.

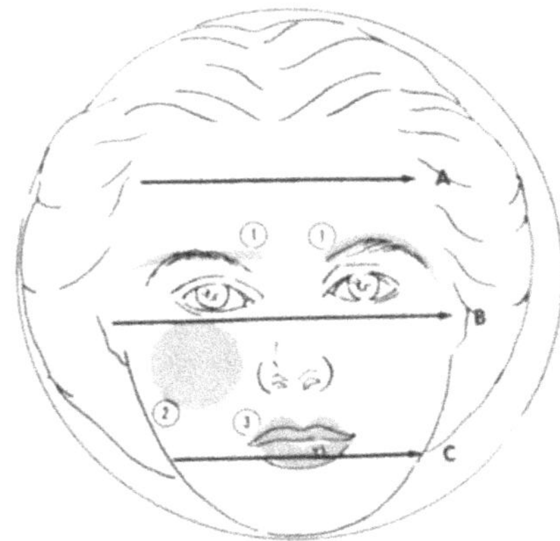

Fig. 69. WRONG MAKE-UP
A, B and C are your caliper measurements. (1) Do not tweeze or pencil the eyebrow too straight or too thin. A straight line on the round face becomes obvious contrast and thereby accentuates the face's roundness. The same unfortunate emphasis results when you create an obviously curved, circular eyebrow. (2) Do not apply cheek rouge (moist or dry) in a round, circular field. This would make the face seem rounder than ever. (3) Do not make up the lips in a high Cupid's bow or in a circular pattern. Note: Occasionally, where there is roundness, there is fullness or a large face. In such instances, the eyebrows and lips should be made up to appear large, full and free. This make-up trick definitely diminishes the appearance of the size of the face.

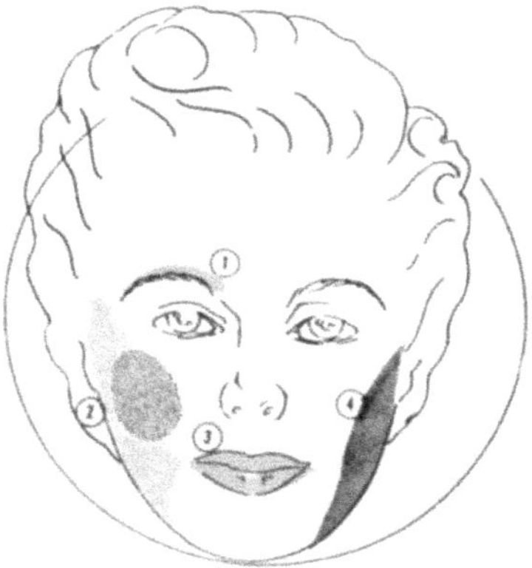

Fig. 70. CORRECT MAKE-UP
(1) Keep the eyebrow full, natural and placed on the high-point of the frontal bone with a well-arched effect. This gives the face the illusion of length. (2) Apply cheek rouge in an elongated field. From the center of the cheek, blend the rouge up, over and back of the cheekbone, then down and back over the jawline. (3) Make the mouth up wide and full to reduce fullness and roundness in the lower part of the face. (4) Consult the section on bases for the procedure to be followed before the application of cheek rouge if the face is extremely round and full.

Fig. 71. Corrective make-up, as shown here, can create an Oval illusion while proper balance is achieved. As a consequence, the face is shown at its best.

MAKE-UP ILLUSION FOR YOUR FACE SHAPE

SQUARE—Straight hairline, square jawline

It is said that the Square face-type denotes plenty of pluck and perseverance. This type can do anything, it is claimed. This could well explain why some of the Square types have turned out to be the world's greatest beauties. Warning: it doesn't take much to make this type stubborn or masculine in appearance.

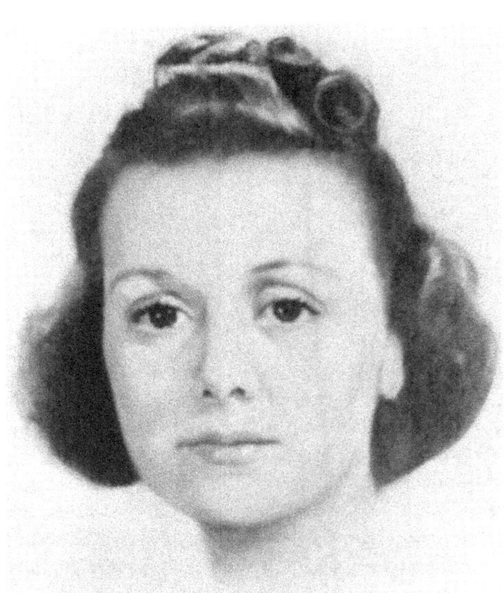

Fig. 72. Square shape minus all make-up.

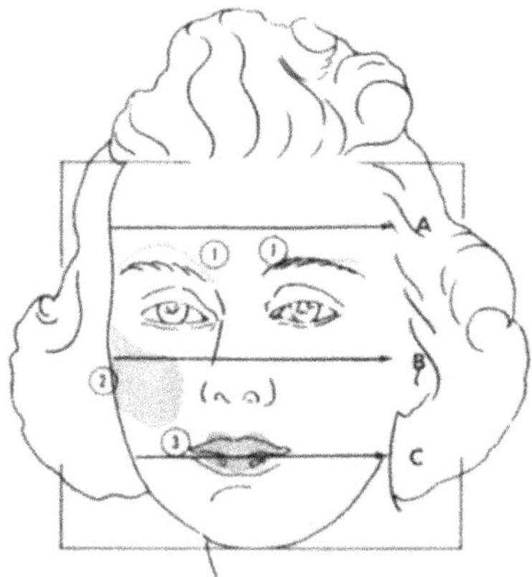

Fig. 73. WRONG MAKE-UP
A, B and C are your caliper measurements. (1) Do not arch the eyebrows or pencil them too thin, high, or angular—or straight with an obvious drooping hook on the end. This accentuates the face's squareness. (2) Do not apply small circular fields of rouge in the center of the cheek. This also accentuates fullness and squareness in the face. (3) Avoid narrow and straight as well as angular lines in lip make-up. This accentuates the width in the lower part of the face.

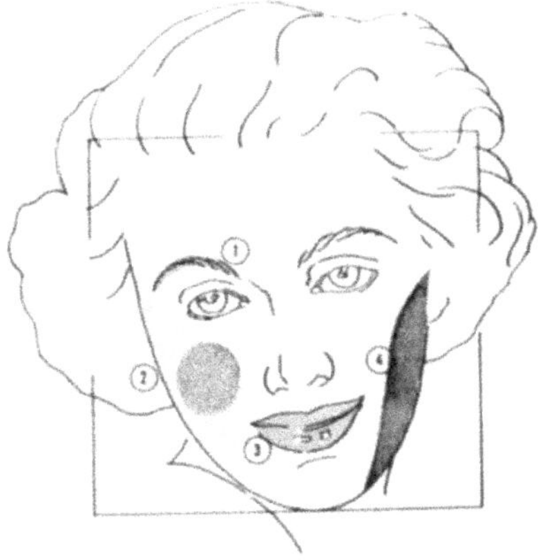

Fig. 74. CORRECT MAKE-UP
(1) Eyebrows should be large and full, with a slight arch and curve. (2) Apply cheek rouge (moist or dry) in an elongated manner. The deepest color should be on the high-point of the smile. Blend the rouge up, down, and over the jawline. (3) Apply lipstick to make lips seem full and large. This make-up trick reduces the width of the jawline from the corner of the mouth to the outside of the jawline. (4) If there is extreme width and squareness in the lower part of the face, refer to the section on bases.

Fig. 75. Here are shown the happy, beautifying results of the proper application of make-up to the Square face-type. Note how the illusion of the Oval has been successfully created.

MAKE-UP ILLUSION FOR YOUR FACE SHAPE

TRIANGLE (Composite)—Narrow forehead, wide jawline and chinline

The Triangle face is slightly wider and more angular than the Round or Square type in the lower part of the face. The make-up procedure for this composite type could be identical to that used by the Round and the Square face-types.

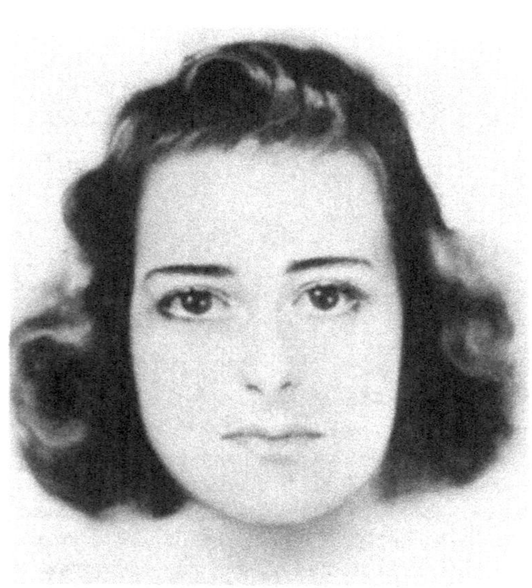

Fig. 76. Triangle shape minus all make-up.

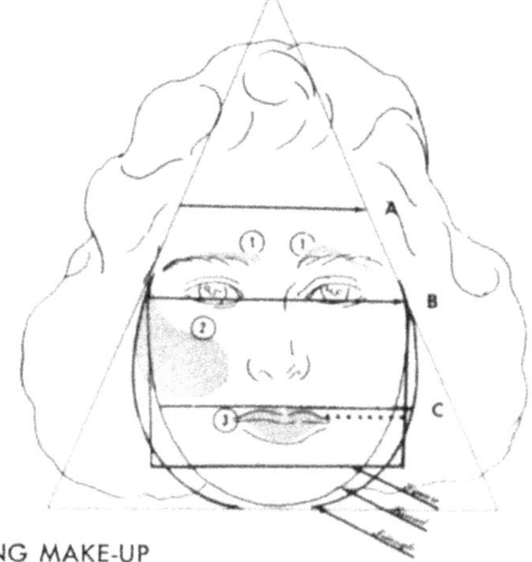

Fig. 77. WRONG MAKE-UP

A, B and C are your caliper measurements. We suggest that you recheck your caliper measurements with this face-type. (1) Avoid the straight, upward slanted, or long angular eyebrow. Any one of these types reduces the width of the forehead. (2) Do not apply your cheek rouge in a circular, high, extended area; this accentuates the width of the lower part of the face. (3) Avoid small, rounded mouth make-up. This again will accentuate any width in the lower part of the face.

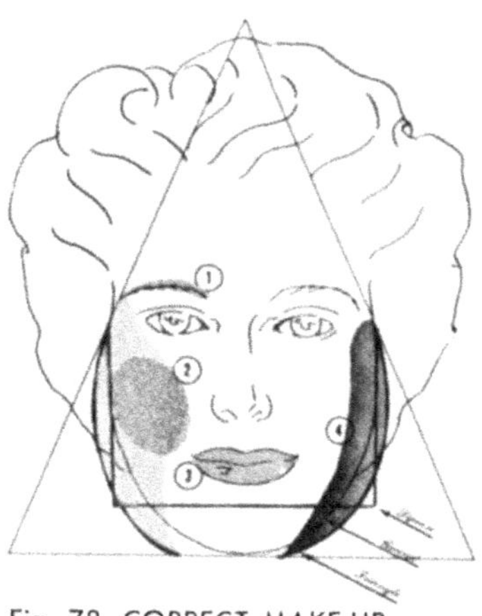

Fig. 78. CORRECT MAKE-UP

(1) Keep the eyebrow full and not too long. (2) Apply cheek rouge in a circular manner on the high point of the smile; blend and taper the rouge up and down, and over the jawline. (3) Make up the mouth as wide and full as possible; this reduces the fullness of the lower part of the face. (4) If there is extreme width in the lower part of the face, refer to the section on bases.

Fig. 79. This reveals the Triangle face corrected through the application of make-up. It might be interesting for you of the composite type to take your caliper and make the caliper measurement C to prove our point of illusion through the application of make-up.

INVERTED TRIANGLE—Wide forehead, narrow chinline

The Inverted Triangle is exactly that. It is a Triangle standing upon its peak. This face-type can have considerable charm. Improper make-up, however, accentuates the width of the forehead and the narrowness of the chin and turns the very assets of this type into liabilities.

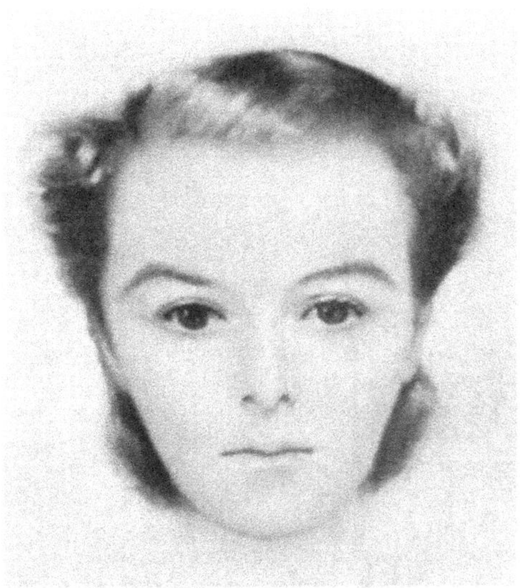

Fig. 80. Inverted Triangle shape minus all make-up.

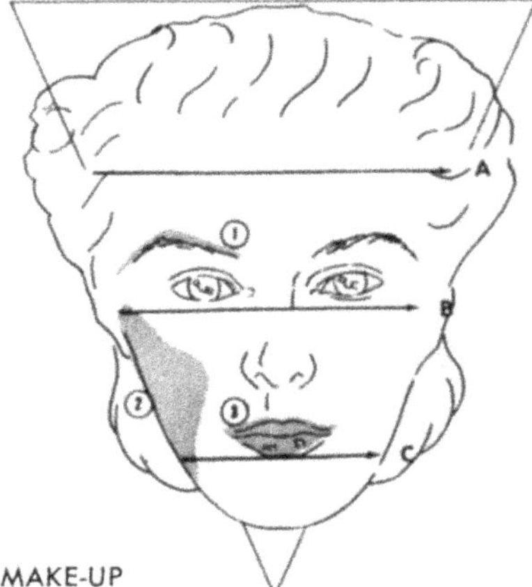

Fig. 81. WRONG MAKE-UP
A, B and C are your caliper measurements. (1) Avoid high, full, or wide masculine eyebrows. Under no conditions extend them. This would create fullness and width in the upper part of the face, and this is undesirable. (2) Do not elongate or taper the cheek rouge down to the chin. This creates thinness in the lower part of the face and accentuates a long, pointed chin. (3) Do not make up your mouth too wide. A too-wide mouth reduces the width of the lower part of the face.

Fig. 82. CORRECT MAKE-UP
(1) Keep the eyebrow line natural—not too full or too thin. (2) Apply cheek rouge on the high point of the smile, tapering rouge up over the high point of the cheekbone. (3) Keep the mouth line natural and the upper lip softly curved, with no angular effects. Arch the mouth slightly, but do not make it too wide. (4, 5) Make up the lower part of the face two shades lighter than the base coloring if the chin is extremely narrow. In illustration 5, the forehead will be two shades darker than the base foundation. This takes careful blending throughout the entire make-up. Check the section on bases.

Fig. 83. Here is shown the subtle beauty to be achieved through the use of proper make-up, and the illusion of balance which can be created in the Inverted Triangle face-type.

MAKE-UP ILLUSION FOR YOUR FACE SHAPE

DIAMOND—Narrow forehead, broad jawline, narrow chin

This face-type, with its broad cheekbones, tapering forehead and narrow pointed chin, is often found among girls of Nordic descent. This face should reveal the sincerity and idealism so often characteristic of this type.

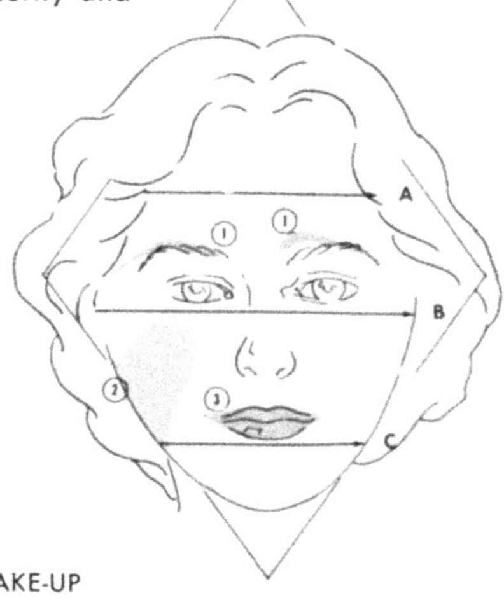

Fig. 85. WRONG MAKE-UP
A, B and C are your caliper measurements. (1) Avoid large, wide, inner hooked, or extended eyebrow line, as this reduces the illusion of width in the forehead which is so necessary to this type. (2) Do not place cheek rouge in the hollows or the centers of the cheeks. This will have a tendency to accentuate the width of the cheekbones. (Caliper measurement B.) (3) Do not make the mouth up too wide, or form the lower lip too pointed and drooping. This only calls attention to the thinness of the cheek line and the pointed chin.

Fig. 84. Diamond shape minus all make-up.

Fig. 86. CORRECT MAKE-UP
(1) Keep the eyebrow natural, with a slight curve to the arch. The brow should not be too thick or too wide. (2) Apply cheek rouge on the high point of the smile. Blend back and upward over the high point of the cheekbone. (3) Keep your mouth completely natural. (4) If the forehead and chin are quite narrow, as in illustration 4, apply two shades lighter foundation than the base coloring to both forehead and chin.

Fig. 87. All of the basic principles in the expert application of your cosmetics are revealed in the make-up for the Diamond face-type.

CHAPTER EIGHT

The How, What and Why of Make-Up

BEGIN YOUR PORTRAIT ON A CLEAN "CANVAS"

Each and every morning of your life you assume a unique and important role. You become a very special kind of artist with a very special goal. You, with the aid of modern cosmetics, paint your individual portrait. It is perhaps the most consistently and constantly viewed and rated effort of your daily life. Your face is looked at, reacted to and rated by your friends, family, co-workers, employer and, however silently, by a good many strangers everywhere you go.

To be blunt about it, your face is on display from early morning until you turn out the light at night, whether or not you want to admit this fact. What you do to your face, and for it, is there for all to see and judge. Can you afford to be any less scrupulous, demanding and skilled in your portrait painting than the artist commissioned to paint a portrait on canvas?

Your face is your canvas. Let it, therefore, be fresh and glowing when you begin your all-important, daily portrait. And when you begin this work, remember that like the artist you must bring skill, persistence and the joy of creative effort to your impossible-to-ignore daily work of beauty.

The simplest, most efficient way of creating your clean, clear "canvas" is with the help of a cleansing cream and skin-freshener. The cleansing cream does exactly that: it cleanses. The skin-freshener freshens and tones the skin and, when properly applied, removes all traces of cream on the face and in the pores.

Use the cleansing cream with a lavish hand so that it can quickly dissolve and pick up the surface and hidden pore grime. Apply it to the face and neck in an upward and outward circular motion. See Figs. 88 and 89. Be certain to work it well into the following areas: The blackhead area at the corners of the mouth; the chin crevice; the nose crevices; and the little squint lines at the corner of the eyes. Remove the cream with tissue, using, as always, an upward and outward circular motion.

After removing the cream with tissue, saturate a cotton square with skin-freshener (the one right for your skin-type). Stroke on gently. See Figs. 90 and 91. Apply skin-freshener twice, if necessary, to make certain every trace of cream and grime and oil secretion have been removed. The skin must be absolutely clean before cosmetics of any kind are applied. The freshener is patted off gently with a tissue, square of cotton or soft towel. The skin is now fresh and glowing and ready for your foundation for a beautiful portrait—the make-up base.

THE MAKE-UP BASE—MOST TALENTED OF COSMETICS

With a bottle or cake of make-up base in your make-up kit, you are, as one actress says, "as close to carrying a spare skin as a woman will ever get." The actress is right, 100% right, for the make-up bases of today, also known as powder bases and foundations, are the most talented of all cosmetics. They color, cover, protect, correct and beautify. It goes without saying that in our eyes the foundation for your make-up is indispensable. If you do not agree with this sentiment, it could easily be because you have never tried a foundation, because you picked the wrong one, or because you tried one and never learned to use it correctly.

As with all good things, if a base is misused, the results can be unfortunate as well as frustrating. Use the wrong color base and apply it too heavily or use it with too dark a powder and you can do nothing but produce a stiff, uncomfortable glaze that makes your face look as if it had just come out of the kiln. Use the wrong type of base—one, for example, that seems to refuse to blend evenly and invisibly over your particular type of skin—and you may feel justified in condemning all bases because of your unwelcome, unrewarding experience. None of these things can happen to you, we insist, if you understand exactly what a make-up base is intended to do for your complexion. You must know the various types, be able to pick the right one for your particular skin-type, and then learn how to apply it correctly in order to use this versatile cosmetic to your utmost advantage.

FIVE IN ONE

There are five specific purposes for a base:

(1) *For color.* When an artist starts to paint a picture, on that fresh canvas we keep talking about, the first thing he does is lay in his ground-tone. This background color, spread over the entire canvas, is what he uses to set the mood and the character of the entire picture. It gives intensity and dramatic impact to the colors that follow.

Fig. 88. Cleansing procedure—upward motion.

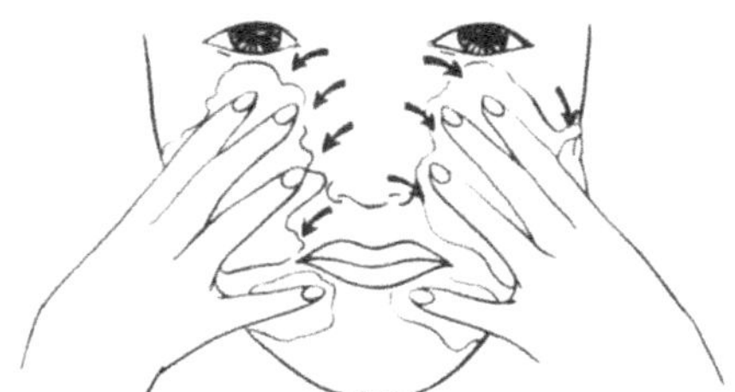

Fig. 89. Cleansing procedure—outward motion.

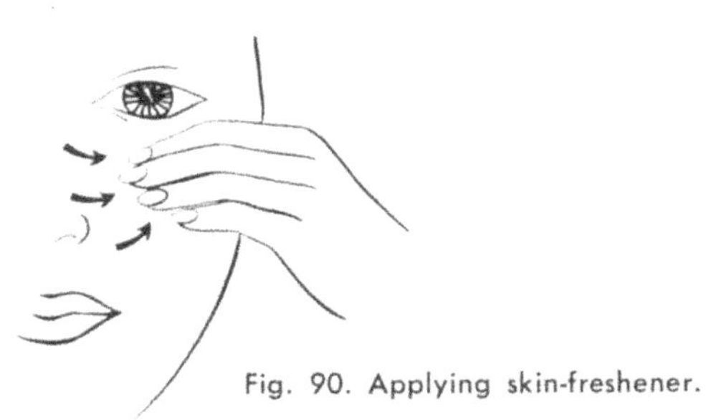
Fig. 90. Applying skin-freshener.

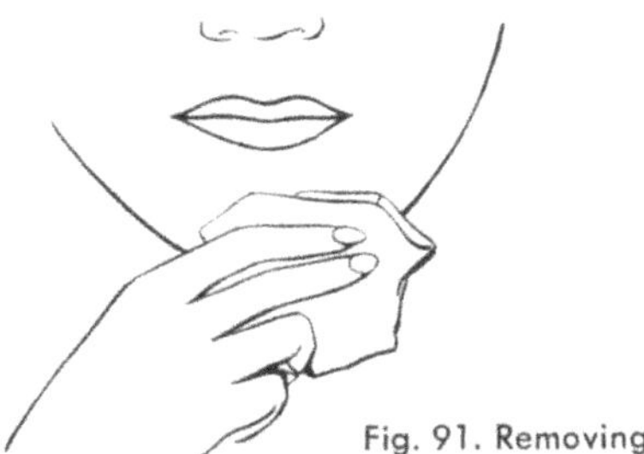
Fig. 91. Removing skin-freshener.

A tinted make-up base is the ground-tone for your facial portrait. It supplies the glow of youth and freshness to sallow, pale, tired or faded skins. It can be used to tone down a florid complexion, to lighten discolorations, to even up uneven pigmentation. If your own complexion has none of these faults, a natural or untinted base will preserve and properly enhance the perfection you now enjoy.

(2) *For coverage (pore protection).* To give the complexion a sheerer, finer-textured, poreless look, spread the base on in a thin film. This permits the make-up base to serve as a buffer between the skin and the other cosmetics to be applied. The lanolin or liquid-oil content of a base acts as an absorbent for the natural secretions of the skin and thereby prevents foreign particles from penetrating the pores. Remember, the pores have a tendency to draw in material drier than the skin itself. So often women say, "Look at my face. I powdered it just a little while ago and all of the powder has rubbed off." In reality, powder does not rub off. Neither does it blow away. In the absence of a base, it is absorbed. As proof, consider the fact that the nose, the most powdered area of the face, is also the most prone to "cosmetic-heads."

(3) *For clinging power.* The use of the base type proper for your skin permits all of the cosmetics used to attain their true effectiveness. Powder, rouge, eye shadow, even lipstick can be applied more easily and can be blended more evenly over the clinging surface a base provides. The proper use of a base gives the finished make-up greater adhering power and, in turn, a freshness which lasts hours longer than it otherwise would. An added bonus is the fact that a base also expedites and facilitates the removal of make-up at night since it literally cooperates with the cleansing cream to bring about a quick disintegration of all the cosmetics used.

(4) *For protective lubrication.* A base helps shield the face from the weathering effects of sun and wind. Most bases have either lanolin or vegetable oil as their main ingredient. Because of this, your make-up gains extra resistance to rain or snow, to pool or sea water. Although a base should never be considered as a sunburn preventive, it does help replenish the facial oils dried out by heat and sun, and prevents the chapping effects of cold weather. In any climate, be it dry, wet, hot or cold, an oil or lanolin content base helps to retain the natural moisture of the skin and to preserve the pliability of the facial tissues.

(5) *For contour correction.* Look to a make-up base for aid in disguising feature faults and creating an illusion of beauty and harmony for

the whole face. As you already know, light and shadow are essential to a beautiful make-up if only because even a proportionate or already pretty face can gain added beauty from make-up tricks employing this most versatile of cosmetics.

THE BEST TYPE OF BASE FOR YOUR SKIN-TYPE

Understand and accept from the beginning that you are apt to have to experiment a little, both in selection of color and in application, before your skin and a particular base fall permanently in love with one another. One reason for this is that, unbelievably enough, most people don't know which skin-type they are. And it is easy to understand why.

You do not, as is so popularly believed, have a problem complexion because your skin has a combination of dry and oily areas. These areas are present in most skins. The facial texture is determined by the manner in which the sebaceous glands function. These are the pesky, yet blessed, little "oil wells" which emit the secretion necessary for keeping the skin soft and young. Every face has its heaviest concentration of sebaceous glands in the center. Thus it is normal for a skin to be slightly oilier on the nose and in the cheek area next to the nose.

Only when the glands oversecrete in the center and elsewhere, giving the face a greasy, coarse-pored look, can the skin be properly classified as an *oily* skin. Only when the glands undersecrete, giving the skin a sensitive, flaky condition, can the skin be properly recognized as *dry*. Dry and oily skins, when caused by irregular functioning of the sebaceous glands, are a health condition and can frequently be helped by diet. Additional classifications include the thin skin, and the thick skin, both of which are inherited characteristics and are yours for keeps.

Having classified your facial texture, let us consider types of products. Bases or foundations come in four general forms: (1) liquid, (2) cream, (3) powder combined with a cream base, and (4) cake-powder make-up. Most of these come in a wide variety of tints including natural.

(1) *Liquid make-up* is a product in which the color is suspended in an oil. In our experience, we have found that the tinted oil base make-up is virtually an all-purpose base in that the product is amazingly adaptable and beneficial to every type and every age of skin. This is a long-standing opinion, for we Westmores were the first to create and use the oil-base foundation as the answer to Technicolor's demand for sheer and naturally lovely make-up. We use this type almost exclusively for screen make-ups and for the street make-up given in our salon. There are many fine brands of liquid make-up available at your cosmetic counter.

It may sound contradictory to say that liquid oil bases are equally good for normal, oily, or dry skins; but there is an explanation for this statement. For the dry skin, the oil acts as an emollient; it protects and lubricates. On an oily skin, the oil base absorbs the natural oil secretions evenly, preventing the secretions from mingling unevenly with your tinted face-powder and forming unsightly streaks and blotches. Any shininess that may become apparent around the nostrils or on the chin can be quickly blotted clean with dry tissue and without disturbing the over-all make-up.

Liquid-oil bases have the advantage of being especially easy to apply and blend. They are featherweight on the skin, have a highly desirable transparent appearance and are effective in disguising minor blemishes.

(2) *Cream base* is the paste or solid type of tinted foundation variously sold in jars, cream-cake or stick form. Practically all such bases have a high lanolin content, thereby generously supplying a much-needed lubricant for a dry skin. If you have a healthy, young, very firm skin, you may prefer using this heavier type of base. Generally speaking, it takes a bit more effort to apply and requires some skill in blending. Although foundations in many instances become strictly a matter of the user's preference, we personally do not suggest a cream base for a very oily skin. In our work, we have found that it tends to absorb the natural oils less evenly than the lighter type of base. This can result in uneven make-up after a few hours' wear.

The stick form of cream base is the most opaque and is very effective for highlighting sunken areas, for covering dark circles, discolorations and skin blemishes. Whether you have used liquid-oil or cream foundation, the stick highlighting can be additionally applied and blended with a small brush.

(3) *Powder combined with base* is a tinted cake face-powder, blended with lanolin or other cream base. It is suggested for those who prefer to apply both cosmetics in one operation. Usually packaged in a mirrored compact, it is convenient for carrying in the purse and excellent for skillful, quick touch-ups during the day.

(4) *Cake-powder make-up* is applied with a wet sponge. For an extremely oily skin, it has a welcome absorbent quality. Although it has become a habit with many women because of its absorbent qualities, we, personally, do not recommend its continued use for all complexion types. If you prefer it above all others, buy the soapless cake type, with some lanolin or oil content.

The slick-surfaced skin, to which base does not adhere, requires a specific foundation application procedure, which will be found described further on in this chapter under the heading Applying Your Base. There is also a rare type of skin—dry, thin and almost poreless—on which all make-up bases are inclined to slip. The possessor of this skin-type sometimes finds that some types of hand or body lotion will alleviate tenderness or burning and act as a make-up base at the same time. A cake-powder, used over the colorless lotion, will supply the desired tint.

THE BEST BASE COLOR FOR YOU

No skin has a single color. It has, instead, a blend of several tones of pinks and ambers. It would be difficult to find a perfect color match in a foundation or base. Even if you could, there would be little reason to use a tint that did nothing but duplicate the skin tint you already possess.

The trick is to decide which tone dominates your complexion and then pick a base to supply the tone you lack. To determine your skin color, simply look at it in a clear, strong light and note whether it is predominantly white, pink, yellow or olive. If after doing this, you still feel uncertain, ask a cosmetic sales person to do this for you and then follow the instructions listed here.

Pale or white-skinned: Use a light flesh pink or light beige base. This will supply the needed color.

Sallow or on the yellow side: Use a pink or rosy-toned base to add a glow to the complexion.

Olive: Use a peach-toned or beige-pink base for a flattering result on a light olive complexion. A copper-toned base gives warmth to a dark or swarthy olive complexion. A pale base does not contain enough tint to keep a dark skin from showing through. Never forget this.

Pink: Use a beige, buff or amber-toned base. This complexion type already has enough of the rosy tint in it.

If you are inclined to blush or flush with exertion, it will be a relief for you to know that the first step in stage make-up for an actor is a liberal coat of white or tan make-up on his ears. He makes sure not to forget it because he knows that the minute he whips up a fine emotional heat the ears—without benefit of this make-up—will show up like red sails in the sunset. The actor who doesn't have to pass close-up inspection uses a thick grease paint. You want your base to be invisible; therefore, don't try to cover up a ruddy skin with a pale pink base. The red will show through. Use a fairly deep tone of amber or a tan to tone down your flush.

Some day, perhaps, every cosmetic counter manager will realize how profitable it would be to have open samples of powder bases to allow the customer to try out a dot of tint. Too many of you take home the wrong shade and promptly decide that foundation does not look well on you. Where cosmetic-counter sampling is impossible, the best method is to hold the bottles up to your face until you find the one containing the color which best complements your own complexion.

Bear in mind that all liquid bases look slightly darker in the bottle than they do on the skin. In average circumstances, the base should be one shade deeper than the face color. This way it can be faded off into the neck, which is slightly darker.

Hair color is a contributing factor to your proper powder-base tint. Very light blondes often make the mistake of thinking their complexion should be equally pale, and the final make-up result is an uninteresting monotone. Avoid having skin-tint and hair so close in color tone that there is no contrast between them. The light blonde gains personality and warmth by using a rosy tone. In summer, a light tan tint is especially becoming.

The brunette, on the other hand, does not want too startling a contrast —such as very black hair and very white skin. Although the poets have written of this combination, it is seldom found in a naturally beautiful form. A brunette with pale skin will gain radiance from a pink or buff tint. In general, a pale skin is rarely a sign of youth or vitality. It is usually a sign of uncertain health or advancing years. Give your skin a glow, a look of radiant health with the expert help of proper base make-up.

Lastly, let us talk about the size of the face. If the face is large and full, stay away from very light-colored foundations. These reflect light, and therefore increase, the big-featured look. Choose a base as dark as the skin can take. This technique permits the base to absorb the light and minimize the physical size of the face. Conversely, if the face is lean, hollow, or very small, never wear a dark base. Such a color absorbs light and makes the face appear even thinner and smaller. Increase size and fullness by choosing a lighter than average base-tone.

APPLYING YOUR BASE

Remember, in using any type of base, a *minimum* amount means *maximum* loveliness! Here are the methods of application for the four common types of make-up base:

(1) *Liquid (oil-base) make-up:* Shake the bottle until oil and color are evenly and thoroughly mixed. Placing finger in neck of bottle, tip out one fingertipful of base. Apply in dots, as illustrated in Fig. 92.

For the "slick" skin on which base is inclined to slip, apply the base with a rubber sponge, creating a stippled effect over the entire face. Blend gradually until color is smooth.

(2) *Cream (or solid) base:* Always keep solid bases at room temperature. Never apply this kind of base when the cosmetic is cold, dry or stiff. To apply the product in this state tends to stretch the skin as you work to blend the base smoothly on your face.

If the cream (or solid) base is in stick form, apply with short swipes of the stick and blend.

(3) *Powder combined with base:* Using the dry puff which comes

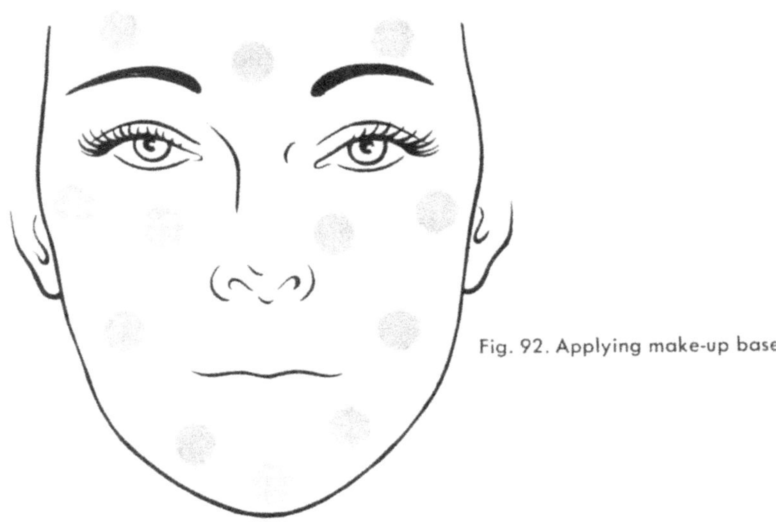

Fig. 92. Applying make-up base.

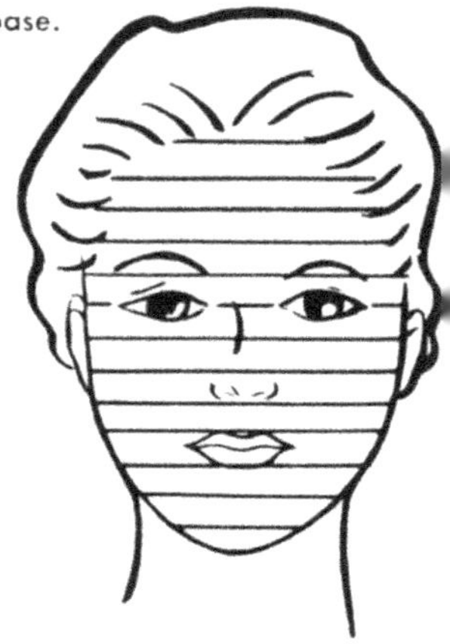

Fig. 93. Over-all blended base.

with the compact, apply according to the directions listed under Blending Your Base, which follows.

(4) *Cake-powder make-up:* Wet the sponge thoroughly. Hold it above the cake and squeeze the sponge dry, allowing its full content of water to spread over the surface of the cake. Next, rub the sponge gently on the cake, allowing it to soak up water and color evenly. Repeat this squeeze and soak-up process about three times until the sponge is well-filled with color. After application, if too much moisture lingers on the face, blot lightly with a tissue. Most women who use this type of base fail to use enough water for proper, easy blending.

BLENDING YOUR BASE

Using both hands, allow the fingers to move smoothly and evenly across the face. Avoid all digging in and undue pressure which would stretch and pull the skin.

If the base being used requires much effort to blend, it is probably because you have not followed directions or because the base is too heavy for your skin. The situation can usually be helped by scattering a few drops of water over the face. The water makes it possible to spread the base evenly.

If the dots of color spread easily, but do not disappear into the next dot evenly, too much base has been used. In this case, blot off the excess lightly with a tissue.

Nose: Begin the coverage of your face with your nose, since this feature is the most prominent and requires the most foundation.

Eyes: Begin at the outer edge of the eyes. Cover under and around them, smoothing the color upward and outward toward the temples. Be certain to work the base well into the little squint-lines at the corner of each eye. If these are merely fine lines, pat in the color with a fingertip. If they are deep, spread them gently apart and smooth in the color. *These crevices, if not evenly covered, will be accentuated.* Cover the eyelids by patting or by gently smoothing the foundation toward the outer corners.

Forehead: Smooth the forehead dots upward and outward to the hairline. Be sure to fade off the color into each small scallop, to avoid leaving a visible line of white skin between the base and the hair.

Cheeks: Work down the cheeks, but move the hands in a series of upward and outward half-circles. Smooth the base well behind the jawbone and well under the chin, "feathering" or blending off the color into the neck with light strokes of the fingers. This is necessary to avoid leaving a line of color demarcation between face and throat.

Mouth: Cover the upper lip from the nostrils down, carrying the base over the red part of the lipline. If there are small crevices running upward from the mouth, or at the corners of the mouth, it is important that the foundation be worked into these. If left uncolored, these tiny lines become doubly noticeable. It is into these small crevices, too, that lipstick is apt to "bleed." See the mouth make-up illustrations for examples of this. Remember that you do not want more than a thin film of base on this area.

After having completed this fingertip blending, you seem to have a perfect job—to the naked eye. Yet, a microscope would reveal many fine ridges of color occurring where you have lifted your fingers from the skin. Admittedly, you meet few people with a microscope handy; but these invisible ridges pick up powder and dust during the day and darken into very discernible lines or streaks. For this reason, it is important to finish off any base application with a *thorough patting*. Using your whole hand, pat over the entire surface of the face. Not until this is done can the application of the make-up base, as shown in Fig. 93, be considered complete.

USING BASE FOR FEATURE MIRACLES

The principle of corrective make-up has its basis in the use of contrasts of highlight and shadow to accentuate one feature and minimize another. In this manner the face as a whole is brought into better and more harmonious proportion. The blending of two, sometimes three, shades of make-up base is an art you can learn. Becoming an expert at it takes time, persistence and practice.

When your daytime make-up must be put on in a hurry, it is best to leave your illusionary tricks to rouge and lipstick. Both are effective in correcting contour and proportion. The good daytime make-up is one that has a transparent look. Unless you have time to blend your two tones of base as thin and smooth as silk, reserve this extra magic for evening wear.

Even then, it can't be done hastily. And, it goes without saying, practice makes perfect. Don't miss the miracles that blended make-up can perform for you simply because you are lazy. These are the rules to remember:

For highlighting: Use a base of the same color as the over-all foundation, but two shades lighter. A liquid make-up base is excellent for highlighting large areas such as the forehead. For highlighting indentations (eye-circles, laugh crevices, etc.) or for covering discoloration, it is best to use one of the stick-form cream bases now available. The correct procedure is to "clean up" the crevices with the highlight stick before applying the over-all base color.

For shadowing: Use a base of the same color as the one used as an over-all foundation, but three shades darker. The shadowing is usually applied after the over-all tint. Important: In blending two shades of base, always finish by patting the areas involved thoroughly. This extra step eliminates any possibility of there being a line of demarcation between the areas covered by different colors of base. This method blends one base color into the other evenly and smoothly.

Base treatment for the forehead: Forehead correction through hair-styling is discussed elsewhere. The following are make-up tricks designed to bring the brow into better proportion with the lower part of the face.

Protruding forehead: Use a darker base over this problem area. See Fig. 94. The lower part of the face, now lighter, will appear fuller by contrast. The shadowed brow will seem less protruding as a result.

Broad forehead: Same treatment as for protruding forehead above.

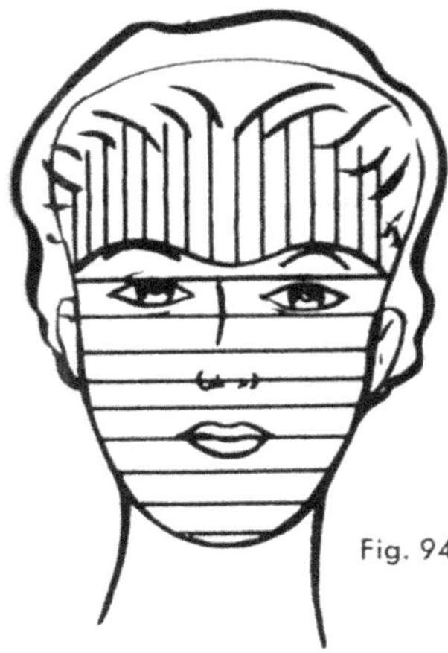

Fig. 94. Wide forehead corrective tinted base.

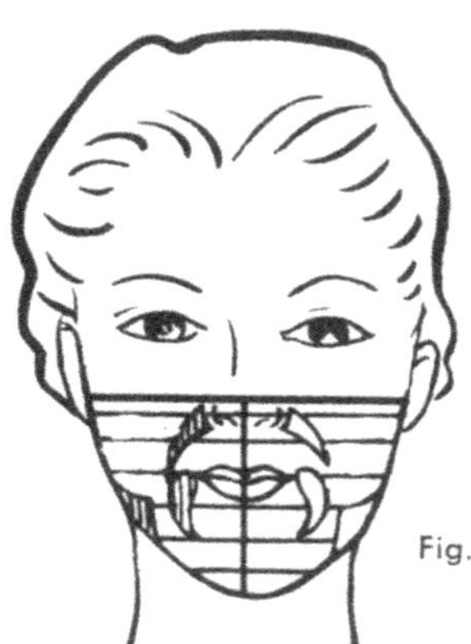

Fig. 95. Corrective tinted base for jawline.

Receding forehead: Use a lighter foundation on this problem area so that the lower part of the face seems darker and the forehead is highlighted into prominence.

Narrow forehead: Same treatment as indicated for a receding forehead problem.

Base treatment for the jaw: Jawline correction is done by bringing the lower part of the face into better proportion with the upper (as we did in forehead correction). See Fig. 95.

Heavy lower face: This type, found in the Round, Square and Triangle face-types, calls for shadowing at the sides as seen in Figs. 96 and 97. This use of a darker shade of base will absorb the light, thus reducing the width of the jawline and giving the illusion of Oval contour.

If the jaw is not too heavy but merely has square bones, soften the angular appearance by applying the darker base over the bone area only.

In both cases, be sure to blend the base well back to the ears and down on the neck. Finish by patting with the hand to eliminate any line of demarcation.

Narrow lower face: This type, particularly where the jaw area is sunken, benefits from a highlighting base, as illustrated in Figs. 98 and 99. By reflecting light, this gives the illusion of fullness in the narrow or sunken areas.

Extreme Inverted Triangle: This face-type calls for special treatment,

Fig. 96. Double chin before base.

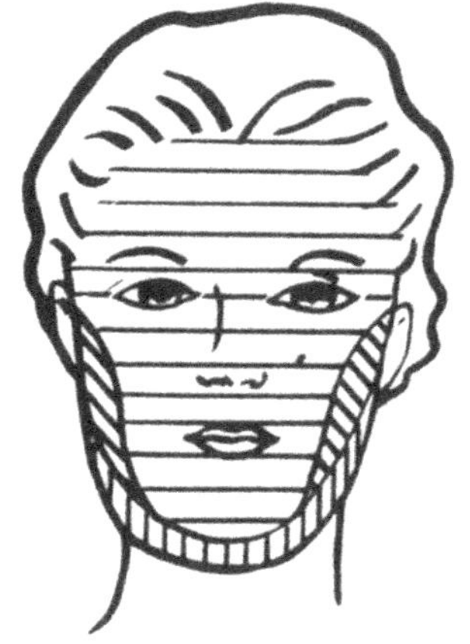

Fig. 97. Corrected double chin.

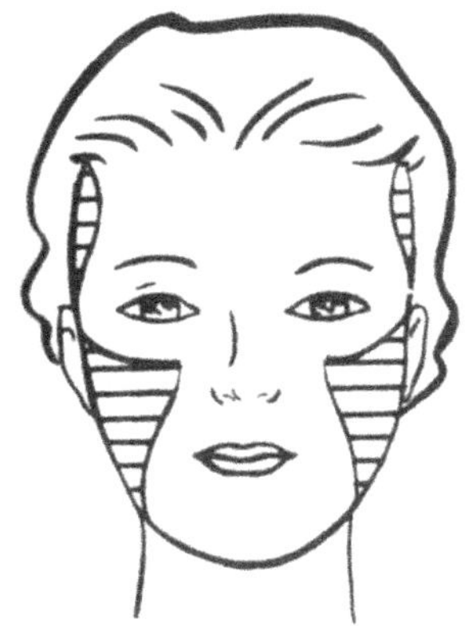

Fig. 98. Thin face before tinted base.

Fig. 99. Thin face corrected.

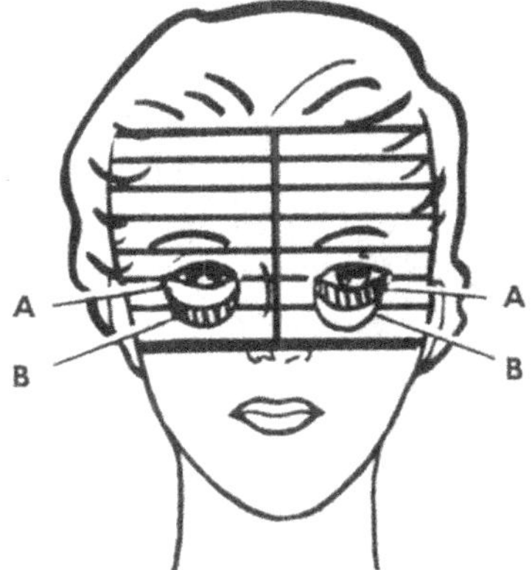

Fig. 100. Corrective eye make-up, pouch and circle.

with three shades of base. First, apply your regular color lightly over the entire face. Then apply the darker shade on the forehead to reduce its width. Use a highlighting base to add fullness to the pointed jawline.

Base treatment for chins: In the case of a broad or jutting chin, use a darker base than on the other features. This will de-emphasize the prominence.

Double or sagging chin: Blend the darker base well under the chin line to minimize the sag in this area.

Receding chin: Use a lighter base to highlight the front plane of this feature and bring it into more prominence.

Pointed chin: Use a highlighting base at the sides of the point to give the chin greater fullness.

Base treatment for necks: You need not be afraid that make-up, if used on the throat, must inevitably transfer itself to your collar. See the instructions for powder application. They contain a valuable hint for keeping the color on your neck instead of on your clothes.

Short, thick neck: Use a darker base than the one you used on the entire face area. This reduces the appearance of thickness.

Long, thin neck: Use a base that is lighter in color than the one used on the face area. This counteracts the thin appearance.

Base treatment for eyes: Deep-set or small eyes and too prominent eyes are specially treated in the eye make-up instructions.

Dark circles: Fig. 100 demonstrates what to do with the hollows of the upper lid, and that unpopular dark shadow under the lower lid. First, apply a highlighting foundation over the hollow or darkened area (as in B). Then apply a darker base over the puff which occurs directly above the discolored part (see A). The principle here is to highlight the sunken circle, and shadow the prominent rim right above it, thereby giving the illusion of smoothness to the entire eye area. Here, especially, it is important to pat gently and thoroughly, so there is no line of demarcation where the colors come together.

Bags or puffs: Fig. 100 shows how to diminish the puff above and below the eyes by covering with a darker shade of base to absorb the light (as in A). Then apply a highlight base on the rim just under the puff (as in B). This heightens the illusion of smoothness between the two. Pat the colors together gently and smoothly.

Base treatment for the cheeks: With prominent or sharp cheekbones, such as are found in the Diamond type, use a darker foundation over the cheekbones. Another effective corrective make-up trick is the use of a highlighting foundation in the hollows of the cheeks and the recession at the temples. This makes the hollows appear filled-out and minimizes the prominence of the cheekbones.

Highlight treatment for laugh-lines: To lighten the laugh-lines—the deep crevices running from the side of the nose to the corner of the mouth—use a highlighting base. This gives a more youthful appearance to this part of the face.

Base treatment for the nose: Don't attempt to shade or diminish a large or prominent nose by the use of a darker base. The darker make-up base will only make the nose look discolored. We correct the appearance of an oversized nose by using a highlighting on the cheek area right next to the nose. The same base is used on the rest of the face as on the nose. Apply highlight in the crevices alongside the nose and on a slight portion of the cheek to make the cheek appear fuller and the nose smaller by comparison.

If the nose is short and flat, give it the appearance of a more definite bridge by running a line of highlighting base right down the center, stopping at the tip. Pat to blend.

A dent in the nose can be smoothed by applying a highlighting base before the over-all face tint is put on.

ROUGE—WHAT IT MEANS TO YOU

Rouge is the color of youth, health and vitality. It is meant to duplicate the natural glow of all these characteristics. Therefore, it must never be applied in harsh or artificial outlines. Rouge is for attraction. Keep your allure on the subtle side if you wish to be beautiful.

In addition, the application of your rouge is one of the most helpful aids to contouring your face. The specific details of this contouring should be noted in the Applying Your Rouge illustrations.

For the most flattering use of both the corrective and the coloring properties of this cosmetic, we use both cream rouge and dry rouge. Cream rouge (or liquid rouge) is always applied before powdering. Dry rouge is used only after, or on top of, face powder.

APPLYING YOUR ROUGE

Cream or liquid rouge: In using cream or liquid rouge over a tinted cream or liquid base, the consistency of the rouge is such that it permits ready blending with the creams or oils of the base, resulting in what appears to be natural coloring.

For application, color is drawn off with the tip of a finger and a few

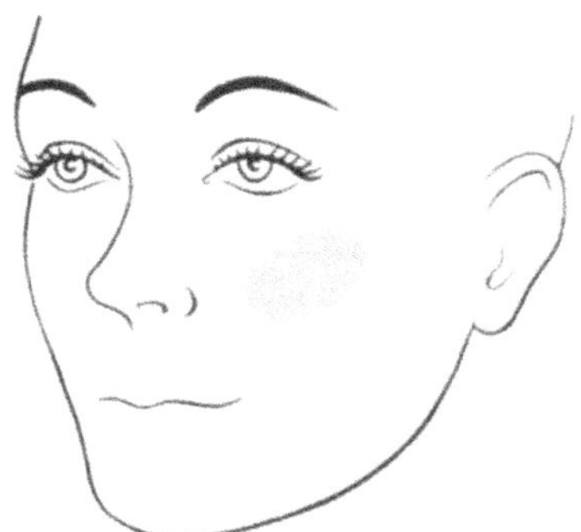
Fig. 101. Oval rouge placement.

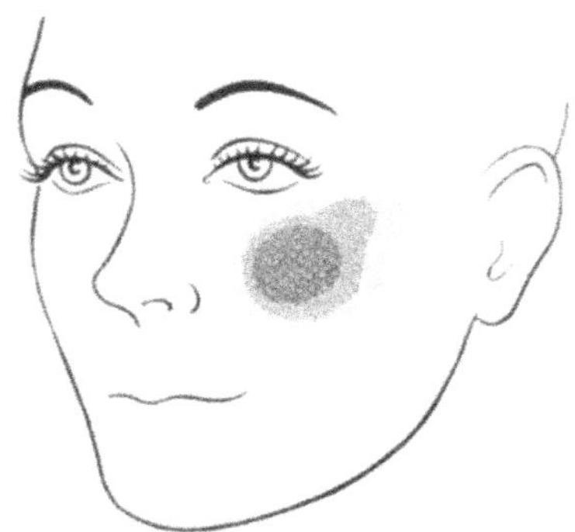
Fig. 102. Oblong rouge placement.

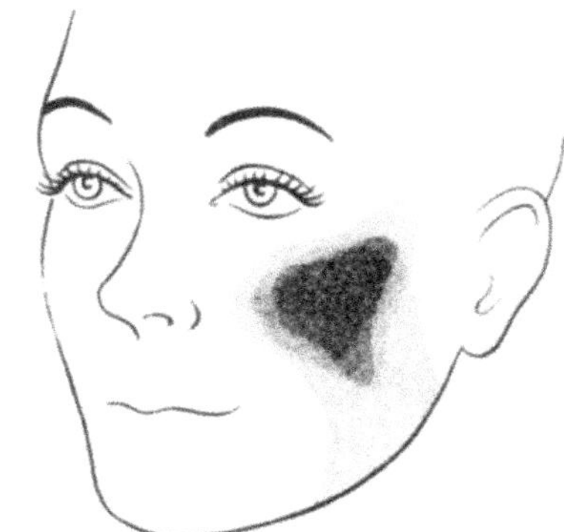
Fig. 103. Composite rouge placement; Round, Square, Triangle.

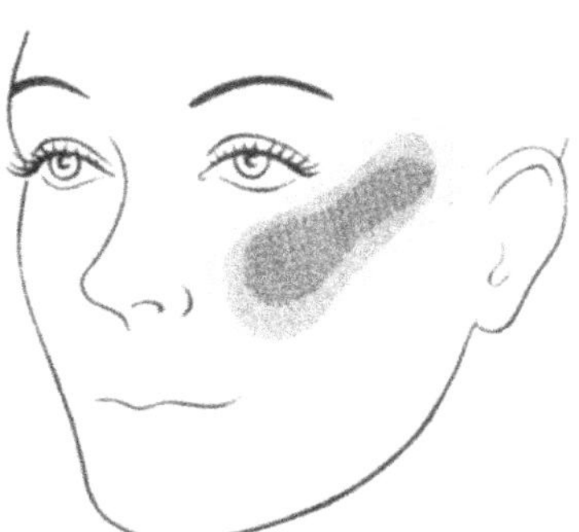
Fig. 104. Inverted Triangle rouge placement.

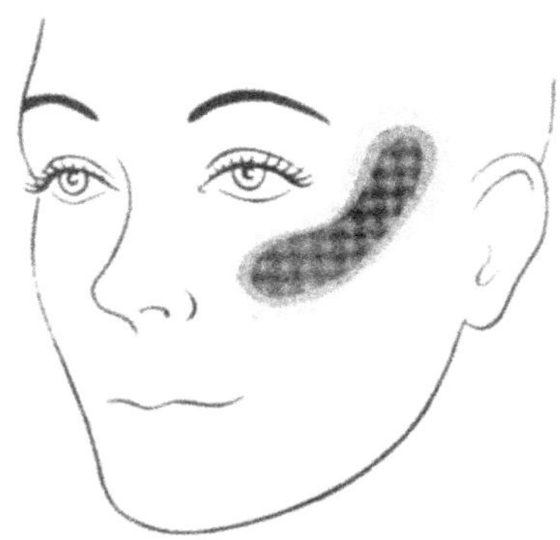
Fig. 105. Diamond rouge placement.

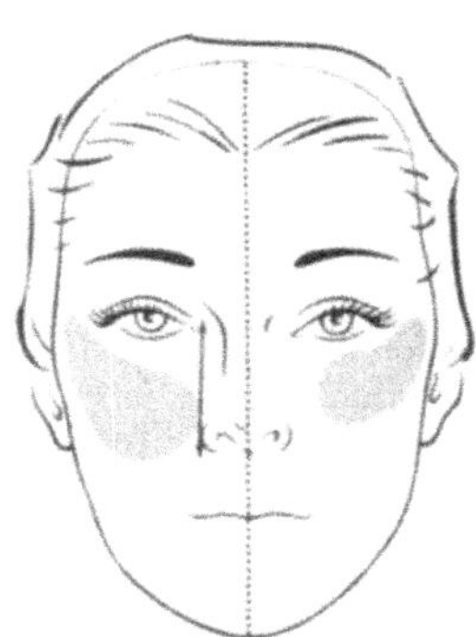
Fig. 106. Wrong and right cheek rouge for large nose.

dots placed on the highpoint of each cheek. With the fingertips, blend it off evenly and lightly. Never end the rouge application in a discernible line. Feather it off with light finger strokes to duplicate the way in which Nature blends off your natural color into the skin. If the cream rouge proves to be hard to spread, or is too dark in color, mix it with a few drops of liquid make-up base. Pour the base into the palm of the hand and mix in the rouge. This helps the rouge to "taxi" more easily over your base.

Rouge of any sort, cream, liquid or dry, is never applied close to the nose. Color in this area crowds and emphasizes the size of the nose. Never apply rouge directly under the eye. It will detract from the color of the eyes and even make them seem dull and lifeless. Never, never try to disguise an eye-circle or puff by rouging over it. This is an unnatural place to find a rosy tint and the rouge will draw attention to the puff or circle rather than minimizing it.

Dry rouge: This is applied only after powdering as seen in Fig. 58. It is dusted on lightly, over the surface and outline established by the original cream rouge application. The purpose of dry rouge is to color the fine pore hairs which may retain powder after the powdering process and intensify the color.

Note: The dry type of rouge is never used over cream or oil base. This would give a streaky or blotchy result. Because it is a dry and powdery cosmetic, dry rouge blends only with another powdery substance.

FACE POWDER—WHAT IT IS AND ISN'T

Face powder is one of the oldest cosmetics in history. Centuries B.C., sirens dusted their noses with powdered marble and crushed chalk. Medieval beauties used starch and flour and even risked white-lead poisoning on cheeks and chin. Early in our own 20th century, although scented and packaged face powders had become available at every "toilet requisites" counter, a buyer's choice was restricted to two shades: ghastly white or gaudy pink. Both were the consistency of calcimine.

To realize fully the advancement and refinement of this cosmetic necessity, we need consider only one fact: It was only a couple of decades ago that a proper mother, should she observe a "powdered hussy" coming along the sidewalk, would take her young daughter by the hand and firmly lead her across the street. In those days a real lady hid away a pat of cornstarch, usually in the toe of one of Father's clean white socks. On special dress occasions, she guiltily socked it across nose and cheeks.

Today, with featherweight textures and natural, skin-toned shades, we are rarely aware that a woman is powdered. We consider her lacking in fastidiousness and beauty know-how when by a greasy, uncared-for skin she makes us aware that she is unpowdered. Since few modern women have to be convinced that they do need a face powder in one form or another, it's unnecessary to point out its virtues. It is more important to discuss the beauty virtues mistakenly attributed to this cosmetic.

THE FINISHING TOUCH

The primary and specific purpose of powder is as a finish. It adds an exquisite, velvety sheen to the complexion. Unfortunately, many women mistakenly expect it to double in other capacities.

Although powder will temporarily tone down or clean up facial shine, it is not, as is commonly supposed, an oil absorbent. To demonstrate this, do this small experiment: Spread a layer of face powder on a saucer and on it drop a globule of oil. (Or drop the oil first, and cover with a layer of powder.) Does the powder absorb the oil? If so, the oil would disappear and the powder would retain its light and fluffy character. Instead, you'll find the oil triumphant. The powder darkens, coagulates and is thoroughly unpleasant to look at or touch.

This is exactly what happens on your face when you do not use a powder base to absorb the natural secretions of your skin. Your powder becomes caked and unpleasantly deepened in color around the nostrils, corners of the mouth, between the eyebrows and on the chin.

The effect of this on today's beauty is immediately visible. As explained in the section on bases, the heavy, oil-soaked powder doesn't rub off nor blow away. It is absorbed into the unprotected pores. Many of the so-called blackheads you see on your face are actually powder-heads or dry-rouge-heads.

Powder has acknowledged qualities as a tint. Where no tinted base is used, powder is correctly relied upon to impart glow and color to the skin. The very common mistake, however, is to add a tinted powder to a tinted foundation.

LET YOUR COLOR GLOW THROUGH

In Nature—in fruit, flowers, and the human complexion—color comes from beneath the surface. It is not spread, like a cookie's thick frosting, upon the top. Natural-looking make-up is one in which the tinted foundation glows through a colorless, translucent finishing powder. To add deeply tinted powder to tinted foundation can only result in an overcolored masklike look.

In corrective make-up, the use of a transparent powder is especially important. This is something we learned years ago in the studios, when doing character make-ups. It was useless, we found, to spend time darkening Mr. Paul Muni's cheeks into hollowness and highlighting his forehead into a majestic bulge if we were going to cover up the light-and-shadow with a heavy layer of opaque powder. When you add beauty to your own face by means of highlight or shadow, remember that the entire effect will be lost if you finish your make-up off with a too-dark or too-heavy powder.

YOUR POWDER—THE TYPE AND THE SHADE

In addition to the ordinary "loose" form of face powder, there is powder in both compressed and liquid form. As a complexion finish, we, personally, like the dusting or loose type of powder. Compressed powder is handy to carry with you as a touch-up. It keeps your purse neat as well as your face. Powder combined with base has already been discussed, along with its application, in another section. The liquid powder, meaning powder suspended in an aqueous or floral-water solution, has some enthusiasts. However, more of it is used on neck and arms.

Powder for tinted base: The proper, flattering choice of a powder-shade is determined by either your base tint or your skin tone. With a tinted base, you will get your loveliest effect with a colorless, luminous powder. There are several of these on the market. They are usually called "finishing powder." If you cannot buy colorless, choose the "natural" or the lightest shade and weight available.

When wearing tinted make-up on throat and shoulders, use ordinary talcum for powdering. Talcum is an old-time professional secret for keeping stage make-up from rubbing off on collars and costumes. You'll find it a precious help in keeping your décolleté evening dress fresh.

Tinted powders for wear without base: When you are relying on face powder for tint, select it to supply the color your own skin-tone lacks.

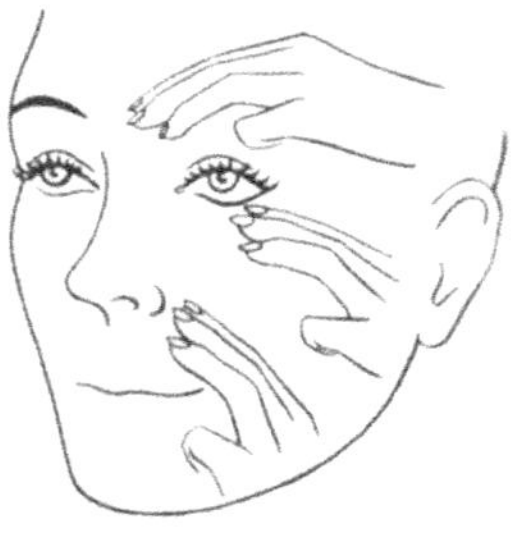

Fig. 107. Retrace before powdering.

Pale, sallow or very white skin: This skin tone lacks pink. Choose a pinkish or rose-toned powder.

Olive skin: This skin tone is on the dark side and requires a copper shade. Don't try to lighten your skin by wearing a light powder.

Pink skin: This skin tone needs a powder containing buff, beige or amber. Don't mistakenly use a pink powder. If your skin is ruddy or florid, don't try to cover it with too light a shade. Pick one with a tan (but *not* a copper) cast.

Suntanned skin: Choose a powder to supply what the tan lacks. If the sun gives you a yellow tan, use a copper powder to add warmth. If the tan is on the reddish side, use a brownish powder—one with no red in it.

When you have determined the most flattering tint (and you are not wearing a tinted base) you normally buy your powder *one shade darker* than your skin. The two exceptions are:

(1) The very large face: The need here is to diminish the size. Wear powder about *two shades darker* than the skin tone. A light shade makes the countenance appear larger.

Fig. 108. Powdering upper face area.

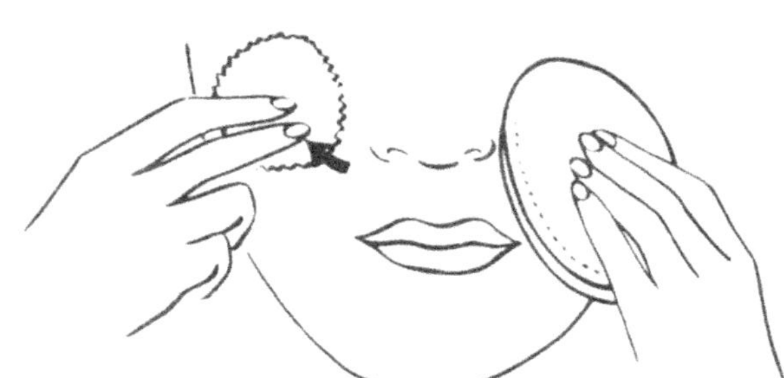

Fig. 109. Powdering lower face area.

(2) The very small or thin face. The need here is to create an illusion of increased size or plumpness. Choose as *light* a powder as your skin will take.

HOW TO POWDER

If powder is used without a foundation, be sure that the skin has been thoroughly cleansed of all cold cream by means of a skin-freshener. Never use a cold cream as a powder base. Among other things, all creams of this sort are made to liquefy. The warmth of your skin or the slightest heat of exertion such as dancing will cause the cream to break down the facial make-up, rather than to help it adhere. Be sure, too, that there is no perspiration on the skin. Apply the dry powder only on a clean, dry surface.

If powder is used over a base and cream or liquid rouge, inspect make-up thoroughly before powdering. See Fig. 107. Be certain there are no lines of demarcation between base, rouge, eye shadow, etc. If there are, the powder will "set" these lines and make them more visible.

Powdering for long-lasting make-up. Never rub powder on your face. Pat it on firmly and generously (see Figs. 108 and 109). Don't be afraid to use too much powder in this first application. Only the amount the base needs will adhere. A make-up generously powdered in the beginning will keep its freshness hours longer than one to which the puff has been too sparingly applied.

Important: One of the most common mistakes made in powdering concerns the little squint-lines and other fine crevices around the eyes. Spread these crevices *gently* apart with the fingers and pat the powder well into them. As explained in the section on the application of bases, these small lines, if left unevenly covered, will be intensified.

Of equal importance are the very fine lines leading up from the lips, the deeper crevices at the corners of the mouth, and the lines in the skin of the throat. These, too, should be gently spread apart and powdered evenly. Powder over both lips, as this adds to the staying power of the lipstick. Check the mouth make-up section for details.

Fig. 110 shows skin being pulled gently downward, preparatory to having excess powder removed. Remove excess powder with light strokes of the powder-brush across all planes and hollows of the face (Fig. 111). If you do not have a powder-brush, a piece of cotton or a towel (Fig. 112) will serve. Use a small, stiff-bristled brush to remove excess powder from the hairline, eyebrows and eyelashes. Don't neglect the space under the eyes and lower lashes. If you wish, a pipe-cleaner may be used for this delicate "clean-up" operation (Fig. 113).

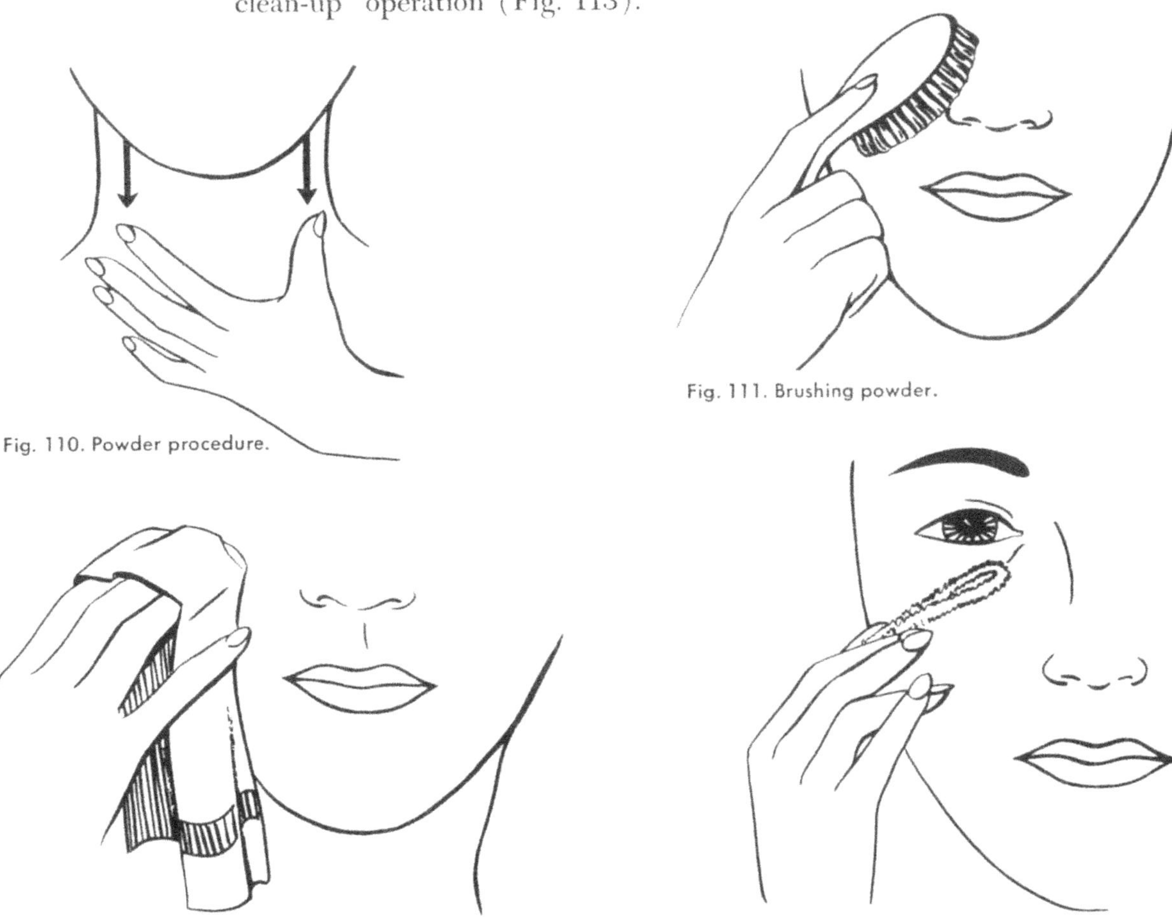

Fig. 110. Powder procedure.

Fig. 111. Brushing powder.

Fig. 112. Damp towel.

Fig. 113. Pipe-cleaner.

SETTING YOUR MAKE-UP

It is a simple matter to set your make-up. Dip a face-towel or cotton square into cold water, wring out, and press gently all over the facial area, being sure to spread apart the eye-crevices and laugh-lines. This eliminates the tense or tight feeling on the skin due to powdering.

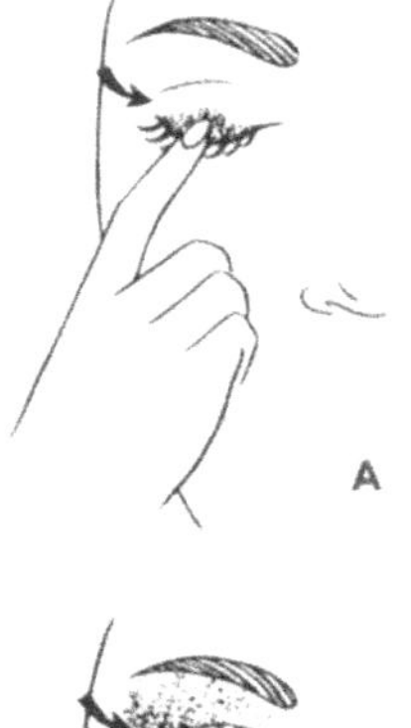

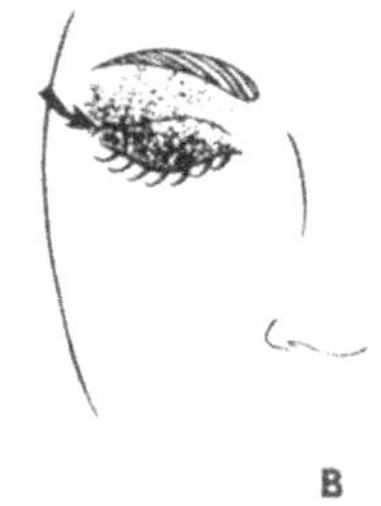

Fig. 114. Normal eye shadow.

EYES AND EYEBROWS

So often a woman will ask us, "You say I should accentuate my best feature—but how can I know which *is* my best feature?"

The answer is, it can only be your mouth, or your eyes. These two are the "live" features, the colorful, movable parts of your countenance.

"The windows of the soul" are where the heart and the mind look out —and can be seen into. The eyebrows add emphasis to what the eyes tell. Surprise sends the eyebrows up, anger draws them together. You must sometimes wonder if the eyebrows are wired directly to our box of emotions. They have been called "the rainbow arch of happiness or discord."

Because these two features, the eyes and the eyebrows, are so important to each other, we treat them together in this section. In the actual make-up procedure, they are separated. The steps are as follows: (1) eye shadow; (2) face powder; (3) eyebrow pencil. At this point, let us consider what we can do to beautify and accentuate the eye itself.

Eye shadow: This cosmetic is used to define the eye and add contrast to the white of the eye. In this way it seemingly intensifies the color of the iris. Except where a theatrical effect is desired for a specific purpose, avoid obviously unusual shades of shadow, such as gold, purple, silver and other faddish colors. The natural color tones are browns, blue, blue-gray and gray. Correctly applied they can add a soft and natural loveliness.

Shadow should be shaded, never applied with the same amount of density over the entire lid. Fig. 114 will help you in your application.

Start the first application, as shown in Fig. 114, at the lash line (A) and blend it up and over the fullness of the eyelid delicately (B). Never use eye shadow under the eye (A). This is demonstrated in Fig. 115. If the eye is very deeply set, use a highlight all around the eye area and don't use any eye shadow at all (B).

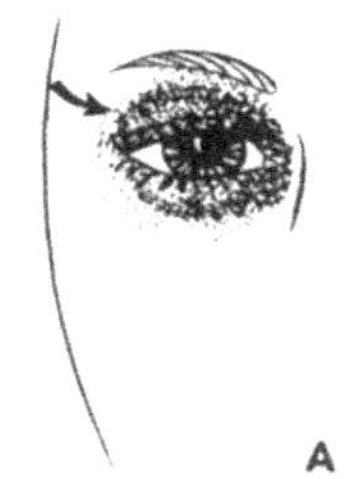

Fig. 115. Eye shadow for deep-set eyes.

Apply eye shadow, as shown in Fig. 116, on the highest and fullest point of the eyelid or frontal bone (A) if you have a protruding, full upper lid. Place the greatest density of color of the eye shadow on the fullest point of the eyelid or frontal bone. Be sure to keep eye shadow away from the nose area (B).

For a full, overhanging or drooping upper lid (A), note Fig. 117. Place the fullest density of the eye shadow at the eyelash line and blend it up and over the puffiness or fullness (B).

Lining the eye: There are two ways to line the eye. For the first, use a properly sharpened eyebrow pencil then soften with cotton swab or pipe-cleaner. For the second, use a lining brush. (This step does not occur until

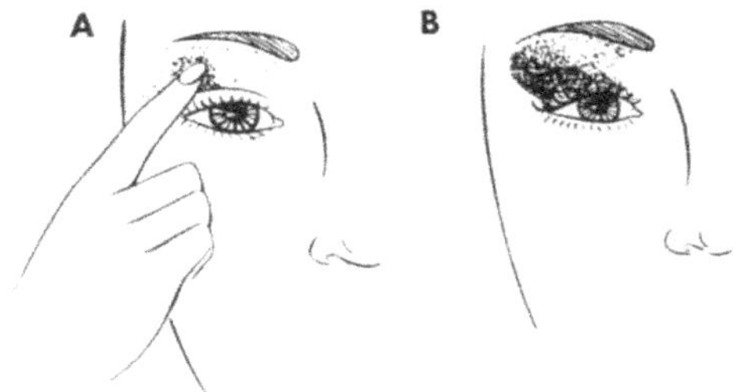

Fig. 116. Protruding upper lid.

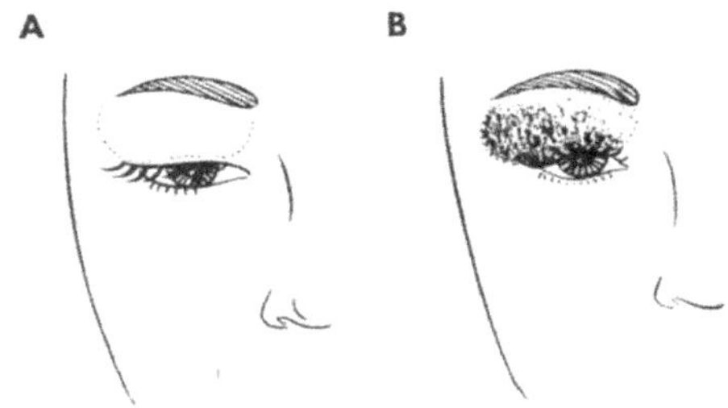

Fig. 117. Full overhanging upper lid.

after powdering.) For subtly done eye make-up, there is nothing so necessary as knowing how to sharpen your pencil properly. See Figs. 118 and 119.

To sharpen, use a single-edged razor blade, holding it as shown. Since pencils contain a lot of wax which softens easily at room or warm temperature, we suggest you either let your pencil set in a little glass of ice water or allow it to remain in the refrigerator for a half hour or so, before sharpening. This will harden the wax and make it easier to work with. Remove the wood first all around the wax part, then pare the wax part almost flat so that it is shaped like a chisel, as shown in the illustration. It is necessary to sharpen your pencil every third or fourth time it is used to obtain clean, clear results.

Figs. 120 and 121 show how to line the eye with either a sharpened eyebrow pencil or a lining brush. The first picture shows placement and the effect of lining. The line blends in with the balance of the eye make-up. Outlining the eye under the lower lashes, as in the next picture, is permissible if the eye is unusually small.

The Hollywood "soot secret" is illustrated in Figs. 122 and 123. Using an eye-liner brush instead of the pencil, it gives a soft subtlety to the eye. Take an old saucer or cold cream jar and an ordinary kitchen match. Allow the match to flame up close to the saucer or jar to have the smoke throw a deposit of soot on it. An artist's brush (No. 00) is suitable for eye-lining use. Roll the tip of the brush in the soot and apply to the eyelid, as shown in Fig. 123. We often use this method here in Hollywood, and it is

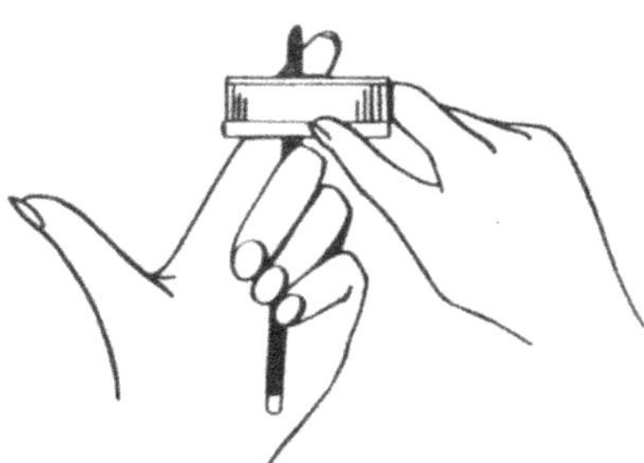

Fig. 118. Eyebrow pencil sharpening procedure.

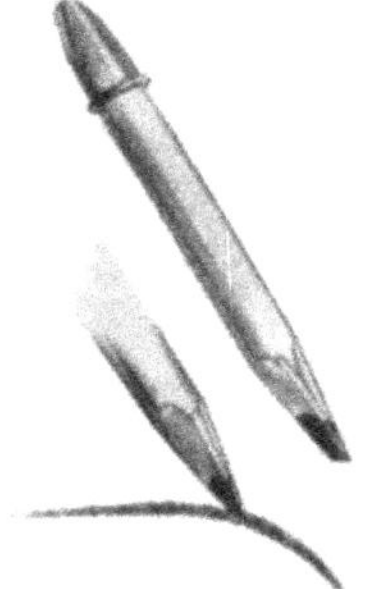

Fig. 119. Eyebrow pencil sharpening.

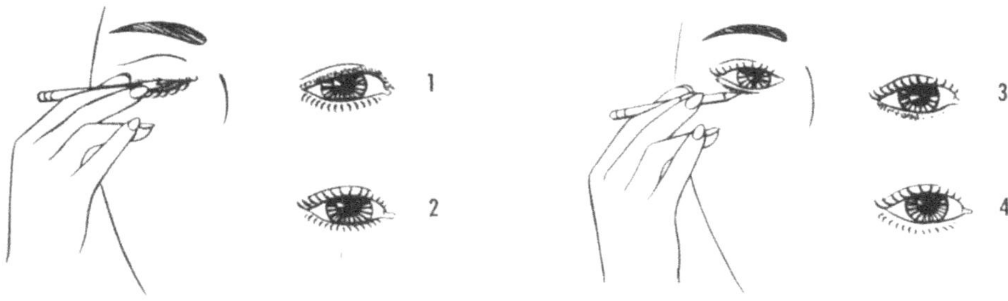

Fig. 120. Placement and effect of lining.

Fig. 121. Outlining eye under lower lashes.

perfectly safe and noninjurious to the eyelid or the eye. You'll be amazed at how smear-proof this soot trick is.

Eyebrows we have seen: Following are some eyebrows sketched from real life. See Fig. 124. The first six of them are distortions and add expression-marks of which the wearer was probably happily unaware. The seventh illustration shows eyebrows in the natural, lovely shape they should be.

Pencilling the eyebrow: An eyebrow pencil can impart added beauty to your face only when it is used with skill and genuine discrimination. Always work with short, definite hair-strokes—never in one continuous hard line. This takes practice, but in time you learn how to achieve a natural result. See Fig. 125. It is a good idea to brace the ball of the hand on the cheek when pencilling your eyebrow, since this gives you leverage and you then have complete control of your fingers and the pencil. Sketching your brow without using leverage results in uncontrolled strokes and an uneven eyebrow.

A black eyebrow pencil should be used only if you have very black hair. The average brown hair is shaded; it is not all one color. Therefore, we suggest two pencils, a black and a brown one. Taking small, quick strokes, alternate the two colors: first the brown, then the black. In this way you get a natural, not-too-obvious effect.

Fig. 122. Preparing Hollywood "soot secret."

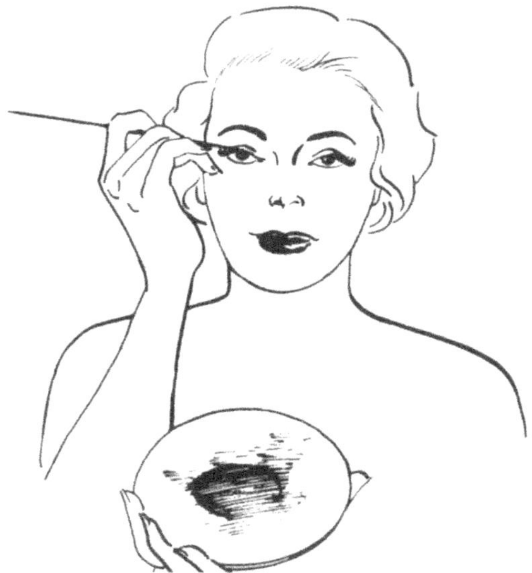

Fig. 123. Applying Hollywood "soot secret."

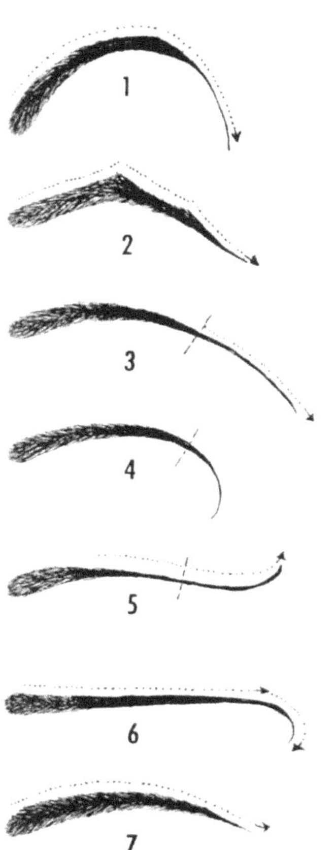

Fig. 124. Eyebrows: wrong and right. (1) A quizzical sky-hook gives the face an expression of continual surprise. (2) A masculine-looking brow gives an angular appearance to the entire face. (3) An elongated, obviously unnatural brow gives a drooping expression to the eye. (4) A woebegone eyebrow gives the eye a sad, questioning look and creates the illusion of too much fullness in the eyelids. (5) A winged brow is unnatural and does nothing to enhance the facial expression. (6) A straight, hard eyebrow gives an expression of undue severity and hardness to the face. (7) A normal, natural arch duplicates the shape of the eye below it and gives added beauty to any face-type.

Fig. 125. Eyebrow hair illusion.

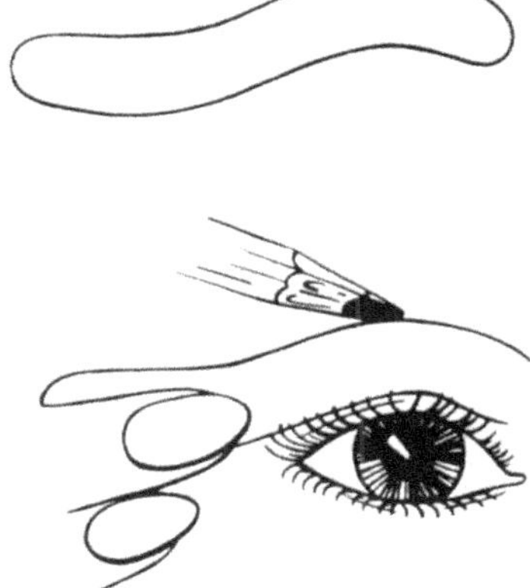

Fig. 126. Templet for eyebrows.

If you have no brows, either because of over-tweezing or a natural lack, draw them on with a templet, as illustrated here in Fig. 126. To make the templet, buy a piece of celluloid or acetate such as is sold in art shops. (This can be washed off, whereas cardboard would become smeared with pencil and mascara.) Now, using your eye pencil, draw on your face the eyebrow you would like to wear. Remember that the arch should conform to the high point of your frontal bone. When you have experimented until you have drawn the brow you want (pencilled on thickly) touch it slightly with vaseline. Now, take a piece of white paper, press it against the pencilled brow, and take off the impression.

The impression on the paper will give you the pattern of curve for your templet. Its entire width should equal the height of your eyelid, so that it may be used as in the illustration. Reverse the templet for drawing the opposite brow.

In this manner, you will be able to draw on your brows exactly the same shape each time.

Applying mascara: Here, in Fig. 127, you see the templet used for control in applying mascara. It helps if you have difficulty with fluttering lids, and it keeps the mascara from being smeared beneath the lower lashes.

Pull the upper lid slightly with the left hand and apply. Follow the same procedure, in Fig. 128, for the lower lid.

Always, when applying mascara, remember that a clean and soft look for each lash is what you're after. If you are dark, black mascara is permissible. For a blonde or auburn-haired woman, black eye make-up gives a harsh and artificial look. Our harmonized color chart, page 50, suggests brown mascara in most cases.

The consistency of the mascara is important for a successful application. Always start with a clean mascara brush. Wipe it off. Dampen the brush slightly and rub on the cake of mascara until a paste-like consistency is achieved. Now brush your mascara on lengthwise, following the growth of the hair from the root of the lash to the tip.

When the lashes are very thin, a second coat of mascara applied a little drier than the first coat will result in thicker-looking lashes. Be sure each coat is quite pasty, and that the second coat is almost dry so that the lashes will be kept separated and will not become stuck together in a heavy, artificial look.

Avoid rubbing or scrubbing across the lashes. Always use water to moisten your mascara. Do not use the common habit of saliva. You can carry an infection into your eye this way. If you have made the mistake of

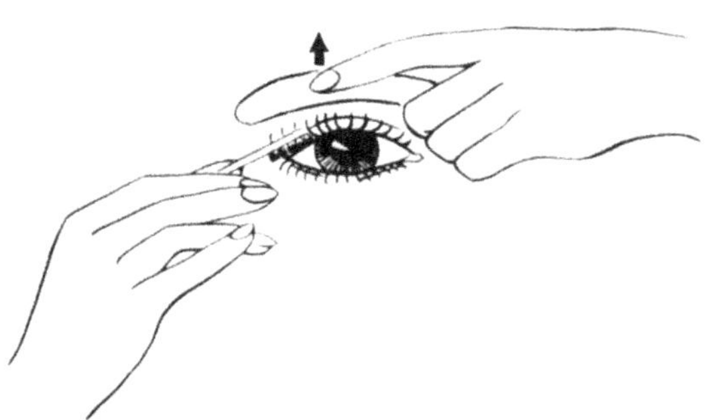

Fig. 127. Control for mascara on upper lid.

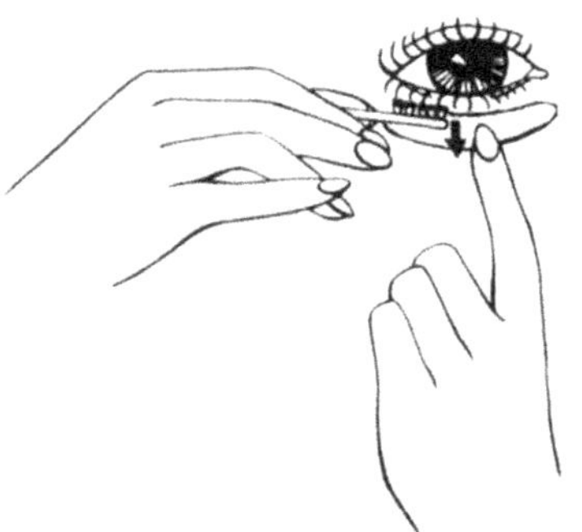

Fig. 128. Control for mascara beneath lower lashes.

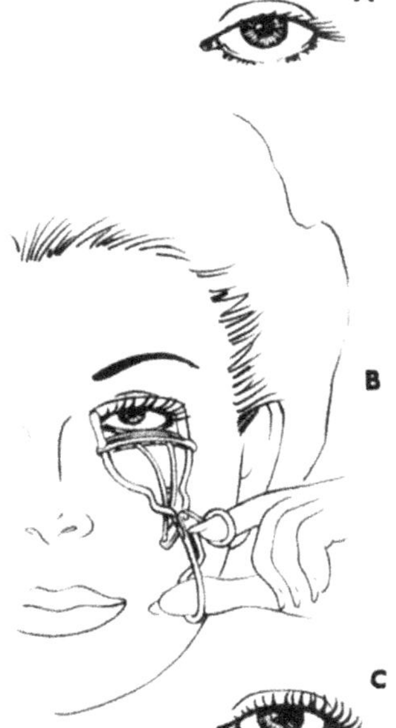

Fig. 129. Eyelash curler.

using too much water and your lashes stick together, before they are fully dry take a small dry brush and separate them. See that your mascara brush is washed clean after each application.

Curling the lashes: If the lashes are very straight, and do not curl even with the use of mascara, use an eyelash curler as illustrated in Fig. 129. Be sure that the rubber lining of the curler is fairly new. Never clamp down tightly on the lashes. A curler should be used by gently squeezing it up and down the length of the lashes. The curler may be used either before or after using mascara. The result is shown in C.

How to make round eyes look almond-shaped: Do not over-emphasize the round effect by lining the entire upper lid. Line the eye from the center to the outer corner only. Avoid a thin eyebrow. Use mascara only on the lashes from the center of the eyes to the outer corners and brush the lashes at the outer corner up and outwards. This will have a tendency to make the eyes appear wide and almond-shaped rather than round.

How to make prominent eyes soft and lovely: Overly prominent eyes can destroy correct proportion in the face. In styling your hair, use a soft, loose arrangement with no small curls or dips. Draw attention to the lower part of your face with your make-up. Don't wear thin eyebrows, but by the same token don't make them overly heavy. Mascara only the upper lashes lightly. Blend your eye shadow carefully over the prominent part of the upper lid, using as dark a shade as possible, and carry it very lightly up to the line of the brow. Do not use mascara on the lower lashes. Do not outline the eyelids.

How to make small eyes look large: If the eyes are small or deep-set, create the illusion of size by arching the eyebrows just a little lower than regularly. Be careful not to exaggerate this effect or straighten the brow too much, since this will give the face a severe expression. Removing just a few of the hairs from the upper edge of the brows and accentuating the lower arch a trifle with an eyebrow pencil will give the desired effect. Line the eye with pencil or liner brush. Also, mascara only the tips of the lashes. With deep-set eyes, use very little eye shadow and none in the extreme hollow of the eyelid next to the nose. See Fig. 115, illustration B and Figs. 120 and 121, illustrations 1, 2, 3 and 4.

Eyebrow and lash helps: For unruly eyebrows (with hair growing in several directions) frequent brushing will help. Use transparent mustache wax or wave-set for control. Brush it into the brow hair, then brush the brow into shape. For scanty or broken lashes, there are several proven lash growers on the market. Use each night and you'll get results. Brush on from the root of the lash to the tip. The brushing in itself stimulates circulation and growth.

Eyebrow tweezing: Go carefully, for in an eyebrow every hair counts. Never touch the top line itself, but take out strays above it. If the brow is too wide, remove one by one the lowest line of hairs and all those below it. The one exception to these general rules is when you are definitely lowering the brow placement for feature-correction purposes.

Before starting the tweezing procedure, run cotton dampened with skin-freshener over the eyebrows and surrounding areas. It will act as a mild antiseptic and tone the skin for less painful pulling.

After tweezing, the same procedure should be followed to lessen the sting of disturbed areas and again act as a mild antiseptic. Also, its application will hasten the withdrawal of reddened surfaces.

YOUR MOUTH, THE MOST MOBILE FEATURE

There has been much poetry and much serious study of physiognomy devoted to the mouth. It is your most mobile feature, capable of showing emotions all the way from tenderness to fear or tragedy. One of the truest sentences ever written about this feature is, "The mouth speaks, even when it does not say a word."

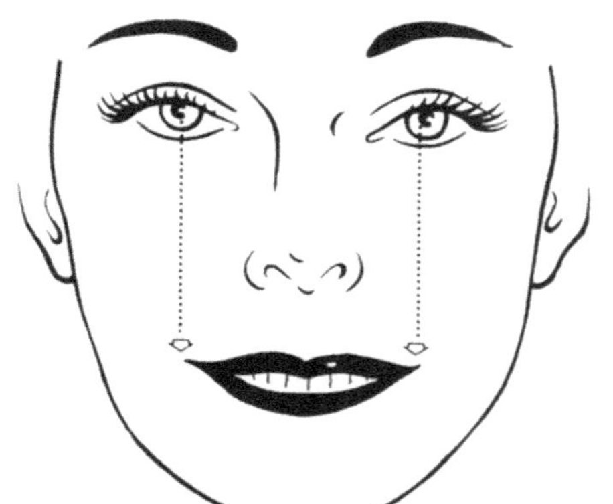
Fig. 130. Full smile.

Fig. 131. High-point lip measurement.

Fig. 132. Practicing lip brush application.

It is also the feature which speaks most loudly about careless or hasty make-up application. Chewed-off lipstick, smeary lipstick, lipstick "bleeding" into lines around the mouth—these are common and displeasing sights.

Mouth make-up, or lipstick, is also a corrective means of bringing your other features into better proportion, as seen in Figs. 130 and 131.

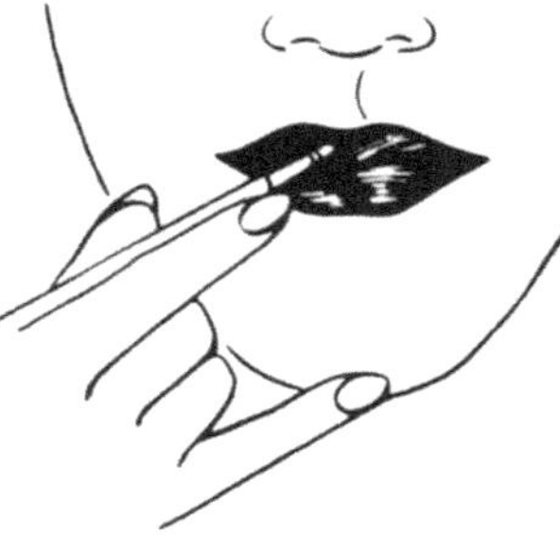
Fig. 133. Actual lip brush application.

Use a lip brush: In the early days of screen make-up, we made many mistakes; the most glaring of these was the "Cupid's bow" mouth. This bee-stung effect was the natural result of applying mouth make-up from a small rouge pot, as it was done before lipstick came into use. A finger was rubbed into the pot and the make-up dabbed on.

A change in the application of lip rouge came about because of our concern with sanitation laws, which objected to the application of make-up men's fingers to the star's lips. One day Perc Westmore used a Chinese marking brush to apply the rouge—and the lip brush was born. From the natural, clean curves achieved in this way, we have known since then that lipstick is most effectively applied only with a brush.

Lipstick procedure: Have your mouth absolutely dry of all moisture when you apply your lipstick.

Use a lipstick of creamy consistency so that there is no need to stretch or distort the mouth to apply.

If you have never used a lip brush, it will require some practice. A good way to start is to apply lipstick in the regular way, then press the mouth on the back of the hand so an imprint is left. Then take the lip brush, with some lipstick on it, and go along the edge of the imprint, changing the line to conform to the shape you want. Practice until you can create a clean, curved edge every time, as shown in Fig. 132.

Now try the brush on your lips. See Fig. 133. Brace your elbow on your dressing table or place the tip of the little finger against your chin to serve as a brace. Start drawing in the outline of your lips with a brush. Outline the lip first, then fill in the color. Start outlining at the highest point of the lip, which is usually directly under the nostril. Draw the outline from the center point out to the corner of the lip on one side, then from the center out to the other corner. Use a steady, even stroke—with a back-and-forth motion.

It is best to have the mouth in a relaxed, normal position (never open) as you outline the upper lip. Don't be afraid to build up the lipline into a better and wider curve than you naturally possess. But make it an even curve so that both sides of the lip match.

When you are ready to fill in the color, open the lips and apply the color with left to right strokes.

Roll the upper lip on the lower one to get an equal fullness. Blot off the surplus lipstick by biting down on a sheet of absorbent tissue. Repeat this until you see no mark of lip rouge on the tissue.

To make the color longer-lasting, press a light application of powder over your rouged mouth and then go over your lips with a second application of lipstick. Again, blot off all the excess. When the lip make-up is complete, be certain of three things: (1) That the mouth is symmetrical, with the line well-defined and unsmudged. (2) That in making it up, due consideration has been given to your face-type. (3) That there is no surplus lip rouge left to leave an annoying stain on your coffee cup—or on *his* clean white collar.

Lip hair: So often it is difficult to apply your lipstick properly due to the tiny pore hairs on the upper lip, which, although sometimes very light in color, nevertheless hinder the smooth application of your lipstick and should be removed. See the section on removing hair from the face.

Illustration 1 shows the desired shape. Illustration 1A shows the unbalanced effect due to pore hair 1B. In illustration 1C is shown the area of correction after removing hair.

Avoid "creeping" lip color: Some women are troubled with lipstick creeping into the fine lines running up and down the upper and lower lip, as in illustration 2. It is not necessary to minimize the lips as in 2A. After applying your lipstick, pull the mouth gently apart and blot well with tissue until no color shows on the tissue. Now, pat powder over lip area, again spreading the mouth as in 2B. Remove excess powder with powder brush or cotton. Retrace your lips with your lip brush but do not retrace the outside edge of the lip. Blot with tissue (2C).

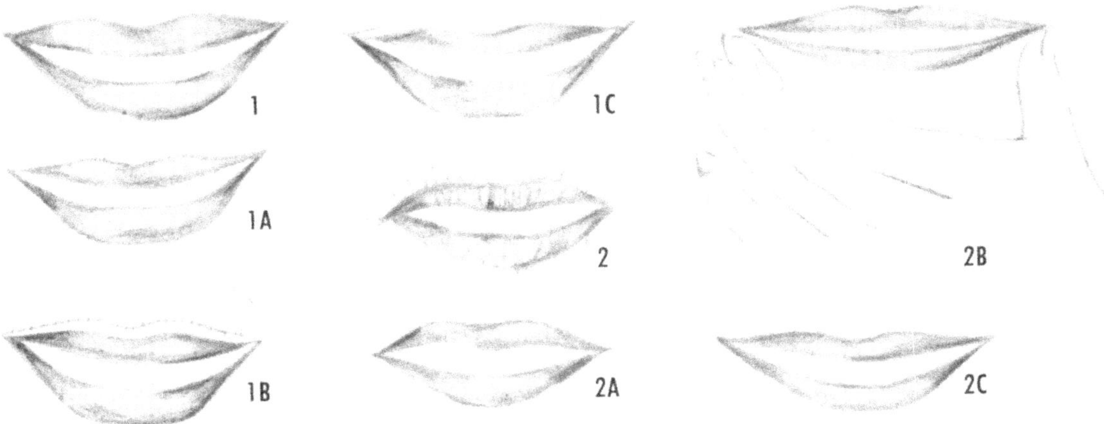

Fig. 134. Lip hair and creeping lip color.

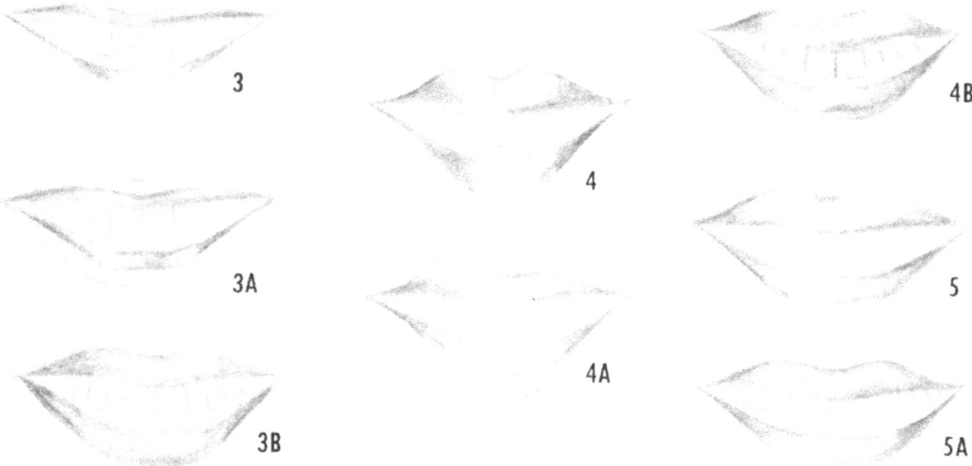

Fig. 135. Problem teeth and lips. (3) The problem of large teeth and thin lips. (3A) The area to be corrected. (3B) After correction, note that the large teeth have been minimized and balanced by the increased roundness of the mouth. (4) The problem of buck teeth, or elongated front center teeth. Building the Cupid's bow high and abrupt creates additional length for these teeth, actually framing and calling attention to them. (4A) If the lip is actually high in the Cupid's bow area, cover the upper lip with two coats of tinted make-up base, each coat to be followed by a colorless finishing powder. Blot with wet puff or pipe cleaner and proceed as shown in 4A to minimize the height of the upper lip. (4B) The result. Note the seeming difference in the height of the teeth. (5) The problem of a full upper lip and small teeth. Simply cut down the height of the upper lip as outlined in illustration 4. (5A) The result. Note the balance achieved.

The types of mouths: Here are outlined the various types of mouths, the wrong lip make-up, the changes made, and results. Most mouths, we find, are made up a little too small. Unless you use a lip brush and use it well you rarely use the complete outline of the lip and rarely apply the lipstick to the outermost edge of the lip. The shaded area in the B illustrations denotes the place of correction.

Note the drooping, thin lips in Fig. 136, 1 and 1A, and the correction in 1B and 1C. So often a reasonably pretty mouth is distorted as seen in 2A. Enlarge this type of mouth only slightly as in 2B and 2C. Do not affect an abrupt Cupid's bow as in 3A. The upper lip curve should be gradual as in 3C.

Illustration 4 is a reasonably pretty mouth; illustration 4A is a pouting, unhappy-looking distortion of it. Check again Fig. 131 for the high point of the bow of the upper lip. It should be directly under the center of the nostril. The correction in 4B and 4C is very slight.

Illustration 5 is an overly small mouth, with an unusually small lower lip. Be sure to increase the height of the upper and lower lip the same amount, as shown in 5B and 5C.

Illustration 6 is a drooping mouth with no upper bow outlined. Do not attempt to minimize the size as in 6A, but do turn the corners up and outline a softly curving bow as in 6B and 6C. Be sure to widen the lower lip to correspond with the height of the upper lip as in 6B and 6C.

Fig. 136. TYPES OF MOUTHS, SHAPED FOR BEAUTY

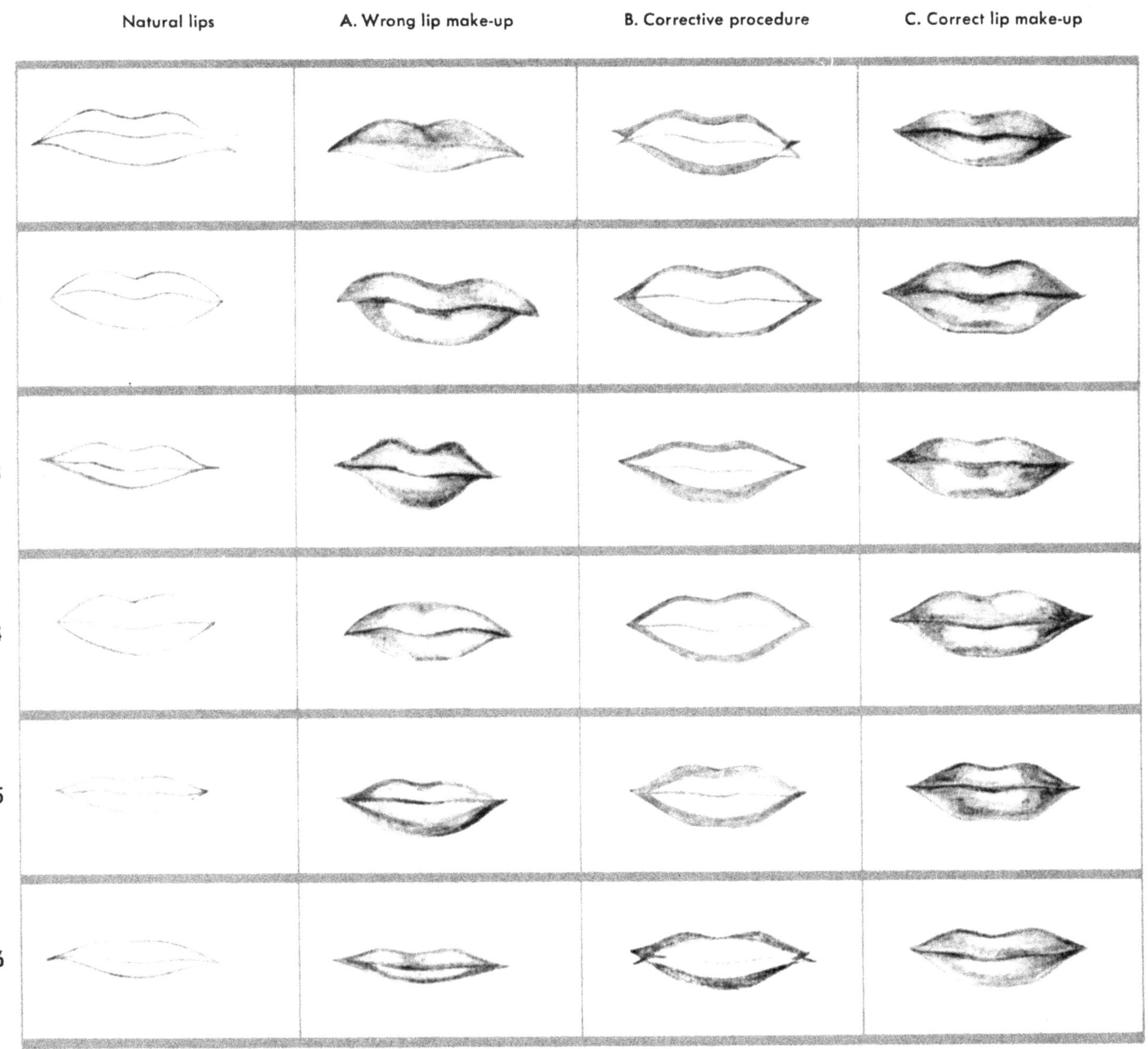

TRICKS WITH A PIPE-CLEANER

The average husband is convinced there is absolutely nothing a woman can't accomplish with the aid of a bobby pin. He'll learn now that there's no limit to the tricks you can perform with a packet of his pipe-cleaners. These little chenille-covered wires are an inexpensive and versatile accessory to beauty. See the next page for illustrations.

Fig. 137. Use a pipe-cleaner to separate lashes after applying mascara.

Fig. 138. As a finishing touch to your make-up, use a pipe-cleaner to brush lashes and eyebrows free of powder.

Fig. 139. A pipe-cleaner can be substituted for a lip brush to run around the edges of the lipstick if you've done a jagged job of application.

Fig. 140. A pipe-cleaner dipped in vaseline, lightly drawn across lids, gives highlight to eye shadow.

Fig. 141. As a manicuring aid, dip the cleaner in oil and use for cuticle massage.

Fig. 142. A cleaner dipped in nail polish remover will remove excess polish from the cuticle or help to shape the moons.

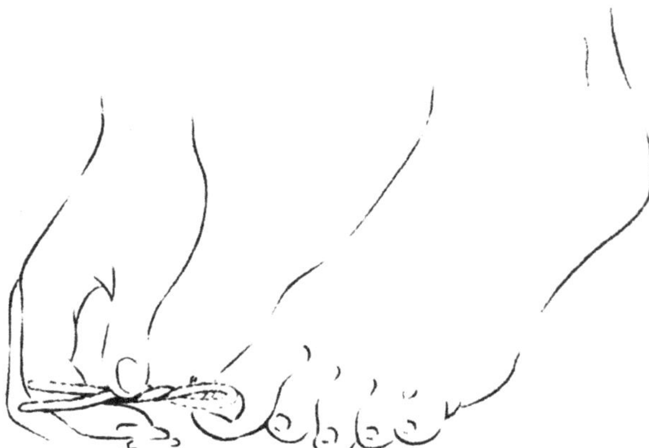

Fig. 143. In a pedicure, a cleaner dipped in nail polish remover will remove excess polish from the cuticle or assist in cuticle massage.

CHAPTER NINE

Facial Care—Creams and Muscle Stimulation

DO UNTO YOUR SKIN AS YOU WOULD HAVE IT DO FOR YOU

It has been estimated that about 85 per cent of the women in the United States have dry skins. Of the remaining 15 per cent, some have normal skins. These should be lubricated to help prevent a later tendency to dryness. The rest have oily skins, which although they do not require as much replacement of natural oils, need massage as a means of keeping the skin soft and supple. In a word, all skins need to be cleansed, lubricated, and stimulated daily.

CLEANSING

Cleansing cream: This product is for cleansing only. It does not take the place of an emollient or skin-food. Its purpose is to liquefy and break down the day's make-up for easy removal. Even if your face has gone without make-up all day, you need a cleanser to remove the dust and grime caught and imbedded by the oil secretion of your face. Cleansers come in both cream and lotion form; use the one you prefer, but use it generously.

Cleansing should always be done with two objectives in mind. First, the cleanser must be thoroughly massaged into the pores and crevices of the face. Second, the correct muscular manipulations of massage must be used to make every face-cleansing a facial pick-up. We cannot repeat too often that the proper facial manipulations must be used every time you soap-and-water cleanse your face, every time you cleanse your face in any way, every time you lubricate or stimulate your complexion.

Always use both hands when performing any cleansing or massage movement. This way you are certain to give both sides of your face equal care. Begin the creaming on the neck, working upward from the collarbone

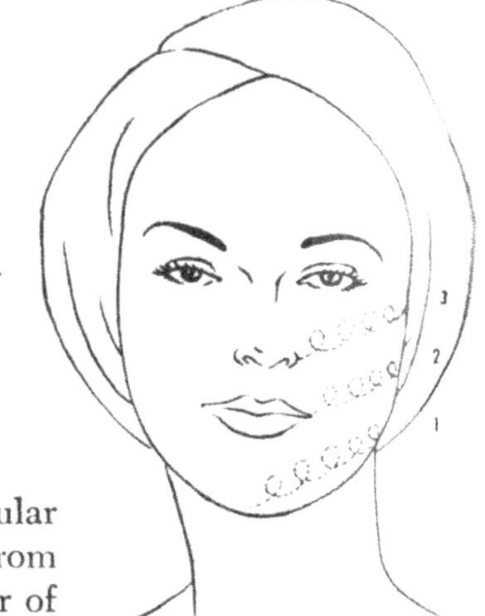

Fig. 144a. Cleansing or massage movements.

to the jawline with the fingers. Then apply the cream in upward, circular strokes along three lines of application as shown in Figure 144A: (1) from the chin to the lobe of the ear; (2) from the mouth corners to the center of the ear; (3) from the nostrils to the top of the ear. Stroke down on the nose, working cream well into the sides of the nose. Apply on the eyelids, working out from the inner corner of the upper lid and then gently in under the eyes. Don't neglect the squint lines at the corner of the eyes. On the forehead, work the cream in upward circles from the center to the temples. (See the complete illustrations for correct creaming movements under Facial Manipulations.)

When the cream has been on the face a full minute, remove with tissues stroked in the same directions the cleanser was applied.

At the end of the day or whenever make-up base must be removed, repeat the cleansing with a second application of cleansing cream. Wait one full minute, as in the first application, then remove with tissue.

Soap and water: In our opinion, this is a most essential cleansing method. For all the women who feel that soap does not do justice to their sensitive (or hypersensitive) skins, we repeat that soap can be used on every skin-type. Not every soap can be used on every skin-type, however. This is what you should learn and remember. Quite frankly, one of the most expensive beauty rituals we've checked recommends a combination of cream and soap and water. Under the dry skin and other classifications of skin-types, note when and under what conditions we recommend such a combination of cleansing methods.

Skin-freshener is applied after the use of a cleansing cream (when you do not follow with soap and water) to remove the last vestiges of the cream. It is used after a soap and water washing to remove any film left from the soap and to give a fresh feeling on the face.

A skin-freshener, not to be confused with astringent lotions, is not ordinarily drying to the skin. It is "washed" across the face with a pad of cotton, with the usual upward and outward strokes. After you have finished, slap the hands gently under the chin and around the jawline allowing the back of the hand to hit the skin with a loose, flapping motion. This helps to firm the throat muscles and stimulates the blood of both the neck and the face.

LUBRICATION

An emollient cream has as its prime purpose the lubrication and moisturizing of the skin cells. It acts to replace the oils and moisture lost by daily weathering and the natural process of aging. It is your greatest weapon against crow's-feet, mouth crevices, all facial and throat lines and wrinkles.

Most skins need an emollient of some sort. There are many "plus purpose" creams on the market to help all types of skins and skin problems.

HELP FOR HUSBANDS—GO PRETTY TO BED

In a spirit of sympathy to husbands everywhere, we want you to know you do not have to go to bed with a grease-coated face in order to get the proper benefit from your lubricating skin-food. All the cream your face will absorb, will be absorbed by leaving it on from twenty to thirty minutes. Then, hold a warm wash-cloth over your face to further increase the emollient's action, and to remove the excess cream from your face. Follow by patting with skin-freshener. Thus, go pretty to bed, with a skin glowing from good care but minus any ugly coating of grease.

COMPLEXION BEAUTIFIERS

"*Problem skins*" are, in this chapter, distinguished from "skin problems," such as blemishes, or those which require the treatment of a dermatologist. It is true that extreme dryness of the skin or extreme oiliness which does not respond to external beauty treatment may be due to internal disturbances. Naturally, if the cause is internal, there is no cure except a specialist's analysis and treatment at the source. Ordinarily, the beauty procedures recommended in these pages will prove rewarding.

Dry skin: This is the most common of all types and requires constant lubrication and protection to keep fine wrinkles from forming. It has several external causes.

For one thing, it may be that the water used for cleansing purposes is too hard. Use a distilled water for washing the face. If this is not possible, the water can be softened somewhat through boiling it before use. With the softened water use a mild, super-fatted soap or a neutral soap. Any druggist will be happy to recommend one.

The nightly cleansing procedure: Remove the day's make-up with two applications of cleansing cream. Each application is wiped off with tissue. Wash your face gently with a soft cloth or the fingertip action described on page 99. After soap and water, the face should be rinsed at least three to four times with warm water to be sure that the face is completely free of soap. In drying, do not rub but pat the surface of the face gently. Morning cleansing should consist only of an application of cleansing cream removed with tissue. The face should then be patted with a piece of absorbent cotton soaked in skin-freshener. The skin-freshener should not be allowed to remain on the face but should be patted off with a piece of tissue.

Whenever possible, cover the face and neck with a film of moisturizing oil and allow to remain on as long as time will allow.

Oil facial for extra-dry skin: A warm oil facial will lubricate and oil the skin. There are excellent oils for this purpose on the market and they can be warmed and applied to the face by means of saturated cotton pads. While the facial is at work, cover the eyes with pads moistened with witch hazel or skin-freshener. Leave pads on for about ten minutes, remove, and apply heavy, oily cream. Finish with skin-freshener.

Oily skin: It is normal for a skin to be oilier in some parts of the face than in others, particularly on the nose and the cheek area next to the nose. This is caused by the sebaceous glands, necessary for normal skin lubrication. A truly oily skin is one in which the greasy condition extends over the larger part of the face. This complexion is usually coarse in texture. (Similar to a citrus fruit, lemon or orange.)

Nightly cleansing should be with two applications of cleansing cream, removed with tissue to rid the face of the day's make-up. Following this, wash your face with warm water and a neutral soap. Do not use a washcloth, but the tips of your fingers, being careful not to use the fingernails themselves since they will spread infection. Work up a good lather with the fingertips over the entire surface of the face. Then rinse as many as four or five times in clean, warm water.

Dry your face with a soft towel, patting gently, rather than rubbing. Following the drying procedure, pat the face briskly with a piece of absorbent cotton moistened with skin-freshener, allowing the freshener to remain on the face. In the presence of oiliness, no night cream of any description should be used.

Morning cleansing should be with soap and warm water, again using the rinsing procedure, followed by patting on skin-freshener. In the morning the skin-freshener should not be allowed to remain upon the face but should be patted off with tissue.

Epsom salt facial bath for oily skin: After regular cleansing, this is applied with benefit to oily skin and blackhead conditions.

To a cup of hot water add one heaping tablespoonful of epsom salts. Dissolve thoroughly. Dip cotton squares in solution. Pat over face. Repeat for ten consecutive nights. The face should be sponged off with cold water after the epsom salt bath.

Large pores: This condition usually can be traced to one of three causes. First, the condition may be hereditary. Second, it may come into existence because of continued incorrect cleansing. Third, it may be due to climatic conditions.

Large pores due to heredity sometimes disappear as the person gets older. If not, there is little one can do.

Large pores which appear where they did not exist formerly often can be traced directly to improper cleansing methods. Extremely hot water should never be used to wash the face. The water should be warm, followed by two or three rinsings in clear water. Soap should be mild and superfatted, and stimulation should be invited through the use of a medium-bristle face brush. Friction should be sufficient only to bring a gentle glow to the face. Following cleansing, pat on cotton moistened with skin freshener.

Where climate is excessively hot and dry, large pores often develop. In such instances, correct cleansing should be combined with lubrication. The skin should have all-day protection through the use of a foundation cream. Following nightly cleansing, a good, emollient cream should be applied to face and neck.

Egg pack for refining coarse skin: Beat the white of an egg lightly, and apply it to the skin, patting in well. Cleansing cream is then massaged into the skin over this pack. Remove, apply nourishing cream, with usual upward and outward rotating motions. After removing this cream, sponge the face with witch hazel. The yolk of the egg is then applied and allowed to dry on the face. This should be removed with towels or cotton dipped in tepid water. Follow with freshener. This should be done no less than once a week—more often if you feel the need.

FACE PACKS FOR STIMULATING, TIGHTENING, BEAUTIFYING

Following are two face-packs or masks which are inexpensive and easy to apply. Either one, if applied to face and throat once a week, will pay off with definitely discernible results. You might try both, determine which suits your requirements best, then stick with it.

All face packs, these and the one given above, are applied after a thorough cleansing of the skin, and after massage with an emollient. Keep your face in a relaxed, normal position when applying, and cover the neck thoroughly also. You may go about your housework for the time required for the pack to stay on, or better yet, lie down and relax awhile.

Honey facial: This is stimulating, refining, tightening, and has a slightly bleaching effect. You'll like it as an all-round beautifier, and it may be used on any type of skin.

Use a tablespoonful of pure, strained honey at room temperature. An emollient massage is given first, with the face cream removed but no skin-freshener applied. Pat on the honey, gently around the eye area, but more briskly over face-planes and neck. Use massage motions to work it into the skin. Then press the fingers on the face and pull away quickly, using the stickiness of the honey to stimulate the skin's circulation. Continue this for about three to five minutes. Allow the honey to remain on the face for fifteen to twenty additional minutes. It will then feel taut and present a stiff-looking surface. Press a warm or hot towel over the face and throat to remove the honey. Follow with a towel dipped in ice-water, then use skin-freshener. Do this every night if you wish.

Buttermilk facial: This treatment will show beautifying effects on all types of skins. Use a powdered buttermilk which can be purchased for facial purposes at drug stores or cosmetic counters. Mix the powder with enough water or milk to form a smooth paste. Cleanse the skin. Then apply the buttermilk emulsion. Give two applications, but do not apply it too thickly.

Apply extra quantities in oily regions such as the wings of the nose and under the chin if it is inclined to be sagging. Do not get the preparation too close to the eyes, but protect and relax them with cotton pads saturated in witch hazel. As you relax, the buttermilk facial does its work. The length of time the emulsion is left on depends on the skin, fifteen minutes usually being the maximum except for very oily skin. Remove with a soft towel or tissue dipped in tepid water. Blood will have been brought to the surface and the skin invigorated. Then apply a lubricating cream and massage in gently. Remove this with tissue, then apply a mild skin-freshener, and apply make-up over a protective base. Buttermilk facials should be given regularly, but one treatment will show results. When the facial is performed at night, leave the lubricating cream on overnight.

FACIAL MASSAGE—WHY AND WHEN

The facial manipulations illustrated and described on the following pages constitute what is known as a "muscle strapping" massage. It may be that you are still too young for your face to require any such detailed treatment, which is usually reserved for those years when the muscles tend to relax.

You are never too young, however, to know the basic principles of massage. By understanding them you are more apt to handle your daily cleansing and creaming in a way to help keep your skin and muscles firm, rather than to break them down. A woman of 40 or more rarely has to be reminded that advancing years bring facial changes—she can see them in her mirror. It is the girl in her teens and early twenties who needs to remind herself constantly that sound beauty habits now will help her to stay ahead of the years!

SIGNS TO WATCH FOR

At twenty, although wrinkles are not now present, they are in the formative stages and should be discouraged. Break yourself of such habits as wrinkling the forehead, squinting the eyes, frowning. If you have already developed one of these habits, correct it now. You may want to select the facial manipulation for that particular part of the face from out of the massage movements in this department, and apply it. Practice the facial exercises illustrated which help to keep the muscles firm and youthful. For skin beautifiers, select one of the face packs recommended under that heading, since these help to keep fine lines from forming.

At thirty, the signs to watch for are horizontal wrinkles on the forehead, frown wrinkles between the eyebrows, and other skin and muscle evidences of bad facial habits. According to your health and the climate you live in, eye-lines or neck creases may begin to be noticeable. Even if your face remains youthful as ever, now is the time to make lubrication an unbreakable habit, to start facial massage as part of your regular routine. This is the way to keep ahead of the signposts that start showing up in the later thirties, such as relaxed eye-muscles and chinline.

At forty and fifty, the muscles are definitely feeling the pull of gravity, and for the neglected face a general "drooping" movement is on the way. This is the period in a woman's life when she must never lose sight of the necessity of a rigid facial routine. If you haven't started as yet, you need little urging to begin lubrication and massage now. It is in these years, too, that women often undertake rigid dieting to reduce the matronly figure. If you do diet, this is another reason for weekly facials. Dieting breaks down underlying fatty tissue on the face, resulting in flabbiness and folds that need stimulating and firming.

At sixty, the muscles of a woman's face have settled, with the result that the reflected age progression of the thirties, forties and fifties assumes permanency. The beauty care or neglect of passing years is now reflected. She is an older woman, but she does not necessarily have to be an aged one. If you have taken good care of your health and beauty, your face may still be fairly firm and virtually unwrinkled. Don't relax your beauty routines now. If your earlier neglect is showing now, it is never too late to start working for improved skin, and more flattering make-up. Muscular massage begun at this point will never, of course, have the preventive benefit it could have had in earlier years. Yet, it will do much to correct fat pads on the cheeks, jowls and chin; to stimulate circulation and muscle health, and to help prevent further deterioration.

HOW TO GIVE YOURSELF A "MUSCLE-STRAPPING FACIAL"

Allow yourself a full hour for the manipulations, and for a relaxation period afterward.

Do your face pack or your muscle-strapping routine at least once a week for best results.

Remember in all facial manipulations, the movement is never meant to stretch or pull the facial skin out of place. The neck is hardier and a good amount of pressure can be applied, but face muscles must be lifted gently. Slapping or patting should never be severe enough on any part of the face, to cause damage to the tiny blood vessels underlying the skin.

All salon facials begin with massage of chest, shoulders and back. This is for the purpose of relaxing the muscles, and for stimulating the flow of blood up into the facial tissues. It is not possible for you to give yourself quite the same relaxing back massage as one done by another person, but the two movements detailed below will start the blood circulation where it is needed.

Using the knuckles of both hands, start at the middle of the chest and work in circular movement up to the shoulders, around back to either side of the spinal column. Here, open out the fingers and rotate them up the spine to the hairline, rotate here three times, then back to base of neck. Do this entire movement, from chest to base of neck, three times.

Now, with the thumb and fingers (thumb forward, fingers back) pick up the cords and flesh along the top of your shoulders, and with a pinching movement work the fingers along the back of neck to the sides of the spine. Rotate the flesh and muscle here three times, then bring fingers back to thumb.

Next, begin your facial proper with the following:

Chin movement: Use the flat of your hands, alternating them in a pressing and lifting movement. Work from the base of the throat up to the point of the chin, around the neck to one ear, back around to other ear, back to center again. Do this three times.

Fig. 144. Chin movement.

Jawline movement: Place two fists pressed against the base of the throat. Work them with pressing and lifting movement up to the tip of the chin. Holding your upward pressure on the neck muscle, knuckle from chin along jawbone to back of ears. In this movement you are working with the knuckles under and along the jawbone itself, rather than above it. At the ears, lift hands from face and return them to the base of the throat for two more complete lifting and knuckling movements.

Fig. 145. Jawline movement.

Lower cheek movement: Placing first three fingers of each hand on chin point move them gently upward and outward in a series of lifting circles to ear, up in front of ears to point even with eye. Here, hold the cheek-muscle lift with two fingers and with third finger gently massage squint lines at corner of eye. Return fingers to chin and repeat upward-circular lift two more times.

Forehead movement: Alternate the fingers of the two hands to lift the forehead in series of light upward strokes from eyebrow line to hairline. Work across the entire forehead from temple to temple, giving the greatest treatment to center forehead lines. This lifts the brow and helps to smooth out the horizontal wrinkles.

This, commonly known as the "headache movement," is for the vertical lines running between the brows. Place the hands across the forehead, fingers overlapping, little fingers over eyelids. Pull fingers apart and across forehead to temples, rotating little fingers on temples. Do this three times.

Fig. 146. Lower cheek movement.

Eye movement: Press (slightly) middle fingers at inner corner of eyelid, let them rest here for a second. Then place first fingers directly above eyebrow. (Thus, you have the two fingers spraddling the eyebrow.) Slide both fingers outward to outside corner of the eye; then let the middle fingers carry on to complete a circle around and underneath the eye and back up to the starting point at indentation of eyelid. Always be very gentle with the tissue around the eyes. Do not press too hard, nor pull at the skin. Do this three times.

Nose and upper cheek movement: Slide middle fingers down the nose. Then, starting at corners of the nose, massage across the cheeks (under cheekbones) with rotary and upward movement to temple. At temple rotate fingers and slide them back across to inside corners of eyes. Lift fingers away from face, and start over with sliding down nose for two more complete movements.

Mouth and laugh-line movement: This can be a routine movement or done with extra concentration, according to your own facial needs. To

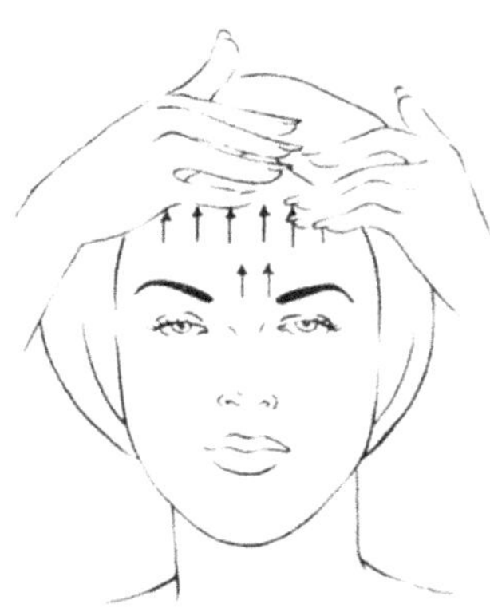

Fig. 147. Forehead movement.

exercise the muscles of the mouth, lift the corners lightly and quickly. Then begin at both corners of the mouth and, with a circular movement, work toward the center of the mouth, lifting the lips to form them into a bow, and exerting only very slight pressure. Place left thumb and forefinger on the upper lip, and right thumb and forefinger on lower lip, and circle from inside out, gently lifting the lips as you go toward the center. Now quickly lift the lips, very gently, first with one finger and then with the other. (When the lips are full, omit this movement, as it tends to develop them.)

To correct the laugh-line crevices, begin at the corners of the mouth; work the fingers in small circles up the lines to the eyes, then gently out under the eyes to their outer corners. Lift fingers from face, return to mouth corners for two more upward circling movements.

Neck lump treatment: Although it is not included in a regular facial massage, an epsom salts treatment is helpful in overcoming the fat lump at the back of the neck which some women acquire. You may want to do it at this time. The treatment is most effective if you can have someone do the back massage for you. If you can reach your own hands to the back of your neck, you may be able to do some effective patting and pinching of your own to help break down the fat cells. If not, the hot salts pack is in itself quite effective. You can increase its action by grasping the ends of the towel, and pulling it back and forth across the back of the neck.

First clean the skin on the back of the neck, and apply a couple of hot towels to open the pores. Now, rub emollient cream across the area, in as vigorous a manner as you can manage. The solution should be prepared as follows: Dissolve four tablespoonfuls epsom salts in a half pint of boiling water. Pour one-half of this into a container, and add a half pint of hot water. The other half of the solution will later be poured over a piece of ice. Now, dip a towel into the hot solution, and apply to the back lump; do this until you have used five towels in succession. Again massage, and finally apply five towels dipped into iced solution. Finish with an astringent.

After the massage, relax. Remove the cream with tissues. Lie down for ten or fifteen minutes, preferably with your feet up. Prepare a couple of eye-pads from cotton soaked in witch hazel, and a towel (Turkish towel) wrung from ice-water, to lay over your face. Lie down for ten or fifteen minutes, wearing the eye-pads and the cold towel. If you do not have this

Fig. 148. Eye movement.

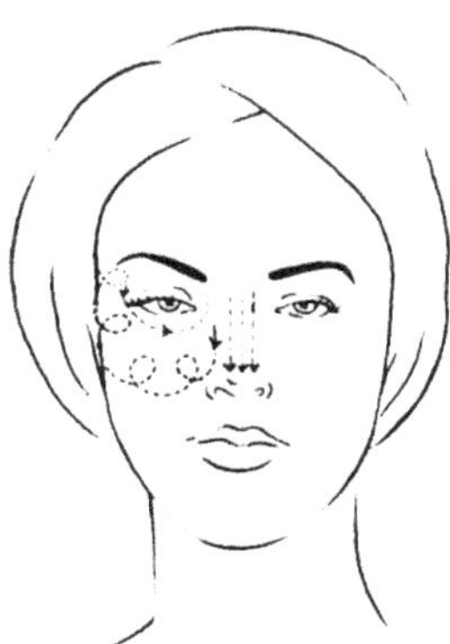

Fig. 149. Nose and upper cheek movement.

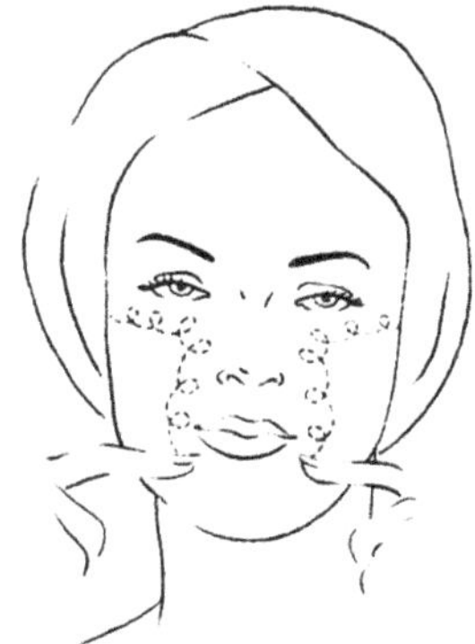

Fig. 150. Mouth and laugh-line movement.

time to lie down and relax, you may want to finish toning your face with cold skin-freshener or with an ice-cube wrapped in a cloth.

YOU CAN BUILD A FACE

You can build a countenance physically, in the same way you can build a body. The right diet, lots of water, exercise, good breathing, plenty of sleep—all these are recognized aids to skin color and hair gloss. Not so often do we consider the fact that the shape of the face can be built up also. Every organ of the human body has its own avenue of connection, through the blood stream and nerve-system, with the face. You have seen the effects of illness upon the features. Consider then what good health can do to tone the muscles, round out the cheeks, firm the nose and chin, and preserve the smoothness of the brow.

How are your mugging habits? Facial exercises (as illustrated here) promote visible results if you keep up the good habit. It's the unconscious exercises, the bad habits of expression capable of building your countenance into a shape you don't want it in which we'd like to discuss first. Look around you, on a bus, in the office, or among your friends, and you can pick out Mr. Squint-Eye, Miss Frowner, Mr. Side-of-the-Mouth Talker, Mrs. Chews-Her-Food-With-One-Jaw-Only, and others. Too bad that all of us can't sneak up on ourselves and be caught barefaced in these mugging habits.

The next best thing is to have a rapid conversation with yourself in a mirror sometime. Try a little smiling and chewing, too—you might be surprised at what's been going on with your face when you weren't looking.

Another countenance builder we can't ignore is character.

The facts of physiognomy are that the facial contour depends not only on bone structure, but on the muscles overlaying it. Each muscle extends fibers into the skin along its course so that there is scarcely a part of the face without its little fiber to move it. The habitual recurrence of thoughts, either good or evil, the indulgence in particular modes of life, calls into play corresponding sets of muscles, which in turn produce folds and wrinkles. Anger, self-pity, stinginess, any of these little mental devils can thus by a sinister kind of team-work give a permanent cast to the features. The only way to beat them is to call up the other emotions, serenity, generosity, joy and laughter, and let them get in some winning team-work of their own.

There's an old saying that when the Lord was creating man, He considered putting a window in front of his heart to let the world see what was going on inside. But then came a better idea—He gave him a face, instead. Remember this!

Frown eradicators. Check your frowning habits. Brow wrinkles often add age to a countenance that would otherwise be quite young. The forehead should be like the "white space" in advertising, an area which by its cool serenity shows off the rich color of the hair above and the liveliness of the features below. Don't wrinkle it by constantly raising the eyebrows upward, or habitually drawing them together.

Illustrated are some effective "wrinkle plasters" you can buy in a drug store or make at home. Those you buy are made of court plaster. If you prefer the home-made variety cut them from gummed brown paper of the type used for sealing cartons for mailing. As far as we know, the glue on this paper will cause no harm to the skin, but if you have a pimple or abrasion play safe and don't use it.

Facial exercises: The exercise to which your face should be most accustomed is that of smiling. True loveliness requires that you be able to smile often, easily, and with warmth. Perhaps the screen stars' trick for a lovely smile when being photographed, will help you. Just before the shutter clicks, the star says slowly and lingeringly, the word "cheese." (This, by the way, is the reason motion-picture publicity art is labeled "cheesecake.") Try it in front of your mirror and see what the word "cheese" does for your own smile.

Following are other facial exercises effective for both relaxing and strengthening the facial muscles. You can make them a practice when you are doing your housework, relaxing, knitting, or watching television alone, or at any other such times.

1. For strengthening the cheek and mouth muscles, and helping to prevent the nose-to-mouth crevices, do the following.
   a. Puff up your cheeks and blow hard against them, as if you were blowing the air into a balloon. Do this six to ten times.
   b. Fill your cheeks with air, then keeping your mouth tightly closed, swoosh the air from one cheek to the other, back and forth. With your mouth still closed, swoosh the air up under the upper lip and down inside the lower lip. Rotate the air rapidly in these four directions a dozen times.
2. "Making faces"—Perhaps you had better wait until you're alone to do this one!

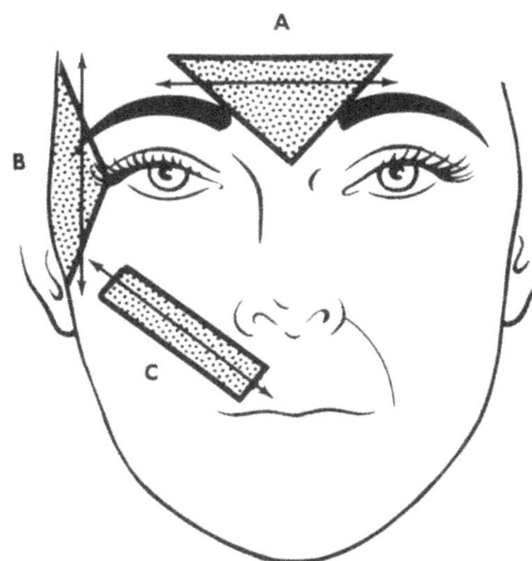

Fig. 151. Wrinkle eradicators. A shows a triangular "frowner" which, applied at night, smoothes out the forehead and circumvents an unconscious frown while sleeping. Worn during the day when you are knitting your brow over household tasks, it helps to prevent a permanent skin-crease between the eyebrows. B illustrates a squint-plaster that will help to prevent and smooth out eye-wrinkles. Apply laugh-plasters, as illustrated by C, for a smoothing effect on nostril-to-mouth lines.

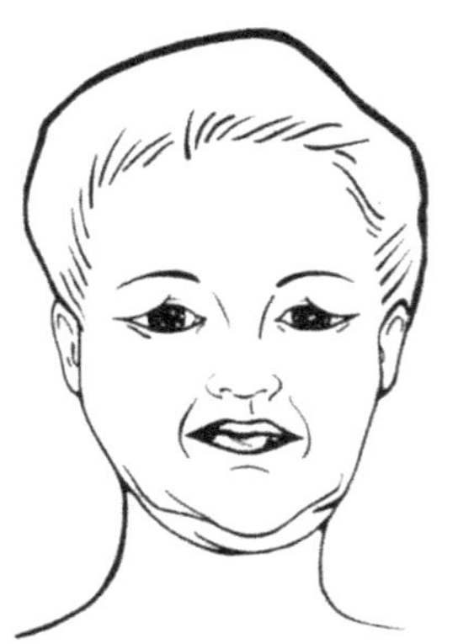

Fig. 152. Full face, before strapping.

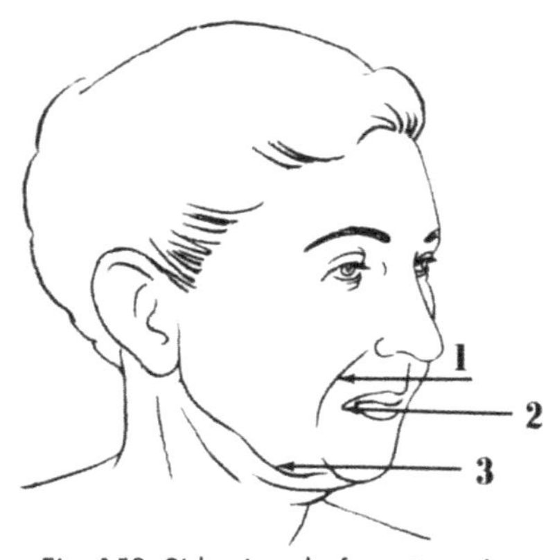

Fig. 153. Side view, before strapping.

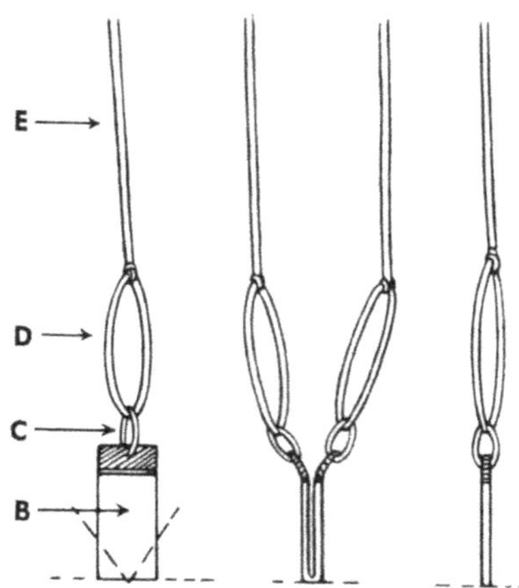

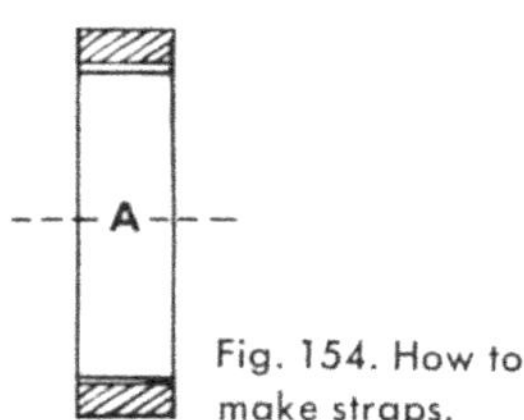

Fig. 154. How to make straps.

Purse up your lips as tightly as you can, at the same time squeezing your eyes together as tightly as you can. Now, open both your mouth and your eyes as wide as you possibly can. Alternate rapidly between the first process of screwing up your face as tightly as possible, and then, opening mouth and eyes as widely as possible. This has a beneficial effect on almost all of your facial muscles, and is usually effective in reducing puffiness around the eyes.

3. For a firm throat: Tilt head back slightly, holding your finger under chin. Now stretch neck up—lift chin forward and over the finger. Done one-half dozen or more times a day, this helps to keep the chin and neck firm.

4. To eliminate a double chin: Drop head forward on chest. Now, leading with your chin turn your head slowly to one shoulder, rolling head up and around until chin touches the other shoulder, then back to front again. The object is to make a complete slow circle with your chin leading at all times. Circle right to left four times—left to right four times.

5. To ease tension: This is particularly good for the office worker who is apt to be sitting at a typewriter or desk most of the day. Clasp your hands behind your neck—head thrown back, elbows straight out at the side. Now, keeping hands behind neck bring the elbows forward until they touch in front at shoulder level. Now, throw elbows back as far as possible. Repeat, bringing elbows front and throwing them vigorously back, five to ten times.

LOSE 15 YEARS IN 15 MINUTES FOR 15 CENTS

The sketches show a temporary face-lift which, you may be interested to know, is known among make-up artists as "The Great Profile." Yes, it was used to take sag-lines out of the million-dollar profile of the late John Barrymore in his stage and film camera appearances.

Since then, it has become a beauty-aid device used by many career women when making public appearances. It will help you, too, to look your best when having a photograph taken or for social occasions. If you are contemplating having a surgical face-lift, by all means try this temporary lift first, to decide what you may have to gain from a permanent step.

Facial muscles, as you know, are very much like a piece of elastic in their consistency. Take any piece of rubber, keep stretching and pulling it for a number of years and it gradually becomes elongated, with less and less power to snap back. In the face, the elongated muscles result in droop-

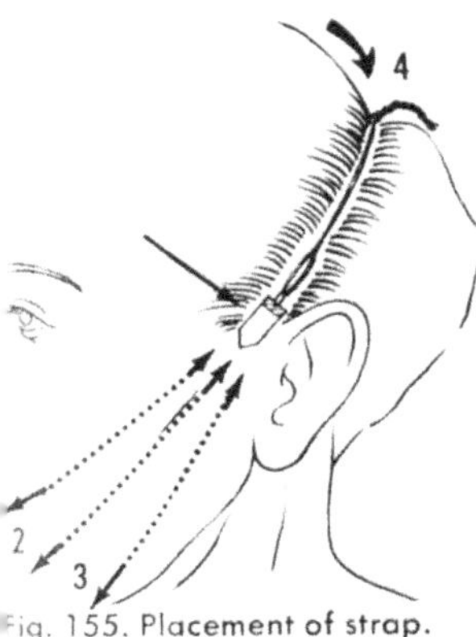

Fig. 155. Placement of strap.

ing mouth corners, deepened laugh-lines from nose to mouth, and a sagging jowl or jawline.

The straps illustrated here use a rubber band as a temporary muscle, to give an upward pull to the face. Other materials needed are a small tab of adhesive tape and a piece of strong linen thread. The whole device is invisible when the hair is dressed over it, and if properly applied it will stay in place as many hours as you wish to wear it. Here are the directions for making and applying the lift, illustrated in Fig. 154.

Use adhesive tape of half-inch width. Cut a piece two-and-a-half inches long. Fold in each end about a quarter of an inch, as seen in A. Fold the tape exactly in half, sticky sides tightly pressed together, and cut in tab shape as illustrated by dotted lines in B.

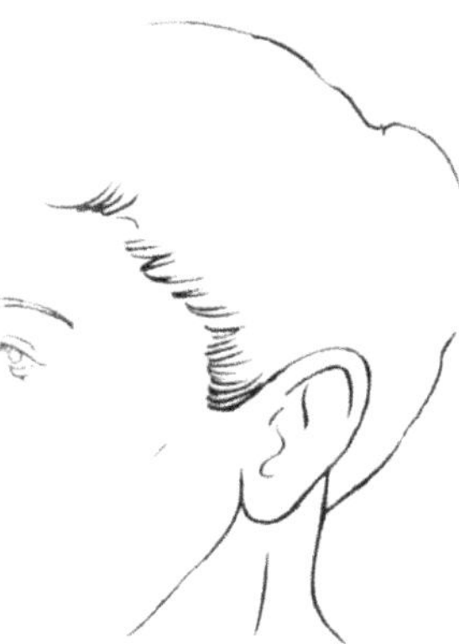
Fig. 156. Hair over strap.

Thread a needle with strong linen thread and, running it through one of the folded margins, create a small loop between the tape and the rubber band, as illustrated by C and D. Use several strands of thread in the loop, and be sure it is fastened securely. Next, loop a double length of thread through the other end of the band, as seen at E. Repeat the thread loop through the other folded margin of the tape, so that now you have two straps as seen in the middle sketch.

Part your hair as in Fig. 155. Next, lifting the top hair at the crown of the head, create a tiny braid from a lock of the under-hair, as seen at 4. Now, sponge off the skin just above your ear with astringent or alcohol. It is necessary that the skin be entirely cleansed of oil or perspiration here, else the adhesive will not stick as firmly as it should.

Take the adhesive and hold it against a light bulb for a few seconds. When the tape is warmed, pull the two tabs apart so that you have two separate straps, one for each side of the face. Press the tab firmly to the skin above the ear. It should be pointed in the direction where you need the most "lift," as in either line 1, 2, or 3. Smile as broadly as you can.

Fig. 157. Side view, after strapping.

When the tab is firmly in place pull the rubber band and thread tautly along the part in the hair, winding the thread tightly around the little braid in the back. Adjust the other strap by the same method, on the opposite side of the face. When you are sure both threads are securely wound around the little braid in back, pin the braided lock flat with a bobby pin and comb the top hair down to conceal it. Dress the sides of your hair over the adhesive on the sides of your ears, as in Fig. 156.

You are now enjoying a face-lift, as seen in Figs. 157 and 158. If you have any doubts about the effectiveness of the straps, try them out at home first. You'll find it's no trick to forget you have them on, and be conscious only of the firmer, more youthful feel of your face.

There are absolutely no damaging effects from using this face-lift according to our directions.

HOW TO REMOVE FACIAL HAIR

One of the most common embarrassments the would-be beautiful woman suffers is the presence of facial hair. If this is your problem, it may console you to know that each time we so much as make mention of it on

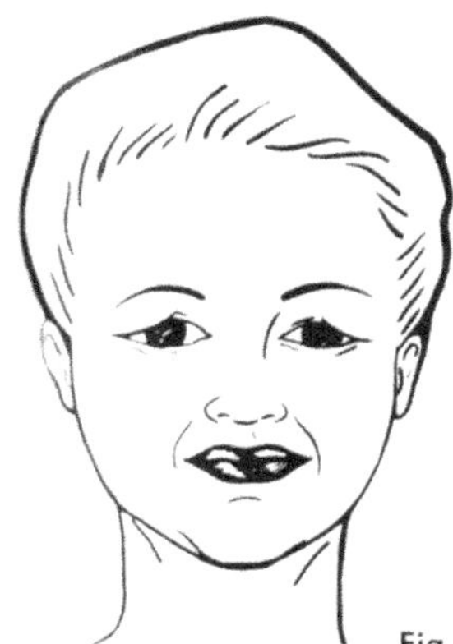
Fig. 158. Full face, after strapping.

Fig. 159. Hair to be removed.

Fig. 160. Powder area.

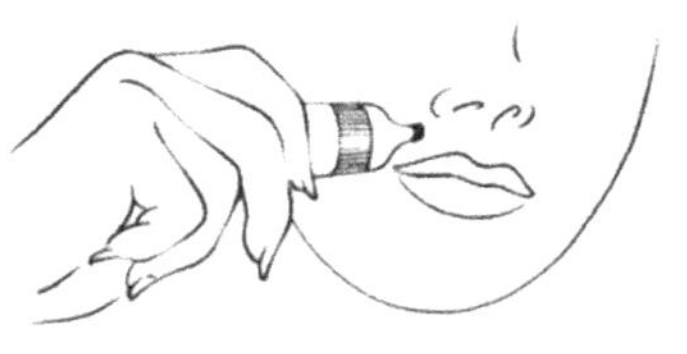

Fig. 161. Apply jelly.

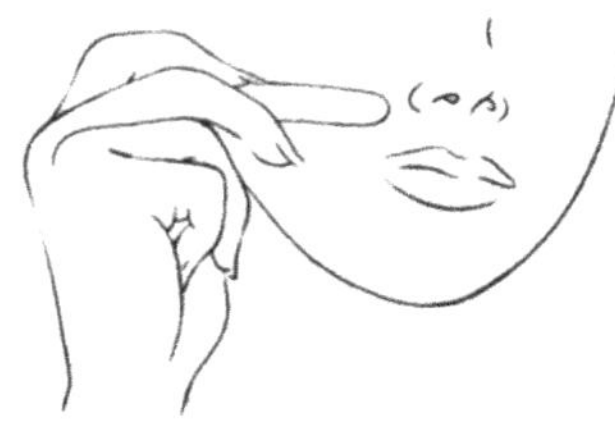

Fig. 162. Spread jelly.

a radio or TV show, thousands of letters pour in asking for a remedy.

There is no method for permanently removing hair, except electrolysis. This sort of decision is up to you and the electrolysis specialist you select.

We offer only a few words of advice. As is true in the solution of any problem, seek a reputable, respected authority in the field in question. If you do not know someone personally who has had electrolysis performed by a reputable electrolysis expert, ask your family physician to recommend one. Failing on both these counts, simply use your common sense and check the electrolysis expert's references in exactly the manner you would check anything of this type.

The hair-removal methods you can perform for yourself at home consist of two types: the hot wax method, and a cold method done with a jelly or cream. Both are used by us; we consider them successful and safe if properly performed. (We cannot recommend or advise on the use of any facial preparation if the individual has a skin-trouble or an allergy.) Neither method is permanent in its results. However, their use tends to gradually discourage the growth of the hair, so that it becomes a decreasingly distressing problem.

Follow carefully and quite literally the directions that come with the product you buy. The instructions given here are general details of procedure only.

Cold method: Wash face thoroughly. Dry carefully. The area from which hair is to be removed must be clean and free from all make-up, dirt, and cream.

Pat face powder or talcum over area from which hair is to be removed, using cotton, facial tissue, or your finger to spread powder.

To make jelly soft and pliable, hold tube under hot water faucet for one minute. Squeeze out a small amount on the area from which hair is to be removed. Never attempt to cover at one time an area larger than the end of your thumb.

Apply evenly in a thin layer over this small area, spreading in the direction the hair grows or lies on the skin.

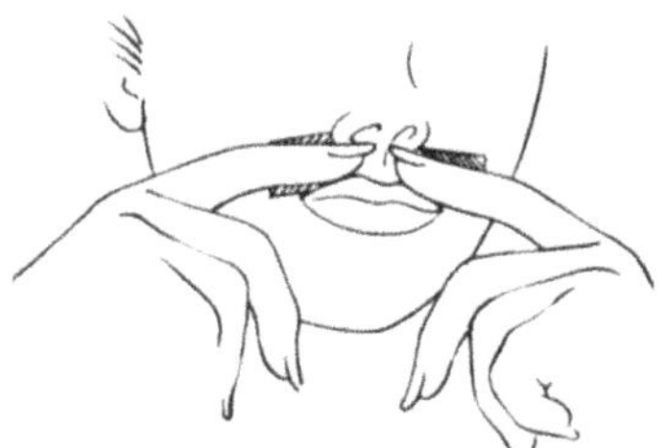

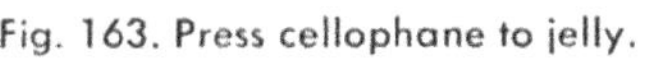

Fig. 163. Press cellophane to jelly.

Fig. 164. Strip off cellophane quickly.

Fig. 165. Press area to prevent swelling.

Fig. 166. Cleanse with alcohol.

To spread jelly: Press a piece of cellophane tightly over the area from which the hairs are to be removed. Press the cellophane with the thumb in the same direction in which the hair grows, rubbing cellophane with strong pressure until all air is pressed out from beneath the cellophane. *The cellophane must adhere completely to jelly to effect proper up-rooting of hair.* The time the cellophane remains on the face is immaterial. Your success depends upon how thoroughly you have made the cellophane stick to the jelly.

After a few seconds pull off cellophane with one swift stroke, pulling in the opposite direction to which hair grows. Do not "peel" the cellophane off.

The above directions can be repeated on areas no larger than the end of your thumb, until all unwanted hair has been removed from any part of the face.

Hot wax application: You will need a pan which you do not intend to use for anything else, and a wooden spatula or old wooden spoon.

Melt wax over low heat; do not boil. (There are also hot waxes on the market which can be melted over hot water.) Test the wax temperature by putting a drop on your wrist. The wax should be quite warm, but comfortable.

For the mouth: After testing wax to be sure it is comfortably warm, powder the upper lip.

Apply wax with wooden spatula or the end of the spoon in strokes going in the same direction as the hair grows. Do one side of the lip at a time. Apply coat heavily enough–1/16 of an inch. Cover wax with small piece of cheesecloth.

When the wax is still warm but can be touched without sticking to the fingers, it is ready for removal. Brace side of cheek with left hand, grasp end of cheesecloth in right hand, and pull wax off in quick ripping motion. (The same as you would remove adhesive tape.)

Immediately press hard on the upper lip with your fingers for about one minute. The pressing is what helps to keep the lip from developing a temporary swelling. Do the other side of the lip in exactly the same manner. When through, clean off with skin-freshener or alcohol. Apply a little night cream for about five minutes.

The same procedure is used in removing hair from any part of the face; hairline, sideburns, hair on jawline or chin. It is also followed for removing excess hair on the arms and legs.

SPECIAL SKIN PROBLEMS

Your dermatologist knows best. The advice given in this section is our best counsel on the general care of average skin problems. We stand ready to be contradicted by your own dermatologist, because he is the person you should see for first-hand analysis and the individualized care and cure of your own specific case.

The skin, as you know, is the body's largest organ. More than that, it is the only organ worn outside our bodies and which the outside world can touch. Its health is therefore uniquely subject to two influences: the state of our bodily and emotional functions within, and our reaction to climate, temperature, bacteria, chemicals, materials, and all the other outside elements with which it comes in contact.

Your dermatologist may discover that the cause and cure of your skin condition is physical or psychological, or both.

How one girl regained her beautiful complexion: As beauty counsellors only, we would like to tell you of a specific case which comes within our own experience. It concerns a young girl who, several years ago, was working in the dancing line of various screen musicals. She was graceful, skilled, and had pretty features, but she suffered from a bad case of "crying" acne. As she attempted to cover it with make-up, her skin grew progressively worse. She became careless with her hair, her dancing showed her attempt to avert her face from the cameras. One day, dance director Busby Berkely looked after her as she passed him, and shook his head. "Too bad," he said. "She's a clever girl. I wish someone could help her."

We of the Make-Up Department made this girl our special project. She had been going to a fine dermatologist, and it was a violation of his orders, of course, when she applied make-up to the infected areas of her face. This was only one half of her trouble, however. We concentrated on the psychological side.

Specifically, we taught her to exert extra care and pride on every other detail of her appearance. She had a lovely natural eyebrow; we insisted it be arched and brushed into an exquisite line. Every eyelash had to be softly colored and curled. We taught her to take extra pains with her lipstick, brushing it into the cleanest, most evenly colored curve she had ever achieved. Extra shampoos and nightly brushing were prescribed for her hair, till her head gleamed and shone with not a hair out of place.

She was soon the most meticulously groomed girl on the stage. She lost the sense of uncleanliness and repulsiveness her running cheeks had given her. She found the spectator's eyes going to her other colorful and well-kept features instead. With her mind focused on things other than her affliction, the doctor's cure took hold. This particular girl today owns and manufactures a facial cosmetic which she demonstrates under the close scrutiny of the TV cameras.

While you are adhering to your skin specialist's orders, concentrate on taking extra pride in your other assets. You'll surprise everyone—possibly even the dermatalogist. If you have an unremovable scar or birthmark, practice with cosmetics to cover it the best you can—but don't make this your life's project. Draw the viewer's eye to the features above it and below it. Remember this about any blemish: The spectator may give it a glance, but then he'll forget it—if you will.

ACNE

This is a skin condition usually associated with adolescence. We suggest that if this condition persists that you see a dermatologist.

BLACKHEADS

Blackheads (or comedones) occur when pores become closely packed with dried secretion from the glands, with cosmetics and possibly with dirt. Blackheads are more apt to appear in oily skins and may often be avoided by proper skin care. They should not be squeezed or forcibly removed with fingertips. Infection is apt to result from a scratch and bruising may leave marks or even scars. The face should be cleansed nightly and kept supple with lubricating cream. With this care, blackheads will eventually decrease through normal drainage.

WHITEHEADS

Most whiteheads are little hard white nubs that form under the surface of the skin. They are made up of thin layers of skin cells with fatty material in the center. Whiteheads occur ordinarily in sluggish skins. Improved health, a more active circulation and more normal elimination are important. Externally, friction is usually helpful. Moderate scrubbing with a washcloth or complexion brush is good for this. In time, the thin skin covering the whitehead may wear away and the nub disappear. Do not squeeze whiteheads with fingertips or open with a needle.

FRECKLES

Pure lemon juice is helpful in bleaching freckles. Apply it to the freckled areas with a small brush; allow it to remain on for fifteen or twenty minutes each day, and then wash it off in the regular manner with a good mild soap and warm water. Because lemon juice has a tendency to be drying, apply a little lubricating cream (night cream) after washing and allow that to remain on for an equal period of time.

The consistent use of a make-up base will protect these pigmented areas against added pigmentation, and eventually, with consistent use, the freckles will become minimized. Wear either a cream or liquid-cream foundation, but it should not be chosen to match the freckles. Complement your normal skin tone.

The tendency to freckle is usually hereditary. Don't worry too much about them, as freckles become a part of personality, and often add a certain charm to a face. Naturally, if you are inclined to "spot" profusely in the sun, the answer is not to expose your face for any length of time. Protect it with a broad-brimmed hat, or a heavier application of a make-up base.

VITILIGO (UNEVEN PIGMENTATION)

This is a condition in which white spots or patches appear on face, hands or body. As far as we know, the medical profession has discovered no real cure for them.

If on the face, they can be covered with a make-up base slightly darker than your all-over tint. Apply this with the tip of a small brush, pat smooth, and then pat on a dusting of talcum or non-coloring finishing powder. Apply your over-all base tint as usual, patting the over-all base tint over the powdered light spots. Powder, brush, and blot with damp puff.

For the body, there are several stains you can make. Try them on a small patch first to test color.

Check as to whether or not you have an allergy to iodine. If not, olive oil and iodine mixed in equal parts will give you a satisfactory body make-up. A minimum application will give you a lighter tone; a heavier application, a darker.

If you do have an allergy to iodine, we suggest that you make a very strong brew of black tea, and apply the strained liquid to these spots.

Please understand that in using either one of these, the color must wear off the body. In other words, there is no recipe for removal.

MOLES

Don't tamper with these. Some are harmless, and some are not. Better check with your physician concerning treatment or removal.

BIRTHMARKS

These may be strawberry color, scarlet color, bluish color, brown color, or wine color. The same procedure applies regardless of the color of the birthmark, or whether the birthmark is raised, uneven, or smooth.

In each case, use a highlight. This means a base three shades lighter than your normal base such as a tinted base stick, or a light color foundation cream. Liquid make-up is rarely heavy enough. Pat the highlight over birthmark area and extend the highlight about one-half inch beyond the birthmark. Be sure to paint the birthmark area thoroughly so that concentration of color is uniform. Pat powder (either talcum or a non-coloring finishing powder) on birthmark area. Brush powder off with powder brush. Apply damp towel or wet puff or wet pad of cotton to powdered area, in a blotting motion. This relieves tension over powdered area.

If the birthmark is not too dark or vivid in color, one application should bring the color of the birthmark up light enough so that it can now be covered with your regular tinted make-up base. If too much of the birthmark color still shows through, apply a second application of highlight in exactly the way you applied the first. Again blot with a damp towel or puff, or cotton.

Now apply over-all tinted base make-up, being careful to pat or stipple it on the treated birthmark area. Proceed with the make-up application.

SCARS, INDENTED AND DISCOLORED

Follow the same application as in highlighting dark circles under the eye. A small artist's brush is best to use.

It is important to make the highlight stronger in the deepest part of the indentation of the scar. Carefully taper the color on each side of the scar, making sure that you do not get the same density on the upper edges or ridges of the scar. Powder the scar area, brush off excess powder with powder brush, and blot with the damp towel, powder puff, or cotton pad. Apply the over-all tinted make-up base, patting or stippling over scar area, and proceed with make-up as usual.

SCAR, RAISED (KELOID)

Use base or stick make-up two shades darker than over-all tinted base normally used, on the raised area. Don't extend color beyond area of scar. Pat powder on and brush off excess powder. Blot with damp towel, puff or cotton. Now apply over-all tinted base make-up, and proceed with general make-up.

CHAPTER TEN

Style Your Hair to Fit Yourself—Design Your Hair to Fit Your Face

MAKE YOUR HAIR WORK FOR YOUR BEAUTY

Having mastered the ways to recognize and know your face-type, having learned the value of showcasing your feature attraction, and having mastered the art of corrective make-up, the time has come to correlate this wealth of new beauty know-how with another of your most important physical assets—your hair.

We are accustomed to speak of the hair as the frame for the face; but it is actually far more than that. When an artist portrays a woman, his greatest help in character delineation is her hair. He fits the fisherwoman into her background of sea and sails by showing her hair wind-blown and free. The bandana-covered head of the peasant girl tells you of her work in the sun-scorched fields. The classically simple coiffure notifies you that the subject on his canvas is a lady. The harridan is immediately recognizable by her frowzy, unkempt hair-do.

First of all, then, your hair—through its care and general styling—serves as an indication to others of your character and good taste. Your coiffure should speak well of your background, your occupation and your over-all personality. One of the greatest mistakes is to copy a hairdress you have seen on an actress or in a magazine without first determining whether or not it fits in with your face-type, the clothes you wear, the places you go and the activities you like best.

Since modern women tend to be practical, on the whole, most of you undoubtedly realize that your hair-style should fit your age. This doesn't mean that if you are on the mature side, you should wear an aged or aging arrangement. It does mean that your head should be a testimony to the poise, the smartness, and the maturity of judgment with which the years have endowed you. If you are a teen-ager, you shouldn't attempt a sophisticated hair-do that you can't match in personality and experience. It takes considerable know-how to be equal to the demands of high fashion. Some of today's most sophisticated women admit cheerfully that it took heartbreak, headaches, constant growing improvement and *time* to achieve that cool, calm, collected look.

The knowledge all women need and few possess is how to put the hair arrangement to work to beautify the facial outline and individual features.

On the screen, as on the painter's canvas, the hair-style is our primary help in changing a star's character to fit her various roles. But the hair's design—its contour, fullness, length and parting—is the important means of enhancing or temporarily disguising her beauty.

Those of us who remember back to the silent screen recall that an actress' hair-style was her trade-mark. To tamper with the Mary Pickford and the Mable Normand curls or with Colleen Moore's bangs would have been the equivalent of having Metro-Goldwyn-Mayer toss out Leo the Lion. Coincidentally, the star of that era had really only one role. Whether ingenue or vamp, she played that one role over and over again, no matter what the plot or title.

To ask you to choose and keep one certain hair-style would be just as ridiculous as assuming you play only one role all your life. Nothing about you should ever be static; change is necessary and stimulating. Nevertheless, there is one basic hair contour, embodying principles related to your face-shape and features, that you should know and observe in every style variation.

At some time or other within your own experience, you have had a hairdress done by a beauty operator, or by yourself, which as a coiffure was a work of art. The waving was expertly and beautifully done, the style seemed appropriate and yet you had the uncomfortable feeling that the whole hair-do, almost as though it were a wig, could be taken off your head and set on someone else's to equal if not to better advantage. When you feel that way—be assured, the hair-style is not for you. When your hair is properly styled for you, it will work beauty magic for you and your features.

Here again the mastery of the basic principles of hair-styling according to face-type will give your face and figure its best balance.

So go on from here and start to put your hair to work for you.

THE HAIR CONTOUR FOR YOU

OVAL—Forehead slightly wider than chin

In dressing the hair, your objective must always be to retain the oval outline. Any distortion in balance will destroy the perfection of features.

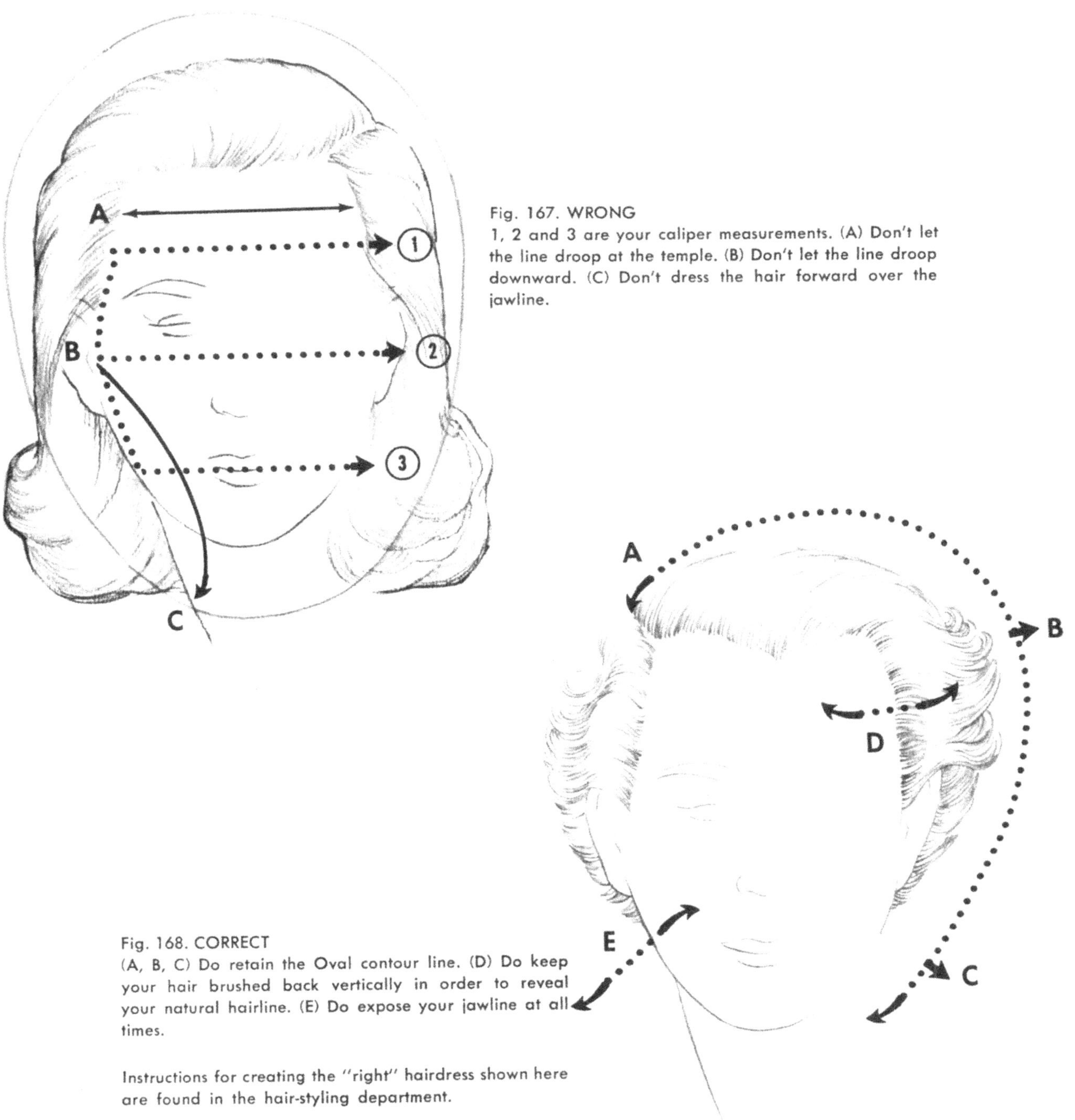

Fig. 167. WRONG
1, 2 and 3 are your caliper measurements. (A) Don't let the line droop at the temple. (B) Don't let the line droop downward. (C) Don't dress the hair forward over the jawline.

Fig. 168. CORRECT
(A, B, C) Do retain the Oval contour line. (D) Do keep your hair brushed back vertically in order to reveal your natural hairline. (E) Do expose your jawline at all times.

Instructions for creating the "right" hairdress shown here are found in the hair-styling department.

THE HAIR CONTOUR FOR YOU

OBLONG—Long and narrow, flat or hollow cheeks

The length and narrowness of features are the problems here. To create an illusion of less length in the face, your hair should be styled close to the top of your head. Soft bangs further off-set face length. By creating fullness behind the ears to a point even with the mouth, an appearance of greater width in the face is achieved.

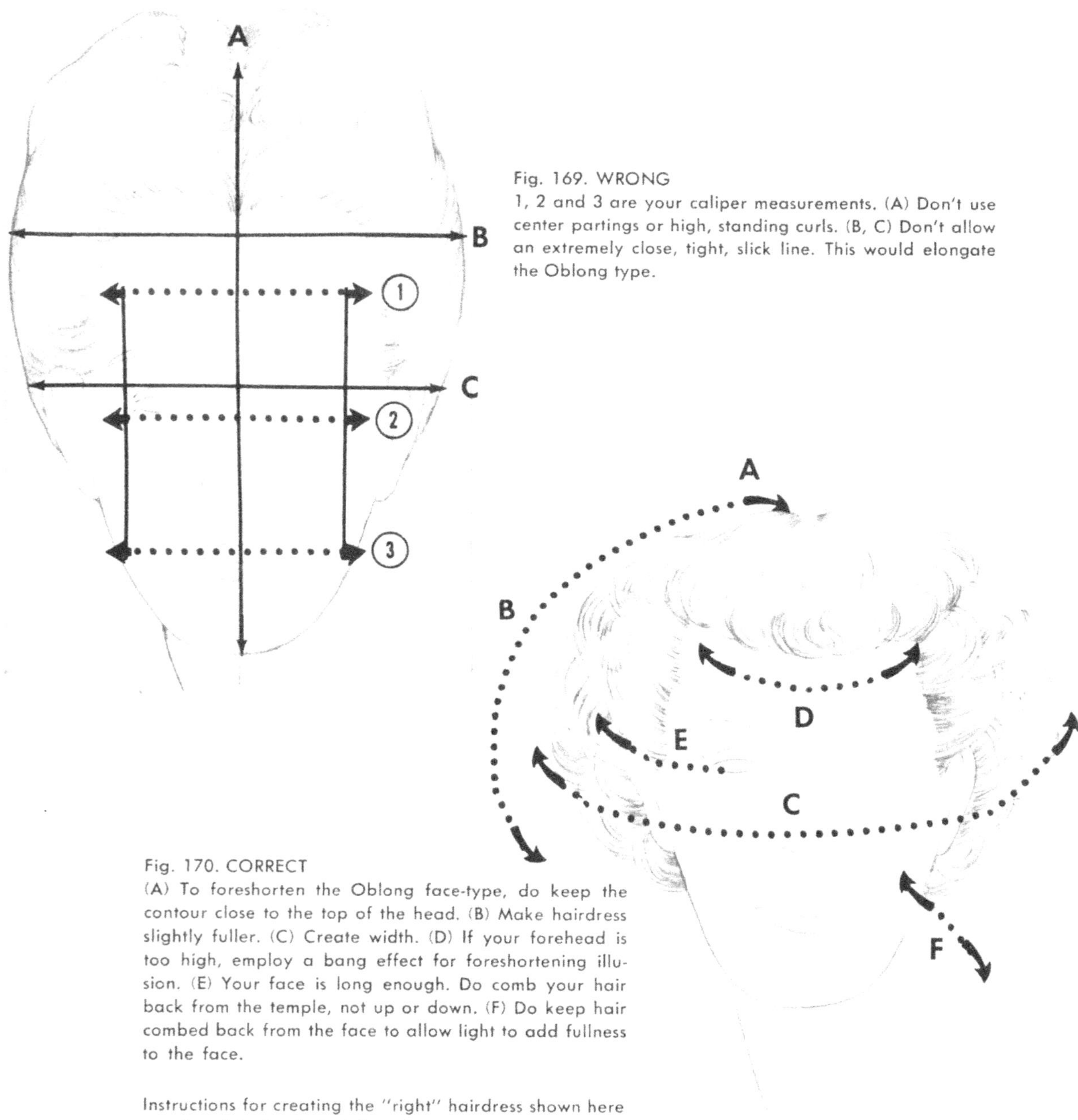

Fig. 169. WRONG
1, 2 and 3 are your caliper measurements. (A) Don't use center partings or high, standing curls. (B, C) Don't allow an extremely close, tight, slick line. This would elongate the Oblong type.

Fig. 170. CORRECT
(A) To foreshorten the Oblong face-type, do keep the contour close to the top of the head. (B) Make hairdress slightly fuller. (C) Create width. (D) If your forehead is too high, employ a bang effect for foreshortening illusion. (E) Your face is long enough. Do comb your hair back from the temple, not up or down. (F) Do keep hair combed back from the face to allow light to add fullness to the face.

Instructions for creating the "right" hairdress shown here are found in the hair-styling department.

THE HAIR CONTOUR FOR YOU

ROUND—Round hairline, round chinline

Your correct coiffure shows perfect balance, providing an illusion of greater length to the face, thereby minimizing roundness. The woman with the large round face is often under the impression that small, tight curls will make her face appear smaller. This is not true. Always remember to keep all hairdressing and pin-curling in large, loose effects to avoid contrast with the size of your face.

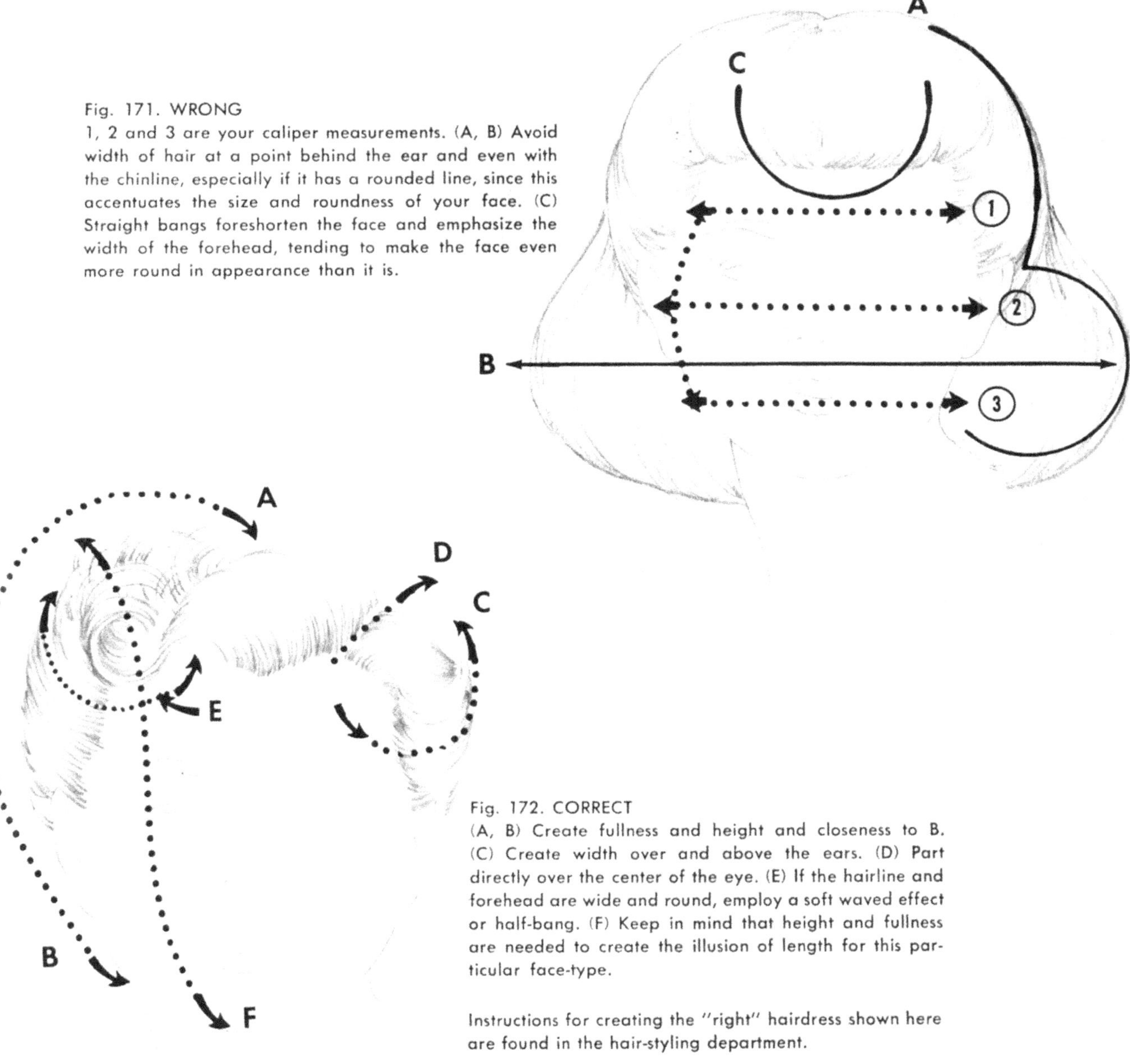

Fig. 171. WRONG
1, 2 and 3 are your caliper measurements. (A, B) Avoid width of hair at a point behind the ear and even with the chinline, especially if it has a rounded line, since this accentuates the size and roundness of your face. (C) Straight bangs foreshorten the face and emphasize the width of the forehead, tending to make the face even more round in appearance than it is.

Fig. 172. CORRECT
(A, B) Create fullness and height and closeness to B. (C) Create width over and above the ears. (D) Part directly over the center of the eye. (E) If the hairline and forehead are wide and round, employ a soft waved effect or half-bang. (F) Keep in mind that height and fullness are needed to create the illusion of length for this particular face-type.

Instructions for creating the "right" hairdress shown here are found in the hair-styling department.

THE HAIR CONTOUR FOR YOU

SQUARE—Square hairline, square chinline

Your correct hair-style is designed to minimize squareness of features as well as to provide an illusion of near-oval contour. Necessary height is provided in styling to give added length to your features.

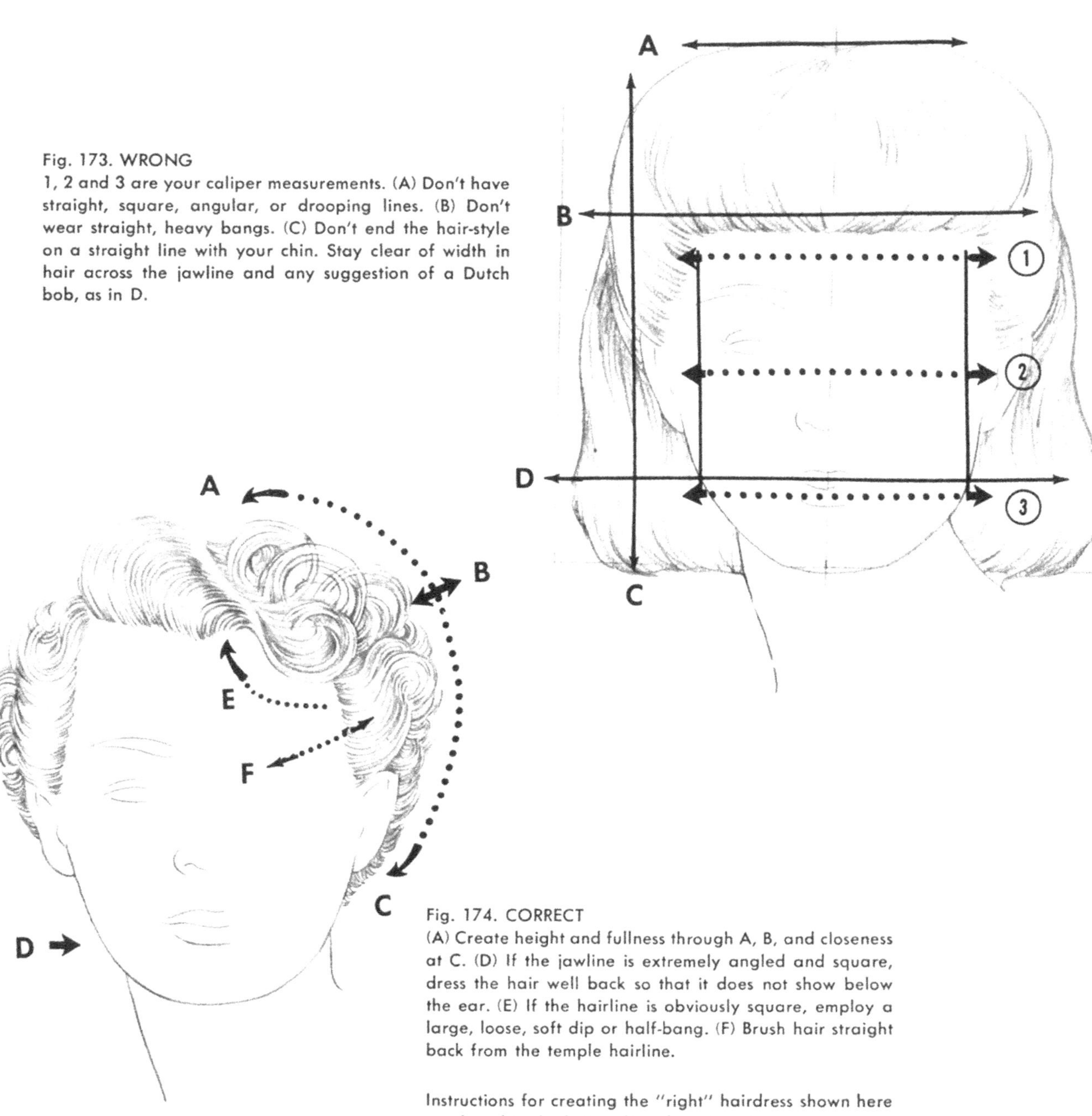

Fig. 173. WRONG
1, 2 and 3 are your caliper measurements. (A) Don't have straight, square, angular, or drooping lines. (B) Don't wear straight, heavy bangs. (C) Don't end the hair-style on a straight line with your chin. Stay clear of width in hair across the jawline and any suggestion of a Dutch bob, as in D.

Fig. 174. CORRECT
(A) Create height and fullness through A, B, and closeness at C. (D) If the jawline is extremely angled and square, dress the hair well back so that it does not show below the ear. (E) If the hairline is obviously square, employ a large, loose, soft dip or half-bang. (F) Brush hair straight back from the temple hairline.

Instructions for creating the "right" hairdress shown here are found in the hair-styling department.

THE HAIR CONTOUR FOR YOU

TRIANGLE—Narrow forehead, broad jaw and chinline

The wide jawline combined with a narrow forehead pose your hair-styling problem. We must style the hair back and up from the temples to create an illusion of width in the forehead, and at the same time counterbalance the width in the lower part of the face. Soft, rounded bangs further disguise the narrow forehead.

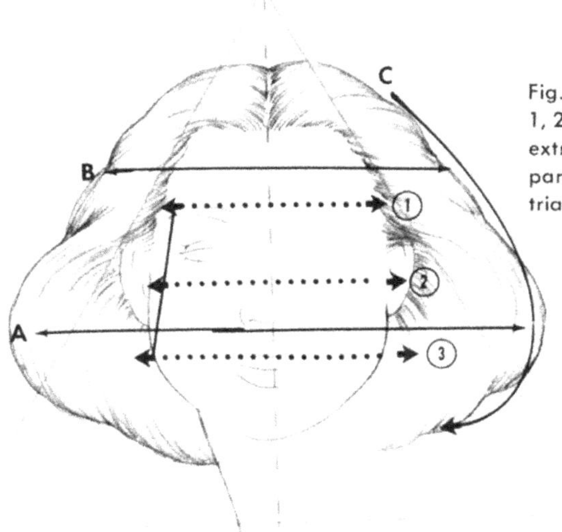

Fig. 175. WRONG
1, 2 and 3 are your caliper measurements. (A) Don't allow extreme width. (B) Don't permit closeness in the upper part of the head through the forehead. (C) Don't use triangular lines.

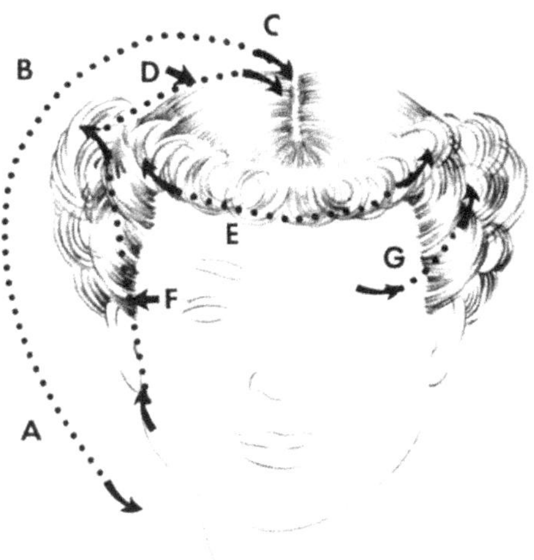

Fig. 176. CORRECT
(A) Do keep the hair behind the jawline. (B) Create fullness and height. (C) Define the short parting at the top of your head. (D) Do keep fullness and roundness to the top of the head. (E) If your temple-points are low and close, employ a softly rounded bang effect, giving the illusion of a lift at the temple, and continuing outward to make greater width for the top of the hairdress. (F) Do keep a fullness of hair up and back at the ear for an ovalized illusion. (G) Brush and comb hair with an upward motion.

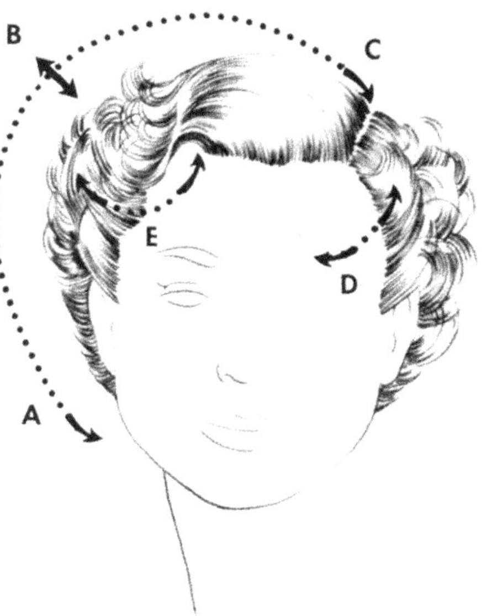

Fig. 177. CORRECT
(A) Do keep the hair behind the jawline. (B) Create fullness and height. (C) If the jawline is extremely wide, part the hair very low, giving width to the forehead and reducing the width of the jawline. (D) Do keep the temple hairline brushed back and upwards. (E) If the forehead is wide or too high, employ a soft dip or quarter-bang effect.

Instructions for creating the "right" hairdress shown here are found in the hair-styling department.

THE HAIR CONTOUR FOR YOU

INVERTED TRIANGLE—Wide forehead, narrow jawline

In your hair-styling, balance must be achieved between the narrow lower portion of the face and the wide forehead. So, we keep the hair dressed easily and closely to the top of the head. And we create the greatest fullness on a line even with the mouth in order to create width across the chinline.

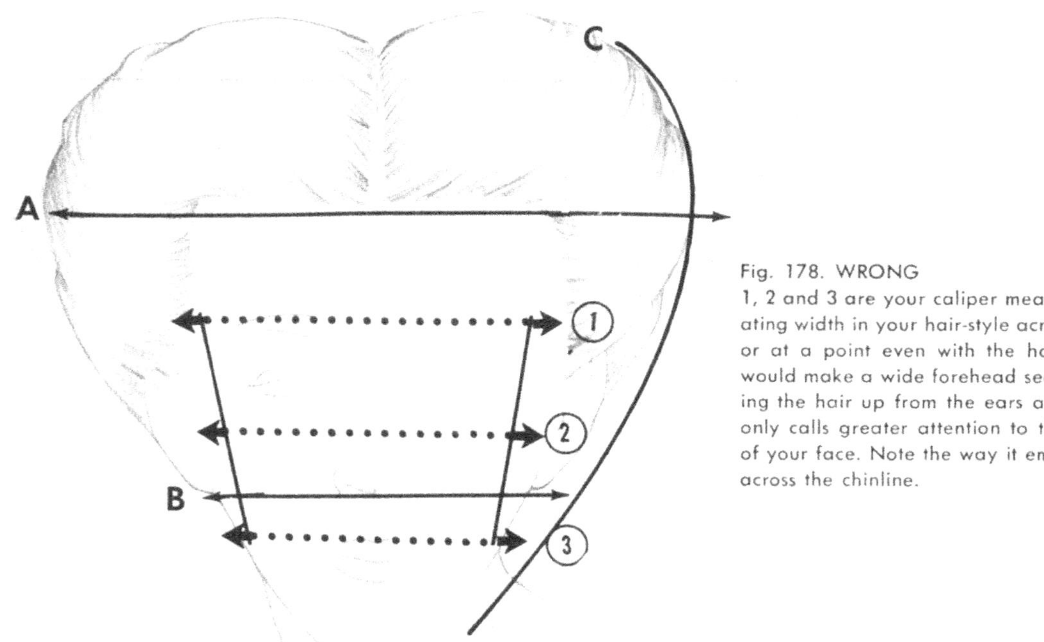

Fig. 178. WRONG
1, 2 and 3 are your caliper measurements. (A) Avoid creating width in your hair-style across the top of your head, or at a point even with the hairline and temples. This would make a wide forehead seem even wider. (B) Dressing the hair up from the ears and the nape of the neck only calls greater attention to the narrow lower portion of your face. Note the way it emphasizes the narrowness across the chinline.

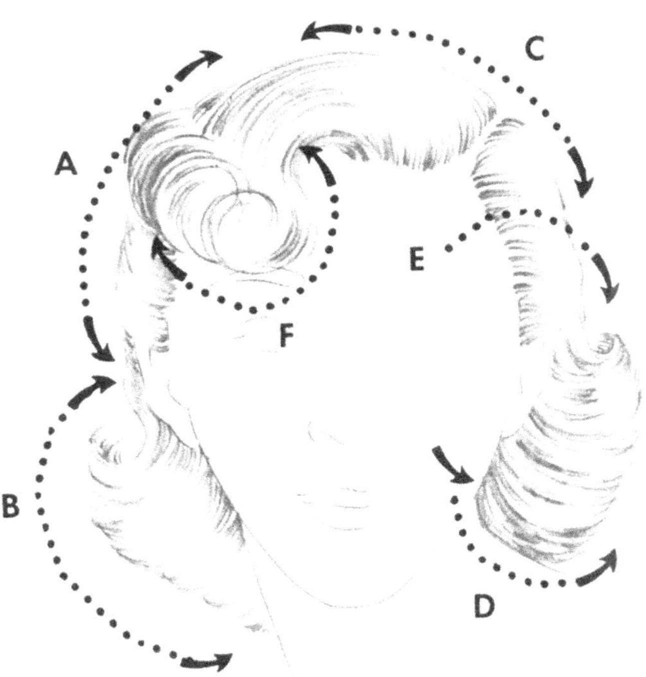

Fig. 179. CORRECT
Since here there is great width in the forehead and a long or short pointed chin, we must style the hair at the top of the head as closely as possible, and let the lower part of the hairdress be full and free. (A) Do keep the waved and curled effects close to the top part of the head. (B) Create fullness. (C) Make the part over the center of the eye. (D) Expose the jawline. (E) Dress the hair back and down into D.

Instructions for creating the "right" hairdress shown here are found in the hair-styling department.

THE HAIR CONTOUR FOR YOU

DIAMOND—Wide cheekbones, narrow at forehead and chin

There are three important points to keep in mind in your hair-styling. The forehead is narrow; the cheekbones are high and wide; the chin is narrow. Fullness of your hair is kept above and below the ears. The hair is combed back and dressed close to the head at the point even with the high, wide cheekbones.

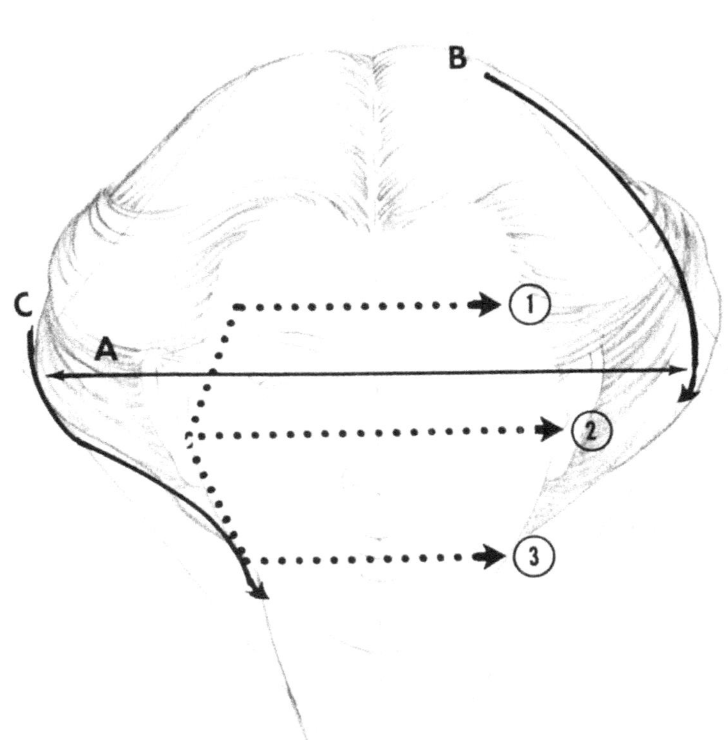

Fig. 180. WRONG
1, 2 and 3 are your caliper measurements. (A) Don't wear the greatest fullness of hair at a point even with the tops of the ears, since this would serve to accentuate width across your cheekbones. (B) Don't allow any slanting line from the top of the head to behind-the-ear fullness. This would emphasize the Diamond shape, as does dressing the hair away from the chinline point C.

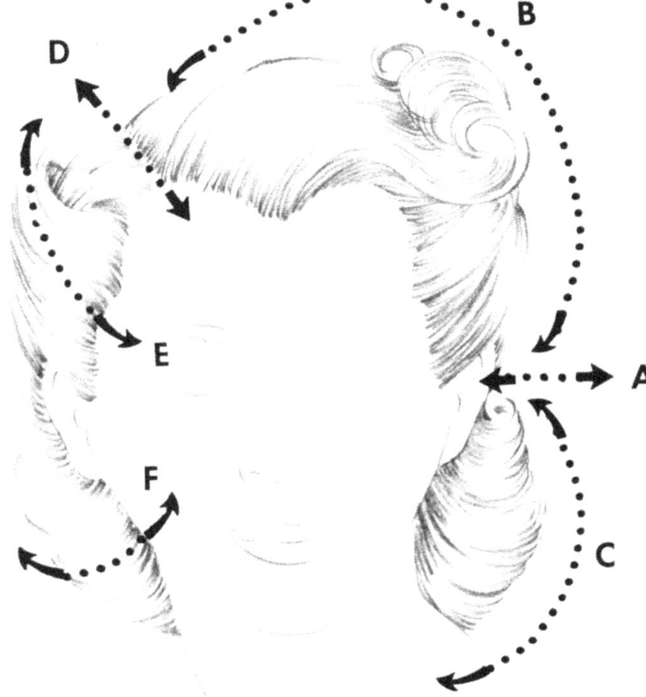

Fig. 181. CORRECT
Since the Diamond face-type has a narrow forehead and a narrow jawline, we must create the illusion of fullness through both the forehead and the jawline, and minimize the width of the high cheekbones. (A) Do keep the hair contour close to the head at the highest point of the cheekbone. (B) Create fullness and height. (C) Create width and fullness. (D) Make the part low to give width to the forehead. (E) Comb the hair back and up full for width through the forehead. (F) Expose the cheek and jawline to reflect light and fullness to the lower part of the face.

Instructions for creating the "right" hairdress shown here are found in the hair-styling department.

HAIR FOR FEATURE CORRECTION

Your forehead may be either wide or narrow, high or low. Use bangs only for softening effects, or to correct proportion. Avoid the drooping effect of hair slanting down from a part; this depresses the whole countenance. With rare exception, every face benefits from a lift at the temples.

From measuring your features, you already know whether your forehead is in correct proportion to the size of your face. To bring the hairline where it should be, give yourself the "Boy Scout salute." Place three of

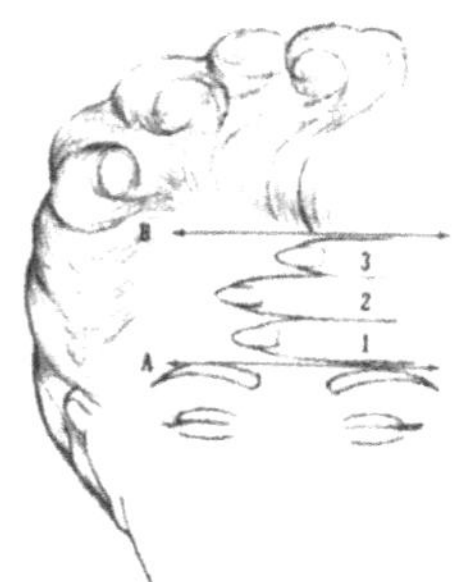

Fig. 182. Normal hairline.

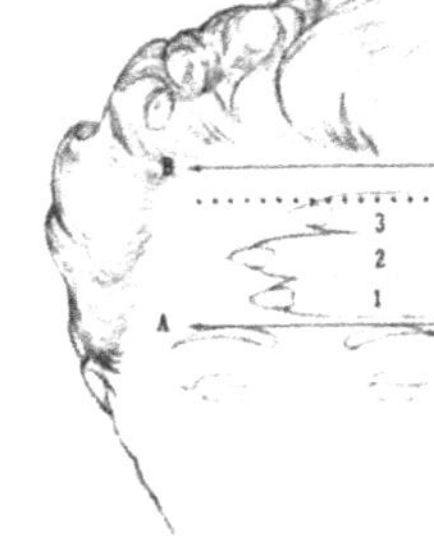

Fig. 183. Hairline too high and too low.

your fingers above the top of your eyebrows, as in Fig. 182. The upper finger and the correct hairline should meet.

If your upper finger overlaps, your hairline is low. Your appearance will gain by dressing the hair away from the forehead. If your natural hairline is higher than the three-finger measurement, bangs will bring down the height of the forehead.

Types of bangs: Bangs are generally divided into three types.

The Dutch bang: This is worn uncurled and flat. It does little to flatter and is best for young faces. At any age, it is not for the Square or Round face-types.

The fringe bang: The most flattering of all bangs for all ages. It should be cut and curled so as to let the forehead show through. This is the ideal softening effect when the hairline is too high, too low, or too wide. It can also be arranged with a horizontal wave to add an effect of width when the forehead is narrow between the temples. This is the bang used to help correct a nose or chin problem.

The French bang: This is a fuller type of bang, cut and curled long enough to brush forward over the hand for arrangement. Brought down, it effectively corrects a too high forehead. Or, it is set for height where the face can benefit from a lengthened effect.

Instructions for cutting and curling the various bang effects begin on page 164.

For a problem nose: The nose could easily take up a whole chapter of this book. In fact, there have been several books written on the nose, its variations in shape, its indications of character, health, and race, and the variety of superstitions attached to this feature.

The nose was considered by the ancients to be the seat of life. Many physiognomists hold to the belief that the shape and size of the nostrils duplicate the shape and size of the lungs. History has been changed and epic deeds accomplished by men made either hero or villain because of complexes at least partially induced by the shape of their noses.

The nose is the one feature you actually feel on your face. There are various theories about this; some scientists have argued with great seriousness that if we had two noses, one on each side of the face, we would be no more conscious of this appendage than we are of our ears.

It has been computed that for every thousand perfect mouths, or perfect pairs of eyes, there is only one perfect nose. More humans (men as well as women) are convinced that their nose is the despoiler of their handsomeness than any other feature. Still, when an ancient Hindu caught his wife being unfaithful, the standard punishment was the one considered most damaging to her allure—cutting off her nose. This usually reformed the ladies quickly and completely. The brick yards did a rousing business supplying ceramic noses to females forgiven by their husbands.

The first thing to do about a nose problem is to remember that you are probably exaggerating its seriousness. Remember that it's an interesting and useful feature. Concentrate on your cleverness in camouflaging its faults.

A prominent nose can be minimized by using hair-styling and glasses to bring it into better proportion with the forehead and chin. Fig. 184 illustrates the combined problem of a receding forehead and a prominent nose. The soft bang brings them into line. If the hairline is normal or low, make it a fringe bang so the forehead can show through.

Fig. 186 shows the combined problem of a prominent nose and a receding chin. Bangs in this instance would serve only to emphasize the weak line of the chin. A soft, upward and backward sweep serves as flattery for both.

With this problem it is important to curl the side hair backward over the ears. See Profile Correction, which follows.

Fig. 184. Wrong hair-styling for problem of receding forehead and prominent nose.

Fig. 185. Corrected hair-styling for problem of receding forehead and prominent nose.

Fig. 186. Wrong hair-styling for problem of receding chin and prominent nose.

Fig. 187. Corrected hair-styling for problem of receding chin and prominent nose.

Fig. 188. Wrong hair-styling for problem of protruding chin.

Fig. 189. Corrected hair-styling for problem of protruding chin.

Fig. 190. Wrong hair-styling for problem of long nose.

Fig. 191. Corrected hair-styling for problem of long nose.

For a crooked nose, one should wear a soft dip or, if the forehead allows, a soft bang worn opposite the crook in the nose. If the bulk of the nose is on the right, you would part your hair on the right and wear your bang or dip to the left to counterbalance the irregularity. If the bulk of the nose is on the left, you would handle your hair in just the opposite manner.

With a long nose, always avoid a center part. The vertical line in the hair seems to continue on down the nose, making it appear even longer. The best trick of all is a diagonal, side part. For side hair arrangement, see Profile Correction.

Fig. 192. Wrong hair-styling for problem of tip-tilted or "pug" nose.

Profile correction: For a receding chin, avoid emphasizing the slant by backward-drawn hair. Dress hair back away from jawline to expose the lower part of the face, allowing as much illumination to the sides of the face as possible.

For a protruding chin, design the hair style with a soft, full-bang effect. Graduate the hair-ends in an upward curve, so you won't be repeating the straight line of the chin. Hair cut too short, or drawn tightly back into a bun on the neck, will leave the chin point without a softening influence.

Fig. 193. Corrected hair-styling for problem of tip-tilted or "pug" nose.

That nose again: For a long nose, it is important to avoid doing the hair too short at the sides. Hair hanging straight down in a vertical line will parallel the length of the nose. Do the ends low, and in a graduated curve.

A tip-tilted or "pug" nose is generally a charming feature. Don't overdo the tilted effect, however, with up-turned curls. Turn the hair ends counterclockwise or back.

Necks, the long and short of it: The illustrations are self-explanatory. They serve as a reminder, too, that it is always good to consider the back effect of your hair and head, as well as the front.

Hair-do's help the figure: Most people, as we've already noticed, have physical differences between the two sides of the body. There is a difference in shoulders, in hips, or possibly in the length of the legs.

If you have one shoulder lower than the other, or any difference that

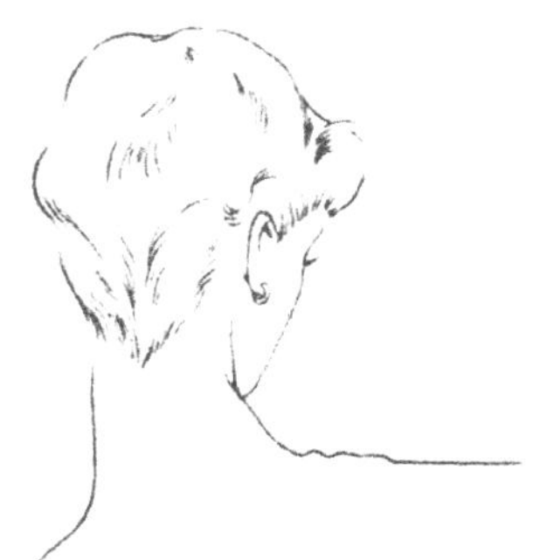
Fig. 194. Wrong hairdress for long neck. Avoid short hair cut.

Fig. 195. Correct hairdress for long neck.

Fig. 196. Wrong hairdress for short neck. Long hair draped over the shoulder submerges the head into the shoulders and foreshortens the front view of a short neck.

Fig. 197. Correct hairdress for short neck. Elongated point gives the illusion of length to the back of the neck.

causes a pronounced droop or limp to one side, never dress the hair flat or low on that particular side. The parting of the hair should be on the opposite side of the drooping feature. Give the hairdress extra height and uplift on this side of the body in order to help the over-all balance.

If you are overweight, wear a medium-full hairdress. A bushy hair-do will add to your size, but cutting your hair all off is even more unflattering. If the breasts are full and forward, dress the hair forward either in a pompadour or full-bang effect to give proper balance to the posture.

The too-thin figure needs to strike a happy medium in hair-fullness, also. Too close a cut emphasizes your over-all thinness; but neither do you want the mop-stick look.

For short figures, don't cut down your height with a long bob or low-on-the-neck arrangement. For overly tall figures, don't add height with an upswept hair-do.

One of the most common errors is that committed by the narrow-shouldered woman with a large head. This woman all too often believes that short, full, fluffy hair disguises the size of her head. Such hair-styling makes her appear more top-heavy than ever and emphasizes the narrow shoulder width.

Most important, this type of woman must dress her hair smoothly. Usually a diagonal side part provides a needed illusion of face length. Since, nine times out of ten, the neck is short, the hair should be kept off the nape of the neck by a high effect or similar treatment. It should not be allowed to show behind and below the ears from a front view.

CHAPTER ELEVEN

Let's Create a Hair-Style for You!

Your Complete Hair Care and Hair-Styling Department

GIVE YOURSELF THAT "SALON LOOK"

The desire of every woman is a head of healthy hair that is curly, lustrous, easy to manage, and smartly dressed. Today, such hair beauty is within the reach of every woman, whether she is near a beauty salon or performs her hair-styling at home.

Hundreds of thousands of home permanent waving kits are sold every year. There are dozens of brands and types, all designed to give your hair the most beautiful wave, in the shortest time, with a minimum amount of experimenting.

Despite all of these easy-to-use beauty aids, an amazing number of women fail to achieve what they particularly want in a home-permanented hairdress—the salon or professional look. Granted that a professional operator has spent more man-hours in mastering the art of giving a permanent wave than the average woman or non-professional; and granted that the professional operator also has the advantage of working totally unhampered from above and behind her subject and with an excellent view of what she is doing—there is still no logical reason why the average woman cannot successfully give herself a beautiful home permanent.

Custom-styling the home permanent to fit your own face is our own theory. From time immemorial, the permanent wave curlers have been set in a horizontal row on the side of the head, and a vertical row from the front hairline to the nape of the neck. Instead, we feel that where an uplift is needed for your face-type on the side of your head, the side-line procedure would be a diagonal placement of curlers. The result is that the waves and curliness-control are set-in to create the uplift where you need it.

The specified setting of permanent curlers for your own face-type is illustrated and explained, beginning on page 147. This does not mean that by following the custom permanent theory you will be confined to any one style or length of hair. It does mean that your wave and curl will be set to fit your own particular face shape and needs.

Before you can have a successful home permanent, you must have a head of healthy, lustrous, carefully cared-for hair. This seems to go without saying—yet how many of you fail to give your hair daily beauty care and expect the home permanent to make up somehow for your constant neglect? Let's correct first things first. Let's begin the home permanent instruction where it should begin—with your hair and its daily care.

HEALTHY HAIR IS LOVELY HAIR

Correct diet and absolute cleanliness are the most important prerequisites for lovely hair.

If your hair and scalp are not in a healthy condition, ask your physician's advice in determining a balanced diet for your individual needs. The hair receives nourishment from a layer of fat under the scalp. If this layer is depleted by improper nourishment, growth of the hair is retarded and, in some instances, results in excessive loss of hair.

Oiliness is caused by overactive oil glands and can be helped by a diet free from oily foods and candy, rich in fruits and vegetables. If your hair tends to be oily, try an egg shampoo to counteract the condition. Be almost fanatical about rinsing. Any trace of soap left in the hair after shampooing irritates the scalp. Vigorous brushing will help normalize this same condition.

Dry hair should always be kept out of the direct sunshine. Protect it with a gay scarf or wear a hat. Be faithful to your daily brushing routine. Use a castile shampoo every two weeks and an oil shampoo once a month to help remedy dry, brittle hair.

Babushkas: There has been nothing worse for hair health in years than the babushka habit. Most people do not realize that the scalp perspires just as any other part of the body does. It needs air to let its pores breathe. A tight or heavy covering worn constantly on the head hampers this. If the hair is kept covered constantly, it is literally soaked in the scalp's perspiration. It is not only unclean, it is bound to show a loss of life and beauty.

Dull hair is usually the result of inadequate rinsing when shampooing, not enough daily brushing and incorrect diet. An egg a day will help keep the dullness away. Include one in your diet for health and for beauty.

Dandruff: There are two types of dandruff. One is powdery and small and is nothing more than a natural shedding of the dry skin cells. This type can be curbed by adequate washing and thorough brushing. The second is a large flaky dandruff and is usually accompanied by an irritated scalp. Follow the treatment suggested for oily hair. Don't neglect your brush and comb if this is your problem. Do keep them clean by sterilizing them daily in a solution of formalin, a teaspoon to a pint of water. If diligent care on your part doesn't help, the time has come to ask your doctor for his advice.

Graying is caused by a lack of pigment in the hair. In older people this is natural. Premature graying is often caused by a vitamin deficiency. Include ample quantities of meat, butter and green vegetables in your diet.

Falling hair is usually a physical matter and calls for a specialist's advice. Meantime, remember that worry and nervousness tighten the scalp and hamper circulation. If you are conscious of the fact that these faults are yours, try keeping your scalp loose and relaxed with daily scalp manipulation and brushing.

Hair-pulling can be a useful scalp manipulation. Grasp a small handful of the hair, pull it hard and away from the scalp. Repeat this for a ten-minute period, until the entire scalp has been exercised. As a daily routine, this should bring beneficial results.

BRUSHING, AN INDISPENSABLE HABIT

Correct brushing is a direct means of attaining beautiful hair.

Brushing stimulates the scalp and, at the same time, removes the accumulation of dirt and dust from the hair. Brushing also frees and removes natural flaking of the scalp. In the case of dandruff, a lanolin ointment massaged into the scalp nightly and combined with faithful brushing will aid in avoiding its recurrence.

When the hair is dry, the cause is usually underactive oil glands. Brushing not only stimulates these glands to greater activity but also helps distribute whatever oil there is right out to the very ends.

If your hair is oily, your oil glands are overactive, discharging excessive amounts. Careful brushing helps to distribute the oil evenly over the hair. It prevents the oil from remaining concentrated at the roots where it will clog the follicles.

The old day of leaning the head down and brushing a hundred strokes went out (generally) about the time long, straight hair disappeared. Nowadays, when shorter hair is worn in a variety of directions—some curled forward, some curled or waved back, some back-sections worn brushed up, and some worn brushed down—hair requires a different brushing technique.

In general, a beneficial way of treating healthy hair in the nightly brushing is to give it a thorough going-over in both directions. That is, first, brush the entire head, section by section, in the opposite direction from which it is worn. The number of strokes is not important. Starting at the scalp, and using a firm, even stroke, brush until all the hair is standing away from the head and the scalp feels live and tingling. Then start brushing the sections back into place, continuing until they are smooth and shining.

If you use care in brushing the hair back into place, this two-way brushing will not be harmful to your wave or curl. You may notice that your beauty operator, when dressing the hair, usually brushes in the opposite direction first. She does this in order to give the curls a "loose" and natural look, rather than a tight, plastered-down appearance. However, remember that the operator is an expert and the home-brusher may or may not be adept. Go cautiously, or you may have your beauty-parlor hair-do brushed out in no time.

Hair that has become damaged and suffered broken ends from over-bleaching or unsuccessful permanents requires special handling. In these cases, do not start the brushing from the scalp. Instead, pick up the ends of the hair in the fingers and give them a gentle brushing to avoid further breakage. Then, moving the brush half-way up the length of the hair, brush from this distance down. Finally, starting at the scalp, brush with fairly vigorous strokes to the half-way point.

No matter whether you choose to set your hair at night or prefer to let it fly loose, brush your hair vigorously for ten minutes before retiring.

Use a good, stiff brush for best results. The ornamental brush contained in your dresser set often is of no use for proper brushing. Choose a plain, stiff-bristled, professional brush obtainable in most drug and department stores.

Keep your brush clean by washing regularly in lukewarm suds to which a little household ammonia has been added. Rinse in clear water. Place it on a window sill or in some other light, airy place to dry. Don't allow the brush to remain wet or damp for a long period, for this will cause the bristles to become loose and eventually to drop out.

SHAMPOOING, HOW AND WHEN

Use a mild and neutral shampoo. Hair should first be brushed and combed thoroughly to remove any existing snarls. Shampoo water should be medium hot. If your faucet water is hard, use either bottled spring water, rain water or water that has been boiled. Hair and scalp should be wet thoroughly before the shampooing process begins.

Shampoo should be used generously, worked vigorously into your scalp to serve both as a cleanser and an invigorating massage. Water should be changed three times, and the shampoo application repeated. Rinsing is done with warm, clear water. Be sure to rinse and rinse and rinse. Most dull-looking hair is directly traceable to incomplete rinsing.

Thoroughly clean hair will "squeak" when a damp strand is pulled through the fingers.

Towel-dry your hair at least partially before setting pin-curls.

Most hair should be washed as often as it becomes dirty, unless the hair is extremely dry. In that case, once a week or every two weeks is enough.

Extremely oily hair: Your best cleansing method is to heat a liquid soap to moderate temperature and work it thoroughly into scalp and hair before applying water. Use a vinegar or lemon rinse.

In the meantime, we suggest that between shampoos you brush your hair from the scalp outward, using shredded cotton in your hairbrush. As the cotton becomes soiled, replace it with fresh absorbent cotton. Dampen the cotton with cologne if you wish. The hair should be brushed in sections.

Between wet shampoos, you might try a cornmeal or orris root shampoo. Apply the meal or powder to the scalp and the hair with a square of cotton. Remove it with a gauze-covered scalp brush, using an upward and outward stroke. The gauze should be changed several times, since it becomes soiled rapidly. Remember that this type of dry shampoo necessitates much brushing to make certain that no residue remains. If your hair appears lifeless after such a treatment, it is probably because you haven't brushed out all of the dry shampoo. After having completed the needed vigorous brushing, promote glossiness by placing the hair in the folds of a coarse bath towel and rubbing briskly.

Dry hair: Where dryness of the hair is a problem, try occasional hot oil treatments. The treatment is a simple one. Heat pure olive oil to approximately body temperature. (A manufactured hot oil preparation can also be used.) Rub the oil into the scalp and onto the hair shafts. Immerse a rough towel into very hot water, wring it out well, and wrap it tightly about your head turban-fashion. When the towel cools, reheat it, repeating this procedure three or four times. The treatment is most effective if done with two towels. This way the head is kept warm and there is no cooling-off period while the towel is being reheated. Following this hot towel application, shampoo with a good liquid soap. Use warm water. Make certain that all of the oil is completely removed from the hair. Rinse at least three times in clear water until a damp strand of hair "squeaks" when pulled through the fingers.

Hand drying is best, particularly for dry hair. Rough towel dry the hair and brush it vigorously. This brushing stimulates the scalp and activates normal oil secretion.

Egg shampoo for dry, brittle, overbleached or dyed hair: There are prepared egg shampoos on the market. If fresh eggs are used, two or three or more are required, according to the thickness and length of the hair. Separate the yolks, and whip well, adding a very little water. Beat the whites to a froth, then blend with the yolks. Wet the hair with tepid water, removing excess moisture with the hands. Dip the hand into the egg mixture and apply with your hand cup-shaped, rotating on the head. When half the mixture is used, rinse with tepid water, and repeat the procedure, using the balance. Rinse with tepid or cool water so the eggs do not congeal.

Bleached hair shampoo: Great care must be taken because this type of hair has a tendency to mat and tangle when wet. Wet with lukewarm or tepid water. Use pure soap, castille or tar. Avoid matting by pouring the soap on very slowly, and always work with the hands under the hair, not on top in the usual way. Finish with a rinse of lemon or vinegar, or a commercial rinse prepared for that purpose. While the hair is still wet, apply a little lubricating dressing for greater manageability and ease in combing.

Salt water accumulation removal: Soap and rinse many times. Massage scalp, since salt may be imbedded with oil and perspiration. Use a mildly acid rinse, either a prepared one or a highly-diluted fresh lemon rinse. Hot oil treatments also are helpful.

Hard-water softeners: In a hard water area use special hard water shampoos, or cream shampoos. If ordinary soap shampoo is used, mix with softening crystals or water softener. Follow with an acid rinse.

Handling frail hair which is inclined to break off: Use a shampoo specially made for such hair and apply with soft or distilled water. Don't rub too hard. Towel dry the hair. Brush only with a soft brush.

Beer rinse for fine hair: Stale beer may be used as a rinse when shampooing the hair in much the same way in which vinegar is used. However, unlike vinegar, it should not be rinsed out of the hair. Beer used in this way tends to give body to fine hair, and it leaves no odor. Be sure that the beer has been uncapped and allowed to stand for at least 24 hours before using.

PARTS OF BEAUTY

The importance of parting: In starting out to custom-style your home permanent, remember that the most important single factor in a hair-style is the parting. A part can determine the natural beauty of the face and hair, and it just as easily can give a complete distortion to the most beautiful make-up and face.

There are a variety of partings: circular, semi-circular, diagonal, center, side, full-length and partial. Here are some rules on hair partings to study and adapt to your own face and head type.

Very thin hair should always have a diagonal part, running from a point on the forehead line to an opposite point on the crown of the head. This provides even distribution of the hair, makes it appear heavier and more generous in dressing.

For the small-boned, well-proportioned face, there is no more flattering hair-style than the three-and-one-half-inch, all-over cut, set in halo curls, with a smooth, saucer crown. No part or suggestion of a part is needed here.

Cowlicks: Where a cowlick is an annoyance, particular attention should be paid to parting and to styling. If the cowlick constitutes a troublesome break at the front hairline, it is often eliminated by parting the hair well over to one side, either diagonally or straight, depending upon which is most flattering to the face. If the cowlick is on the crown of the head, a semi-circular parting disguises it.

A widow's peak is one of the most coveted natural hair beauties. The hair should not be parted in the direct center, but to one side of the widow's peak, allowing its full effectiveness to remain. If your face is young and regular in outline, the hair can be worn straight back without a part of any kind. This is the ideal where a widow's peak is present, drawing full attention to it through an open, smooth, clean forehead.

A long nose or a long face should never wear a center part. The safest

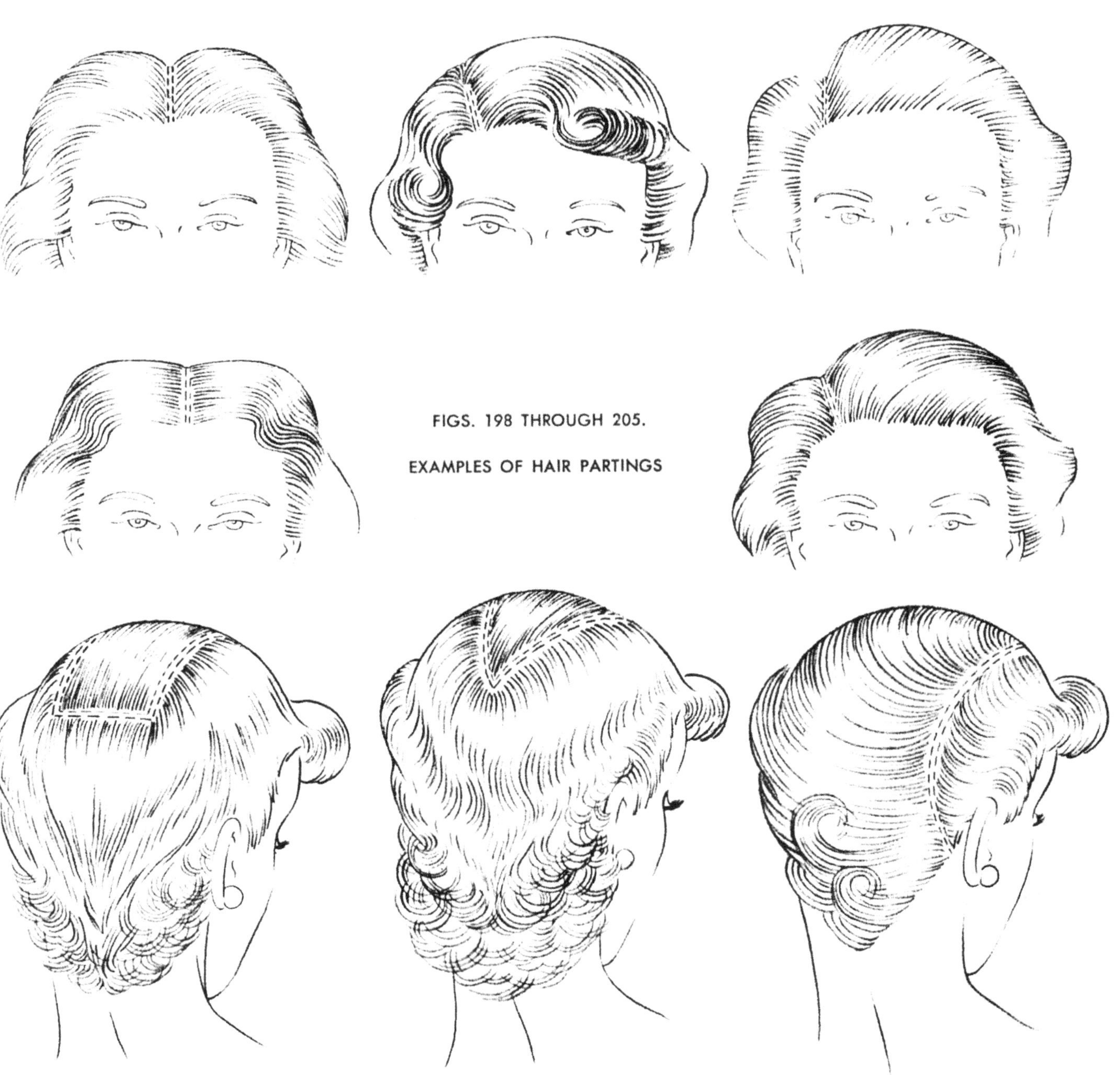

FIGS. 198 THROUGH 205.

EXAMPLES OF HAIR PARTINGS

bet is a diagonal side part. The same is true for the very round face. A Diamond face-type must not forget that the center part exaggerates a pointed forehead and chin.

The egghead: If you have what is commonly described as an "egg-head," the most flattering treatment is to have a three-and-a-half-inch, all-over cut, with the hair tapered in length in the back and at the nape of the neck, from a part that runs completely across the top of the head.

Start this parting at the top of either ear, and go across the head just back of the actual crown.

The hair in back of the part is set in soft pin-curls. When combed out, they provide a balancing fullness to the front, so that the so-called "egg-shape" is effectively disguised.

The flat head: When the back of the head suddenly falls off from the crown and becomes flat in appearance, the same short cut as for the "egg-shape" is recommended. In this instance, however, a full-length diagonal parting is flattering. Starting just above either the right or the left temple, the hair is parted diagonally across the head to end just behind and below the opposite ear. Curls in front of the part are set forward; curls in back, away from the part and downward.

In conclusion: No matter what the parting, keep it a clean line. Straggling hairs or an uneven parting destroy an otherwise lovely coiffure. A clean, true parting indicates a fastidious, appearance-conscious woman.

CUTTING YOUR HAIR

There are many procedures and techniques used in cutting hair professionally. Both scissors, thinning or conventional, and razors are used. We do not recommend razor cutting, since this type of cutting splits the ends of the hair.

Fig. 206. Blunt cutting.

We do suggest that you consult and patronize a professional hair stylist, particularly when changing the style of your hair. For those of you who wish to cut your own hair, or must cut it yourself, the illustrations in this chapter, if followed closely, will enable you to do a good job.

If you are going to do your own cutting, invest in a good pair of barber scissors, or barber shears, as they are called. Don't chop away with kitchen scissors. The success of any job is determined by the tools used, as well as the skill with which they are employed.

Blunt and tapered cutting: There are two methods of cutting hair: blunt cutting and tapered cutting. Blunt cutting can result in a bold, hard, unmanageable end. Taper cutting is done by running the scissors in a quick, light scraping motion toward the scalp, starting at the point where your fingers are holding the hair. The result is a tapered end, which is softer, curlier, and more manageable for the average head of hair.

Fig. 207. Result of blunt cutting.

Sectioning the head: Before cutting any of your hair, it should be sec-

Fig. 208. Taper cutting.

Fig. 209. Result of taper cutting.

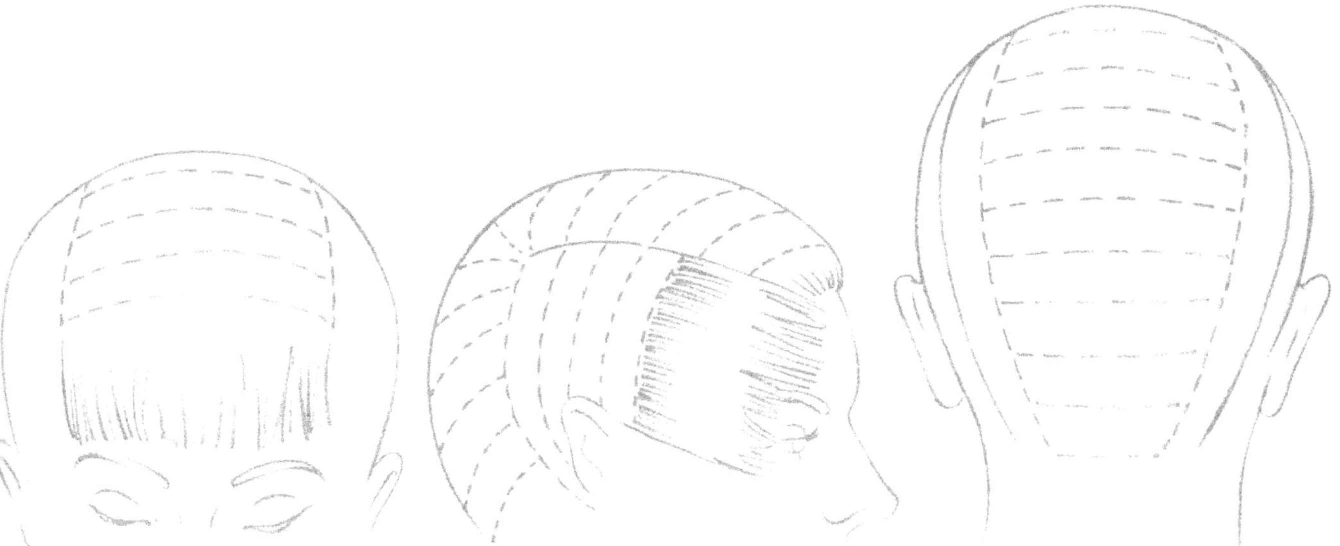

Fig. 210. Front section for haircutting.

Fig. 211. Side section for haircutting.

Fig. 212. Back section for haircutting.

tioned off into four equal parts. The three parts not being worked on are pinned on top of the head out of the way. Remember that regardless of the section to be cut, the hair is first combed forward. The four sections to be parted off are:

1. From the crown of the head to the forehead.
2. From the side of the head to just behind the ear.
3. From the other side of the head to just behind the ear.
4. From the crown of the head, down the back of the head.

Here are the partings, plus the amount of hair to be cut at a time, all over the head. You will notice that the hair has been combed forward into individual, one-inch horizontal sections, and then cut. In the succeeding sketches, the second, third, and additional layers of hair have been combed forward and cut. This is the procedure for cutting the forehead section or bangs.

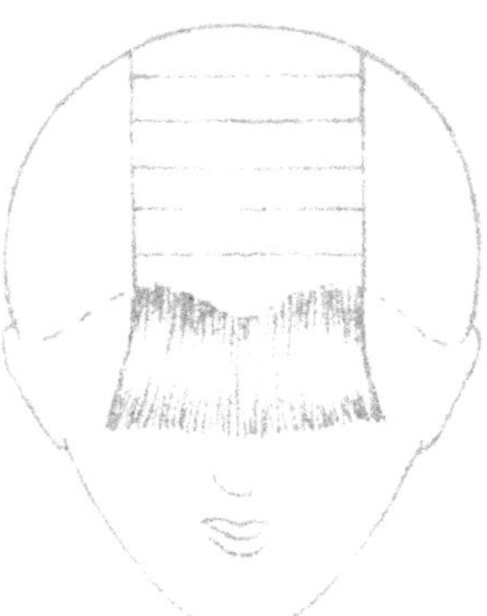

Fig. 213. Bang cutting.

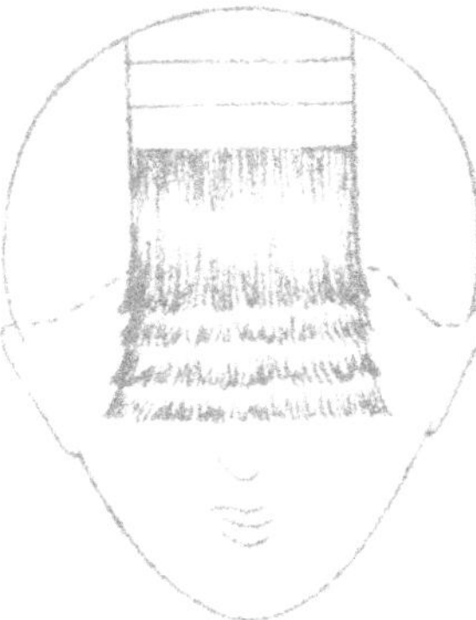

Fig. 214. Bang cutting—continued.

Fig. 215. Bang cutting—conclusion.

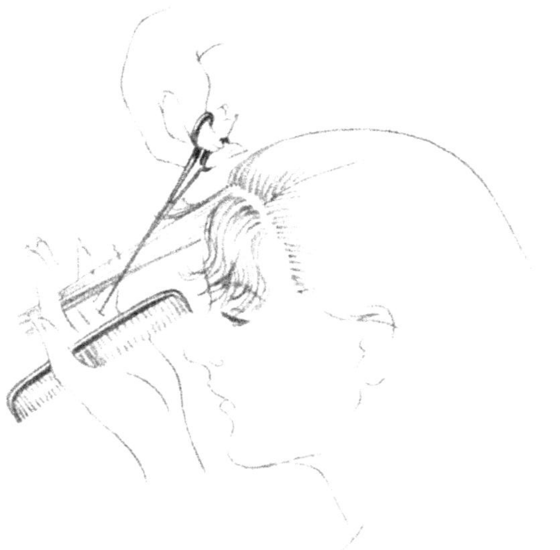

Fig. 216. Cutting front section.

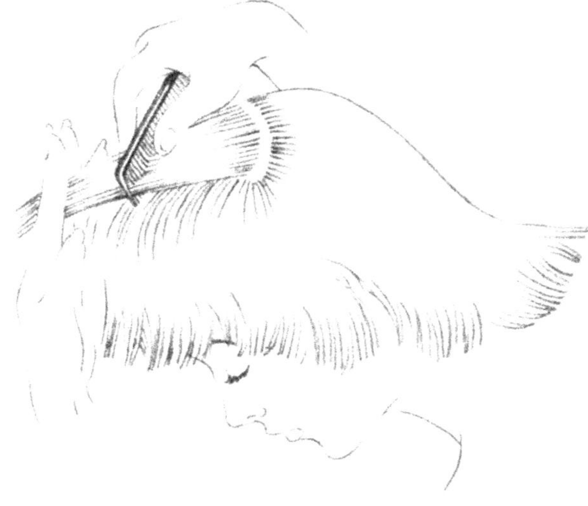

Fig. 217. Backcombing front section.

Fig. 218. Combing forward, and backcombing side section.

Fig. 219. Taper cutting forward side section.

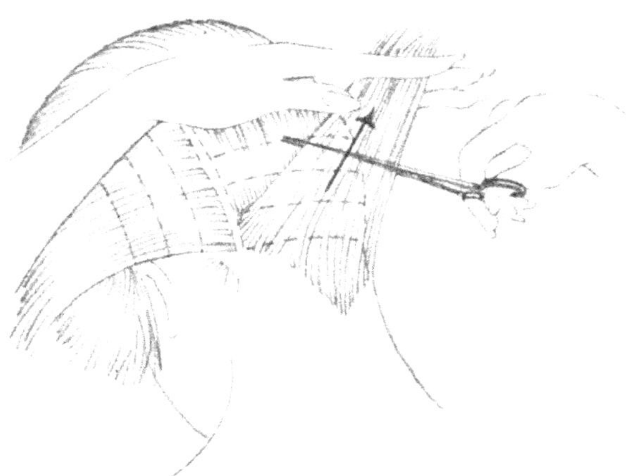

Fig. 220. Cutting back section.

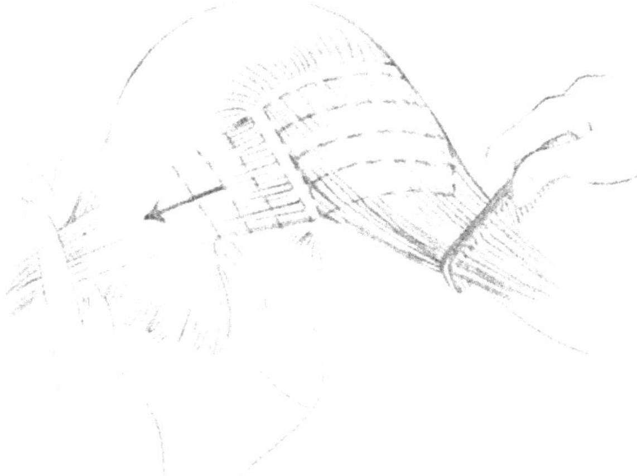

Fig. 221. Combing and complete cutting, side section.

The hair has been cut from the crown and combed back out of the way, and the last layer of hair is being cut.

For a soft, tapered effect, each section of hair, approximately one square inch in size, is backcombed slightly and the ends extending beyond the backcombed area are then cut.

Here the hair has been combed forward, backcombed and cut.

Each one-inch layer of hair from the crown of the head down the back of the head is parted off, pulled up, backcombed slightly, and then cut, clear down to the last layer of hair on the neck. Now comb hair out as you intend to wear it. If you have missed any ends, they will show and can easily be snipped off. The same procedure is used in cutting hair, whether you are cutting bangs or the complete head.

As in Fig. 213, the hair is combed forward in individual one-inch horizontal sections and cut.

The second, third, and fourth layers of hair have been combed forward and cut, as shown in Fig. 214.

Additional sections of hair have been combed forward and cut, as in Fig. 215.

The same procedure as we have stated above applies to the sides of the head.

A blunt cut, in which the hair is cut straight across the end of the section, is recommended for the heavy head of hair, particularly if the hair is cut in layers. A thin head of hair can be cut blunt, but it should not be layered.

YOUR CUSTOM HOME PERMANENT

We appreciate the fact that there are many of you who prefer to have your permanent waving done at a beauty salon. The instructions in this chapter are particularly designed to be of help to the woman who gives herself a home permanent.

Whether you dress your hair yourself, or have it dressed, you should have the knowledge and understanding of how hair-styling is executed. You will know better then how to ask your beauty operator for the effect you want, and how to care for and maintain the hairdressing between times.

Practice makes the perfect permanent: The natural looking permanent wave must be a happy medium—enough curl but not too much curl. To achieve this, there are three points which cannot be stressed too strongly.

Always choose a nationally advertised brand, whether you are having your wave done by a beauty salon operator or are giving yourself your own home permanent. These well-known brands have had months of testing before packaging. Most of them present a choice of solution according to your specific type of hair. Follow the directions on the package, observe the timing exactly.

If this is your first home-given permanent, remember that practice makes perfect. Rehearse your wave before you pour out the solution. Practice rolling your hair on the curlers until you can effortlessly make smooth, cleanly-rolled curls of uniform size. It doesn't matter whether you do this practice rolling on wet or dry hair; the object is to become skillful at it before the solution is applied and it's too late to experiment.

The test curl is a must: Always make a test curl with the solution before applying it to the entire head. Take a piece of hair on the back of the head where the strand will not show if there is any discoloration, such as sometimes occurs on overbleached or improperly tinted hair or when there are systemic conditions such as extreme acidity. This test curl is important, too, for determining whether or not the timing is right for the amount of curl you desire.

When not to permanent wave: Wait at least a week after tinting or dyeing. Wait at least a month after surgery or the use of an anesthetic. Best results may not be obtained after a cocktail party when the alcohol is still in your system, or during monthly periods.

Pre-cutting for a permanent: Always allow your entire head of hair to be one-half to three-quarters of an inch longer than you intend to wear it. Thus, if the ends show kinkiness, you can trim them afterwards and achieve a soft, loose curl.

For soft, up-turning ringlets, the ends should be slightly tapered. Stubby ends do not make an up-turning curl. Ends tapered too thin will result in frizziness.

If you have long hair with a tendency to curl, and you intend changing it to a shorter style, have your short cut done two weeks before your permanent. As you know, more men have curly hair than women, the reason being that they wear it short. Your own hair may have enough natural curl when short to make a permanent unnecessary. In our salon we always feel it's senseless to put an artificial wave over a natural one. During the two weeks, you may discover that your head needs only a pick-up curl here and there.

Do or don't shampoo? If your hair is clean and only moderately oily, it is not necessary to shampoo it before a permanent. The natural oil sometimes helps create a softer wave. Dirty or excessively oily hair should be shampooed first. If you have any foreign material on your hair such as lacquer, spray dressing or rinses, shampoo and rinse the soap out thoroughly. Any of these materials if left on will retard the action of the solution. Substances such as face-powder or cold cream in the hair around the face will sometimes cause discoloration at the hairline.

PROCEDURE FOR PERMANENT

Dividing the hair for curling: In rolling the hair for any kind of curl, the hair mass should be divided into squares (sections) of equal size at the scalp. Check the illustration, Fig. 222. This applies to curls for permanent waving or pin-curls, flat, standing, rolled or hanging curls and even for waves. Dividing the hair into squares or sections of equal size assures you of curls of equal thickness, Fig. 223. It also provides an easy-to-manage amount of hair. One-inch squares are generally accepted as the most satisfactory and manageable amount of hair to handle at any one time. Since there is a definite relationship from one curl to another, it stands to reason that if a small section of hair is used for one curl and, just below it, a larger section of hair is used for a larger curl, there will be no smoothness in the waves, Fig. 224. Without proper blocking, frizzy and uneven results are obtained, Fig. 225. The exception to the one-inch rule is the hair at the nape of the neck. This is rolled and curled tightly and in small sections to secure tighter, longer-lasting curls.

If your selected hairdress requires waves in a vertical position at the sides of the head, they should not be rolled horizontally. By the same token, if the hair-style requires waves in a horizontal position at the sides of the head, they should not be rolled vertically.

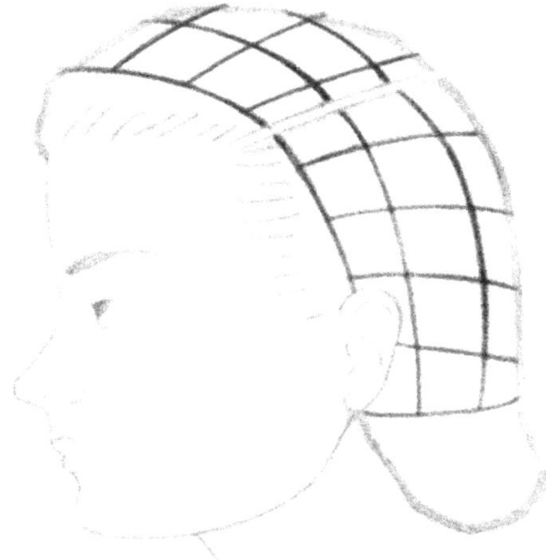

Fig. 222. Dividing the hair into squares before pin-curling.

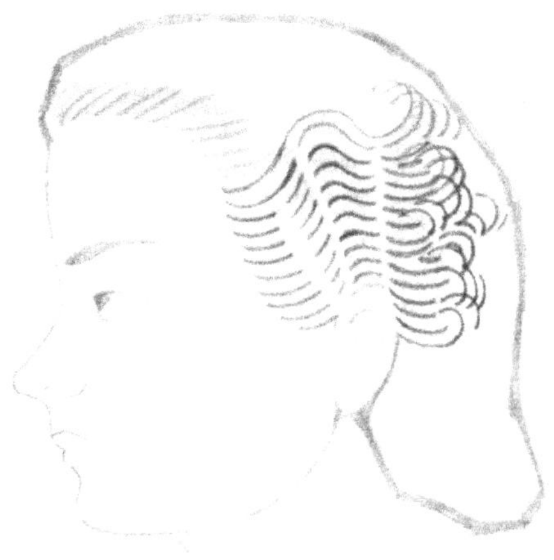

Fig. 223. Result of proper blocking pin-curl section.

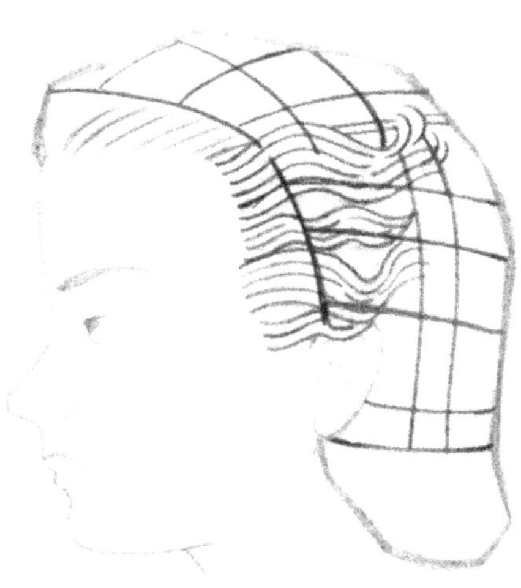

Fig. 224. Improper blocking.

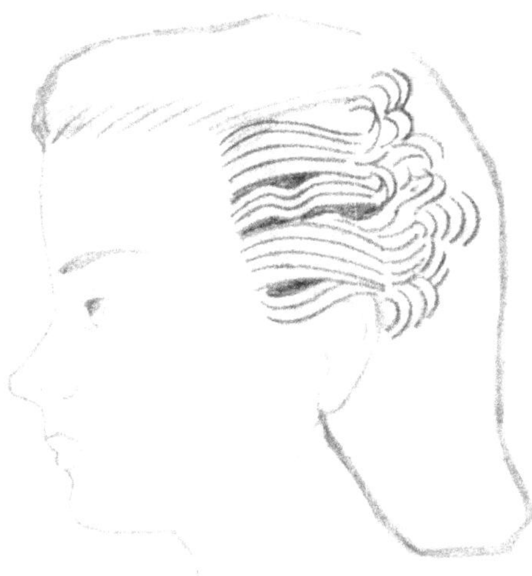

Fig. 225. Result of improper blocking and pin-curling.

In combing each one of these hair-sections preliminary to rolling, combing should be thorough from the scalp outward to the points, or ends, of the hair. Make certain that there is no disheveled hair within the strands. Failure to do this will result in fuzziness or kinkiness when you comb out for your finished hair-style.

How to roll your hair for best results: Assemble all the tools and ingredients you will need before you start working; this will help you in controlling your timing. Having followed our pre-permanent advice, rehearsed your rolling technique, and performed your actual test-curl, you are ready to apply the solution.

Procedure: Apply the solution evenly. Very often when certain curls turn out weaker than others it is because they have been improperly dampened. Too much solution on the ends will result in frizziness. Ends are always more porous than the rest of the hair-shaft, and this is especially true where a trace of old permanent remains. Apply the solution starting about one-eighth of an inch from the scalp and brush along two-thirds of the length. Then comb the solution through the entire length.

Avoid stretching and pulling the hair when winding. Wind the ends around the curler firmly but not too tightly. If you stretch or pull on the strand when you are wrapping it, the hair, when it is released, will spring back into a kinky curl.

Naturally curly hair being permanented to give it more body requires a milder solution and less time than perfectly straight hair. However, too little time may just relax the natural curl into straight hair, so watch your timing carefully.

We don't recommend saving unused solution from one wave to another. Freshly-opened solution for each wave will be more economical in the long run since it will give better results.

Wool-crepe, if you can buy it, will help in getting those short lengths of back hair around the curlers. If you can't buy the wool-crepe, go to the variety store and purchase a cheap hair-roll or rat, and pull this material apart. Cotton may also be used. Cut the wool-crepe about an inch longer than the hair, then holding it under the hair start your winding and the real hair will be caught up in the process.

Too much curl: If your best and most careful efforts still result in a wave that is overtight, the curl can be relaxed by wetting it again with the solution. Let the solution remain about five minutes, combing it through the hair thoroughly, then remove.

For naturally kinky hair, we do not recommend home-straightening unless you cannot manage to have the work done by a professional operator. In this case, you may have some success by combing through a waving solution as suggested above. Comb continuously for about ten minutes, then remove with shampoo. Do not leave the solution on overnight.

After your wave: Rinse the solution thoroughly. Do not shampoo unless the specific product you are using so instructs you.

HOW TO CUSTOM-SET YOUR HAIR-STYLE

In the following sketches, illustrating placement of permanent wave curlers, we have three types of movement: horizontal, vertical and diagonal.

The arrow indicates the forward procedure in rolling the hair, clockwise or counterclockwise.

The proper placement of the curlers will give the proper result, so follow the arrow.

You are ready now to set your custom-built hair-style for the greatest flattery to your own face-shape, as shown on the pages immediately following.

OVAL

Fig. 226. Front placement of permanent wave curlers for Oval type.

Fig. 227. Side placement of permanent wave curlers for Oval type.

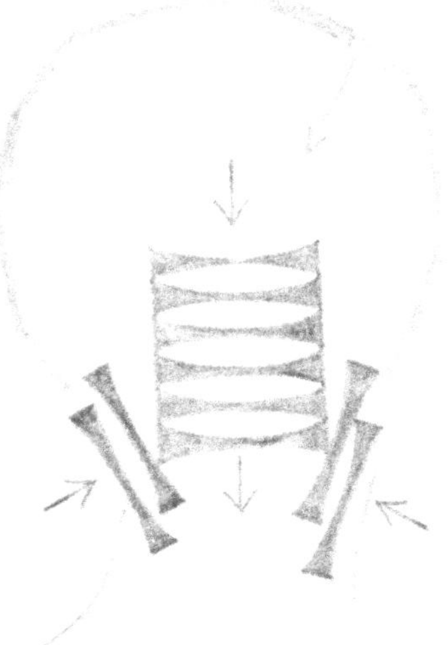

Fig. 228. Back placement of permanent wave curlers for Oval type.

OBLONG

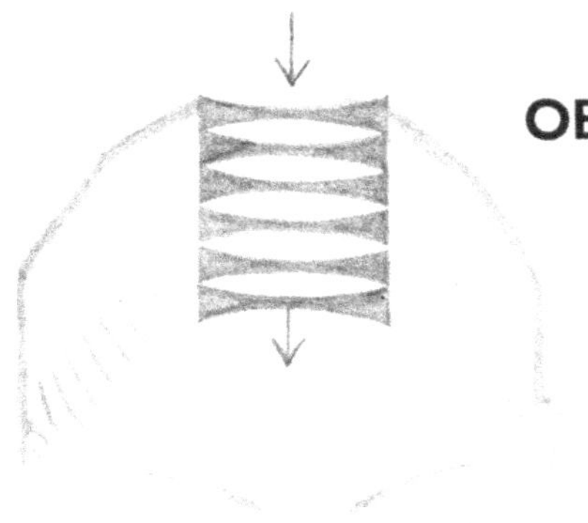

Fig. 229. Front placement of permanent wave curlers for Oblong type.

Fig. 230. Side placement of permanent wave curlers for Oblong type.

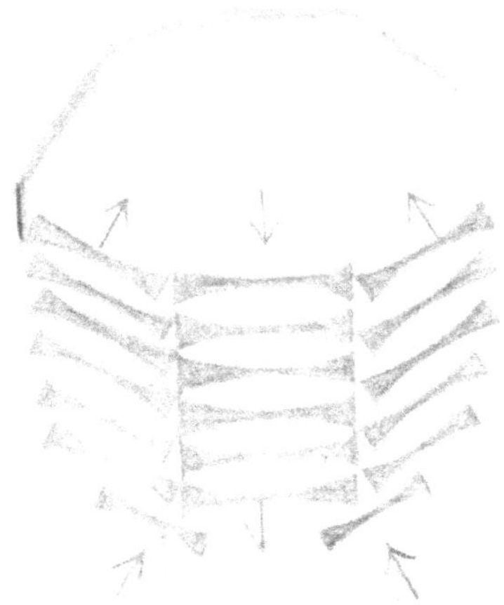

Fig. 231. Back placement of permanent wave curlers for Oblong type.

ROUND

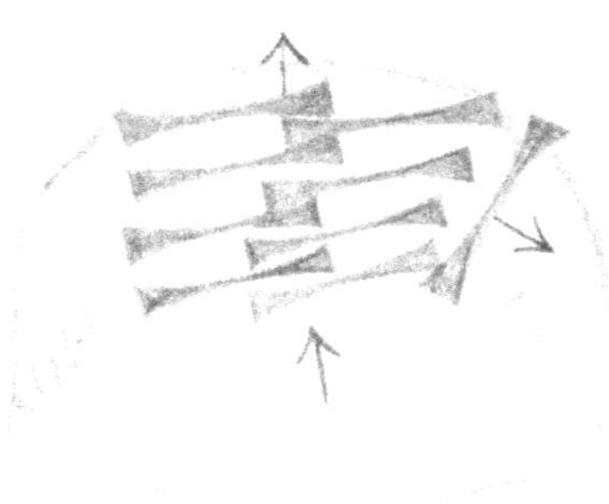

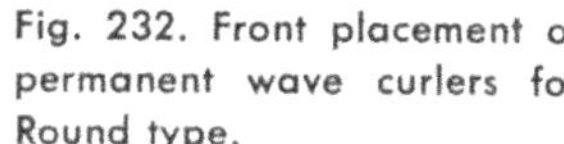

Fig. 232. Front placement of permanent wave curlers for Round type.

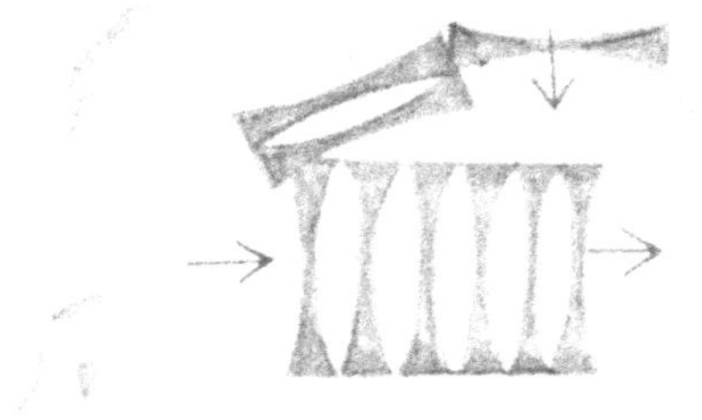

Fig. 233. Side placement of permanent wave curlers for Round type.

Fig. 234. Back placement of permanent wave curlers for Round type.

SQUARE

Fig. 235. Front placement of permanent wave curlers for Square type.

TRIANGLE

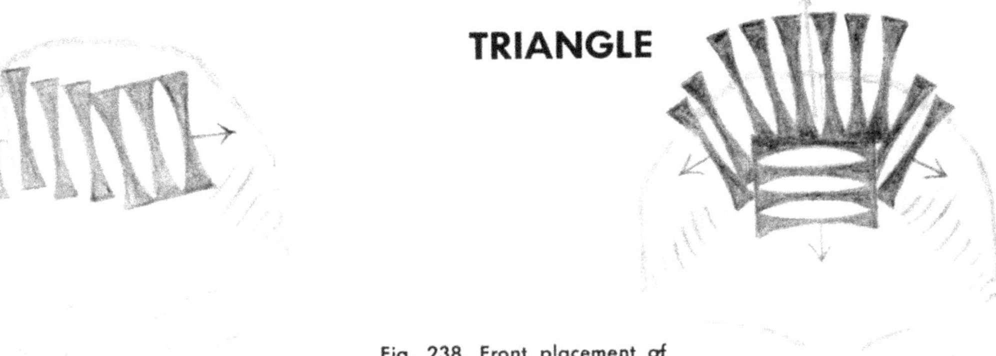

Fig. 238. Front placement of permanent wave curlers for Triangle composite type.

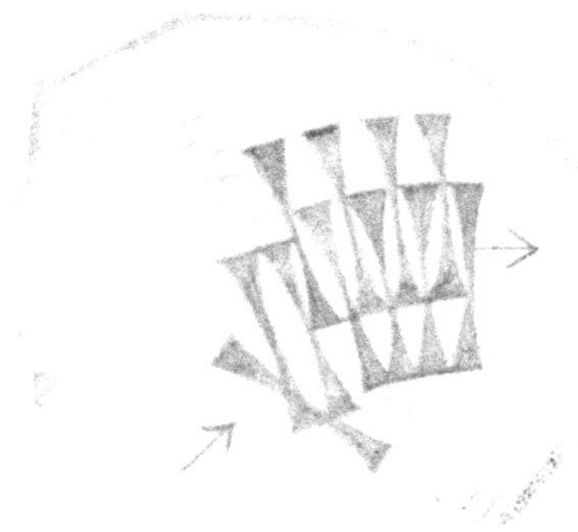

Fig. 236. Side placement of permanent wave curlers for Square type.

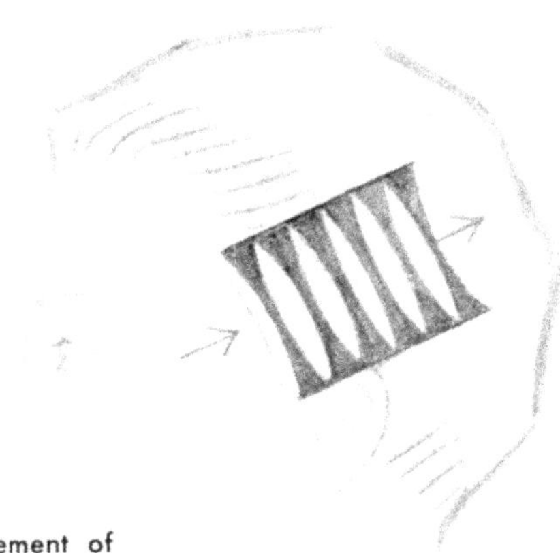

Fig. 239. Side placement of permanent wave curlers for Triangle composite type.

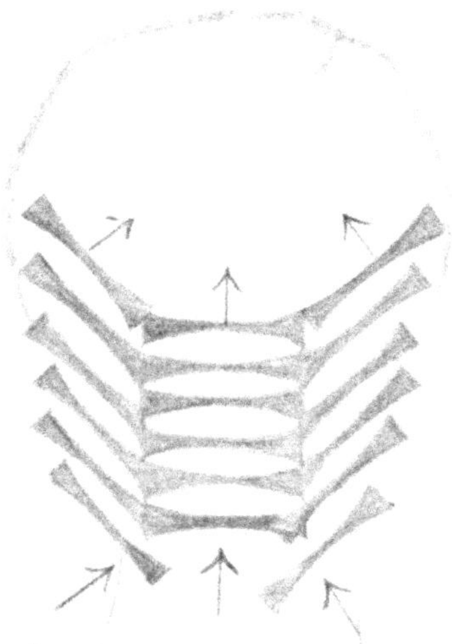

Fig. 237. Back placement of permanent wave curlers for Square type.

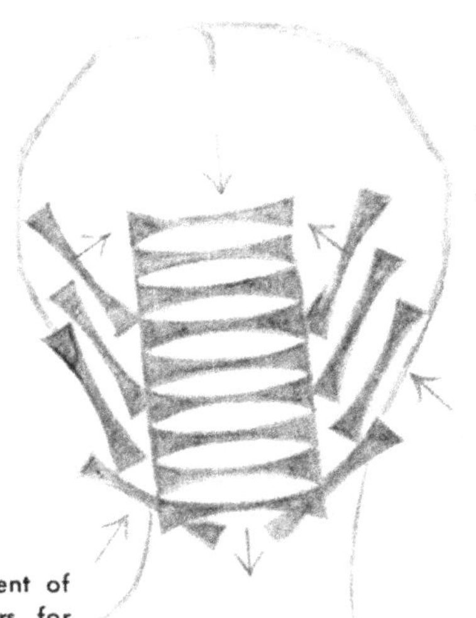

Fig. 240. Back placement of permanent wave curlers for Triangle composite type.

INVERTED TRIANGLE

Fig. 241. Front placement of permanent wave curlers for Inverted Triangle type.

Fig. 242. Side placement of permanent wave curlers for Inverted Triangle type.

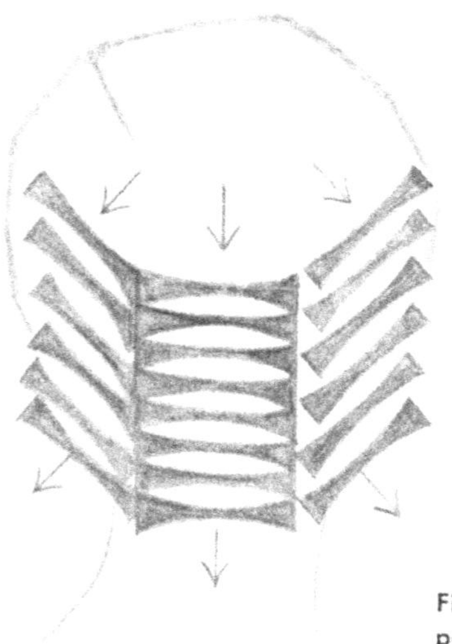

Fig. 243. Back placement of permanent wave curlers for Inverted Triangle type.

DIAMOND

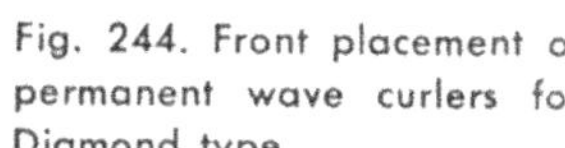

Fig. 244. Front placement of permanent wave curlers for Diamond type.

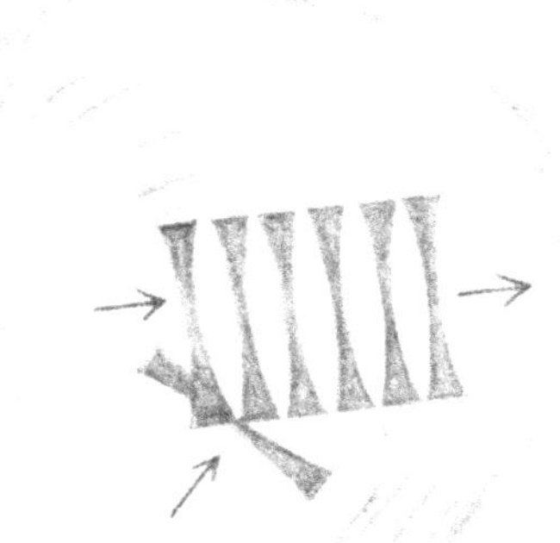

Fig. 245. Side placement of permanent wave curlers for Diamond type.

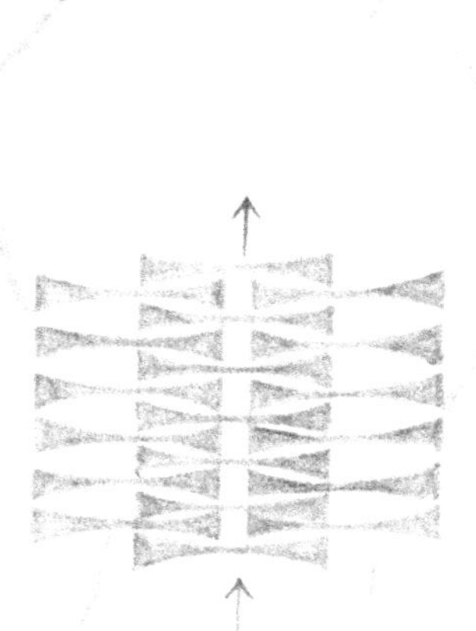

Fig. 246. Back placement of permanent wave curlers for Diamond type.

PIN-CURLING

Types of pin-curls: There are several types of pin-curls. These are the simple forward and backward pin-curls, the forward and backward pyramids (as illustrated) and the roll curl. (Figs. 247 through 251.)

The final deciding factor in choosing the direction of the curl is whether you want to dress the hair toward or away from the face, or draw it up to the top of the head with curls lying away from the face and sides of the head, or dress the hair toward the face and sides of the head.

Where a single bobby pin is used for fastening, the bobby pin is opened (*not* with the teeth!) and inserted into the body of the hair on the scalp inside the circle of the rolled curl itself. The open end is pushed over the curl and is then allowed to close. Only the ends of the bobby pin, on opposite sides, hold the pin-curl in place. See Fig. 252. This method of placement avoids hair breakage and any pin-kink in the dry curl.

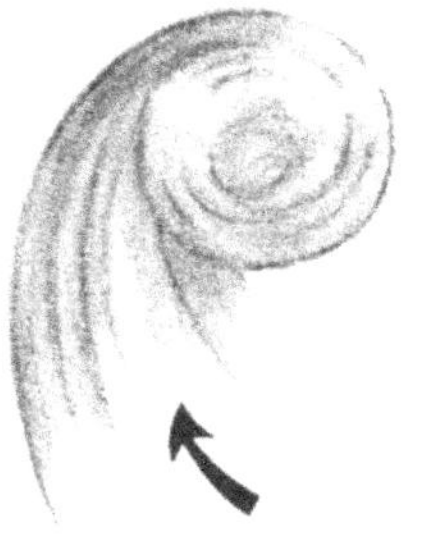

247. Forward pin-curl.

Fig. 248. Backward pin-curl.

Fig. 249. Forward pyramid.

Fig. 250. Backward pyramid.

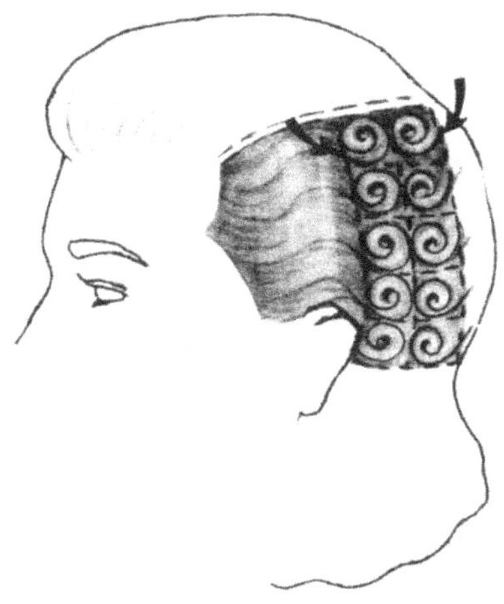

Fig. 251. Roll curl.

Fig. 252. Placement of bobby pin in pin-curl.

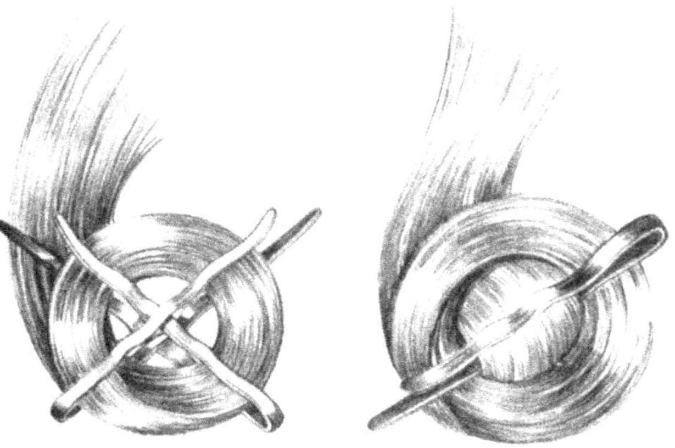

Fig. 253. Alternate methods of securing pin-curls with bobby pins.

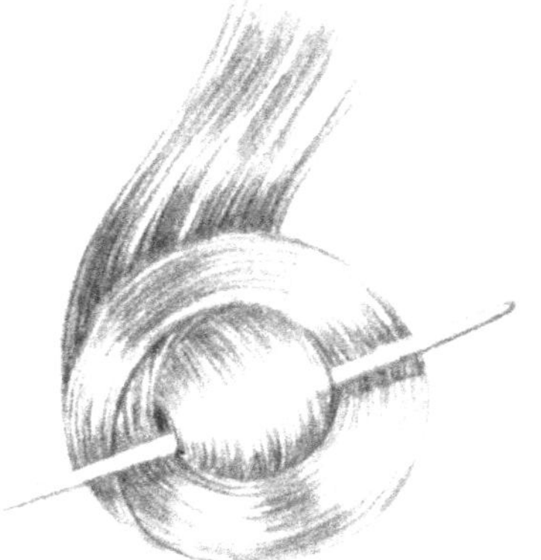

Fig. 254. Securing pin-curl with toothpick.

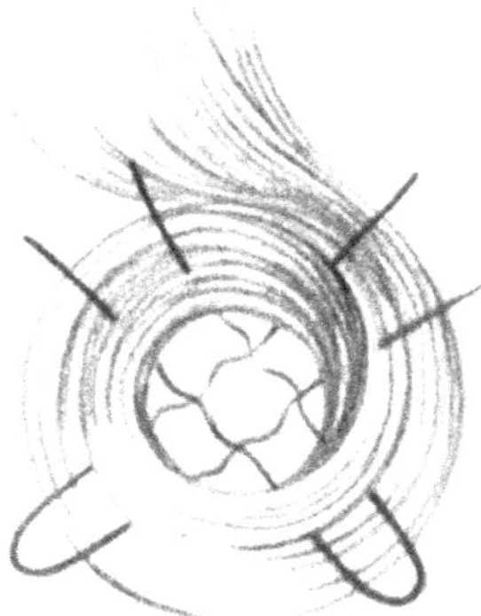

Fig. 255. Securing pin-curl with hairpins.

Fig. 253 shows alternate methods of securing pin-curls with bobby pins. Fig. 254 shows the method of securing a pin-curl with a toothpick.

When hairpins are used to hold a pin-curl in place, two pins are used. The undersides of each pin are inserted into scalp hair under the pin-curl. The tops of each pin cross the top of the curl. Method of insertion of the two pins should be such that they form an X across the curl proper, as illustrated in Fig. 255.

We must always keep in mind the importance of the proper placement of any one of these bobby pins, hairpins, or clips to avoid crimping the hair (Fig. 257) and uncoordinated rolling and pinning of the hair (Fig. 258). A is wrong; B is right.

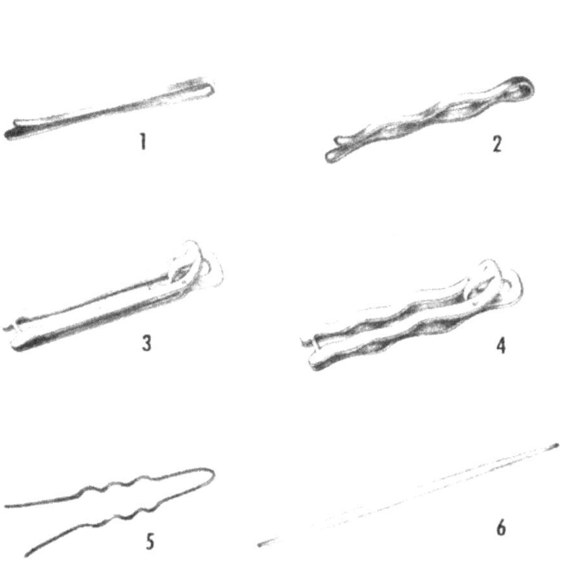

Fig. 256. Devices used in securing pin-curls. (1) Straight bobby pin. (2) Crevassed bobby pin. (3) Straight pin-curl clip. (4) Crevassed pin-curl clip. (5) Invisible hair-pin. (6) Round toothpick.

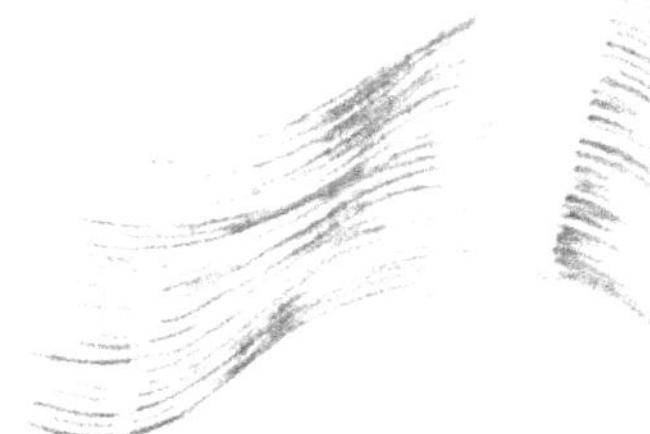

Fig. 257. Result of wrong placement of bobby pin.

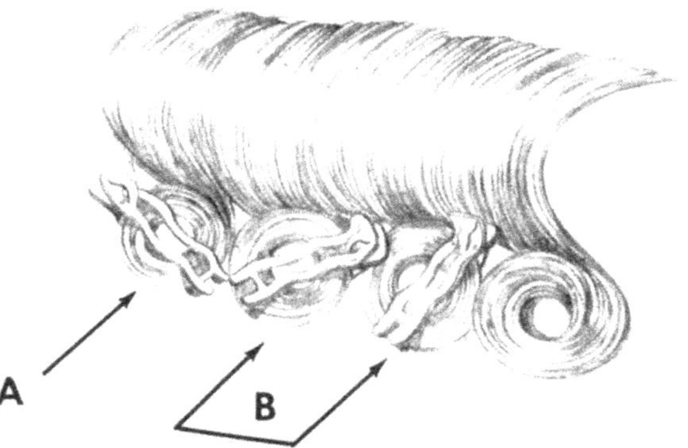

Fig. 258. Rolling and pinning. (A) Wrong. (B) Correct.

Fig. 259. Placement of this pin-curl clip will cause crimp in hair.

Fig. 260. Correct placement of pin-curl clip.

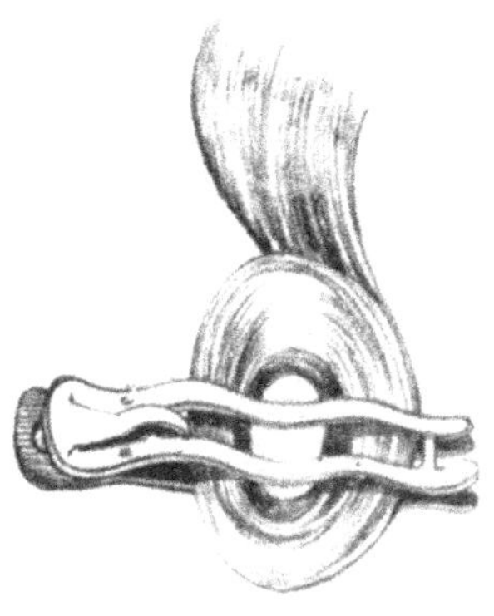

Fig. 261. Placement of this pin-curl clip will pinch curl.

Fig. 262. Correct placement of pin-curl clip.

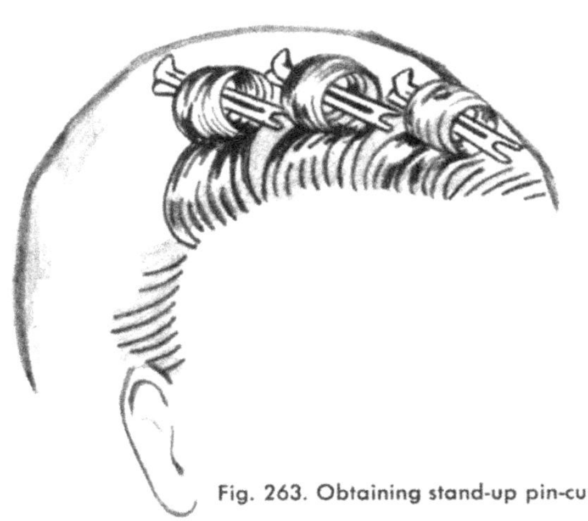

Fig. 263. Obtaining stand-up pin-curls.

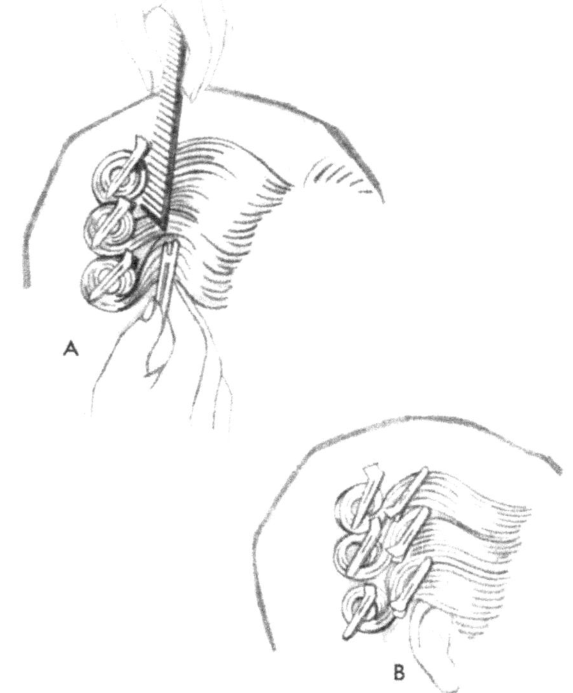

Fig. 264. Obtaining smoothness at the temples.

For stand-up pin-curls: Use a hair clip or bobby pin placed through the standing-up curl. For smoothness at the temples, comb hair back and place clips as shown at A and B.

Following are five sketches, showing one method of rolling a pin-curl. Always start with the section of hair to be curled pulled straight up from the scalp and thoroughly combed through.

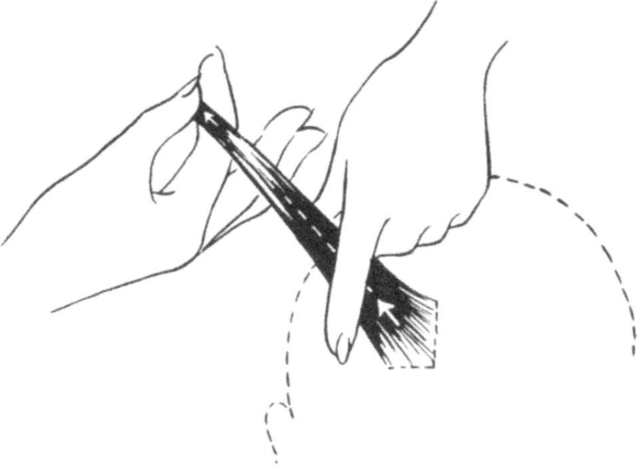

Fig. 265. Pin-curl procedure No. 1.

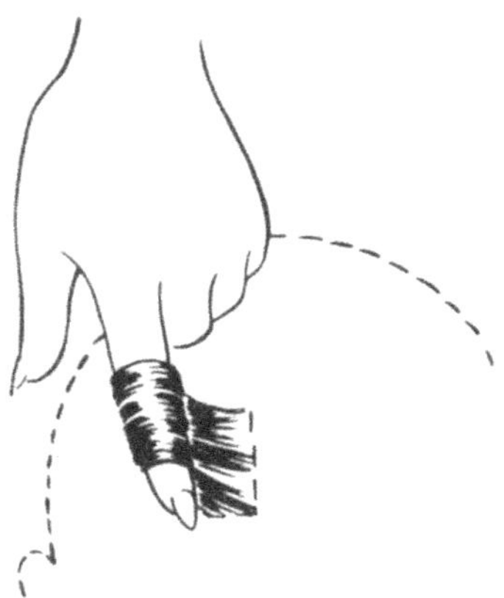

Fig. 268. Pin-curl procedure No. 4.

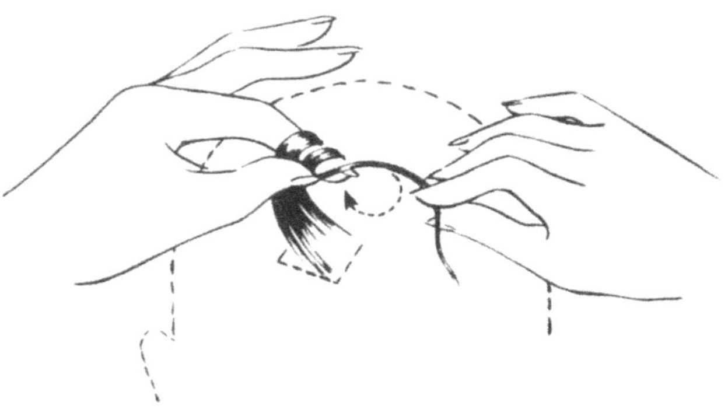

Fig. 266. Pin-curl procedure No. 2.

Fig. 267. Pin-curl procedure No. 3.

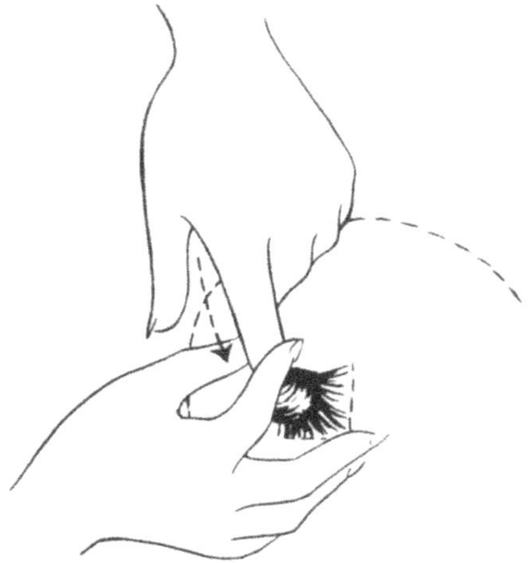

Fig. 269. Pin-curl procedure No. 5.

SUGGESTED HAIR-STYLES

Type of haircut: The perfect haircut for the hair-styles illustrated, both in the sketches immediately following and on pages 162-163 (Suggested Hair-Styles for the Seven Face-Types), ranges from a front length of three and one-half inches to four and one-half inches in back, measuring from the crown of the head. Graduated length—in two layers at front and sides—three layers in back, permits great variation in styling.

The Finishing Touch: If you set your pin-curls exactly as diagramed, after your set has dried, you will find that a simple brushing and combing will give you the proper hair-style suggested by us for your face-type.

Oval: In dressing the hair, your objective must always be to retain the Oval outline, as in the hair-style below. Any distortion in balance will destroy the perfection of features.

Note the smart, flattering simplicity of the finished coiffure, achieved by brushing front pin-curls into waves and resetting the ends into soft curliness.

OVAL

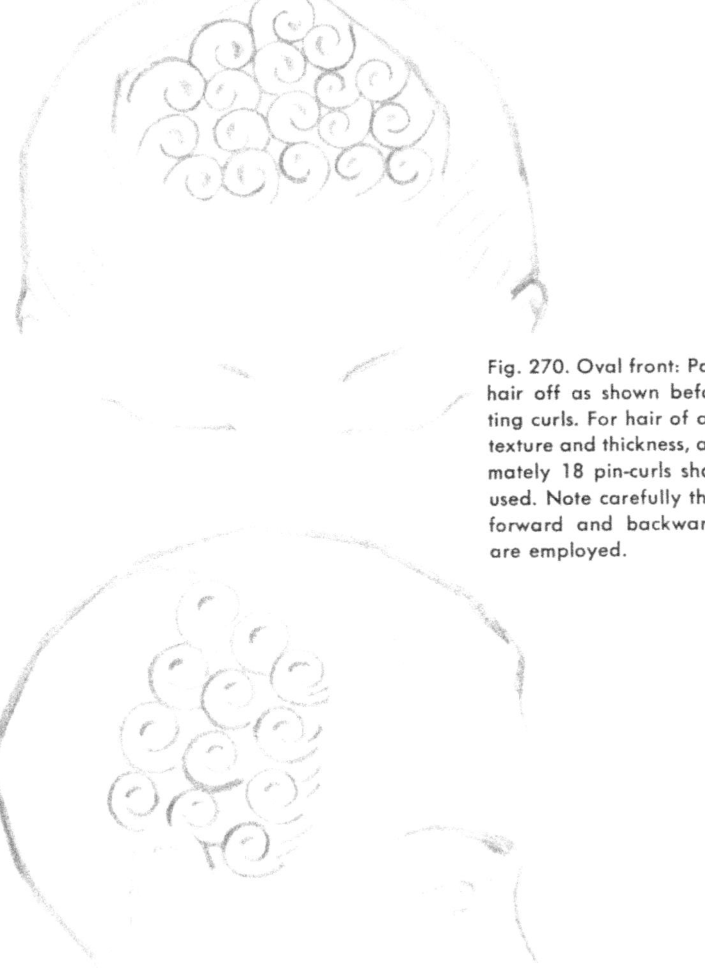

Fig. 270. Oval front: Part your hair off as shown before setting curls. For hair of average texture and thickness, approximately 18 pin-curls should be used. Note carefully that both forward and backward curls are employed.

Fig. 271. Oval side: Approximately three rows of four forward pin-curls are used. Clearly illustrated here is the use of preparatory, one-inch blocking. Both side sections are identical.

Fig. 272. Oval back: Note carefully the direction of the pin-curls. Again, some are forward, some are backward. Back treatment requires approximately 25 pin-curls.

Oblong. Length and narrowness of features are the problems here. To create an illusion of less length in the face, your hair should be styled close to the top of your head. Soft bangs further offset face length. By creating fullness behind the ears to a point even with the mouth, an appearance of greater width in the face is created.

OBLONG

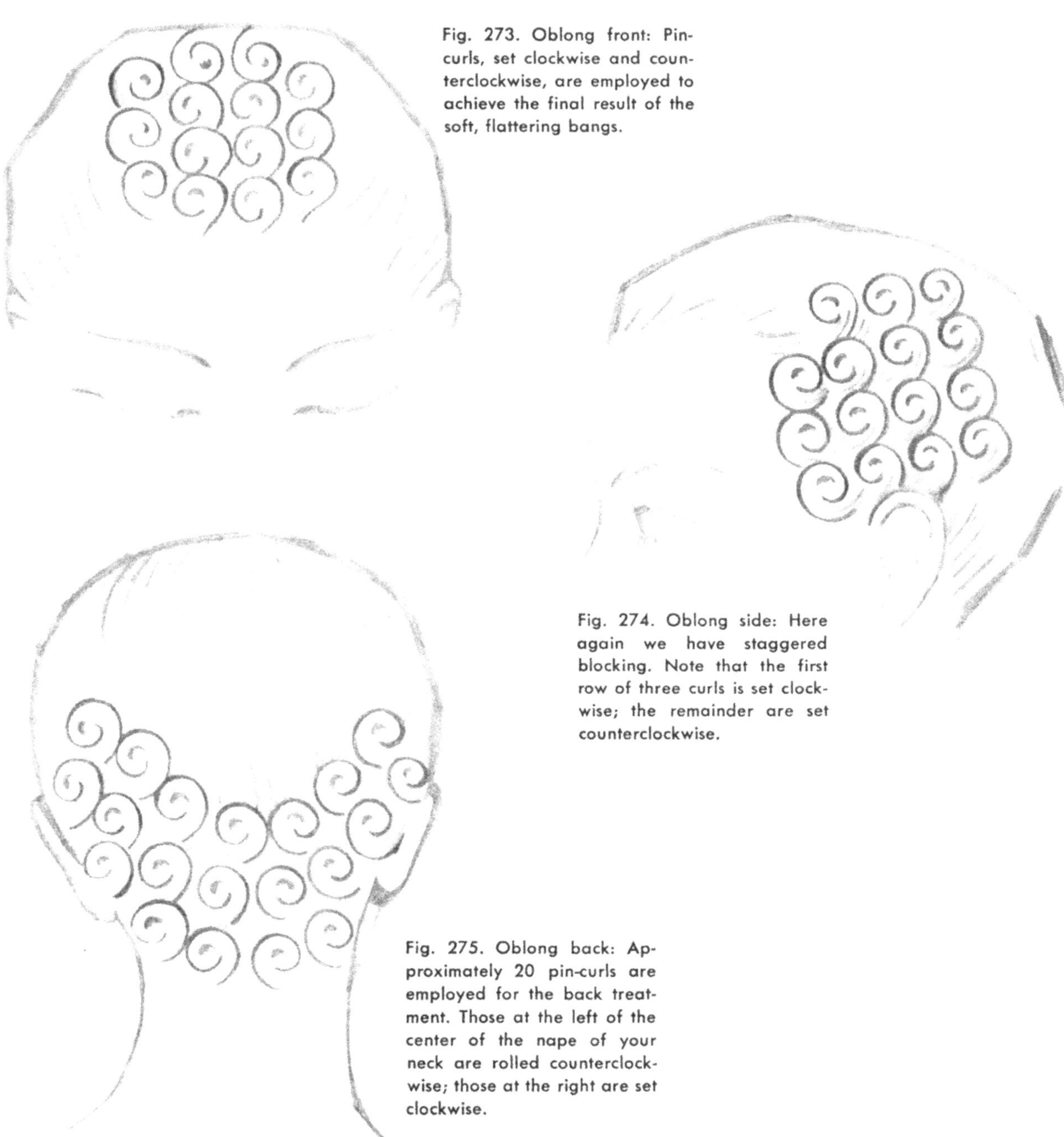

Fig. 273. Oblong front: Pin-curls, set clockwise and counterclockwise, are employed to achieve the final result of the soft, flattering bangs.

Fig. 274. Oblong side: Here again we have staggered blocking. Note that the first row of three curls is set clockwise; the remainder are set counterclockwise.

Fig. 275. Oblong back: Approximately 20 pin-curls are employed for the back treatment. Those at the left of the center of the nape of your neck are rolled counterclockwise; those at the right are set clockwise.

Round. Here, the coiffure shows perfect balance, providing an illusion of greater length in the face, thereby minimizing roundness. Note the slightly diagonal part to reduce the width of the forehead.

ROUND

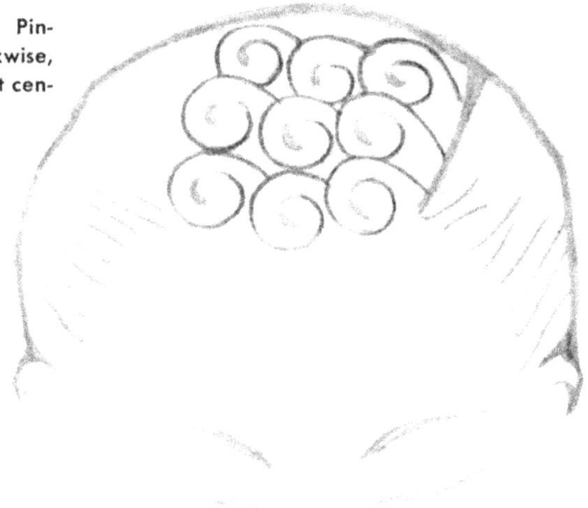

Fig. 276. Round front: Pin-curls, rolled counterclockwise, are employed in the front center section.

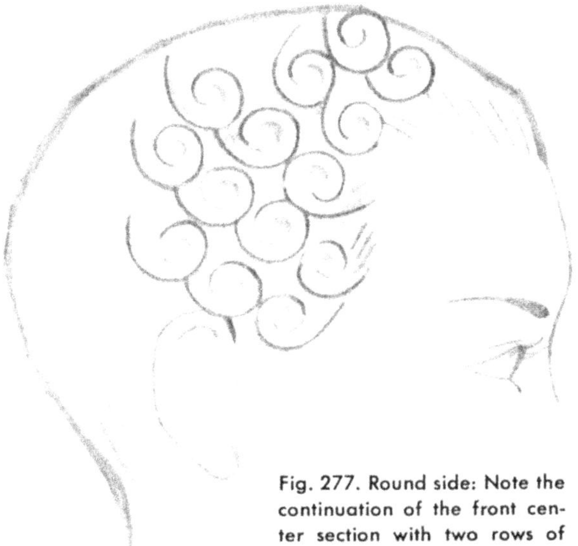

Fig. 277. Round side: Note the continuation of the front center section with two rows of two each counterclockwise pin-curls. The first row of pin-curls at the temple line is forward, or clockwise; the remaining seven curls in this parted-off section are backward curls.

Fig. 278. Round back: The continuation of the parting is carried diagonally over the crown of the head to a point in back even with the tops of your ears. Careful consideration must be given to the varying direction of the pin-curls.

Square. Clearly defined is the perfect balance achieved in this hairstyle to minimize squareness of features and provide an illusion of near-Oval contour. As on the Round type, a diagonal part is employed. Necessary height is provided in styling to give added length to your features.

SQUARE

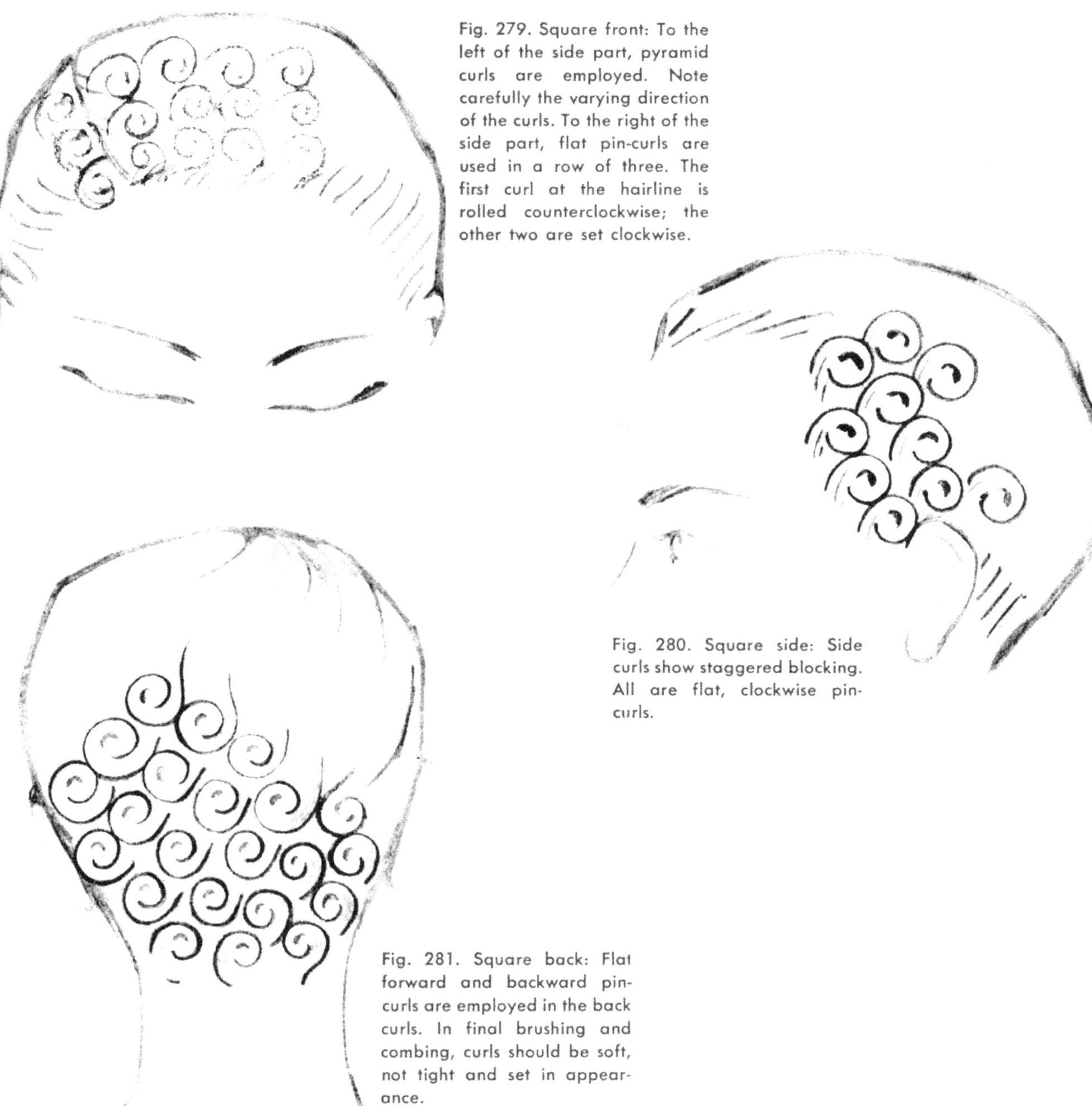

Fig. 279. Square front: To the left of the side part, pyramid curls are employed. Note carefully the varying direction of the curls. To the right of the side part, flat pin-curls are used in a row of three. The first curl at the hairline is rolled counterclockwise; the other two are set clockwise.

Fig. 280. Square side: Side curls show staggered blocking. All are flat, clockwise pin-curls.

Fig. 281. Square back: Flat forward and backward pin-curls are employed in the back curls. In final brushing and combing, curls should be soft, not tight and set in appearance.

Triangle. The wide jawline in contradiction to a narrow forehead poses our hair-styling problem on this type. We must, then, style the hair back and up from the temples to create an illusion of width in the forehead and at the same time counterbalance the width in the lower part of the face. Soft bangs further disguise the narrow forehead.

TRIANGLE

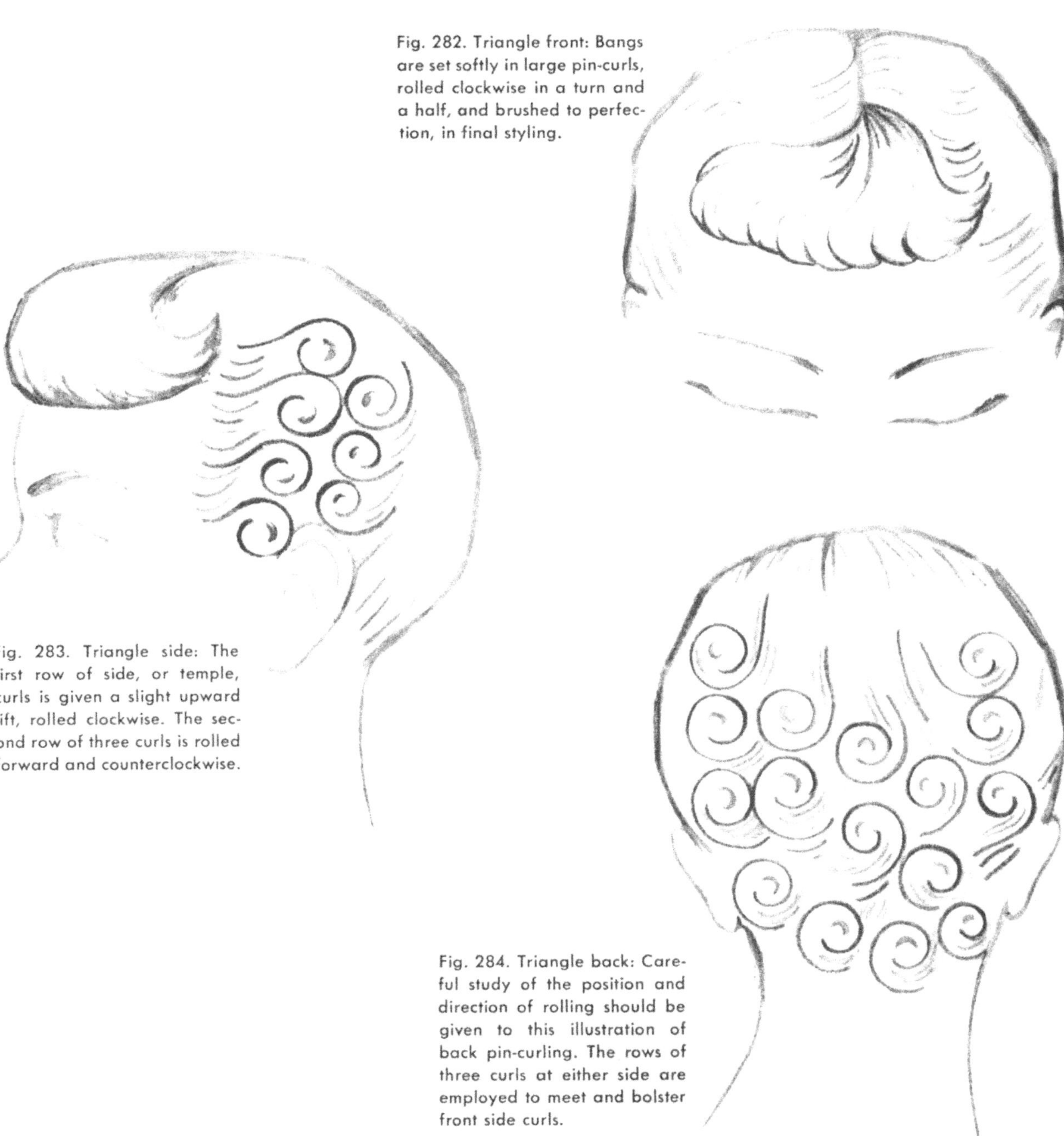

Fig. 282. Triangle front: Bangs are set softly in large pin-curls, rolled clockwise in a turn and a half, and brushed to perfection, in final styling.

Fig. 283. Triangle side: The first row of side, or temple, curls is given a slight upward lift, rolled clockwise. The second row of three curls is rolled forward and counterclockwise.

Fig. 284. Triangle back: Careful study of the position and direction of rolling should be given to this illustration of back pin-curling. The rows of three curls at either side are employed to meet and bolster front side curls.

Inverted Triangle. In hair-styling for this type, balance must be achieved between the narrow lower portion of the face and wide forehead. For this reason we keep the hair dressed easily and closely to the top of the head and dress it for the greatest fullness on a line even with the mouth to create width across the chinline.

INVERTED TRIANGLE

Fig. 285. Inverted Triangle front: From the left side part, pin-curls are started at staggered, slanting lines to permit an initial smoothness. Note the varying direction of setting in the curls before starting your pin-curling.

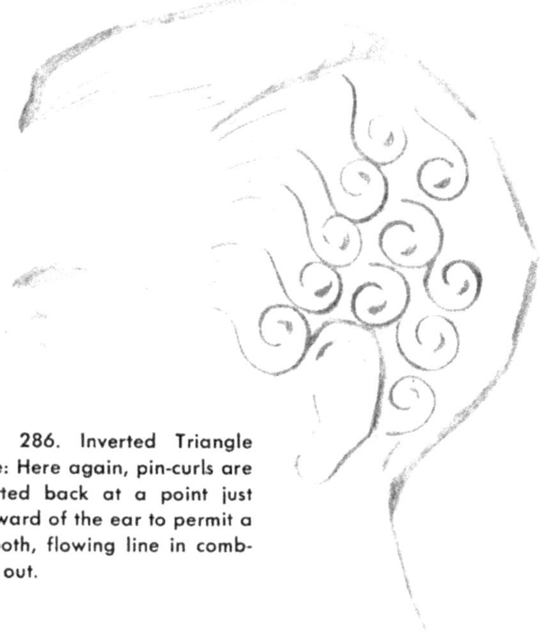

Fig. 286. Inverted Triangle side: Here again, pin-curls are started back at a point just forward of the ear to permit a smooth, flowing line in combing out.

Fig. 287. Inverted Triangle back: Combining clockwise and counterclockwise curls in this manner assures the necessary fullness needed in this hair-style.

Diamond. There are three important points to keep in mind in hair-styling for this type: The forehead is narrow; the cheekbones are high and wide; the chin is narrow. Fullness of the hair must be kept above and below the ears. The hair is kept back from and dressed closely at the point even with the high, wide cheekbones. Notice, too, that a short, diagonal part is employed to further an illusion of forehead width.

DIAMOND

Fig. 288. Diamond front: The first row of pin-curls should be started well away from the part. Notice the staggered blocking of the row of curls nearest the left ear and the reversed rolling of the two curls at the hairline.

Fig. 289. Diamond side: The row of pin-curls nearest the part is rolled clockwise; the other two rows are rolled counterclockwise. To create the desired, finished hair-style effect, remember to brush your pin-curls out thoroughly and reset the ends with comb and fingers into flattering soft curls.

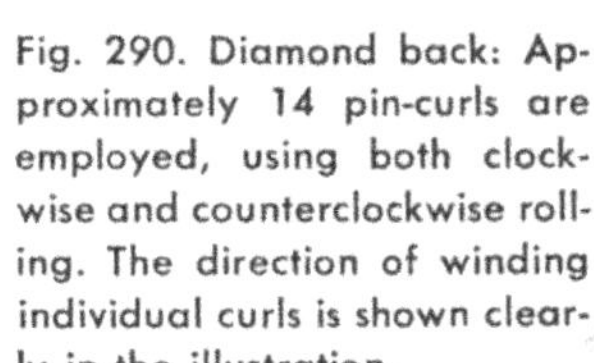

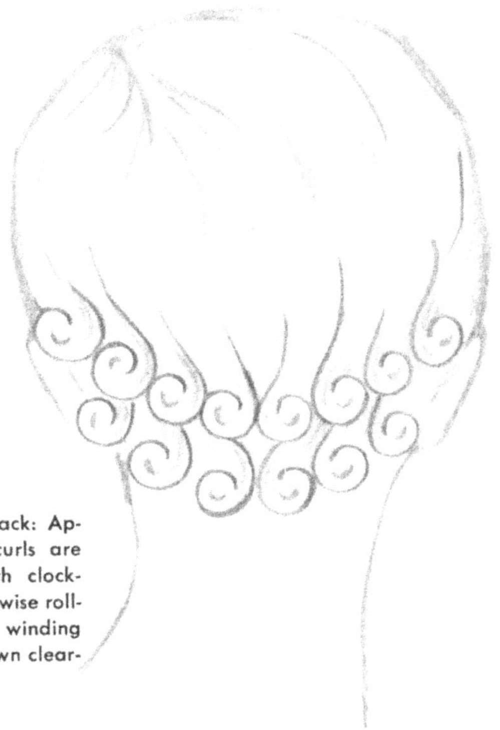

Fig. 290. Diamond back: Approximately 14 pin-curls are employed, using both clockwise and counterclockwise rolling. The direction of winding individual curls is shown clearly in the illustration.

SUGGESTED HAIR-STYLES FOR THE SEVEN FACE-TYPES

Fig. 291. For Oval type.

Fig. 292. For Oblong type.

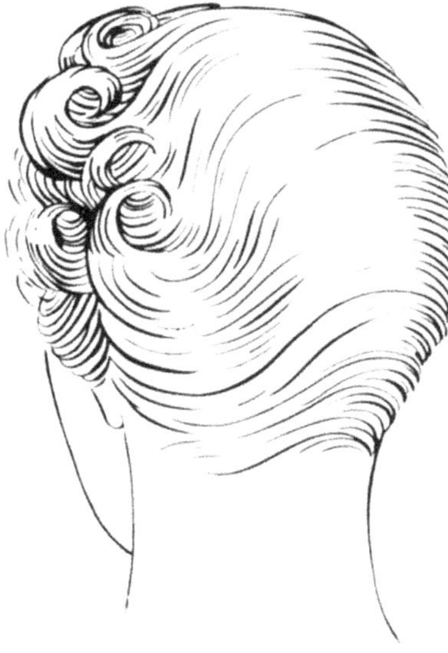

Fig. 293. For Round type.

Fig. 294. For Square type.

Fig. 295. For Triangle type.

Fig. 296. For Inverted Triangle type.

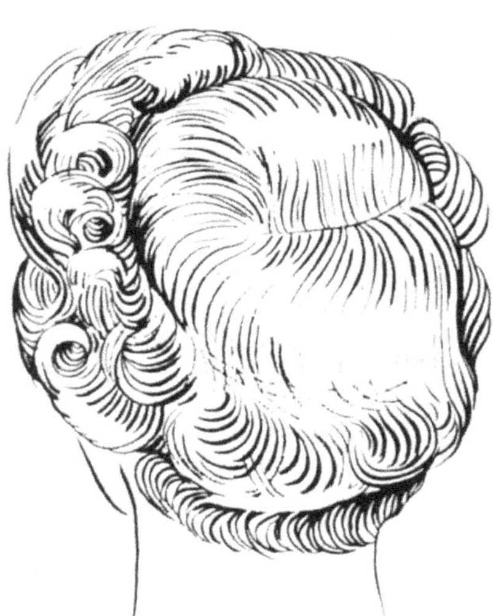

Fig. 297. For Diamond type.

Fig. 298. Composite (for Round, Square or Triangle type).

Fig. 299. Composite (for Round, Square or Triangle type).

Fig. 300. Composite (for Round, Square or Triangle type).

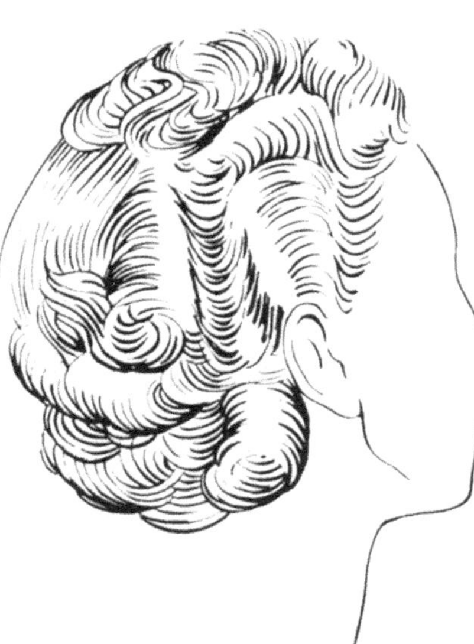

Fig. 301. Composite (for Round, Square or Triangle type).

Fig. 302. Composite (for Round, Square or Triangle type).

TYPES OF BANGS

Full Bang. Hair is cut approximately 3½ inches in length. Hair is pin-curled, as in Fig. 276, in fairly large pin-curls. Brush hair forward, and push in wave.

French Bang or Fringe Bang. Hair is cut approximately 2 inches in length, and is pin-curled, as in Fig. 285. Start pin-curls a little closer to the part. Hair is brushed back and then forward to gain lift near parting. Brush in soft curls at side of head.

Dutch Bang. Hair is cut approximately 3 inches in length, and is pin-curled, as in Fig. 270. Set pin-curls rather large and loose. Hair is brushed over hand until smooth and almost straight.

Girl Scout Bang. Hair is cut exactly the same as for the Dutch bang, and is pin-curled in the same procedure. This or the Dutch bang can be effectively used for one having too high a forehead.

Janey Bang. Hair is cut approximately 1½ inches in length. Pin-curl as in the first three rows of Fig. 270, except that your pin-curls are rolled clockwise on one side of the part and counterclockwise on the other side of the part. Brush hair smooth and almost straight, allowing ends to curl.

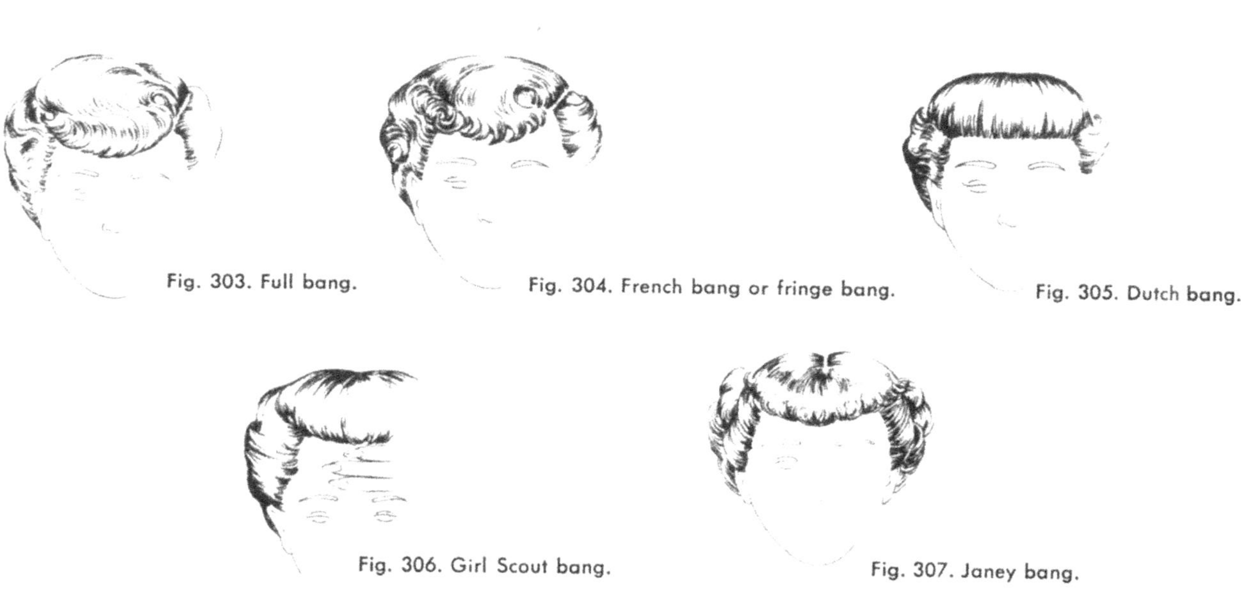

Fig. 303. Full bang.

Fig. 304. French bang or fringe bang.

Fig. 305. Dutch bang.

Fig. 306. Girl Scout bang.

Fig. 307. Janey bang.

HAIRDRESSING CONTROL

The type of brilliantine used should vary with the texture of the hair. We mention brilliantine first of all, because it is the simplest solution for hair which picks up a static electric charge. If the hair is very fine, the brilliantine used should be of a thinner consistency. It should never be applied directly to the hair. Place a small amount in the palm of one hand, rub the palms of both hands together briskly and then pass them over the hair.

If the hair is heavier and coarser, then a heavier brilliantine cream or pomade should be used in the same manner.

Lacquer should be used only when you are facing an outdoor, windy day. It then should be used in minimum, because it tends otherwise to give the hair a hard look. Then, of course, "invisible nets" can always be used.

How to make your own hair-dressing: Following is the way to prepare the home-made substitute for hair lacquer.

Cut two lemons in slices and add only enough water to cover them. Boil until the thickness of water indicates that all lemon juice has been extracted. Now strain—and the remaining lemon juice and water mixture is used for dressing the hair in exactly the same manner as when lacquer is used.

For your information, this is one of the very finest hair dressings. We make use of it consistently at the studio.

HAIR-COLORING

Doing something for the hair: Hair-coloring has always been a subject for feminine experiment. Henna is older than the Sphinx, and the ladies of ancient Rome sat in the sun by the hour wearing bleaches made of alum, black sulphur and honey. Today, with every type and shade of rinse and tint packaged for home use, millions of women frankly "do something" to their hair.

Although we frequently advise individual women not to bleach, or to let their gray hair stay gray, there are just as many others to whom we do suggest a color change. Forty per cent of the American population possesses hair of a lifeless color. If you are one of these, it can be that a touch of color will add warmth and emphasis to your whole personality.

As an example, there is the story of Faye Emerson, one of the first and most exciting ladies of television. In her early days, Faye was a minor player at Warner Bros., discouraged by her scarcity of roles and not making much of an impression in the ones she did get. One day Ann Sheridan, already a star, took a kindly look at her. "What you need," she said, "is a change of color. You're not getting anywhere with brown hair. Why don't you turn blonde?" As Miss Emerson told a reporter, "My whole life improved with that bleach."

The same can happen to you, if you use care and judgment in making the change.

"Try on" the tint first: Let us begin by putting your mind at ease. Hair-coloring by modern methods is not injurious to the hair, provided that the manufacturer's directions are carefully followed and application is made with some degree of skill and care. Thousands of women tint their hair so successfully at home that friends are never aware of the fact that their hair is artificially colored.

Popular opinion to the contrary, there is surprisingly little difference between a dye and a tint. Both are liquid and are mixed with peroxide to develop the color. Both color by penetration of the hair shaft and do not wash off. Many women think a tint is temporary coloring and not so effective or lasting as a dye. Basically speaking, the modern tint does color gray hair completely and wears about as well as dye. Don't confuse tint with a rinse. The latter is applied after a shampoo and washes out readily. It is, in a word, a temporary coloring.

Helps on choosing your best shade: It is logical to assume that the very next thing you would want to know about hair coloring is how to get the right color tint or dye for yourself. In the final analysis, the best way to assure yourself of success is to make a color test on a small strand of hair before applying the tint or dye to the whole head. This also helps you to determine how long the tint or dye should be left on the head. Remember that hair should be washed and dried before a color test is made. You should also try to take a strand of hair that is cut as close to the scalp as possible. Once you have made a satisfactory color test, keep this sample to check your color work from time to time. You cannot carry a color in your mind. You only think you can. If you have a strand of hair which has been dyed the color you wish, you have an accurate check. If you make a drastic change in your hair color, cut a strand of hair before coloring. This way you have a color guide at hand in case you ever decide to return to your natural hair color.

Note: As an added help for those of you who have white or gray in your hair and who wish to improve your natural color rather than make a drastic change from, let us say, brunette to blonde, bear the following suggestions in mind: If your hair has almost no white, select a color two shades lighter than the natural color; if your hair is quite gray, select a shade one shade lighter than the natural color; if your hair is very gray or entirely white, use any shade desired. If your hair is soft and fine, it is usually best to use one additional shade lighter than the color indicated. If your hair is coarse and resistant, use one shade lighter.

If you frequent a beauty salon or when you change beauty salons for any reason whatsoever, make certain that a record is kept of your hair-coloring history. Take this record with you wherever you go for beauty treatments so that you can assure yourself of the best results. This is helpful to you and essential to the beauty operator.

No matter what your natural hair color is at the time you decide to make a color change, we advise one and all not to undertake extreme color changes without the aid of professional advice. Breakage and brittle hair can result from improper hair-coloring or overbleaching.

In any event, take heart in the fact that overtinted hair is not a hopeless problem. There are preparations known as restorative products on the market. These are designed to correct such problems.

In ordinary occupations, a drastic change in color is inadvisable. For one thing, it commits you to a definite, impossible-to-ignore hair-coloring schedule. You must touch up the grown-out or light roots regularly. How often this must be done depends, for the most part, upon the rate at which your hair grows. If your hair grows at an average rate, this would probably mean you would need a retouch on an average of every two weeks; if you are very lucky, perhaps once every three or four weeks. (Many pale, pale blondes have a hair-part touch-up about once a week.) For easy upkeep, it is better to pick a color only a few shades brighter or darker than your natural color.

Another reason why it is a serious step to go from dark hair to platinum, for example, in one step, is that it gives you no chance to try on the new tint. When Nature planned your original color-scheme, she tried to coordinate hair, eyes and skin in terms of color. If you want to improve on Nature, fine. But experiment with a soft shade first. If it proves to be becoming to your complexion type, you can gradually increase the change.

It should also be borne in mind that a color change from dark color to palest blonde is not only dramatic but drastic. It is not a change to be undertaken lightly. You have only to look at a color guide arc and see the various shades you go through to pass from brunette to pale blonde to see how complete the color change really is. The change is one that can be done safely, effectively and beautifully. It is also one that should be done with a full knowledge and appraisal of the steps involved and the commitment made in terms of time, energy, budget and beauty expenditures and returns. We recommend professional help if you plan to change to any of the high-fashion blonde shades. It should be pointed out at this stage that every head of hair reacts differently to the same dye or tint. Some hair takes color faster than others. These individual reactions can be checked, controlled and used to advantage if you just remember to make certain to adapt the color change and hair-coloring method to your head of hair. Common sense, some skill, strict adherence to the instructions on the package, and a little patience and practice should help you accomplish the happy colorful result you wish.

We have one last precaution to mention with respect to color itself. Avoid high-fashion tints unless you have sophisticated clothes and work and live in the surroundings that go with such sophistication. On a model or at a fashionable tea, pink-blonde, fluorescent blonde, and other high fashion colors are delightfully effective. When worn while shopping for groceries or working at the office in a sweater and skirt, they can look out of place and artificial. This is just another way of saying, adapt your hair color to your way of life as well as to your personality and complexion type.

Gray hair, we repeat, is natural and lovely, although we accept the fact that many women feel it is an employment hazard. Some women feel, too, that their husbands prefer to see them with a youthful, vibrant hair color. There is nothing wrong with this, except that too many women make the mistake of dyeing gray hair a harsh black or a strong brown. Perhaps this was the color of their hair in their teens, but the complexion has changed in tint since then.

If you are in your middle or later years, always choose a dye or tint a couple of shades lighter than you remember your hair to have been. (Actually, few of us can accurately recall the color of our hair during our teen years.) Skin pigment fades or perhaps grows ruddy, as time advances and a softer tone makes a more flattering frame for your face. When in doubt, get help from a trained, informed salesperson, or, best of all, seek professional help.

If you have made a noticeable change in your hair color, perhaps going from brunette to blonde, or from brunette to a light shade of red, you may find that your dark eyebrows have suddenly taken on a harsh, black look. This is understandable, since Nature designed them for your natural hair color. Many women find that lightening the eyebrows will naturalize their new "color-scheme." In giving you this bit of information, we wish to call attention to the fact that using any dye or bleach near the eyes is extremely dangerous. There is risk of getting it into the eye itself, which has been known to cause permanent injury. Please do not attempt to change the color of your brows yourself—and don't allow anyone else to do it unless you are sure your eyes are tightly closed and covered. We, personally, do not ever advise dyeing the lashes.

RINSE, TINT OR DYE?

Variety of types: There are as many different types of hair-coloring preparations as there are shades and hues. Each manufacturer has his own specific method of application; it would be impossible for us to give you detailed instructions on each one. We can classify the various types of products for you, and give the general purpose of each. After that, it should be easier to decide among them.

When buying, study the label while you're still at the cosmetic counter. Be sure you understand it before you take it home. Most saleswomen are informed about the product and willingly answer your questions about it. If your saleswoman can't give you some accurate, satisfactory information, then go buy the product from someone who can.

Basically, hair-coloring products are divided into temporary colorings, penetrating colorings, and bleaches.

TEMPORARY COLORINGS

Rinses: These coat the hair with a very slight coloring that can be removed with the next shampoo. For this reason they are easy to experiment with, and they come in a wide range of hues. A "shampoo rinse" is poured through the hair after the final shampoo rinse. A henna rinse, which gives the hair a reddish tint, is usually poured through with the last shampoo rinse water. Rinses are generally used for a brightening or slight lightening of your natural hair color.

For gray or white hair, there are various rinse preparations—some merely to remove the yellowish cast from the gray, others to lend the faintly blue or violet cast which some women find becoming. All of these products are temporary colorings. They wash out with a shampoo.

Hair crayons or pencils: These are primarily used to cover up grown-out roots until the next thorough touch-up. They are good to even up streaked hair, or to color the gray at the temples. (For brown or black hair that shows gray at the roots or the temples, you can use a small brush rubbed over an eyebrow pencil.)

PENETRATING COLORINGS

Tints: These are the colorings that penetrate the hair and cannot be washed off. They require a retouch as the hair grows out and shows a line of demarcation. Generally speaking, these colorings are applied to the hair strand by strand. They are usually used to restore faded hair or to change it to an entirely different color.

In some instances, the actual coloring is preceded by what is known as presoftening. Presoftening concerns the proper preparation of the hair for the new color. This is considered essential when the color change is dramatic or the natural hair color (of the new hair growth) contains a mixture of gray.

Most tint manufacturers insist on the preliminary patch test and warn you that the product cannot be applied to the eyelashes. We second both of these details. We do not recommend dyeing the eylashes and do not practice it in our salon. If any burning, itching, swelling, irritation or eruption is experienced in or around the test area at any time during the patch test period, then the person is predisposed to this preparation and must not use the product.

Dyes: Basically speaking, when mixed and applied in the same fashion, a dye and a tint produce just about the same effective, hair-coloring results. As we have said earlier in this chapter, when you are going from your natural color to a marked change in hair color, such as from brunette to palest blonde, we recommend that you seek professional help or better yet, have your first tinting done by a professional. Also remember to learn to leave highlights in your hair because every natural head has variations of shading. Without these variations, dyed hair is harsh and wig-like in appearance.

Bleaches: Although these are considered hair-colorings, they actually remove color. They can be prepared at home from ordinary peroxide and ammonia, but you'll do better buying one of the oil-bleach preparations. These keep the hair in much better condition, and help you to avoid the harsh, brassy look. All of these are color-controlled, and give you a choice of ash blonde, silver blonde, champagne and other blonde variations. Always be sure the peroxide you mix with them is 20-volume and guaranteed to be "live."

The importance of properly choosing your materials: For home coloring and bleaching, buy good materials. Don't try to save a few cents at the expense of your hair. Always use fresh materials—never a bottle that has been opened and partially used some other time. The best of chemicals are believed to deteriorate with exposure to air.

Choose a nationally advertised brand and follow the directions explicitly. They have been scientifically pre-tested by literally hundreds of people to make certain the directions were accurate and sufficiently detailed. Measure the portions carefully and observe the timing faithfully.

If the preparation is new to you, take time to make two very important tests:

(1) *The predisposition test, also known as the patch test.* This test is essential and is recommended by all manufacturers of hair-colorings. Many states require a beauty salon to make this test before applying a tint. The reason for the test is that penetrating tints and hair dyes contain certain ingredients known as aromatic amines. Because some individuals may be hypersensitive to these, just as people may be hypersensitive to certain foods, a patch test is recommended. The procedure is simple. A small area of skin back of the ear or in the fold of the elbow is washed with soap and water. A small quantity of dye or tint is prepared according to the directions outlined on the package. This is applied to the test area and allowed to dry. If no burning, itching or swelling is observed at the end of a 24-hour period, the tint or dye may then, and only then, be applied. Please note that the test area must be left undisturbed for the entire 24 hours.

(2) *The action test.* This test is to determine how quickly your hair reacts to the color. Does it grab color, take it slowly, or react in the average way? This test is made just before you start the coloring job and after you have shampooed the hair thoroughly (the strand to be tested). The hair is shampooed in order to make certain that the hair being tested is free from dirt, lacquers or excessive oils. Cut a small lock of hair for the test. Try to get it as close to the scalp as possible. Color it, then give the hair time for the color to develop. Dry thoroughly. This is the only way you can tell if the color is what you want it to be.

Don't plan a permanent wave and a tint or bleach for the same day. Do your permanent wave first and the hair-coloring three days later—no sooner.

Oil tends to remove color from treated hair, so if your hair is in need of an oil treatment, do it the night before your hair-coloring treatment.

How to "fix" the color: After your coloring job, brush your hair thoroughly. Brushing helps to "fix" the color. Waving lotion is apt to affect the hue if applied when the hair is wet. As a general rule, it is better to let the hair dry, at least partially, before waving or curling. Or, dry it entirely, then dampen for curling.

The best shampoo: Pure soap shampoos, castille or tar, are best for hair that has been artificially colored. Never use extremely hot water when washing and avoid powdered dry shampoos. Hair follicles in some instances tend to be more porous when they have been colored, and the powder is almost impossible to brush out. In hard water areas the cream shampoos prove especially soluble and are, therefore, easy to use. If you wish, they may be followed by a mild vinegar rinse.

GENERAL CARE OF COLORED HAIR

Shampoo or soap of any kind must not be left on touched-up hair, since it may cause streaks or marks. In hard water areas where soap is difficult to remove, follow a shampoo rinse with an egg application. Mix the yolk and white together and pour on the scalp. Rub in lightly, then put your head under tepid water. Rinse, rinse, rinse, until thoroughly clean.

Hair that has been colored should never receive too much exposure to the sun. Bleached hair is particularly vulnerable to heat of any kind. Wear a scarf or beach hat when sitting near salt water. Salt is a bleaching agent and the porous follicles will absorb the salt spray. Always wear a cap when swimming, particularly in the chlorinated water of swimming pools. A band of chamois tied around your hair under the swimming cap will help to keep out salt and chlorine water. If some seeps in, rinse it off with clear water at once.

Observe these general rules, and you'll keep your colored hair healthy and lustrous. If you decide to slip over to a beauty parlor between home touch-ups, be sure to tell the operator which products you have been using on your hair. Some preparations contain chemicals which do not mix well or easily with other types of tints. If applied over another product, they can prove to be damaging.

APPLICATION OF HAIR-COLORINGS

General suggestions: On applying a tint or bleach, you'll get your most professional results by working on one section of the head at a time, rather than by hit or miss application. Part your hair into four sections. Run a center part from the forehead down to the back of the neck. Then run a horizontal part from the crown to the back of each ear. Pin off the sections you're not working on with bobby pins.

Pick up small sections of hair at a time, and hold them away from the head. Apply bleach or color to the topside of the strand, then to the underside. Work from the scalp outwards.

As stated previously, it is vital to follow the directions on each product carefully. The following are general suggestions only.

Bleaching: For a virgin bleach, the hair is shampooed first, rinsed thoroughly and dried. Section the hair as instructed. Start at the roots and apply the bleach to the ends. Complete the entire head this way, and allow to remain on no longer than one hour. During this hour, reapply bleach to any area that has become dry. When you think the desired color is about reached, test it by washing out one strand from roots to ends with soap and water. Rub it dry so you'll get a good idea of how the bleach will look.

For a bleach touch-up, start the application at the darkest spot—which is usually the widow's peak, the crown, or just above the ears.

Apply the bleach over the dark growth to within 1/8 inch of the old bleach. Your bleaching preparation should be thick enough so it will not run more than this tiny distance. Do not overlap the new bleach and the old one.

Bleaching, properly and carefully applied according to the manufacturer's instructions, has no injurious effect on the roots of the hair. It will not, of itself, prevent growth nor cause hair to fall out. Overbleaching or improper use of any hair-coloring product can result in harsh and brittle hair, as previously noted in this chapter. When the hair is in this overbleached condition it is as porous as blotting paper, so be careful when applying color.

Overbleach treatment: An effective treatment for overbleaching is an oil treatment. Buy a good reconditioning oil, or use olive oil or sweet almond oil. Since extreme heat is bad for bleached hair, have the oil no more than tepid. In this case you are treating the hair, not the scalp. After rubbing in the oil with a rotating movement, take each strand between the palms and work the oil into it. Dip a Turkish towel in warm water and wring out. Wrap tightly about the head. Resaturate the towel again during the 20 to 30 minutes the treatment requires. Take this oil treatment at intervals until there is a noted improvement in the condition of your hair.

Rinses: All rinses (temporary colorings) should be preceded by a thorough shampoo. The type of shampoo, oil or soap, does not affect the coloring process.

Although there are many good rinses designed to be simply poured over the head, this is advisable only if your hair is in very even color and good condition. For streaked or sun-bleached hair, and for ends made porous by a permanent wave, it is better to apply the rinse strand by strand. The porous hair will absorb more of the color than the normal hair, so watch this carefully.

Brightening rinse: On natural hair, apply with a swab of cotton, wetting the streaked or porous sections less than the other. Start at the back on the under hair; separate all strands and apply the rinse close to the scalp. Apply about three-quarters down the strand, comb through to ends. If ends are porous, blot them slightly with a towel after they have absorbed enough color.

On bleached hair, apply the rinse with a brush or applicator. Remember, overbleached parts will absorb the color faster and to a greater extent than just normally bleached hair, and it is difficult to wash out.

When ends or any other portions become over-colored, give these sections of the hair a mild soaping before the clear water rinse. All color rinses should have a clear, tepid water rinse to remove excess color from the head which might rub off on pillows, collars, and the like.

Bluing rinse for gray hair: Where there is a yellow tinge on gray or white hair, bluing rinses are effective for toning it down. The amount used depends upon whether you wish only to whiten the hair, or to give it a decided blue cast. There are prepared rinses which give a sophisticated violet or greenish cast. Always follow directions closely, and make a color test on a strand of hair first.

Where the hair is partially gray and partially dark, the darker portion will take on the darkest tone. Therefore, apply to the gray strands first and tone in the darker hair afterwards.

Henna rinse: You can purchase henna leaves and steep them in hot water as you would tea, if you wish. The most popular form, however, is prepared powdered henna. The powdered form of henna must be followed by one soaping, else the hair will be dry, clouded and dull.

Henna pack: In making a henna pack, it is important to heat the paste thoroughly, stirring out all lumps while the mixture bubbles. Keep the paste warm by covering it while you shampoo. Soap just once and rinse with clear water. Towel dry your hair, but leave it slightly moist. The henna will take better on a slightly damp head.

Apply the paste warm, but not hot enough to burn you. It is best to start application about an inch away from the face, and apply to within about an inch and a half of the ends of the hair. Then go back and comb through to all the ends. Lastly, comb the henna carefully into the hairline around the face, working upward so that you will not discolor the skin.

Test by washing out a single strand, and drying. All henna packs should be well shampooed, with two or three soapings to remove discoloration from the scalp.

It is suggested that you be sure the henna you use is strictly fresh, or you may get a very dull shade. For a dark auburn, a mixture of black walnut is popular. Follow the directions on the package.

Do not apply a tint or dye *over* henna. Henna should first be removed, particularly if you are changing to a lighter color.

Peroxide rinse: This is used for a highlighting or brightening effect. Use 17-volume peroxide, from half an ounce to a full ounce in a quart of water. Pour over the head and allow to remain on for 10 to 15 minutes, according to the degree of lightening desired. Rinse off with clear, tepid water.

Tinting: Be sure to make your allergy and your color tests first. If a tint is used, it is not necessary to shampoo the hair first unless it is excessively oily or dirty. If so, use a mild soap, only one soaping, and shampoo gently rather than vigorously.

After parting the hair into the usual four sections, pin off three of them. Tint the lightest section and its lightest strands first. Lift each strand in the hand, apply tint to the top side, then turn the strand away from you and tint the underside. (If retouching a previous tint, tint only the grown-out portion.) Apply the tint from the scalp to within an inch and a half of the ends. After all the hair has thus been saturated with preparation, comb the hair through to the ends. Make sure you don't skip any of them.

Hair ends are naturally lighter than the rest of the head. This is one reason for leaving them until the last, so that the tinting job will have a natural look. If your ends are porous from a permanent, it is a good thing to protect them by rubbing in a little hair cream or pomade. This will keep them from picking up the tint until you are ready to comb it through.

If you are tinting a partially grown-out permanent wave, apply color to all portions of the unwaved hair first. Wait until the tint starts to take in the grown-out hair before combing it down into the waved part. The part still retaining the permanent will tint in approximately one-third the time it takes the unwaved part.

Make a color test from time to time, by wiping one strand with a wet piece of cotton. Rinse it off by holding a small dish of water to your head. Dry with a towel and stretch taut with your comb to see the true color. If still too light, recolor the strand and let the tint stay on the head a little longer.

On hair that takes the color quickly, the first section sometimes develops too quickly. If you are a slow worker, it is better to use a darker shade of tint than used ordinarily and to dilute it with water. This will slow up the action and give you more time for the all-over job. If the tint develops too rapidly near the scalp, comb through this part with a wet comb or spray on a little water to slow up the developing action.

Dyeing: The application of hair-dye is, in general, the same as that followed in putting on a tint.

RETURNING TO NATURAL COLOR

In restoring any kind of artificially colored hair to its natural state, the process can be helped along by giving the hair frequent hot oil treatments. We recommend seeking professional advice for this.

Bleached hair: The best way to keep your hair looking attractive during the growing-out period is to tint the bleached portion to match the new growth. Choose a shade a little lighter than your natural color. Apply the tint just over the end of the grown-out portion, and do the ends last.

Tinted, dyed and hennaed hair: There are many removers and restorative preparations on the market for each. We suggest that you buy the restorative product from the same manufacturer whose coloring product you used. Don't forget the hot oil treatments.

In conclusion let us say that that research in the field of hair-coloring is continuous and productive. Thousands of chemists are at work daily to make hair-coloring more effective, longer lasting and more natural looking than ever before. They also are dedicated to the task of making the procedure simpler and simpler for the do-it-yourself hair tinter.

Even as we go to press there are new and exciting developments being made in the hair-coloring field. One such development is the use of a tint in cream consistency. It is now being used in some salons throughout the country and may later be made available in the home hair-coloring kits. In any event, rest assured that more and more fewer and fewer people will hesitate to color their hair because of the ever-increasing beauty of lasting color that such products continue to bring to you and your hair.

CHAPTER TWELVE

Figure Fascination

BODY CONTOUR

The exercises we have illustrated for your body contour program range from all-over conditioners to so-called "spot" improvers.

To be factual, any effort that will directly benefit a slumped shoulder, an over-padded flank, or any other spot can't help but make its influence felt at various points north and south. To parody the song, "the arm muscle is connected to the bust muscle—the waist muscle is connected to the abdominal muscle—the thigh muscle to the leg muscle"—and so on.

Many health and beauty troubles are overcome or greatly helped by regular exercise. Among these are poor elimination, poor circulation and cold feet, sallow skin, some female disorders, insomnia, and mental depression. Even if you are in perfect health and figure, you benefit from regular physical action. Deepened breathing and increased oxygen intake, an enlivened pulse, all these blood stream stimulants work in one vital circle from your brain to your toes.

When your problem is too much weight, a course of body massage and steam baths will quicken the reducing regime. If such treatments are beyond your budget, don't waste your envy on the woman who can afford such beauty procedures. You can create your figure at home.

Use common sense: In your figure improvement project this is the only commandment.

If you're not accustomed to exercise, you needn't start off like a trained athlete. If you've led a sedentary life for some time, remember it's not possible to make up for it all in one week. At any age from the teens up, you'll reap your most beneficial result by slow, building perseverance, rather than by a sudden burst of vigor.

We suggest that before embarking on any new and strenuous schedule, exercise or diet, you ask your doctor's advice and permission. If you haven't had an examination lately, have one. Know yourself, then you won't do anything to jeopardize your well-being. Certain physical conditions, such as a tendency to hernia, can be helped by one type of exercise, aggravated by another.

When the doctor has approved your plans, start the contouring regime slowly. We recommend a ten-minute period to start. Never more than 30 minutes. It is normal that hard breathing and a rapid heartbeat should result from extra exertion. This is a desirable reaction; it means the heart and lungs are being exercised and invigorated, too. As your physical training progresses, breath and pulse will return to normal with increasing promptness. It is also healthful to perspire. This shows increased metabolism. And as for that first unpleasant soreness, it proves that muscles almost atrophied from disuse are coming to life again.

Your exercise must belong to you, just as your clothes and cosmetics do. In each of the body departments, we have given you a choice of several types of movement, done from various positions. Select the ones most important to your own figure needs for body building, weight reduction, or as a means of retaining your current trimness.

Narrow your selection further by trying out the various positions and movements. Some may be easier for you to perform than others. Note which action gives you the greatest sense of accomplishment. Unless you feel an exercise under your skin pulling, lifting, tautening those inner cords, it's not doing enough for you. You may want to combine several of the movements detailed. At any rate, you'll get more result from six good exercises well done than from sixteen performed half-heartedly.

Arrange your selected exercises to suit your preference, they may be performed in whatever order seems most natural to you. Do them all at once, or divide them to fit into your daily schedule. The important point is, *do* them.

Have a time and place: It will bolster your determination some to have a regular place and time. Equip yourself with a pad, a rug, or a blanket folded approximately two by six feet, and designate it as your exercise mat. Find a household space in which you can bend and kick without damage to furnishings or yourself, and think of it as your gym. Don't begrudge yourself "time out" in the morning. The resulting physical pep will carry you through the day's chores easier and faster.

If your only possible exercise period is in the evening, you are more apt to think you are "just too tired" to go through with it. But fight off the temptation to shirk, and you'll be surprised at how much the exercise does to alleviate the weariness. In fact, you'll soon learn that at any hour you happen to be feeling weary, depressed, foggy, heavy in mind and body, a session of stretches and bends will pep you up and give you a happier perspective.

Remember, frameworks differ. For an added morale booster, chart your figure improvement. Before you begin your exercising program, jot down your weight and important measurements: Bust, hips, waistline, abdomen, derriere, upper and lower thigh. Choose the dress or suit which shows you to your worst advantage, put it on and study yourself in front of a mirror. Make mental (or written) note of where you protrude (and shouldn't), where you strain a seam, or fail to fill it out. Hang this particular garment away for a month at least, as a standard for your progress.

It helps to set a goal of pounds or inches, lost or gained. Don't compile these statistics according to some envied friend's measurements. What is attractive padding for her bone structure may be too much, or too little, for yours. Keep in mind that frameworks differ. You can vary as much as 10 or 15 per cent from any standard table of "correct" weights and measurements, and still be in perfectly good form.

If your objective is weight reduction, don't be disappointed if the scale doesn't show an immediate drop. Flab weighs less than solid flesh; it is possible to lose girth and gain weight at the same time. Always, in any sort of a contouring effort, the inches are more important than the pounds.

Finally, the first hundred bends are the hardest. Go at them with a will, because once your figure has been reconditioned, it will take far less work to keep it fit.

Basic rules for exercising follow:

1. Begin slowly and work up to the more difficult exercises.
2. Never exercise immediately after eating. Wait two hours.
3. Note the breathing instructions accompanying the exercises. These are important and must be followed to obtain the proper results.
4. Don't exercise in a draft.
5. The warmer the clothing, the better for reducing. But be sensible about it. Don't weight yourself down. Just bear in mind that athletes exercise in sweat shirt and sweat pants.
6. Start your exercise period as a ten-minute session. Work up to 30 minutes—no longer.
7. When you are tired, stop and rest, then continue.
8. Take no hot showers or tub baths after exercising. Relax until the heartbeat has returned to normal; then shower or tub.
9. Wear ballet slippers or go barefoot when exercising.
10. Do not undertake any of the exercises or any exercise program without the specific approval of your doctor. This is a must.
11. Exercise regularly, daily, and briskly for reducing. Exercise slowly and every other day for building up.
12. Never forget that exercise must be supplemented by diet for weight reduction. Your doctor will furnish you with a diet suited to your individual needs.

POSTURE

A beautiful figure is often self-created. Nature gives us our body structure, but we have to learn how to handle it for ourselves. It's good posture, good carriage and good exercise that make a good figure. If you lack any of these, it will surely account in great measure for the bad shape you're in.

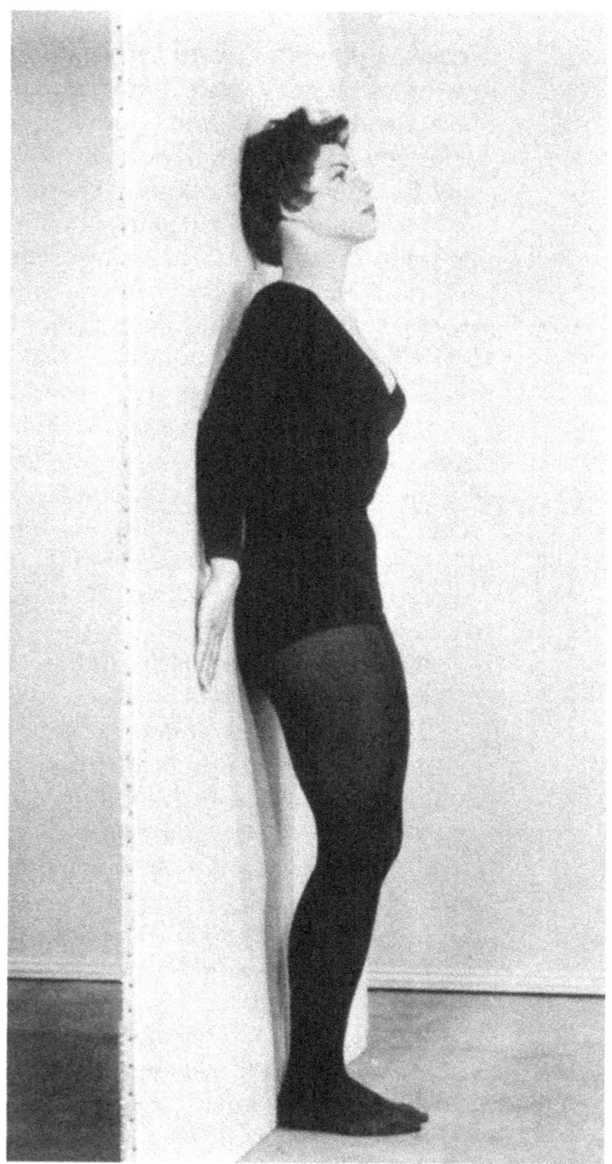

Fig. 308. Posture.

How do you carry yourself? Let's make a mirror test and see. Line up sideways and stand in your natural everyday pose. If your posture is good, you'll see the following: (1) Neck straight from hairline to shoulders. (2) Shoulder blades flat. (3) Bosom high. (4) Shallow curve in back at waistline. (5) Abdomen flat, buttocks normal. (6) Feet straight ahead.

If your posture is bad, you'll see this: (1) Head forward, neck curved. (2) Protruding shoulder blades. (3) Chest caved in. (4) Deep curve in lower back at waistline. (5) Abdomen bulging, buttocks protruding. (6) Feet turning out.

A "MUST" FOR THE MOST—THE TWO-WAY STRETCH

If you could do only one exercise faithfully each day, this should be it. Not only does the slow-motion stretch work on muscles hard to get at, but you actually *feel* slimmer from the moment you start it. It tautens the entire middle section, the midriff, waist and abdomen. It will help to prevent, or to melt, those high-pockets of fat at back and sides, and on the flanks. Arm and breast muscles feel it, too.

We suggest it as a morning wake-up and limber-up movement, but at any time of the day it should be done slowly and deliberately.

1. Stand erect, feet parallel and about 15 inches apart.

2. Arch (round) clasped hands overhead as high as you can reach without stretching the arm muscles. (You want to put the muscle-pull elsewhere.)

3. Now, comes the upward stretch. Using mid-section muscles only, pull yourself slimmer. Raising the shoulders or stretching the neck isn't the way to do it. Make the middle muscles do the work of pulling the waist up and away from the hips, and ribs up and away from the waist. You are now slimmer, flat in the abdomen, and taller. Hold it now, for the sideward flexion.

4. Bend sideways at the waist and sway the lifted arms as far as possible to the left. Keep the hands clasped, the head held normally rather than bent backward or forward. Breathe out as you bend, breathe in as you swing back up to starting position.

5. Still maintaining upward stretch, bend sideways to the right. Because of the number of unused muscles this exercise affects, two or three times is enough to start. As your body becomes more supple you will enjoy performing ten or twenty bends.

Fig. 309. The two-way stretch: upward.

Fig. 310. The two-way stretch: sideways.

FOR POSTURE, THE PUSH-UP

Ten million G.I.'s can't be wrong about the results of this one. Its primary purpose is to promote a fine posture, but for arm, chest, and shoulder development it can't be beat. The soldier performed it twenty times, but six times will be enough for you.

1. With hands on the floor about 15 inches apart, hold body in a straight slope from head down to feet.
2. Bend elbows until you are flat on the floor.
3. Now, push up with the arms until elbows are straight and body is back in the original head-to-foot slope. Breathe *out* as you lower yourself, breathe *in* as you push up.

Fig. 311. The push-up.

THE SEMAPHORE FOR A LOVELY, LIFTED BUST

To enliven the breast muscles, tauten the underarm, straighten the shoulders, and melt fat from the shoulder blades, do this energetically a generous number of times.

1. Sit cross-legged on the floor, slumped forward a slight bit. Cross arms so that the right hand rests near the left knee, left hand near right knee.
2. Swing arms swiftly up and out as far as you can. In this wide spread the hands should be well above your head, and the arms so far back that your shoulder blades are telling you about it. Return hands to crossed position at knees, and repeat swings to a rhythmic count.

Fig. 312. The semaphore: arms crossed.

Fig. 313. The semaphore: arms outward.

Fig. 314. The up-and-over: front.

Fig. 315. The up-and-over: back.

THE UP-AND-OVER

This is one exercise you can perform in front of a mirror and feel as though you're getting places. Done faithfully, it will lift and firm the bust, and teach you to carry your shoulders so that the improvement is visible.

You may want to make yourself a baton from a sawed-off broom or mop handle. (If not, use a small Turkish towel pulled taut.)

1. Stand tall, stomach in, head straight. Hold the baton straight down in front. The firmer the grip, the greater benefit to the muscles.
2. Breathing deeply, raise the baton straight-armed over your head.
3. Keep a firm, straight-armed grip as you bring the baton down behind you.
4. Let the breath out now as you bring the baton back up, over, and down in front. The whole procedure should be a slow one. Two or three times will be plenty at first; you'll eventually do eight to ten.

DUMBBELL DRILL

If you're serious about developing, or preserving, a beautiful bust, it's worthwhile to assemble the props required. Not everyone has a pair of dumbbells handy, but there are several household substitutes. If you're on a reducing diet it would be a nice touch to use weighted fruit-juice cans as pictured here. (Be sure the substitute dumbbells are of equal weight, about 4 pounds.) The drill can be done standing up; it is more comfortable using a piano bench, or a cocktail table that will support your weight. Proceed as follows:

1. Lie flat, with head and hips on bench. Grasp the dumbbells firmly and hold them toward the ceiling, keep elbows straight.
2. Lower the dumbbells forward, down to the sides, out at the sides, and bring them up again to original position. Start with three or four of these wide circles, work up to ten daily. Breathe *in* deeply as the arms are lowered, let breath *out* as arms are brought up again.

Fig. 316. Dumbbell drill.

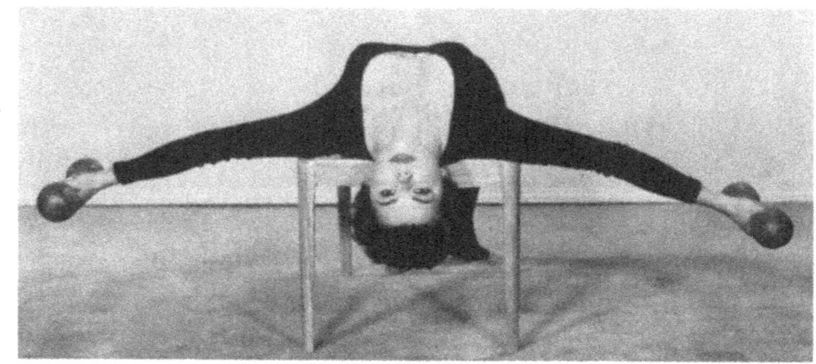

Fig. 317. The turtle-dove.

THE TURTLE-DOVE

Continue the dumbbell drill by moving up on the bench, putting a healthy stretch on the throat-line while the head hangs backward.

1. Hold the dumbbells straight-armed, and lowered to the sides. Start raising the weights slowly, moving the arms in a series of small, flying circles until the dumbbells are straight overhead.

2. Lower the arms to the sides again, describing the same slow circles all the way down. Do Dumbbell Drill and Turtle-Dove on alternate days, or divide the daily ten between the two.

LIMBER FROM THE WAIST

The new and easier version of the familiar touch-the-floor routine has the same beneficial results in flattening the diaphragm and whittling the waistline. Bent knees are not only permissible; they are a requirement.

1. Stand erect, feet about 15 inches apart.

2. Bend forward, knees bent, slumped, head and arms dangling downward. Enjoy this limp droop for a second.

3. Now, slumping and twisting the body as much as you wish, touch the floor behind the left heel with the fingers of the right hand. Breathe *out* as you bend to touch the floor. Breathe *in* as you return to erect position. Repeat droop, and touch floor behind right heel with left hand. Begin with five times; soon you'll do ten to twenty bends without too much exertion.

Fig. 318. Limber from the waist: limp droop.

Fig. 319. Limber from the waist: twist.

Fig. 320. The tire-less touch: part one.

Fig. 321. The tire-less touch: part two.

THE TIRE-LESS TOUCH

If your sacroiliac objects to bending while standing, here is a horizontal way to get at that midriff "bicycle tire." Many physicians recommend it for reconditioning the mid-section after pregnancy.

1. Lie on your back, arms above head.

2. Keeping head and shoulders flat on floor, raise left leg straight up and forward until you can touch it with the right hand. Breathe *out* as leg and arm are lowered to original position. Breathe *in* as you raise right leg and touch it with the left hand. Alternate leg-touches slowly at first, work up to rapid pace. Perform ten to twenty times.

KNEE-CHEST FLATTENER

The familiar knee-chest exercise has long been recognized not only as a figure beautifier, but for its beneficial effect in various organic weaknesses. It is one of the most effective of all abdomen flatteners, strengthens groin and pelvic muscles as well. Choose one of three movements given, or do them all.

Movement one:

1. Lie on the back, arms at sides or overhead, legs straight out on floor.

2. Pressing the knees together, draw them all the way up to the chest, so that the upper legs press down on the stomach. Kick the legs out straight again. Repeat knee to chest, repeat kicking legs out straight. Start slowly, increase speed and vigor. Ten to twenty times.

Movement two:

1. Lie on back, arms overhead or at sides. Bend knees and draw them up to chest.

2. Now raise legs straight up toward ceiling, at the same time contracting the abdominal muscles strongly up and in. Lower knees to chest again. Ten times.

Movement three:

1. Lie on back, hands clasped under head, legs straight out on floor.

2. Bend right knee and bring it up across chest to touch left elbow. Return leg to floor. Bring left knee up to touch right elbow, then return leg to floor. Repeat with increasing speed, ten times.

Fig. 322. Knee-chest flattener.

MAKE A "V"

An abdomen flattener, which also helps to trim the rear.

1. Lie flat on back, arms over head.

2. Start by bringing your arms forward, followed by the head and shoulders. Lift the legs, knees straight, simultaneously with the shoulders until the body forms a "V" (with only the buttocks resting on the floor). Hold for a short count, then return to flat position. Perform five to ten times, depending on what other abdominal exercises you are doing.

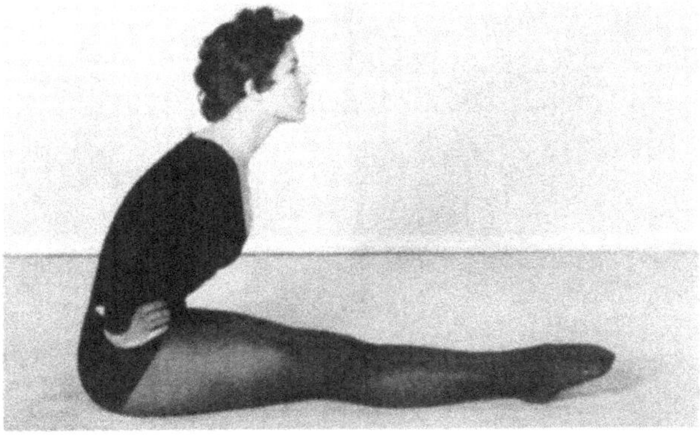

Fig. 323. Make a "V."

SLOW SIT-UP

This is strenuous until you're used to it, but it does very fine things for both back and stomach muscles.

1. Lie flat on back, arms stretched over head or clasped behind neck.

2. Keeping the legs pressed to the floor, bring body to a straight sitting position. Breathe *out* as body returns to flat position, breathe *in* as you sit up again. It is important to pull the body up by back and stomach muscles alone; don't use arms for assistance, or raise legs from floor. Do five times.

3. Same as 2, except that after sitting position is reached, keep bending forward until the abdominal flesh presses against the thighs. Return to straight sitting position, then back to flat position. Perform this floor-to-thigh movement five times.

Fig. 324. Slow sit-up.

THE BICYCLE FOR TAPERED THIGH AND LIMB

Long practiced as a leg and thigh slimmer, the bicycle position has other benefits as well. While you are upside-down your organs are getting a relief from the sagging feel induced by the prolonged sitting and standing you do most of the day.

1. Lie on the floor, arms at sides.

2. Raise your body straight in the air until it rests on shoulders and neck. On your first tries, you may have to use your hands to help hold the hips aloft, but later you'll keep your arms on the floor.

3. Now, pedal an imaginary bicycle. Start easily, then increase pace and vigor. Make wider and wider revolutions so that while one toe is reaching for the ceiling, the opposite knee is almost down to your chest. Ten to twenty turns, both morning and evening if you wish.

Fig. 325. The bicycle: part one.

Fig. 326. The bicycle: part two.

THE SCISSORS

We give you the scissors exercise in two parts, both very effective in slimming the thighs. The preliminary movement has the added benefit of making the ankles more shapely. The scissors proper does more for eliminating fat on the inner thigh.

Preliminary:

1. Lie flat on floor, arms at sides or above head, legs straight.

2. Curl toes of one foot up, pushing heel down. Raise leg to right angle. Now, press heel toward ceiling and pull the toes down. Return leg to floor, and repeat with other leg. Ten times each leg.

Scissors:

1. Same position as above. Holding both legs straight out, raise them about 8 inches off the floor.

2. Without allowing legs to touch floor, lift and lower them alternately, as if they were the blades of a scissors. Keep them as close together as possible, to get at inner-thigh flesh. Do rapidly, counting to twenty.

Fig. 327. The scissors.

THE SIDE ROLL FOR A CONTOURED HIP AND DERRIERE

A real friend to both waistline and upper hips, you'll feel it tautening your upper leg muscles, also.

1. Lie on the back, shoulders firmly pressed to floor, arms above head, legs straight out.

2. Raise left leg straight in air, toe pointing to ceiling. Now, cross this left leg over and touch the floor on your right side with your toes. Try to keep your shoulders flat while doing this; put the twist in the waistline, and a rolling motion in the hips.

3. Return leg to straight-up position, then lower to floor. Repeat the performance with right leg, touching toes to floor on left side of body. Ten to twenty times, medium speed.

Variation: This hip roll may also be done as a knee-chest procedure. Keep the shoulders flat, roll the torso so that the knees touch the floor first on the left side, then on the right side. Keep the knees drawn up close to the chest, and pressed together when touching the floor.

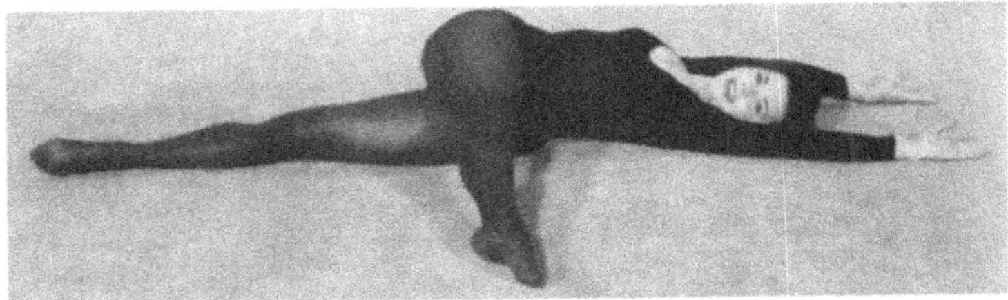

Fig. 328. The side roll.

Fig. 329. The side roll: variation.

MOVE TO THE REAR

If there's plenty of room for improvement in both hips and derriere, you'll want to divide this into two movements. Movement one is for those "high pockets" of fat over the hip bone, also for the fleshy pads on the outer thigh where your girdle ends. Movement two works directly on the buttocks.

Movement one:

1. Lie on the side, legs straight out. Raise head and shoulders, bracing yourself with your arms.

2. Lift legs about eight inches from the floor, so that all the weight is centered on hip and thigh. Now, perform a vigorous scissors movement, moving one leg forward as far as possible while the other goes backward as far as possible. Be sure the flesh-pads you want to work on are massaging against the floor.

Movement two:

1. Same side-lying position, upper torso raised. This time leave the feet on the floor.

2. Using feet and arms for bracing, lift hips off floor. Twisting to the right, bounce right buttock smartly against the floor for as many counts as you can accomplish. Return to original position. Be certain not to hit the spinal column.

3. Lift hips again, twist left and bounce left buttock. Keep the bounce rapid and vigorous, perform exercise five to ten times.

Variation: The buttocks bouncing can be done while lying flat on back, but there is some danger of hitting the end of the spine. The side-twist is a bit more difficult, but safer.

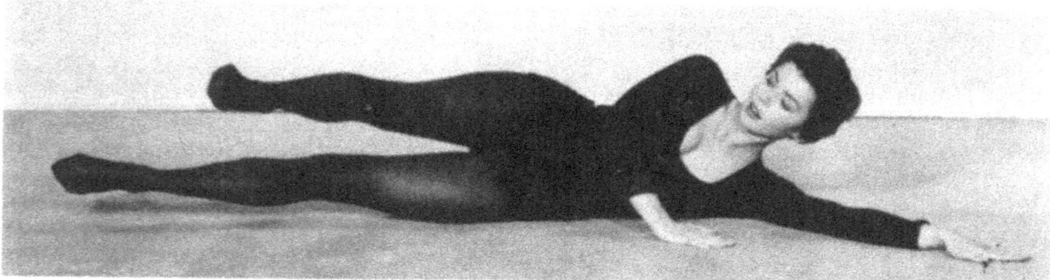

Fig. 330. Move to the rear: movement one.

Fig. 331. Move to the rear: movement two.

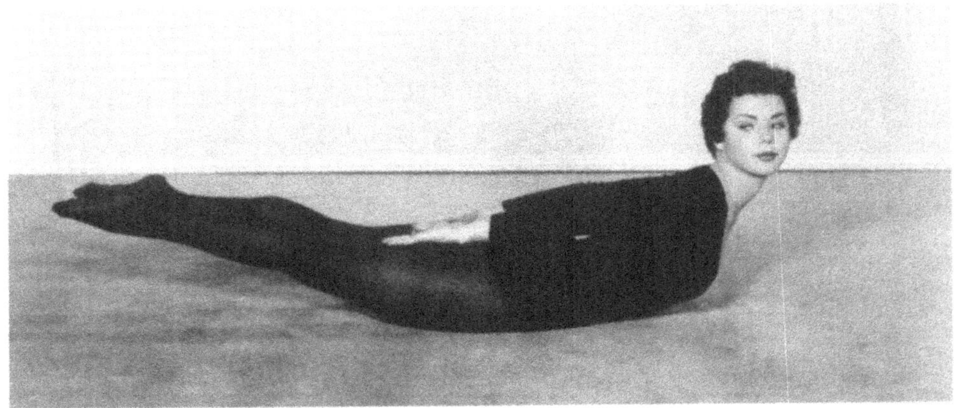

Fig. 332. Spine tingler: movement one.

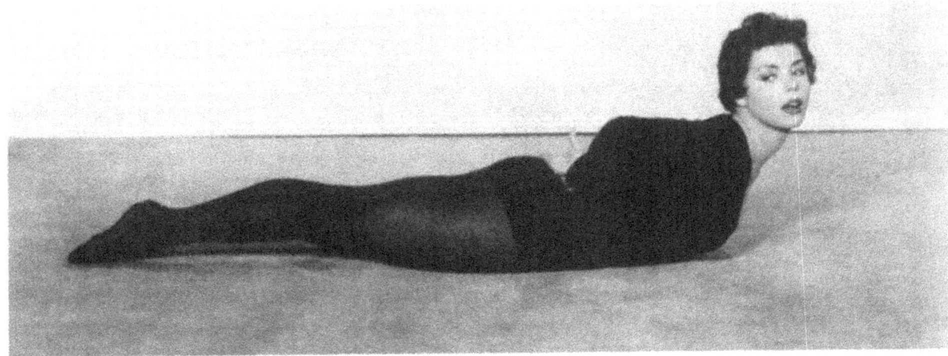

Fig. 333. Spine tingler: movement two.

SPINE TINGLER

In both its movements, this one helps to straighten the spine and strengthen the back. Movement one is of benefit in streamlining the thighs, also.

Movement one:

1. Lie on stomach, hands clasped behind back.
2. Keeping the face down, raise both head and feet until you're curved like a rocker. Hold for a count of three, then return to flat position. Breathe *in*, as you repeat the head-and-foot lifting procedure, breathe *out* as you lower them. Perform five to ten times.

Movement two:

1. Same position, flat on stomach and hands behind back.
2. Breathing *in*, raise upper part of body as far off floor as is possible without lifting your feet. As you raise the head, twist it around until you can see both your calves and heels. Breathe *out* as you lower head to flat position.
3. Repeat five to ten times, keeping feet on the floor, twisting head alternately left and right for a backward look.

CHAPTER THIRTEEN

Beauty Points East and West

SHOULDERS AND CLEAVAGE

Décolleté make-up: For many years, the average woman's idea of neckline propriety was pretty much dictated by the Johnston office, which tells the movie industry what's proper for public gazing. Then along came the uncensored ladies of TV, encouraging and emancipating many another lovely throat and bosom.

Most women discover that an uncovered chest does unexpectedly fine things for the neck and chinline. This is particularly true for those of you who may have been spotlighting a double-chin by wearing white too near the face. By contrast, flesh does not reflect flesh. Drop your dress to a flattering "V," allowing an expanse of throat between face and material, and you'll find you've accomplished a cleaner, down-sweeping line.

Hints for bosom beauty: There are make-up tricks to give an illusion of fullness to a small bust, and to deepen the cleavage. But those are finishing touches. Bosoms and shoulders suddenly exposed to décolleté usually need some preparatory work.

A recommended skin-reconditioner is both simple and inexpensive. Fill a small cheesecloth bag with equal parts of oatmeal and almond meal. Add a drop of your favorite perfume and drop the bag into your bath water. A very few skins are sensitive to almond meal. If yours is, use just the oatmeal.

For make-up, you will want to accent shoulders, throat and bosom with the same tones that complement your facial complexion. A liquid-oil make-up base spreads easily over large surfaces and gives a smooth sheen to shoulders and back. A tinted cream-cake or beauty-stick is better for covering small blemishes, if you have them. Be sure that throat and face make-up blend smoothly at the jawline and under the chin.

For setting make-up base so that it will not rub off, pat talcum powder over the entire made-up area. Pat it on generously with a large puff. Remove the excess with a powder-brush.

Be sure that throat and face base blend smoothly at the jawline and under the chin. The base of the throat is usually darker than the face or back, so here it may be necessary to blend in a lighter shade of foundation cream.

Collarbones often need special attention. When the clavicle is prominent, a lighter base blended into the hollows on either side of the bones will smooth down the sharpness.

A blending of two shades of basic make-up can be helpful in correcting arm faults, also. A darker foundation cream will help disguise a large upper arm, while the woman with too-thin arms will find that a lighter foundation shade seemingly adds plumpness.

Always be sure that chest and bosom make-up extend a good inch below the top of your gown, so that a sudden slip or move doesn't show a startling line of demarcation. A strip of cellophane tape pasted inside the frock will protect it from make-up stain.

And always give the back of your neck and shoulders the same careful creaming and powdering that you've expended on the frontal area.

Now, here are the make-up tricks to beautify the bust.

To give a small bust the illusion of fullness, highlight the upper part of the breasts with a very light base, and use powder very sparingly. Highlights can be given by using cold cream or cocoa butter, and toning it down with tissue. Keep the cream or cocoa butter from contact with the dress.

Last of all, run a thin line of rouge down between the breasts. You'll be surprised at this deepened, more intriguing cleavage.

Fig. 334. Loving cup ears.

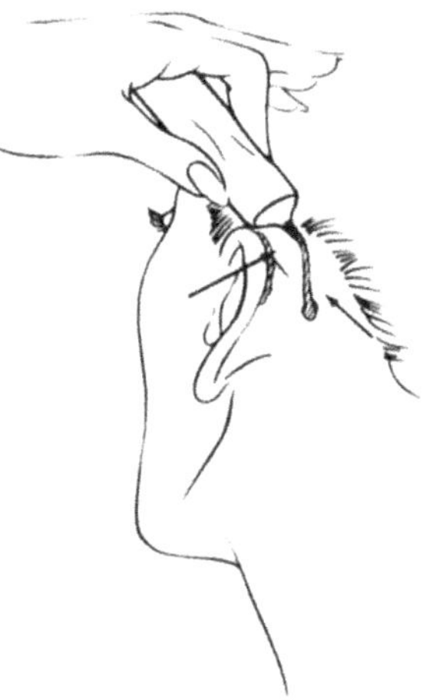

Fig. 335. Procedure for applying liquid adhesive.

HINT FOR "PINNING BACK" THE EARS

You needn't be sensitive if you have "Clark Gable" or "loving cup" ears. It may be that you would like to show off a naturally beautiful hairline with an up-do style, but are prevented from it because the ears do not grow close enough to the head. If so, here is a help employed by many a lovely actress, in which you use a liquid adhesive regularly carried by druggists.

Fig. 334 shows the ears before correction. Clean off the area in back of the ears and the mastoid bone with alcohol, so that no oil or grease will interfere with the adhesive.

Fig. 335 shows how to apply liquid adhesive on the mastoid bone (bony curve behind the ear). Apply liquid adhesive on the back rim of the ear itself. Allow both to dry for about three to five minutes, and then press the ear rim against the area covered with adhesive. Do one ear at a time.

Fig. 336. Ears after correction.

Fig. 336 shows the ears after correction. Liquid adhesive is very easily applied, and very easily removed. Simply peel it off, and cleanse the skin again with alcohol.

JEWELS OF WISDOM

Just as colors in clothes either complement or detract from certain skin types, so, too, do jewels. Here are some facts on gems and beauty. They apply to jewelry worn on the skin—not on the dress.

It goes without saying that a healthy, clear, flawless skin is emphasized by any jewel. In the case of sallow or ruddy skins, it's an entirely different story.

Since the predominant color in a sallow skin is yellow, wearing green, blue or yellow stones points up the sallowness of the skin. Life and color can be added to this complexion type by the pale glow of moonstones, the iridescence of opals, the soft glow of rose quartz. In metals, silver, platinum or palladium are more flattering than any shade of gold.

Since the predominant tone of ruddy skins is red, rubies and topazes should be avoided, as well as deep blue sapphires and amethysts. Emeralds, too, offer unwelcome contrast to this skin-type.

Diamonds, crystal, aquamarines, star sapphires, black or ivory pearls complement ruddy skins. In metals, yellow and green gold can be worn, while pink gold should be avoided. Platinum, palladium and silver are most flattering.

As a generalization, if you are deeply tanned, silver and yellow gold offer most telling contrast. If your skin is very pale, a rose gold provides added warmth.

PALE HANDS OR TANNED

So often we hear the expression, "She has him wrapped around her little finger." Or, "She has him in the palm of her hand." This is more than picturesque speech, because to most men there is nothing more synonymous of femininity than a soft, graceful, and daintily-kept hand.

There was a time when rough, work-worn palms and broken nails were the honorable, if pitiable, proof of being a housewife and mother. Today, with rubber gloves, hand lotions and nail-polishes available at a low cost, well-kept hands are the rule with American women of all classes. The exception—the chapped, reddened hand with broken or overly short nails excites pity not so much for the owner's lack of means as for her lack of personal pride.

Since your hands are such an important part of your beauty, guard and protect them before they become roughened and stained. Don't wait until they require reconditioning.

Here are five "do's":

1. Wear work gloves, rubber gloves to keep hands out of hot water and strong soap powders, cotton gloves or an old pair of leather gloves when doing work that promotes calluses or stains.

2. Before polishing furniture or silver, gardening, or other such tasks, dig the nails into a bar of wet soap to keep stain and dirt from getting under the nail. Afterward, when you wash out the soap, the soil will come with it.

3. Dry your hands thoroughly after washing them, and immediately rub on a soothing lotion. If you are going out into cold weather, protect your hands against chapping by rubbing in a good lotion before putting on your gloves. Learn to wear your gloves rather than carry them. Literally keep hand lotion handy.

4. If you smoke, use a holder to keep stains off the fingers. Remove household stains quickly before they have a chance to become imbedded in finger crevices. Lemon juice is a good all-over bleach for hands, and for some type of stains. Fruit and berry juices from canning, medicine and dyes will usually yield to chlorine bleach.

5. At least once a week, or oftener if you need it, give your hands a good bed-time massage with face cream, or with warm oil (baby oil, olive oil or sweet oil). Beginning at the fingertips, stroke the cream or oil down over the back of the hands and past the wrists. Wear a pair of roomy cotton gloves to bed to keep the lubricant from rubbing off. If your cuticles need softening, wrap each fingertip in a piece of cotton or gauze soaked in the warm oil, before pulling on your night gloves.

Elbow care: Elbows, so important to the beauty of your arms, are an almost incorrigible feature. In youth they tend to become roughened or to appear dirty. They are one of the first parts of the body to show wrinkling and aging. To keep them looking their best requires constant scrubbing, massage, and lubrication.

Use a hand brush and plenty of soap when washing the elbows. A grainy cleaner will give them a cleaner and smoother look. So will the use of a toilet pumice. A rich eye cream is the best lubrication of all. Massage it into the skin over the bone and the area surrounding it, including the elbow crease in the front of the arm. Leave the cream on for at least an hour before washing it off.

It is a good idea to apply a non-greasy elbow lotion several times a day, massaging well each time. The woman who makes a habit of this will stave off elbow-wrinkles many years more than the woman who prefers to forget them.

Handy hints for manicuring: Hands are rightfully said to "speak," and beautifully kept nails are their exclamation points.

Always harmonize the color of your lacquer with the lipstick and rouge you are wearing. The depth of shade should be determined by the size and

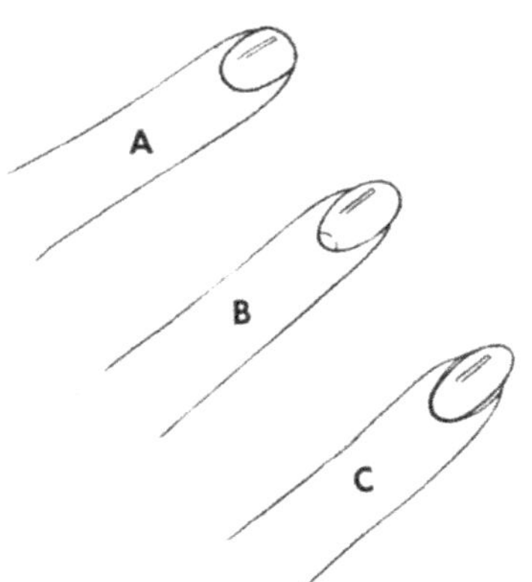

Fig. 337. Short finger.

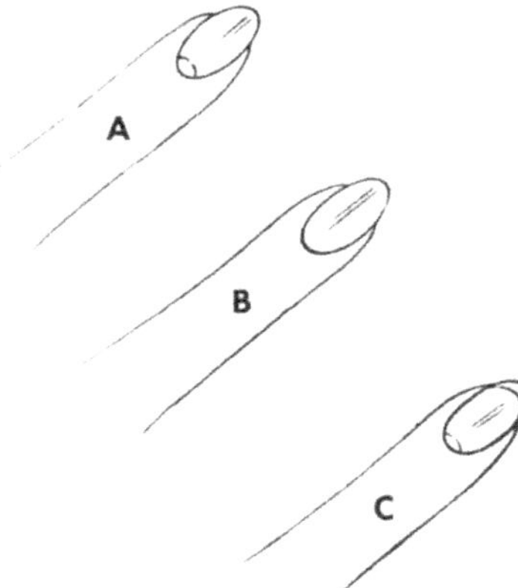

Fig. 338. Average finger.

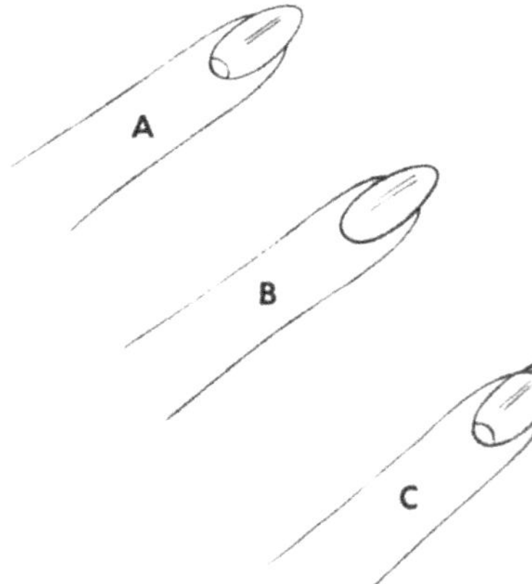

Fig. 339. Types of long nails.

shape of your hands. Colored polish seemingly shortens the fingers, therefore the darker shades are lovely on large hands, or long slim fingers. Small hands, or short and stubby fingers, benefit most from the medium or pale shades.

To make a nail look longer, paint its entire surface covering both moon and tip. To shorten a nail that is long and narrow, leave the moon and the tips unpainted. Here, too, the Oval is considered the ideal shape, and much can be done to add grace to your fingers by using polish to lend ovalized illusion to the nail.

Fingernail illusion: Fig. 337 shows a short finger made to look stubbier by the shortness of the nail, A. In B, the same nail has been allowed to grow a little longer, given an oval shaping. In C, both nail and finger are slenderized and lengthened by the application of the polish. Note that a small, curving rim has been left uncolored on each side, thus helping the ovalized appearance.

Fig. 338 shows an average finger with an oval nail, A. The tip has been allowed to grow just slightly beyond the fingertip and has been shaped to conform to the shape of the bottom of the nail. Entirely lacquered as in B, the nail lends length to a short finger. C, with moon and tip uncolored, seemingly shortens the finger.

Fig. 339 shows three types of treatment for a long, narrow nail—quite impractical for the typist, but decorative on the woman who can keep her manicure protected.

MANICURING PROCESS

A well assembled manicure kit or tray includes the following: a nail brush, emery boards, cuticle pusher or orange stick, nipper or scissors, buffer, cotton squares, cuticle cream, polish remover, colored lacquer, base coat, and sealer. Add to this equipment a bowl of warm, soapy water, a towel, massage cream, and antiseptic.

Care of your nails: The manicuring theories and process detailed here are ones we know to be effective not only in preserving healthy nails, but for growing them. Proceed as follows.

Remove old polish with a cotton square moistened (not soaked) in polisher remover. Press the square down, then rub it from the base of the nail to the tip, working carefully so that the dissolving polish does not stain cuticle or fingers.

Shape the nails with an emery board, rather than a metal file. Nails should never be shaped until they have grown beyond the finger, so that it will not be necessary to file down into the corners. To develop nail strength, let them grow out square at the corners, then shape into an oval.

When shaping, slip the emery in under the nail and work from the sides to the middle, as in Fig. 340. Avoid bevelling the edges. Nails are formed in layers and a bevelled edge leaves some layers protruding beyond the others. The slightest pressure will cause the layers to separate from each other. This causes peeling nails. It is best, therefore, to keep the flat surface

Fig. 340. Shaping fingernails.

Fig. 341. Massaging cuticle.

Fig. 342. Cuticle care.

of the emery board at right angles to the nail edge. In this way you get a good even edge, with each layer assured proper support from the others.

Remedying peeling nails: For nails already in a peeling condition, buff all edges after shaping. The buffing will bind the layers together, thereby ending the peeling condition. If you have paper-thin nails, form a habit of tapping them against a hard surface now and then. This will encourage a denser structure.

Fig. 341 shows cuticle massage done with a cuticle oil or cream. This softens dead cuticle for easy removal and helps to stimulate circulation at the end of the fingertips.

For nails that break easily, massage is an absolute necessity. In fact, all nails are kept stronger and healthier by thus encouraging the blood stream to carry minerals and other vital chemicals to their base. We suggest that instead of confining the massage to the fingertips, you massage the hand as follows:

Cover the wrist, fingers and thumb of one hand with a good massaging cream. Begin at wrist, massage along palm to the end of each finger. Pause at each tip to massage the cream well in to the cuticle. Then massage the joints and sides of each finger and thumb, travelling downward over the back of the hand and to wrist. Repeat with the other hand.

When you have finished the massage, immerse the hands in the warm, soapy water and let the cuticle soak and soften for several minutes. Use a nail brush to rub away as much of the dead cuticle as is possible and to remove all oil from the nails. Dry the hands thoroughly, because the polishes will have no staying power if applied to nails that are either oily or wet.

Use an orange stick to clean under the nails. Then wrap the orange stick in cotton, as seen in Fig. 342, and run it around the cuticle. Lift the cuticle very gently and run the stick under it, all around the nail, pushing it back as you do so. You may use a metal cuticle pusher for this purpose, but we personally do not recommend scraping the nail or cutting the cuticle.

With nippers or nail scissors, remove the hard skin at the top corners of the nail. When this dry or callused growth is allowed to remain it causes the nail to curve and split. If your nail is already curved, soak it in a strong soap solution until it softens. Then, with your orange stick, insert cotton under the nail until the in-curve is straightened out. Allow the cotton to

Fig. 343. Applying base coat.

Fig. 344. Applying false nail.

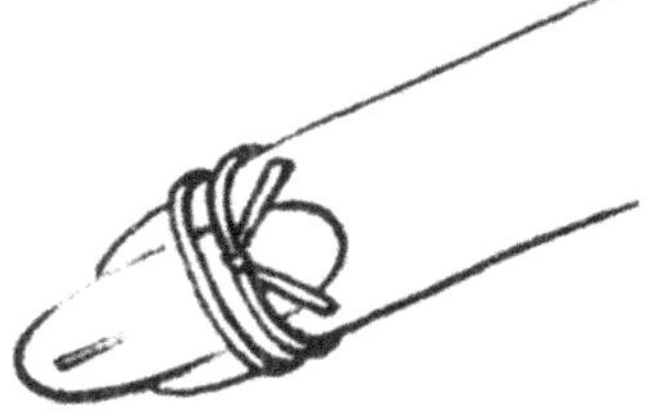

Fig. 345. Fixing false nail.

remain until the nail has thoroughly dried. To mend a split nail, buy nail-mending paper and follow the directions carefully.

Now, bracing your fingers on a tray or dish as in Fig. 343, apply your first base coat. Stroke from the base to the tip, covering the entire nail, carrying the base coat over the edge and under the tip. Allow the base coat to dry until it is hard and slick.

To give real protection and to encourage growth of the nail, we recommend two coats of base, two coats of lacquer, and one coat of sealer. Each coat should be thoroughly dry before the next coat is applied.

In applying the color, use long steady strokes. Outline the nail first, then fill in the center, always working down toward the tip. Be sure to carry the color over the edge of the tip. When the second coat of color is dry, apply the sealer.

Figs. 344 and 345 show the procedure for applying false nails. These are successfully worn when your own nails refuse to grow to a pleasing length, or are temporarily broken off.

False nails can be bought in most variety and drug stores, and usually come complete with the fixative or glue for applying. With an emery board, shape the artificial nail to fit your own fingertip and nail base. Apply the fixative to both your own nail, and to the underside of the false nail. Press the two together firmly, then wrap the finger with thread or a rubber band until the fixative is thoroughly dried.

PEDICURE PROCEDURE

In doing the toes, follow the same method as in manicuring. Instead of a curved tip, however, shape the nails straight across. The feet are especially liable to infection so avoid cutting into the nail corners, or filing the nails down too far. Carry the polishes over the edge, not only for better appearance, but because this gives a smoother nail less likely to snag the hose. To prevent smudging when applying the polish, separate the toes with little rolls of cotton.

EXERCISE AND MASSAGE FOR PRETTY FEET

Figs. 346 and 347 show two relaxing exercises for tired and aching feet which also help to strengthen the arch. In the first, the toes are curled down repeatedly over the edge of the book. In the second, the foot is rolled

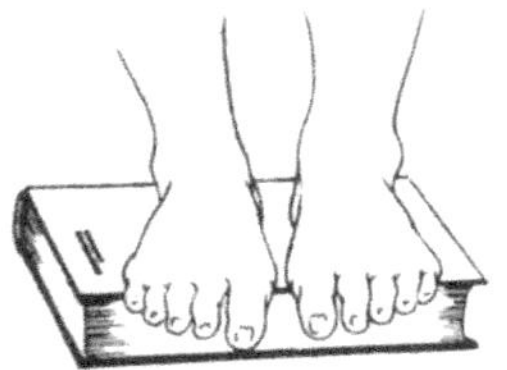

Fig. 346. Foot relaxation.

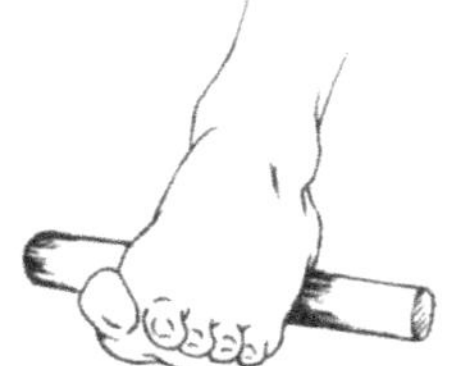

Fig. 347. Foot relaxation: variation.

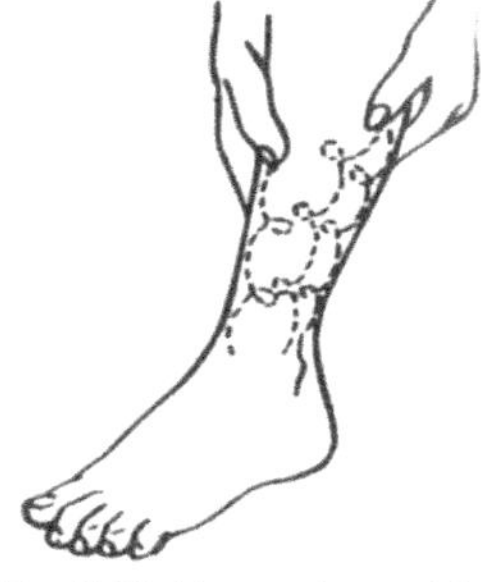

Fig. 348. Massaging ankle and calf.

over a section of sawed-off broom handle. Fig. 348 shows a relaxing massage movement for the ankle and calf. Figs. 349 and 350 show exercises for strengthening the ankle.

THAT PRECIOUS SMILE

A dentist we know once said, "In designing the human body, there is only one place the good Lord slipped up. With just a little extra effort, He could have given us a third set of teeth." Considering how careless some people are with the teeth they do have, an extra set wouldn't go too far either, we add.

Each natural tooth you have has in many instances been legally valued at $1,000. This is the amount people have collected as damages for teeth lost in an accident. If your teeth are sound, well-shaped, and well-cared for, there's no price high enough to equal their value to your health and beauty.

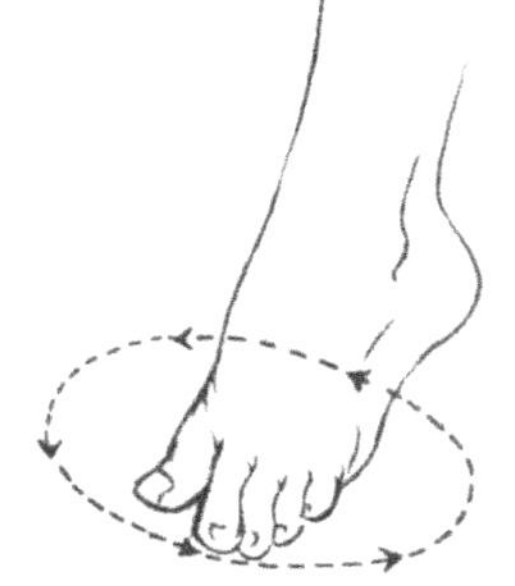

Fig. 349. Circular foot rotation for ankle.

Heredity is one of the most important factors in the formation of sound and beautiful teeth. However, it is possible for you to inherit the large teeth of one parent and the small mouth of the other or vice versa. Many a woman has gone through life made unattractive by this or some other sort of dental malformation. If this should happen to be your problem, don't deny yourself corrective dentistry.

Good teeth are a gift: Good dental care begins with prenatal care. A high calcium diet, containing orange juice, tomato juice, milk and natural cheeses is often prescribed by the obstetrician. It is well to abide by this if you want to give the gift of beautiful teeth to your children.

There is no longer any reason to believe that women must suffer damage to teeth during pregnancy. Once we have become adults, and our permanent teeth are full grown, a tooth does not lose calcium whatever our health or food intake. The bones, which includes the jawbone, of course, can and do lose calcium which has to be replaced by proper diet. The high percentage of cavities which occur to some women when they are carrying a child is sometimes brought on by an increased intake of sweets. No matter what the cause, there is no longer any credence given to the old superstition that dental work is harmful or useless when pregnant. Unless your physician objects to it for some specific reason, it is always better to have a cavity repaired before it grows larger. Going to your dentist twice a year is a sound beauty and health rule.

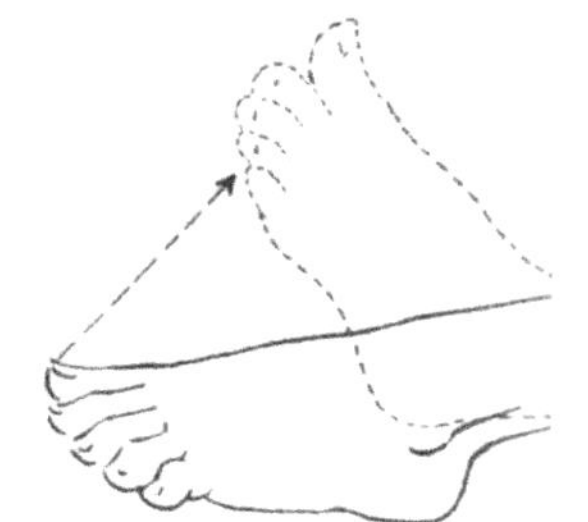

Fig. 350. Up and down foot rotation for ankle.

One of the most important developments in the search for better care for and the preservation of beautiful teeth, was the discovery of fluorine. This chemical combines with the enamel of the tooth to make it 40 per cent more resistant to decay. Many large cities in the United States today are placing fluorine in the drinking water supply. In many cities which have not yet adopted this plan, fluorinated water is available in bottled form. For children's teeth the application of sodium fluoride is often recommended by a dentist. It is swabbed on the tooth when the child is about three, and repeated every three or four years until thirteen.

Keep them gleaming: Remember that tooth color is related to complexion color, though most people feel that their teeth are darker than they are. If a color sample could be taken of the individual tooth, one would find Nature has created a good blend with the colors surrounding it. If your teeth are stained, or are naturally dark, a solution of peroxide will act as a slight bleaching agent. Use 3 per cent hydrogen peroxide by itself or diluted with an equal amount of water. This is recommended in daily mouth hygiene as a mild germicide.

Teeth and gum tissue should be brushed at least twice daily, with an accepted dentifrice. Both the dentifrice and the brushing are necessary for healthy gums. The sooner you brush after a meal, the better. The greatest damage occurs within the first fifteen minutes after eating. Rinsing will not clean the teeth the way a brush does, but it will remove the larger food particles. Therefore, rinse your mouth if you are out somewhere with no toothbrush handy.

A most vicious habit, dentists tell us, is that of opening bobby pins with the teeth. If you sew a lot, remember that continually biting threads can wear a groove in the tooth enamel.

In general, one should brush the teeth from the base downward in the upper jaw and from below upward in the lower jaw, thus stimulating the gums and cleaning between the teeth. Use the top of the bristles to clean the top, biting surfaces.

Improper use of the toothbrush may cause damage at the gum line. Cross brushing cuts notches in the teeth. Contrary to popular opinion, everyone can use essentially the same type of brush. It should be straight in design and have widely spaced bristles of two or three rows. The bristles should be firm.

New teeth for old: Corrective dentistry is today a highly developed aid to beauty. Improvement of profiles and facial reconstruction are very definitely allied to the realignment and replacement of the teeth. Closing of the bite is probably one of the greatest causes of change in profile, and should be carefully studied by the dentist at time of treatment.

In cases where Nature has not been too kind, it is possible, without destroying the health of a tooth, to remove the enamel and reconstruct the tooth by the use of a plastic or porcelain jacket. Many motion-picture stars have been thus treated to gain the beautiful teeth that would otherwise handicap them in a profession which necessitates so much close-up photography. In some cases temporary so-called "Movie Facings" are constructed from plastic to be used when a personal appearance or picture demands beautiful teeth. These are then removed and used when the occasion demands it.

It is no longer necessary to fear having to wear dentures, or "false teeth" as they were once called. It is now possible to duplicate exactly the teeth which were originally in your mouth, as to shape, size, and color. The material now used in place of the gum tissue is so life-like, it is difficult to tell it from your own.

Sometimes there is a psychological complex against the wearing of a denture. In this case you will have to teach yourself to think, not of losing your own teeth, but of gaining a new attraction. Do it in the same high-hearted way, and with the same feeling of accomplishment with which you do or buy anything else for self-improvement. Whether your teeth are the ones you started out with or ones you have acquired is not important. It is only important to realize that your beauty depends on your ability to smile—often, freely, and with loveliness.

CHAPTER FOURTEEN

Eyeglasses—The Added Decoration Can Frame Your Face with Beauty

FRAMES FOR BEAUTY

"Eyeglasses," although a literal description, is a cold and unpicturesque term. We sometimes wish they were called "eye-frames," because properly selected, your glasses can frame your eyes with added beauty and give added emphasis to your entire personality.

Very often one whose eyes require eyewear will say to me resentfully, "Why is it a star never wears glasses in a picture—unless you're purposely trying to make her look like a Plain Jane or her own grandmother?"

This is a two-part question and it has two answers; eyewear is avoided as much as possible in pictures because the lenses reflect the filming lights and cause photographic difficulties. Whenever eyewear is used to add a character make-up touch, the lenses are omitted and only the empty frames are worn.

The second part of the answer is that many Hollywood stars do wear eyewear in real life, with no detraction to their glamour. Many of them consider eye-frames to be the final touch of decoration they can add to a smart costume, and possess several pairs framed in different colors to match their various accessories.

When in screen make-up we create a "Plain Jane" disguise, the frames we use are purposely unflattering. To be factual, glasses play an important part in the character make-ups done by my brothers and myself for films. Often it needs only an oversized pair of spectacles to create a comic-type, or a monocle to designate a German officer. Just as often, however, we use a good-looking pair of eye-frames to change an undistinguished actor into a prosperous looking business man, banker, doctor, or other professional type.

EYEWEAR CAN REFLECT *YOU*

Your eyewear can be an indication of your personality, occupation, and general good taste. The wrong frames can make you appear to be a "character" foreign to what you really are. From my observation and experience, frames are selected and purchased either too small, too large, too wide, or too narrow for the individual wearer's face. To the spectator, this wrong-sized or unbecoming accessory you are wearing, becomes a *disturbing* factor.

To better explain the effect of this, it might interest you to know that to become a star on the screen, your appearance must be minus any *disturbing factor.* For instance, to the best of our knowledge, no male or female has ever become a star who had tight, kinky or frizzly dark-brown hair. Why? Because to be an adornment, hair must be lustrous, loosely curled or waved, and adaptable to any style trend. The dull kinky head would subconsciously be unpleasant to the viewer's eye, disturbing the effect of the film role he or she was playing. For the same reason, no dentist of today would think of putting a gold crown tooth in the front of your mouth to draw attention to the fact that you had a bad tooth.

After more than 30 years at Warner Bros. Studios as Director of Hair-Styling and Make-Up, I have devoted most of my time to personal consultation in our Hollywood salon, creating hair-styles and make-up for the average woman. Naturally, I come in contact with many hundreds of women who wear glasses, in an amazing variety of shapes, styles and sizes of frames. From daily experience, I know that often the difference between attractiveness and plainness is merely the difference between right and wrong eye-frames.

EYEWEAR—ANOTHER COSMETIC

Opticians and frame manufacturers are constantly striving for new shapes, newer and more decorative materials. However, there has been little written about the cosmetic qualities of frames as applied to the individual wearer. Many times, neither the woman selecting her glasses nor the fitter who is absorbed with seeing that the lenses meet her visual requirements, seems to be concerned or even aware of the cosmetic details that will enhance, or perhaps distort, her facial beauty.

In my consultation work in the salon, I use a Polaroid (one minute) camera to photograph the subject "Before" and "After." Often I have, by a newly designed hair-style and make-up, created a lovely woman—then watched that woman put on a pair of rimless glasses that aged her ten years in two seconds. An eyeglass without frames seems like a magnifying glass placed over every eye-wrinkle, puff, or dark circle the wearer possesses. The illustrations following will give you a visual example of what eyewear can do to add youth, or detract youth, from your appearance.

There is a right shape of frame to enhance your face-type, Oval, Square, Diamond or whatever it may be. If eyeglasses are requisite to your visual comfort, take full advantage of all the new, exciting, decorative colors and materials in which frames are now being manufactured. Frames are now available to match your accessories and accent your every color combination. You'd be surprised to know how many ladies are actually envious of the woman who has a real reason to require this important decorative accessory. Opticians supply many of these fashion-wise eye-frames to women who actually don't need eye correction.

FRAME SIZES AND SHAPES

In the following illustrations we hope to give you the knowledge and understanding of frame sizes and shapes to fit your face and your individual features. The top of your frame, as you will note, by specific illustrations, can reveal or it may cover your eyebrows. The eyebrow, as we have stated in our make-up discussions, is one of the most expressive features of the face. If you have a thin eyebrow, the frame may actually give you the illusion of a fuller brow. Always be sure that lashes worn behind eyeglass lenses are mascaraed cleanly and attractively, each lash colored softly and evenly. Blend your eye shadow to a lovely smoothness; don't let your lenses magnify a streaky application.

The temples of your frames are important to the line and design of your make-up. Too often a woman who has waved her hair into a youthful uplift at the temples will destroy its lovely effect by wearing frames with slanted bows, thus creating a down-pressing line on each side of her face and head. Don't accept a frame that pinches the sides of the nose; the

Fig. 351. Rimless frames, exposing discolorations, lines and circles.

Fig. 352. Deep lens and low frames, reveals circles and pouches.

Fig. 353. Comparison, right and wrong frames: (A) Covered pouch. (B) Exposed pouch, denoting age.

Fig. 354. Flattering frames, provide coverage for lines and pouches, add youth to appearance.

Fig. 355. Avoid width in bridge which gives appearance of foreshortening.

Fig. 356. Correct for a short nose: Choose a high-arched bridge to create length.

Fig. 357. Avoid adding to appearance of length in nose with high-arched bridge.

Fig. 358. Correct for a long nose: Select a deep-set bridge to foreshorten.

Fig. 359. Avoid narrow saddle-type bridge if nostrils are broad and heavy.

Fig. 360. Correct: Use wide keyhole-type bridge to diminish broad nostrils.

Fig. 361. When the jawline is heavy, avoid trames which are narrower than the temple line.

Fig. 362. Correct: Select a frame equal in width to widest point of face, thereby diminishing heaviness of jawline.

Fig. 363. Close-set eyes: Avoid narrow bridge and small lens size.

Fig. 364. Correct for close-set eyes: Create as much width in the bridge as possible, choosing a proportionately larger lens size.

Fig. 365. Wide-set eyes: Avoid wide bridge, also extra width at outer frame.

Fig. 366. Correct for wide-set eyes: Narrow bridge and less width in upper line of frame, deepened lens size.

Fig. 367. Small eyes: Avoid crowding eyes with small lenses and heavy-weight frames.

Fig. 368. Correct for small eyes: Lighter weight frames and larger lenses give illusion of larger eyes.

Fig. 369. Large eyes: Avoid narrow, light-weight frames, insufficient for size of eye.

Fig. 370. Correct for large eyes: Heavier frames, with enough width and depth of lens to give eye freedom of expression.

depression marks caused by this can become permanent marks on your skin. If you select a mottled frame such as tortoise shell, avoid one with the darkest brown color in the bridge. In contrast with the lighter color of the lens rims this dark line at the top of the nose will seemingly increase the width of your nostrils.

We realize that this knowledge is sometimes not too easy to apply. Although it is always possible to obtain lenses ground to your individual requirements, it is not always as easy to find the most appropriate frame. Too often, the buyer is given a choice of two or three frames and told that the frame she prefers is not available. This situation can be one of those commercial stalemates, created by public supply and demand. When, in the interests of variety, a new eye-frame fashion is introduced, it is immediately adopted by a large number of buyers. An example of this is the "harlequin" frame—so lovely on many faces, so absolutely wrong for others. When such a style shows great popularity, most makers swing to similar design. Less popular designs are then dropped by the manufacturers.

BE YOUR OWN JUDGE

Learn to choose or reject your eyeglass frames by intelligent judgment of their suitability to your own face, not by prevailing fashion. In the illustrations in this chapter you will see how it is possible to diminish or exaggerate the size of your nose by the wrong bridge—how the total width of the frame affects your face shape—how the tilt or wide part of the lenses can accent the length of the face—how the depth of your frame is important in covering an eye-puff, rather than helping to magnify it. As increasing numbers of women begin to choose basic frame shapes with the same care as hair and dress styles, frame makers will follow the same guideposts in their eagerness to meet the needs and tastes of their customers.

By greater knowledge of the cosmetic value of your eyewear, you can create eye beauty for yourself. Above all, you needn't risk the neglect of your vision by the fear that you can't wear glasses attractively.

TIRED EYES ARE UNLOVELY EYES

Let us not forget that the sense of vision through the use of the eyes is similar to the senses of hearing or taste or smell. Over-use of any of these senses cause fatigue and diminished function. Yet we should no more think that we are injuring the eyes by extensive use than we would think of over-tasting, over-smelling or over-listening.

These marvelous organs—the eyes—serve in two important ways. To the owner they report the whole outside world. They will make a valiant effort to report it well, even if vision is defective and unusual effort is required. To all others they reveal not only the owner's varying emotions, but his state of health and well-being. In good health the eyes fairly shine. On the other hand, fatigue produces a lackluster or haggard expression, reddened eyes and lid margins, or tearing. These local symptoms can be caused by uncorrected visual defects, improper glasses, poor lighting, prolonged use of the eyes or general body fatigue. General symptoms of headache, inattention, petulance, dizziness and indigestion are often associated with eye fatigue.

Thus it would follow that beautiful, expressive eyes are eyes that are not tired. Observance of very few rules of ocular hygiene accomplish wonders:

1. Periodic eye examination by an eye doctor is essential. If glasses are prescribed, wear them as directed, and allow the lenses to relieve unnecessary effort.

2. Have good lighting, *not in front of the eyes,* for reading or close work.

3. If bright sunlight is bothersome, wear *good* sunglasses, not the less-expensive and fatiguing kind. Take them off indoors. It is sometimes dangerous to become accustomed to them.

4. Avoid intense lights such as welding machines, or looking directly at the sun. Eye damage from such light sources can be permanent.

5. Eye exercises or gymnastics, unless prescribed by your eye doctor, are usually worse than worthless.

FEATURE FLATTERY THROUGH EYE-FRAMES

We have previously explained in the section on eye and eyebrow make-up how you can increase or diminish the size of the nose through proper shaping of the eyebrow. The bridge of your eye-frames can work the same corrective illusion, enhancing the attractiveness of various features.

THE RIGHT FRAME FOR YOUR FACE-TYPE

You have never seen a picture that did not gain beauty and importance by proper framing. A rimless eyeglass is an unframed picture—like the rimless canvas, it impresses you with a sense of lack. More than that, the frameless glasses signal to the observer that here is a defect—weak eyes wearing "specs" from necessity. Add a frame—the appropriate and flattering frame—and you have a "plus" instead of a beauty "minus."

Before considering the specific details for fitting glasses to your particular face-shape, remember this: It's not enough to choose your frames for beauty, they must be *worn* for beauty also. Glasses slipping down on the nose not only encourage you to peer over them in "granny" fashion, but they are apt to push ridges in the skin and flesh of the nose. Frames that become loosened or bent from wear are quickly straightened or tightened. Don't neglect having them adjusted often. Remind yourself with this jingle: When your frame begins to slip, the optician's glad to tighten your grip.

Many present-day frames are enhanced with lovely ornamentation. Choose frames with the detailing at the point you would accent—on the browline to move with the upsweep—or a cluster at the end to give width. Never permit the detail to be closer to the nose than the inner corner of your eyebrow. Avoid a horizontal decoration on a wide nose.

Before going on to the end of this chapter, I want to say that I recently had the privilege of attending, in Chicago, the world's largest convention of eyewear and eye-care experts. After seeing the great variety of frames, both conservative and spectacular, I decided on one piece of advice which I consider it a privilege to pass on to every one of you:

Remember that romance occurs within a distance of three feet or less. Make sure that when "he" looks closely into your eyes, they are clear, rested, and shining. Don't be afraid that carefully selected eyewear will detract from your attractiveness. Take care of your vision, make your eye-frames an adornment. "Wear them and dare them!"

THE RIGHT EYE-FRAME FOR YOUR FACE-TYPE

OVAL

As previously discussed, the Oval face is the ideal. In choosing frames, do nothing to distort or destroy the ovalized effect.

Fig. 371. WRONG
(A) Don't wear round, or angular frames. (B) Don't wear round bridge. (C) Don't wear large, heavy frames.

Fig. 372. CORRECT
(A) Harlequin or pear-shaped frames can be worn to the widest point of the facial contour. (B) Bridge should be softly curved. (C) Lower part of the frame should cover discoloration or circles.

THE RIGHT EYE-FRAME FOR YOUR FACE-TYPE

OBLONG

The Oblong is a long, narrow face. In choosing eye-frames, our purpose is to achieve an effect of foreshortening.

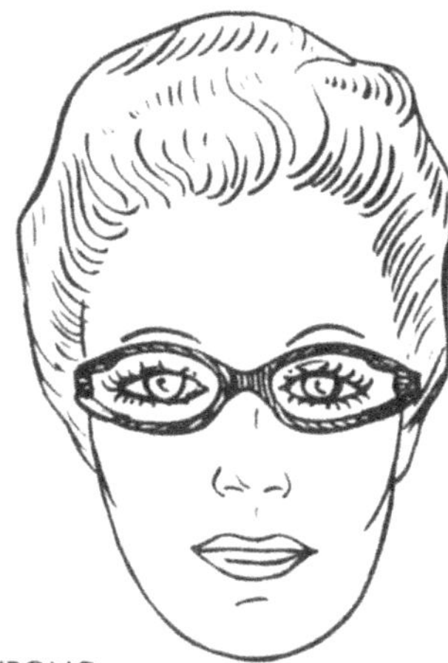

Fig. 373. WRONG
(A) Don't wear frames wider than the greatest width of the face. (B) Don't wear an extremely wide, straight bridge. (C) Don't wear high-arched or low-drooping lines in frame. This accentuates length.

Fig. 374. CORRECT
(A) To create the illusion of more width in the face, keep frames within the margin line of the widest point of the cheekbone. (B) Bridge should be softly curved, as in the Oval "Correct" type.

THE RIGHT EYE-FRAME FOR YOUR FACE-TYPE

ROUND

The Round face shape is a fine example of the vibration created by exterior decoration. At some time or other you have probably tossed a stone into a pool of water, and watched it create a series of ripples which became larger and larger circles. In selecting eye-frames, we want to avoid adding still another circle.

Fig. 375. WRONG
(A) Don't wear conspicuously round frames. Don't wear them narrower than the widest point of the face. (B) Don't wear a straight bridge. (C) Don't permit heaviness or emphasis in the lower half of the frame.

Fig. 376. CORRECT
(A) Because of the fullness and roundness of the lower face, create an illusion of slenderness by wearing frames slightly wider than the widest point of the facial outline. (B) Bridge should be wide as possible, and slightly arched. (C) There should be a noticeable upsweep to the lower part of the frame.

THE RIGHT EYE-FRAME FOR YOUR FACE-TYPE

SQUARE

The Square-shaped face tends to strong lines, heaviness and fullness in the lower part of the contour. In eye-frames we avoid all accentuation of the lower face.

Fig. 377. WRONG
(A) Don't wear square or angular design of lenses and frames. Frames must not be too straight-sided, or too narrow. (B) Don't wear a straight bridge line. (C) Don't wear a straight line in lower part of frame. Also avoid obvious roundness here as this would accentuate squareness in the lower part of the face.

Fig. 378. CORRECT
(A) Create width by wearing a frame slightly wider than the widest point of the jawline. (B) Bridge should be arched, to create length from the bridge to the point of the chin. (C) Lower part of the frame should have a slightly upswept curve.

THE RIGHT EYE-FRAME FOR YOUR FACE-TYPE

TRIANGLE

The lower part of the Triangle face is extremely broad in comparison to the close temple points and narrow hairline. In choosing eye-frames we try to create width for the upper part of your face, to contradict the heaviness and fullness of the lower face.

Fig. 379. WRONG
(A) Don't wear frames any narrower than the widest point of the facial contour. (B) Don't permit a high arc to bridge, which would accent triangular effect. (C) Don't permit excess width and droop in the lower part of the frame, which might point to the jawline.

Fig. 380. CORRECT
(A) Create as much width as possible by wearing upper frames slightly wider than the widest point of the jawline. (B) Bridge should be softly curved and form part of a flowing upswept line, to accentuate width in upper part of face. (C) Lower part of frame should repeat gracefully upswept movement.

THE RIGHT EYE-FRAME FOR YOUR FACE-TYPE

INVERTED TRIANGLE

The Inverted Triangle is the exact opposite of the Triangle. The forehead or upper part of the face appears much wider and broader than the lower part of the face. The lower part of the face is smaller, and the chin is sometimes pointed.

Fig. 381. WRONG
(A) Don't wear extreme width and harlequin effect in frames. (B) Don't wear V bridge line. (C) Don't permit an upward, outward sweep to lower frame.

Fig. 382. CORRECT
(A) Keep width of frames within temple hairline. (B) Upper line of bridge should be softly curved. (C) Lower part of frame should be full and downswept to the outer jawline.

THE RIGHT EYE-FRAME FOR YOUR FACE-TYPE

DIAMOND

The Diamond face requires careful consideration so that perfect balance may be achieved. In choosing eye-frames we do not wish to accentuate the width of the high, broad cheekbones—nor do we wish to add extra "point" to the narrow forehead and the often pointed chin.

Fig. 383. WRONG
(A) Don't wear frames that are wider than the high-point of the cheekbone. (B) Don't wear the high-arched bridge. (C) Don't permit excess width and definite upsweep in lower part of frame.

Fig. 384. CORRECT
(A) To create fullness in the upper face, accent the width above the cheekbone as with a modified harlequin shape. (B) Use wide, flowing upper bridge line. (C) Lower frame should be full and downswept to the outer jawline.

Let me leave you with these last thoughts on the subject of eyewear. It is clear to everyone that the proper eye-frames serve a multitude of beneficial purposes. They can add youth to your appearance, concealing circles and pouches under the eyes. They can help solve face and nose problems. They can aid in making your hair-do appear more becoming than it would be by itself. Problem eyes can be tastefully camouflaged. In addition, properly-chosen eye-frames can serve a more light-hearted purpose, displaying to best advantage the charm which attracts people to you. They can be gay and decorative, matching your accessories and going far to add to the impression that here is a personality whose eyewear reflects her—rather than on her!

CHAPTER FIFTEEN

Beauty Is Always in Season

Summertime is the time for going places and seeing new faces. A complete change of scenery and environment is wonderful for you, if your circumstances allow a vacation trip. If not, summertime is still the logical time to take a vacation from yourself. At home or abroad, what you want and need is to get away from the monotony that's settled down over your outlook and personality. Fortunately, no woman is ever so budget-bound that she can't meet a new face in her own mirror. New complexion and make-up shades, a cooler, more casual hair-do to go with informal clothes and outdoor activities—these are not only in season but are also psychologically good for you.

The sun, of course, is your best ally in the search for new color and new vitality. But don't forget that this dear friend is also your severest critic. The skin that got by on overcast days may show up muddy and blemished when subjected to the searching white light of summertime.

IN SUMMER MORE OF YOU SHOWS

A good all-over skin conditioner is the oatmeal bath recommended elsewhere in the book. Fill a small cheesecloth bag with oatmeal and drop it into your bath. When the oatmeal is sufficiently moistened to turn the bath water milky, pat the bag over your face and neck. Let the oatmeal dry on the face, removing just before you leave the tub. This treatment will bleach and soften face and body at the same time.

You'll want to be scrupulously free of body hair. If legs show a dry scale after shaving (or if you have this scaly effect on arms or shoulders) rub the skin with a lanolin-based lotion in which you have mixed a tablespoonful of table salt. Condition the elbows, or roughened knees, with some of your extra heavy and rich eye-cream.

Remember that a suntan is beautifying only if you keep it well-lubricated. Keep away from a parched or leathery skin by replacing the natural oils lost during the day, with a good rich face cream each night. A couple of tablespoonsful of a lanolin-based lotion dropped into your bath water once or twice a week, will do an all-over "lube" job.

Don't make the mistake of leaving oils, butter and cream out of your diet. In hot weather it's customary to have lighter meals, with a predominance of vegetables and fruit juices. These are very necessary to your health, of course, but so is a certain amount of fat. During the war, many service women stationed in dry or hot bases of operation found that their skins became painfully dry and started to peel. The condition was alleviated when they included extra butter and cream in their diet. If you want a smooth and supple skin with a glossy tan, remember that the oil glands have to keep functioning.

The tanning process: You may have your own favorite suntanning lotion. However, here's one you can make at home which we personally use and highly recommend. You can make any amount of it you wish, but the proportions are as follows:

One-fourth ounce of cider vinegar (for the tannic acid it contains).

Two ounces caron oil (this is the basic ingredient of all burn-healing salves).

One-and-a-half ounces iodine (for color; if you have an allergy to iodine, you will have to omit this).

One-half ounce baby oil.

Four ounces of your favorite cologne. (Never put cologne or perfume directly on your face when going out in the sun. It can result in a permanent burn).

Suffice it to say that a lotion, or sun-screening preparation of some sort, is your best protection against a painfully burned face. Untanned skin will not brown unless some sunburn occurs first. Without the aid of a suntan preparation, the skin will set up its own defense against the harmful rays and this results in a coarsened texture.

A suntan cannot be acquired all of a sudden. It should be acquired very gradually if it is to be painless and attractive. If the skin is sensitive and burns quickly, avoid exposure at first between the hours of ten in the morning and three in the afternoon. Five minutes is quite long enough for exposure on the first day. The time limit can be increased by five to ten minutes on successive days.

Sensitive skins require constant use of a suntan lotion and rigidly timed exposure to the sun. Some skins, let's face it, are not for tanning.

Remember that it is possible to get a severe sunburn even on a cool or a cloudy day. Sunburn is most likely to happen at the beach or near snow-covered mountains because of the reflected glare from the sand and water or from the snow. A fresh application of lotion should be made at frequent intervals and especially right after coming out of the water. No one can err in using too much of a suntan preparation, but it is easy to go wrong by using too little too infrequently.

Severe burn or blisters require a physician. If the sunburn is not severe but still annoying, there are soothing preparations available that will relieve the slight burning sensation and soothe and cool the irritated skin.

If possible, start your sunning in some private spot where you can wear less bathing suit than usual, so that your tan will start below the top and above the end of the suit you mean to wear later. After your first burn, your line of demarcation is pretty well fixed for the summer. The white lines from your shoulder straps will mar the effect of a peasant blouse or off-the-shoulder décolletage if they are not browned with the rest of your back and chest.

It is well to remember that an *excessively* deep tan can be injurious to health.

Sunglasses are important to prevent squint lines around the eyes, but try to let a little bit of sun get on your eyelids, and the area around the eyes. If you make the mistake of leaving large white "spectacle" circles here, be sure to even them up with a dark make-up base.

Brighter face and breezier hair: The deepened face-tone is, of course, the best excuse in the world for throwing away your old lipstick and trying something entirely different. A browned blonde can get stunning effects with the orangey or pepper shades—the browned brunette challenges attention when wearing a bright battle-red.

You never change your lipstick color without following through in the nail polish department, of course.

Meantime, don't forget that mouth make-up helps to prevent sun-blisters and wind-burn of the lips. At the beach, or riding in an open car, renew your lipstick often, and under these outdoor circumstances don't blot it after applying.

The greatest all-out spirit-lifter for any time of the year, is a new hair-styling. For the carefree months wear it shorter, freer, more natural looking. If you're getting a new permanent, get large, loose curls—not too much curl, and not too little (which is the secret of a good permanent, always.) Get a cut you can brush up or back, with a breeze-swept look.

Don't forget that the sun can turn any hair into straw if you over-expose it. Because the scalp perspires just like the other parts of the body, warm weather calls for extra shampooing. A hot oil treatment for sun-exposed hair is a "must" at least once a week. Rub one of the lanolin-base hair-conditioners (or else, plain olive oil) into your hair and scalp, and make a turban of a steaming hot Turkish towel. After about three hot-towel applications most of the oil will have been absorbed, and you're ready for shampooing.

This is just about the point where it's impossible to meet that new face of yours without feeling inspired to follow through with figure and wardrobe changes—which is exactly what we started out to prove: That no woman is ever too budget-bound to "go places" in self-improvement!

AUTUMN—TRANSITION SEASON

The fall of the year is the time when the average woman looks into her mirror and realizes that the "dingy days" are upon her. The summertime tan is subsiding from a glowing brown into a yellow tinge, and the more delicate glow that comes with cooler weather and "indoor" care is still several weeks away. Fortunately, make-up base will help you make the complexion transition beautifully. While your skin is on the yellow side, use a base with more pink in it than you will want to wear later in the year.

A lemon bleach will help fade the tan. Use pure lemon juice, patted on the face and allowed to remain for no more than five minutes. If your skin has any dryness or flakiness left over from the suntanning, a tablespoonful of table salt mixed in your cleansing cream will help to get rid of the dry particles. The salt treatment is stimulating; you'll be pleasantly surprised at the soft glow of your invigorated skin.

If you can hibernate for a day away from friends, cover your face and neck with one of the new moisturizing oils, allowing it to remain on for as many hours as possible. A rubdown after your bath a couple of nights a week with the same oil, allowing it to remain on all night, will beautify your body and restore the natural oils dried out by summer heat and sun.

The use of a foundation liquid or cream is of as great importance during the winter months as during the summer months. They serve as a daytime lubricant and a protection against cold and chapping.

Greater attention should be given to your hands, for chapping is a common ailment. Use a hand lotion after each washing, and a gentle hand massage with warm olive oil before retiring at night.

WHEN WINTER COMES

Winter is the elegant season, of course, bringing holiday parties and celebrations. You'll want to match up the deeper colors and richer fabrics of your wardrobe with a more formal hairdress. Undoubtedly your last permanent has suffered from wind and sun. Recondition your hair to its former gleaming beauty through rich oil treatment.

One leftover from summertime is worth keeping. You're undoubtedly several pounds slimmer than you were when the hot weather and outdoor exercise began. Watch that natural inclination to eat more, sit more, and gain more now that you're indoors. A few simple exercises will maintain your trimness. It will take a lot more work to get rid of the extra pounds once you put them on again.

CHAPTER SIXTEEN

Look Who's Talking—The Men!

The above title was borrowed from an article by Hazel Rawson Cades in *Woman's Home Companion*—which was based on the results of a questionnaire sent out by the *Companion* to a list of important advertising executives and posing the question, "What Do You See When You Look at Women?" The answers from over 1300 men may surprise you. Perhaps you'll find it interesting to run through the questions with your own man and see how his answers compare.

Question: "What feminine attraction do you notice first?"

Answers showed "Face" first by 529 votes. "Figure" second with 459 votes. Only 96 males noticed "Legs" first, and 91 voted for "Carriage" as an attention getter. "Eyes" drew 53 first glances, and "Hair" drew 46. Other features in order of votes, "Bust," 11 votes; "Lips," "Skin" and "Voice" drew 4 votes apiece; "Personality" was voted for by 2, and "Clothes" was last with only 1 lone male checking it.

Question: "About the female form divine—which type do you prefer?"

Answers: The "Tall, slim fashion model" drew 496 votes as against the "Petite" gals' 392. 345 preferred "Junoesque proportions" and 46 wrote in their own classification, "Medium."

Question: "What type of gams (legs) do you prefer?"

Answers: "On the slim side," winner with 783 votes. "On the full side," 471 votes. "Medium," 34 votes.

Question: "Do you have definite ideas about your best girl's crowning glory? How do you like her to wear it?"

Answers: "Curled" hair was a decisive winner with 629 votes; "Short" satisfied 532 males; "Long" enticed 473 votes; "Upswept," 183 votes; "Sleek" scored 149; and 33 went for "Bangs."

Question: "Do you like her to conform to current trends in hair-styling?"

Answers: "Yes," 403. "No," 401. "Not necessarily," 185, "Depends on the girl, the time and the place," 105.

Question: "How do you feel about the color of her hair—do you like her to do things to it, if the process is not obvious?"

Answers: "No," 866 males. "Yes," 409 votes.

Further questions on hair-coloring proved that 645 men were moved to wonder whether pretty hair was colored by Art or Nature, as against 619 who looked, admired, and didn't question the source. 783 males thought they could tell the difference between artificially colored hair and natural; 452 said they couldn't; and 60 "weren't sure."

On the subject of hands, 999 men thought grooming was more important than anything else (as against 204 who thought it secondary). 553 males preferred "Capable-looking" hands, to the 336 who voted for "Delicately artistic." Nail polish drew 743 votes for "Light" colors; 180 votes for "Dark"; 222 for "Bright"; and "Others" racked up 163 undecided votes.

Perfume opinions: *Question:* "What type attracts you?"

Answers: "Light, floral," 352 votes. "More exotic," 187 votes. "Depends on the girl," was checked off by 726 men. 413 males had "a favorite perfume," as against 838 who didn't. "If so, is the scent connected with someone special?" drew 264 "Yesses"; 149 "Noes"; and 24 husbands added "Connected with wife."

Question: "Where do you think women show their age first?"

Answers: "Eyes," by 502 votes; "Skin," 415; "Neck," 391; "Hips," 224; "Hands," 178; "Mouth," 177; "Hair," 97; "Legs," 28.

Question: "Do you object to women making up in public?"

Answers: "Yes" drew a strong 690 votes, "No" was answered by 252 tolerant fellows; 131 didn't mind "Just lipstick," and 216 objected to "Lipstick and nose powdering" especially.

Question: "Do you have definite preferences in women's clothes colors?"

Answers: "Soft pastels" preferred by 523, "Black or other dark colors," by 355, "Brilliant shades" by 255, and 52 said, "Depends on the girl and time."

Question: "What colors do you like the woman in your own life to wear?"

Answers: "Blue," 291; "Green," 254; "Black and dark," 248; "Red," 217; "Brown," 162; "Gray," 126; "Yellow," 62; "Pastels," 61; "Tan," 50; "Navy," 31.

Question: "Are there styles, color, particular items you don't want your wife to wear—and would you care to name a few?"

Answers: "No, I like my wife in everything," scored 562 gallant votes; "Yes," scored 502. Items disliked on a wife were: "Plunging necklines," 132; "Sweaters," 47; "Bikini bathing suits," 45; "Red," 26; "Tight dresses," 26; "Extreme hats," 22; "Extreme clothes," 17; 'High heels," 15; "Slacks," 14; "Ankle straps," 14.

Question: "We're sure you've always wanted a chance to air your grievances about women's grooming faults. Here it is—which ones bother you most?"

Answers: "Bad posture," 815; "Chipped nail polish," 487; "Fussing with hair," 279; "Fussing with make-up," 311; "Sloppy or over-done make-up," 898; "Talking about diets," 178; "Neglecting to use deodorant," 694; "Neglecting to remove unsightly hair," 606; "Lipstick remains on glasses, cups, etc.," 567; "Eyebrows over-plucked," 432; "Eyebrows weedy," 201; "Affected mannerisms," 855; "Awkward gestures," 318; "Crooked stocking seams and drooping stockings," 37; "Poor smoking manners," 28; "Talking too much," 26; "Lack of clothes consciousness," 20; "Slip showing," 20; "Falsies," 18; "Unpleasant voice," 18; "General poor grooming," 14; "Poor drinking manners," 12; "Adjusting girdles, straps, etc.," 9.

Question: "Anything else you'd like to get off your chest?"

Answers: "It would take too long—but the girls would need more space on us."

"All women are wonderful; thank God for women."

"Perhaps I'm an old fogey but I hate everything obvious—be it make-up, clothes, manners, or voice. I admire naturalness in appearance, dress, and actions, even though it may actually be cultivated. I might turn and stare at an overdressed, exotic looking female—but I wouldn't be seen with her."

"Tell them to adopt the current styles to their type and natural personality (you can see that I'm a conservative cuss)."

"Good grooming is most important. Taste, neatness, call it what you like, is apparent when not in evidence. Regardless of so-called 'styles' women can do best for themselves by using good judgment."

"Set the dress line just below the knees and quit foolin' with it."

"A good figure attracts me first—especially a beautiful bosom. I'm in favor of falsies if the gal needs them."

"Yep—falsies. In an age of . . . shall we say . . . bosomless wonders, I get a wallop out of the clumsy efforts of a lot of gals to give themselves an all-too apparent 'lift.' Who do they think they're fooling?"

"I dislike having a woman continually ask if I like this or that detail about her clothes, jewelry, hair, make-up, etc. There's only one safe answer, but then my conscience usually bothers me—and I feel tricked."

"I heartily subscribe to Shakespeare's observation in *King Lear* that 'her voice was ever soft, gentle and low—something rare, but excellent in a woman.' "

"When logic leaves a woman's argument, her tactic (and usually successful) is to make the guy feel guilty. He knows he's right. She knows he's right. So—he apologizes for being right."

"Life is complicated enough without tight sweaters."

"Yes, a desperate 'viewing with alarm' of the style forecast of a return to the flapper girl. I look forward with no anticipation to learning the Charleston."

"Women are sheep—they submerge individuality in the frantic effort to be *au fait*. The result is that pretty gals are a dime a dozen and they all look alike."

"About the only other thing I would like to add is the fact that in spite of all gripes the average stenographer is the best dressed, best groomed, and best looking package in the world."

CHAPTER SEVENTEEN

Beauty Is an Ageless Thing

If there is one single piece of advice we would give all women, it is: act your age. The reasons why this is wise—not just beauty-wise—are many.

Every woman goes through several beauty stages in her life. Each one is precious and a once-in-a-lifetime experience. Each one comes only once to every woman. And every woman, inevitably, goes through all of these beauty stages. This thought alone should teach you that envy of or uncharitableness toward any one age is futile and unrealistic.

A very young woman is a thing of beauty and innocence. She can, at this stage, take full advantage of her innocence and the beauty only innocence can have. After her teens, she becomes the youthful, vital, anxious-to-learn kind of beauty. Wide-eyed wonder, and the kind of beauty it has, comes only once.

Thence the woman turns into the still young, ever-alert, more knowledgeable and more adaptable kind of beauty. This woman has learned at least part of the score of life and is anxious to learn the rest. This beauty is easy to look at, less easy to deceive. And so a woman can finally approach the true beginning of maturity in the fullest sense—mental, physical, and emotional. This is the kind of true beauty that can and should have no equal. It is a beauty every woman has to earn. It is, by the same token, a time when a woman can begin to relax and enjoy the fruits of her earlier, learning, blossoming years. The assurance, poise, and generosity of heart and mind that can and should be part and parcel of the woman at this stage of life create a kind of enduring and durable beauty of mind and body that can be truly irresistible. A knowing woman is a beautiful woman—and she is one who learned in her teens that every stage of her life has its own, richly rewarding and enviable beauty.

TRIBUTE TO TEEN-AGERS

Perhaps you know that drug and cosmetic associations frequently make surveys to see what kind of beauty products are being bought and used by the women of various age classes. Such a survey was made on teen-agers not too long ago, and the results were a tribute to the general good taste, intelligence, and good beauty habits of these young women.

In our opinion, there's something unusually lovely about a young girl who's found a way to keep the natural freshness of youth while she gradually acquires the privileges in make-up and dress that come with young womanhood. Statistics show that 92.7 per cent of this age group uses lipstick. This is perfectly permissible and understandable since colorless lips are never attractive on any woman at any age. Most of the lipstick was bought in light, clear shades. This would be our own best advice to you. Rouge should never appear on schoolgirls' cheeks in daytime—and, happily, all but 7.5 per cent of you skip this cosmetic. If you are entirely without natural color, a slight bit of rouging may be required when wearing a party dress at night. This, we hope, accounts for the 7.5 per cent of sales.

Clean-cut statistics: Always, in talking to teen-agers, we try to impress upon them that cleanliness and personal daintiness are the most precious habits they can acquire. When a child is born, the first precaution taken for its welfare is absolute cleanliness. Everything that touches it must be washed or boiled. Strangely enough, it is only as humans grow into childhood and make more contact with grime and soil that this rule of physical hygiene is relaxed.

The teens, then, are the time when we must again become aware of the necessity for hygiene, neatness and grooming.

The statistics show that 86 per cent of the feminine teen-agers wash their hair once a week. As for neatness, 83 per cent of you put your hair up in curlers nightly. Home permanents are practiced by 60 per cent of the schoolgirls. Regarding personal daintiness, the all-out winner in teen-age purchase and usage is the deodorant, by 93.4 per cent. Fourth highest is cologne (used by 61.6 per cent).

With an appreciative eye on all these impressive figures, we feel that the teen-agers of today are, for the most part, more conscientious and better educated in the matter of beauty care than most of their mothers were at the same age.

Don't be a tween-ager: The few young girls of today who do call for special criticism include what we call the tween-agers. These are the young misses who get themselves up to look like something that's half-way 'tween a girl and a boy.

It's rarely a "happy in-between" because this group also seems unable to make a choice between over-make-up or downright untidiness. From the neck up, they are feminine—in a confused sort of way. Too much lipstick, most of it too dark or too bright in shade, used on faces that are either overpowdered or downright greasy from lack of any powder at all. Hair becomes a wild mass of uncombed frizz—or a straight pulled-back job sticking out stiffly like a horse's bang-tail. From the neck down, these might be boys—except that few fellows would be seen in such ill-fitting shirts and baggy bluejeans, or in such dirty saddle-shoes.

Daintiness, softness, and prettiness are strictly feminine privileges.

Don't throw away these particular qualities in which no boy can match or exceed you. Certainly, bluejeans, slacks and other such comfortable wearables have their place in sports and activities too active for skirts; but exercise your prerogatives by looking slim and trim in them.

Remember that boyish attire should never be topped by a frizzed-up hair-do. The "pony-tail" style is clean-cut and appropriate because of its simplicity, but only when the hair is softly tied and well-kept. Otherwise it's not a hair-do, but a sign of being too lazy to "do" your hair.

Beauty is as beauty does: The beauty habits you form during your teens are ones that can benefit you for a lifetime. One of the most important of these is care of the skin. It's at school age that problems of skin irritation, acne, blackheads and oiliness are apt to become the most depressing thing in a young person's life. These troubles are a part of growing up. They can happen to anyone and it is comforting to know they don't last too long.

If you do have an adolescent complexion problem, look in our section on skin problems, page 114, and read the suggestions there. Meantime, remember that all beauty is based on physical well-being. Drink at least eight glasses of water a day; get at least eight hours sleep nightly; sleep on a fairly hard spring and mattress to keep your spine straight and to attain true restfulness. Too, this is a good time to form a habit of sleeping without a pillow. This will help you to grow up with a firm chinline and throat.

Most importantly, while you are trying to clear up your skin, don't let your complexion trouble make you unhappy or depressed. When we are very young and every trouble seems like a great crisis, the nervous system itself can promote bad skin health.

Let's talk about make-up: As for make-up, most of the high-school and college men we've talked to are equally divided between their dislike for "a greasy-faced girl who doesn't care *how* she looks" and "the girl who's so floury-faced and gooey-lipped you don't want to get near her."

There's a happy way for teen-agers to have color and keep a fresh-washed look, too. If you have no skin eruptions but your trouble is skin oiliness, a liquid make-up base may help you on dressy occasions. Ask your mother first if she approves of your wearing it. Under no condition, ever use enough of it to give a caked-up look to your face. Just a small dot of foundation is enough to cover one whole cheek if properly smoothed into the skin. Use just a light coating of clear, uncolored face powder.

As we have said, a teen-ager has a perfect right to use a lipstick if she learns to apply it for a natural effect. Use only light, true reds—never the dark or purplish red. Rouge, as we have mentioned, is best skipped, except perhaps a very slight application for special occasions—a prom, for example. Forget about mascara and eye shadow until you are older. They are apt to make a young face gaudy and harsh.

Pretty in public: It's all right for a girl to make slight make-up repairs in public, if she absolutely has to. That is, rather than see a young woman wearing a smeared lipstick or a really shiny nose, most fellows would prefer to have her fix it. They dislike seeing a girl constantly gazing into her vanity case, however, and their real plaudits go to the girl who manages to look pretty without making you conscious of how hard she works at it.

And a special word to the girl who's constantly wearing a babushka to cover up the pin-curls underneath. This a fine way to ruin the quality and sheen of your hair. Healthy hair needs to breathe. The scalp perspires, just as every other part of the body does, and sun and air promote the evaporation of this stale moisture. The healthy scalp is constantly exchanging new hair for old. Sun and air stimulate this process, also.

While you're in school, don't indulge in long, red-painted nails. Any fingernail more than a quarter of an inch longer than the finger length is in bad taste.

Remember, it's lovely to be young—and you're never too young to be lovely.

THE ENCHANTING TWENTIES

This is the time when you are frankly looking for a man in your life. And why not? It is normal and right that the sexes should want to enchant and be enchanted by each other. This is your time for parties and dates and romance; it is a time to put your brightest personality and your loveliest face forward.

Beauty course by male: Your best beauty instruction then is by male. Your reflection in the masculine eye is an even better perspective on yourself than the one in the mirror. Pay attention to it.

The man you work for may, or may not be, the type of boss who says, "That new haircut is very becoming, Miss Jones—" but your intuition knows when your own fresh and pleasing appearance helps to get the day off to a smooth-working start. Few men are fashion experts; but all men are experts on what pleases them in a woman.

Therefore, if the men in your particular sphere react more alertly or cooperatively when you're wearing a clean-looking pink or a clear, bright blue, look for more of the same shade. The biggest mistake some girls can make is to cling to the "smart black." Occasionally, it *is* smart—but don't let it become a uniform. In fact, it's a mistake to adopt any habit of appearance in dress, make-up or hair, simply because it's fashionable. You may not have a great deal of money to spend on clothes, but this needn't keep you from dressing attractively. Look for the simple styles, and add the individual touches that give you some help in standing out from the crowd.

Can I attract him—can I win him? What does a man want in every woman in general, but above specifically all else in his own best girl? He wants her to be feminine, which, physically, means all the things he is not. He wants her soft and gentle, of womanly flesh and fragrance. He wants her colorful, red-lipped, clear-eyed, her hair richly dark or bright.

If you would be that girl, the unavoidable fact is that you must first catch a man's eye before he can learn how much you mean to his heart. You don't have to be gorgeous, but you do have to be attractive. After you've won that first glance, then you can concentrate on displaying all those other feminine gifts—fun, sincerity, companionship, humanness—the attributes which make a man want to own and cherish you.

Too often, the girl who has failed to find Mr. Right is the girl who has been so blocked by self-consciousness she could not step out and meet him half-way. Sometimes, her lack of sparkle is due to enviousness of her more attractive friends. Never forget, you are adding to a rival's advantage if you fail to make the most of what you have.

To each, your own: It's a comfort to know there is no woman on earth who is beautiful to every man. It's even more comforting to know that every woman is beautiful to some man. Your own man is waiting for you somewhere. Go on out and find him and be prepared for that meeting—because you *can* win him.

THE EXCITING THIRTIES

These are the creative, the "building" years. As a business woman, you are on the way to achieving a career. Or, as a housewife and mother, you are creating a home and rearing young citizens. Either way, man is still your best mirror. The chances are that it is now one man in particular—a man who needs the knowledge that his love and admiration are important to you, because this fact makes him important to himself.

Housewife's hazard: It is in these years that all women, and housewives especially, are vulnerable to what we call "creeping carelessness." It would be a rare wife who knowingly set out to lose her attractiveness. Rather, she becomes sidetracked by the rush and responsibilities of daily living into a gradual habit of letting herself go. For some of you, they are necessarily the "thrifty thirties," when family expenses and duties strain the budget and absorb most of your time and energy. Still, don't let these things become an excuse for the "self sacrifice" of your personal appearance and well-being.

Please remember that this third decade is the most unique, most decisive period in your whole beauty-life. In the early thirties, youth and natural good looks are still predominant enough to furnish encouragement for putting off until next week, or next year, the self-care you're "too busy" for at present. In the late thirties an off-guard look in your mirror—or in your husband's eyes—is apt to make you do a double-take one day. The reflection you see can be one still vibrant, still exciting with youth and attractiveness. Or it could be that of a woman dully wondering how face, figure and spirit ever arrived at the worn state they're in.

The mistake made by too many brides is to think that once the wedding bells have rung, the chase has ended. Instead, this is where it really begins. To win him, you kept every facet of your personality and appearance polished to its brightest. You creamed, and tried out new hair rinses, and guarded your hands with scented lotions. Admittedly it's more difficult now to be as diligent in all these self-improvements, but it's even more vital.

As a young wife, you may still be a working woman—even though one with special privileges. As your mate's co-partner, you're keeper of the key to all the things he holds dear, his home and children—and his plans for your mutual future. If you're smart, you'll remember you're still in competition with those other co-workers of his—the wide-awake and pleasant-tempered females who give him a bright "Good morning" at his place of business.

Don't give up the chase: For this reason, we think the most helpful advice we can give any wife is to ask her to think back once in a while to the time when she was a hard-working, ambitious career girl. The woman in the business world has no guilt complex about making her own appearance her number one concern. As you'll remember, you performed your beauty care then as a part of your working schedule—skin and hair care at night were a necessity for getting out early in the morning. Your cosmetics were necessary working expenses. Whether your salary was large or small, you found a way to provide yourself with them. When you were tired or nervous you found a way to conceal it, and enjoyed and displayed good disposition and good health instead.

All these former accomplishments of yours must be maintained now. Perhaps it's impossible to run yourself and your home on an office schedule, but you can apply to it the same ingenuity and enthusiasm with which you once solved your working problems. These are the exciting, productive years for you and your mate. Never forget how completely you, as an attractive wife, will symbolize his success.

THE GLAMOUROUS FORTIES AND THE FABULOUS FIFTIES

Two decades ago, a woman dreaded her fortieth birthday as the beginning of age and the end of attractiveness. Today, most women of forty and many women of fifty are more lovely, more glamourous than they were in their twenties.

There is nothing truer than the remark inspired by Marlene Dietrich and Gloria Swanson: "Being beautiful is something you need to be experienced at." There are many women in private life still just as attractive as these two public "Glamour Grandmas."

Those added attractions: The well-groomed woman has no age. In her later years she has not only the knowledge of how to be lovely physically, but the added attractions of poise and deepened knowledge and experience. With most women, this is the age when they are beginning a life of their own, one free of family responsibilities. The only way to make it an unhappy time is to refuse to accept maturity gracefully. In other words, by "letting yourself go" or—worst of all—by aping the youthful.

What makes a man conscious of a woman's resentment of her age? Mostly ill-advised use of make-up. The too vivid lipstick, the red-red cheeks and overly tweezed eyebrows restored with a harsh pencil line. Blatantly dyed hair tops the list.

Allure can be mature: Here are the main points for mature allure. Your skin and hair both have changed slightly in color. Use soft make-up colors. Choose them carefully so that the all-over effect is harmonious and no one feature is overly outstanding.

When applying make-up, strive to recreate the curves your features had in youth. With tweezers or eyebrow pencil, soften the line at the top of your eyebrows with a gentle curve just above the brow.

The Cupid's bow mouth has long been replaced by the natural lip line. Just a touch of filling in of the outer mouth edges is permissible if necessary. However, never let your lip brush or pencil go more than the maximum of one-sixteenth of an inch above the regular lip outline—rather, flatten out the center. Dark lip rouges, most especially the purples, are out for gray-haired women.

Use a foundation that is light in weight and apply only a little. The heavy bases line the sides of wrinkles, forming cracks that make them more noticeable. Top with a finishing powder and brush it away.

With good health and enough sleep, there should be no circles under your eyes. A little dark brown mascara will add brightness. Apply it lightly to your upper lashes only, and brush with a clean brush when dry.

Don't fight it, flatter it! It is usually around the age of forty that a woman begins to take on more weight. A tightly corseted figure is never a youthful one. Although the previous years were the logical years of prevention, it is not too late to do some figure conditioning. Be sensible, and don't start out too vigorously. Consult your doctor and take his advice on what exercises you may perform.

In clothes, watch line and color. A flattering silhouette is more important to a mature figure than the latest creation, or copy thereof. Wear soft colors.

Don't wrap up your neck to hide a line you might be conscious of. Better still, wear something on your lapel or shoulder that will attract attention.

Tint your hair if this gives you a lift, but don't feel you have to do this.

THE SPARKLING SIXTIES

Making the most of maturity. Accept maturity without making excuses for it. Make the most of it with the attitude that a new phase of life is beginning.

And, we add, it is. And it's an exciting one unlike any other period.

And it is, for the Sparkling Sixties offer a woman advantages no other age can offer. During this time a woman can, if she is wise and has planned accordingly, be her most unique and beautiful self.

The full flowering of beauty. It is at this age, above all others, that the mature woman can relax in the knowledge that this is when her particular type of beauty asserts itself and is in full flower. It is at this period of her life that a woman, blessed with the assurance of experience and the wisdom of maturity, can make those around her believe in and happily accept the rare and individual beauty she has created and nourished throughout her creative, growing years. The sixties are the years when life's richest rewards should and can be enjoyed. It is an exciting, unusual and bountiful period for the woman who has planned for it. The smart woman refuses to be deprived of the privileges and benefits of any beauty period in her life.

REACHING A BEAUTY CONCLUSION

At this point in your Westmore planned beauty program, you have learned to turn your debits into beauty assets. This, understandably, might lead you to believe that your beauty life has been settled once and for all. This is hardly true since, as we have carefully pointed out throughout this entire book, beauty is not static. Beauty is an ever-blossoming flower and one that needs to be nourished and cared for each and every day of your life.

You and your beauty change with the years—and happily so. Your basic beauty care changes little, however. Each and every day of your life you must, we repeat, give beauty its due if you would reap its rich rewards. And so it is that you will discover that this beauty book which has given you your daily and basic beauty plan has other advantages and bonuses still in store for you. As the months go by, you will find yourself returning to this book for a periodic beauty check-up. It may concern your figure, your hair, your make-up. A quick recheck of certain chapters in this book, plus some of the special progress charts and other charts included in various appendices of this book, should provide the answer to your new beauty challenge, as we like to call such beauty checks.

In a word, the more you learn to use this book as a continuing beauty reference book, the more you will keep you and your beauty up to date. Basic beauty care changes little, though your beauty needs may vary considerably. Learn then to use this book in part, as well as in its entirety. We Westmores have planned it so. Our beauty plan for you is one designed to give you the daily beauty plan that keeps pace with your ever-changing, more and more beautiful self.

Ten Ways to Westmore Beauty

1. *Beauty begins in the heart.*
2. *Lifetime beauty depends upon daily beauty care.*
3. *Know your face- and skin-type so you can put your best face forward.*
4. *For a fresh and glowing complexion, follow the Basic Rule of Three: cleanse, lubricate, stimulate.*
5. *The best make-up is the one you don't see.*
6. *Know your feature attraction and feature it.*
7. *Keep in shape—you have to catch a man's eye to win his heart.*
8. *Beauty changes with the seasons, so plan ahead.*
9. *Make the most of every beauty stage of life.*
10. *For all-time beauty knowledge, keep this book handy.*

APPENDIX A

Photographic Make-Up

For Professional or Amateur Motion-Picture or Portrait Photography

PROFESSIONAL MAKE-UP

The right make-up is the first step toward good photographic results, either motion-picture or still. In this appendix, we acquaint you with the basic techniques of "glamourizing" make-up as used on the Hollywood stars.

As you well know, it is a physical impossibility to retouch each individual frame of a motion picture. Therefore, the retouching is done on the face before photography, by means of corrective make-up. Eye hollows, wrinkles and facial blemishes which would ordinarily show up on the negative, are eradicated by means of base application before the subject is lensed. This, with proper lighting and camera technique, ultimately results in a perfect close-up.

Before engaging in any kind of photography, whether you are the photographer or the subject, read the chapters on make-up and hair-styling. The procedure and principles are identical with those of street make-up, except that different lighter and darker shades of cosmetics are used. The purpose, of course, is to reveal the true and natural personality of the subject, glamourizing but not altering their individuality.

Color photography: For color photography, make-up for women is kept to an extreme minimum and the colors applied with subtlety. Lipstick, as well as cheek rouge, should be two shades lighter than that used for the street, because the film accentuates the basic colors of red, blue and yellow. Black eyebrow pencil or black mascara should be used only if the subject is a very dark brunette. When selecting a brown eyebrow pencil, avoid a reddish brown. Remember, when color photography is projected, the colors used are intensified.

This intensification of shades was something we learned in the very first color film make-up test made. The subject was former Follies star, Marilyn Miller, then starring in the film, "Sunny." On the blonde and fragile Miss Miller, we used a peaches and cream base, and a pink powder.

In addition, she was seated at a table with a red-checkered cloth. In the projection room, when viewing the test, it was hard to tell whose face was the redder, Miss Miller's flushed and blotchy screen countenance, or ours. The light had reflected from the red-checkered cloth and created the blotches on her face.

Your tinted base make-up application is the most important step in photographic make-up. The over-all tinted base—whether it be liquid, cream or cake—should be applied before eye and lip make-up, or powder. Special care must be taken to pat (with the finger) after it is applied, particularly where lines of demarcation might show. The slightest streakiness or unevenness, while invisible to the eye, will register photographically.

Always use a colorless, transparent finishing powder. If a tinted powder is used, and there is any unevenness in application of the tinted base, the tinted powder will deepen the concentration of color. If the base has been applied unevenly, the high mounds of the base will absorb more powder, and an even deeper concentration or streak of color will show up photographically.

Very little actual corrective work can be done for color photography since, as we have previously mentioned, the amount of make-up must be kept to a subtle minimum. However, in the event that the subject has an extremely florid skin, the use of a flat beige tinted base will cut down the amount of red in the finished picture. Of course, no rouge at all should be used on this type of coloring.

For hilation on the lips and other features, use same effects as described for hilation in Black and White Photography below, but blot well with tissue. Only half the sheen permitted for black and white is allowable in color.

In most cases, for men, no make-up at all is used, except in the presence of a heavy beard. If this is the case, a tinted make-up base matching their own skin tone is used over the bearded area only.

Black and white photography (motion-picture or portrait): Quite a bit of corrective make-up can be done for black and white photography. For shadowing, we suggest the use of a tinted base make-up two shades darker than the over-all base color. For highlighting, use a tinted make-up base two shades lighter than the over-all color.

Shadow is applied to those areas larger, rounder, or more prominent than those on a perfectly balanced face: sides of nose, jawline, forehead, chin, and cheekbones. Shadow is never applied all over the nose to reduce the size, but is applied to the sides of the nose. If the nose is broad and flat, the bridge is highlighted. A prominent jawline or cheekbone is shadowed, and a too-prominent forehead can be minimized in the same way.

Highlighting is applied and used in the crevice of the circle under the eyes, in the laugh-lines by the sides of the nose, on the bridge of the nose if it is flat, in hollow cheeks, hollow temples, and on a forehead that is narrower than the jawline, to bring these features into seemingly better proportion with the rest of the face. A protruding chin is shadowed, to provide the illusion of a normal chin. The front of the throat is highlighted in width equal to that of the jawline, with highlight continued to the base of the throat. If the head is very large and the neck very small, the entire throat is highlighted back to a point past the ears. Be sure to blend both highlight and shadow effect, so there is no definite line of demarcation. This is best done by patting the area where the two colors join, with the fingertips.

No rouge is used in black and white photography, with the exception of possibly a little for a "mental lift" for the subject. It must, however, be in a very light shade, otherwise it will photograph as a smudge.

For hilation on the lips, a little cocoa butter can be used, or the subject can moisten the lips before each "shot" is made. A clean, scrubbed look can be achieved by using a little vaseline or cold cream patted lightly on the cheekbones, bridge of the nose and in a vertical line up the forehead above the center of the eyebrow. This application gives a faint sheen to the bone structure of the face, and is applied over the finished make-up.

We do not suggest using any make-up on children, for it tends to destroy their natural charm.

The charts herewith for black and white and color photography are self-explanatory, with this exception: If you desire a mat finish, you will powder the over-all face with a *non-coloring transparent finishing powder.* These charts will alleviate and eliminate any of the technical problems, for better photography, portraiture, or home motion-pictures.

MOTION-PICTURE MAKE-UP

For black and white screen photography: The actual steps in make-up and cosmetics used, with exceptions of cream rouge and shades of foundation, remain identical with those outlined for street make-up. Because cheek rouge creates a dark shadow in black and white screen photography, no cream rouge is used. When a feminine star's make-up is completed a very light dusting of dry rouge is made simply for mental "lift." The amount of make-up used is comparatively the same as used for a good evening make-up.

Corrective make-up application is based on the premise that shadow absorbs light; highlights reflect light. Thus, to minimize any structural prominence a dark foundation would be used; to bring structural weakness into relief, a light foundation, or highlight, would be used. In the examples which follow, a shadow is a color three to five shades darker than the over-all base color, and is applied before the highlight. A highlight is three to five shades lighter than the over-all base and is applied after the shadows and before moist rouge and powder.

If a chin has a tendency to recede, we use a foundation three shades lighter than that used on the remainder of the face. Where the two shades meet they are blended expertly together by patting with the fingertips. Creation of such highlight on the chin brings it into a stronger relief.

When a protruding forehead is a problem, we choose a foundation three shades darker than that used on the remainder of the face, following the same blending process. The darker foundation becomes a shadow, accepts light, thereby minimizing forehead prominence.

A sagging, double, or prominent chin is disguised with use of a dark foundation.

When the greater prominence lies in the cheekbones, a dark foundation is used over the cheekbones, a light foundation in the hollows of the cheeks and the recessions at the temples. The remainder of the face is made up with foundation matching normal skin tone.

These examples best explain the principles of corrective make-up and the use of highlights and shadows.

Character make-up: In the creation of a straight character make-up for the screen, where latex (sponge rubber) is not used to change facial structure, the subject's face is treated as an artist's canvas.

An over-all base, or primer (base color in keeping with character), is first applied to face and neck. Using artists' flat sable brushes, numbers ranging from 1 to 20, highlight and shadows are applied in broad brush strokes, are then blended with the fingertips. Wrinkles are accentuated with

COSMETIC COLOR CHART FOR BLACK AND WHITE PHOTOGRAPHY

	Tinted make-up base	*Eye shadow*	*Powder*	*Pencil*	*Rouge*	*Mascara*	*Lipstick*
BLONDE Light, medium or dark skin	Rose beige*	Brown	Trans-parent finishing	Brown	Light pastel	Brown	Light orange red
REDHEAD Light, medium or dark skin	Light tan buff	Brown	Trans-parent finishing	Brown	Light pastel	Brown	Pepper red
BROWNETTE Light, medium or dark skin	Peach buff	Brown	Trans-parent finishing	Brown	Light pastel	Brown	Pepper red
BRUNETTE Light or medium skin	Peach buff	Brown	Trans-parent finishing	Brown	Light pastel	Brown	True red
BRUNETTE Dark skin	Copper	Brown	Trans-parent finishing	Brown or black	Light pastel	Black	True red or garnet

*Use two shades darker base make-up than shade normally worn for street on platinum blonde, light gray, or white-haired subject, to gain contrast between skin and hair if proper contrast is lacking.

Tinted make-up base for shadowing should be two shades darker than over-all make-up base.

Tinted make-up base used for highlighting should be two shades lighter than over-all make-up base.

pencil. To promote an appearance of age on the mouth, base is carried over the lips, and pencil is used to stress normal lip wrinkles. Hair whitener is used to age eyebrows and temples. A wig is used for white hair.

To create an age make-up, all hollows, crevices and lines of expression are first covered with a dark brown foundation. When this procedure is finished, the face should somewhat resemble a skull. The subject's forehead is then forced into the deepest possible wrinkles, and all foundation is carefully wiped off the mounds of the wrinkles. As a result, the brown base is

COSMETIC COLOR CHART FOR COLOR PHOTOGRAPHY

	Tinted make-up base	*Eye shadow*	*Powder*	*Pencil*	*Rouge*	*Mascara*	*Lipstick*
BLONDE Light or medium skin	Ivory*	Blue or gray	Transparent finishing	Light brown	Light pink	Brown	Light pink
BLONDE Dark skin	Peach buff	Blue or gray	Transparent finishing	Light brown	Light pastel	Brown	Light pink red
REDHEAD Light or medium skin	Deep ivory	Blue or gray	Transparent finishing	Light brown	Light pastel	Brown	Light pink red
REDHEAD Dark or florid skin	Peach buff	Blue or gray	Transparent finishing	Brown	Light pink red	Brown	Pepper red
BROWNETTE Light or medium skin	Rose beige	Light brown, blue or gray	Transparent finishing	Brown	Pepper red	Brown	Pepper red
BROWNETTE Dark skin	Peach buff	Light brown, blue or gray	Transparent finishing	Brown	Light true red	Brown	Light true red
BRUNETTE Light or medium skin	Peach buff	Light brown	Transparent finishing	Brown	Light true red	Brown	Light true red
BRUNETTE Dark skin	Copper	Brown	Transparent finishing	Dark brown	Medium blue red	Black	Medium blue red

*Use one shade darker base make-up than shade normally worn for street on platinum blonde, light gray, or white-haired subject, to gain contrast between skin and hair if proper contrast is lacking.

retained in the wrinkle crevices. Next, the subject squints one eye to obtain the deepest possible corner wrinkles, then the other, and the same procedure outlined above is followed. Then the lips are pursed, and the same method is followed on the wrinkled area surrounding the mouth. With completion of the mouth, all wrinkles and natural expression lines are accentuated.

In applying your over-all make-up bases, the wrinkling process must be used during each application and each application must be powdered and brushed.

A choice of shade for the over-all foundation would be dependent on the character to be portrayed. If a ruddy skin is characteristic, then a dark basic color (two shades lighter than the brown wrinkle base) would be used; if pale, a lighter shade of over-all base. Over-all base should not be used in the shadow areas, such as temples, cheek hollows, etc.

Shadow work now comes into play. In the wrinkling process, dark brown foundation was used in all hollows, including temples and cheeks. These same areas are now retraced with shadow. Care should be taken not to disturb the original application. Shadow placement is at the temple line, inside corners of the eyelids, down the outside planes of the nose, and from the nostrils to the outside corners of the mouth. For extreme gauntness, shadow is applied in the cheek hollows.

Highlights follow shadows. Previously applied foundation is retraced with highlight; when it crowds onto the wrinkle areas, the wrinkling process should be repeated so as not to destroy previous work. Highlight coloring should be applied to all protruding points of the head's bone structure; i.e., frontal forehead bones, nose bridge, cheekbones, nostril sidewalls.

Eye shadow should be used only in the inside corners of the eyelids. On men, red foundation is used on the lower eyelid ledge, but is not extended beyond the outer corner of the eye. On women, no lining of any kind is used.

For powdering, use plain talc and repeat the entire wrinkling process while powdering. Excess powder is removed with a powder brush.

On men, no lip rouge is used; on women, very little is used, and the lower lip is thinned and the corners droop.

Hair whitener is used on eyebrows to conform with hair. No mascara is used and powder is allowed to remain in the lashes.

To age the neck, chin and neck are stretched backwards, and shadow is applied on either side of the neck cords. Powder is applied. After shadowing, highlight is applied to the mounds of the cords. Again powder and brush. The chin is then dropped, and revealing lines or wrinkles are traced with brown pencil, and the mounds of the wrinkles highlighted.

In straight make-ups, no hand make-up is used unless the general make-up is very dark or very light. Hands should then be made up to match the face, because dramatic action often brings hands into play close to the face. To age hands, shadows are created between the sinews and veins. Hands are hung in a drooping position until the veins are outlined, and blue shadow is then used on the veins proper and between the sinews. The hands are then closed into fists, the tops of the knuckles highlighted, and, from the ends of the fingers, a highlight is carried back to the wrist, accentuating sinews and cords of each finger. No over-all base is used.

Historical character portrayals or extreme old age make-ups (Agnes Moorehead in "Lost Moment"), where change of bone structure is needed for the first, and sagging and loose tissue for the latter, are handled with the use of latex (sponge rubber), otherwise called appliance make-ups.

Appliance make-ups are very effective, but they are prohibitive from the standpoint of cost to the layman. Not only does their employment demand a complete laboratory set-up, but the formulas themselves are secret, varying with various requirements.

Make-up as such, however, is applied in exactly the same way over rubber as described in the foregoing. It is also the same make-up, with the exception of the base. Known as rubber grease, it is an evaporated oil base, necessary because any regular oil base discolors and deteriorates rubber.

For color screen photography: Continued experimentation with color film has necessarily brought about some changes in make-up principles. Where formerly the basic tone for a screen color make-up was light gray, the basic tone now is a light gray-green which is warmed with the desired shades through the use of primary mixing colors. The mix is according to part requirements and the story setting. For instance, if it is an outdoor picture, men's make-up would have a tendency to be on the brown side. Bases for women are brought up to the desired pink tone, dependent on individual coloring, although if it is an indoor, or drawing-room type of picture, the mix has a pinker tone. Only pre-picture testing can prove or disprove a correct color make-up.

The amount of corrective work done for color motion pictures is held at a minimum. While the principles remain the same, shadows and highlights must be handled much more subtly. Very little shadowing is done, and any highlights or shadows used are mixed with the base color so that only a suggestion of their use remains after application. Great pains are taken in blending highlights and shadows, since absolutely no hint of demarcation can remain.

All color make-up is applied in absolute minimum, a straight make-up for women, for instance, utilizing only about half the amount of that customarily used for a street make-up. For women, both moist rouge and dry rouge are used, the former directly over the base and before powder, the latter after powder. Moist cheek rouge is first mixed with base color to avoid a "hot" rouge color. Matching colors in lipstick and cheek rouge are of the greatest importance, and those used for women are on the cameo-pink side because of the intensification of red in photography.

No cheek rouge is employed on men, and any lipstick is on the brown side. Applied very lightly, it is wiped off, the very limited residue serving to provide a faint definition.

Brown eyebrow pencil is used. All desired depth is acquired with brown. The use of black pencil results in an undesirable harshness. Mascara, too, is preferably brown, although sometimes there is occasion to use a dark brown shade on a very dark brunette.

Powder must be neutral (finishing powder) so that the color value of base tones, highlights or shadows is not changed.

PHOTOGRAPHIC MAKE-UP, AMATEUR AND PROFESSIONAL

For 8 and 16 mm. use, the make-up procedure as given for black and white motion-pictures is correct. If in color, the best possible make-up is that designated for street, with the exception of cheek rouge and lipstick. In color, these should be two shades lighter than that customarily worn by the subject for street.

The most important single make-up item, photographically speaking, is the base. Not only is it flattering to the subject, but its use saves hours of retouching. Base color is that used ordinarily by the model for street wear. Exceptions are platinum or bleached blondes, when skin and hair tones are so often similar that definition is lacking. The same is often true of brunettes with olive skins.

For blondes who pose this problem, foundation liquid or cream should be at least two shades darker than that used for street; for brunettes, one shade lighter.

In black and white still photography, Hollywood photographers often skip the use of powder if a subject's skin is unblemished and freckles not too apparent. They use only cream or liquid foundation without powder. The result is lustrous, highlighted skin, with normal skin texture showing through.

For color stills or home movies, eye shadow should be used very sparingly. If brown is used, it should be mixed with a little of the base, using only enough base color to bring the eye shadow down to a smooth tan instead of brown. After mixing, it should be two shades lighter than in its original form. Blue-gray shadow should not be mixed.

For black and white portraiture, the subject should pass the tip of her tongue lightly over both upper and lower lips before each shot. The result is the nice lip hilations seen in Hollywood portraiture.

Interesting hilations on bare shoulders are achieved by smoothing on a very little cold cream or vaseline, then toning it down with tissue.

If a bathing suit model has an even, over-all tan, it can be effectively highlighted by covering it with an application of baby oil and removing the excess with tissue.

TELEVISION MAKE-UP

A perfect television make-up for a woman, whether blonde, brunette, brownette or redhead, is a good summer tan.

Of course, people can't keep a summer tan the whole year around. Therefore, we have to achieve the same result with a dark make-up. The base, then, should be a dark, or suntan, shade.

This is necessary, not only on account of the extreme amount of light used, but television has a tendency in transmission to wash out reds and make the performer appear white.

Eye shadow should be a true brown, with no apparent red in it.

The perfect lip rouge is a purple or brownish red.

Highlights are applied to the cheekbones, hollows of cheeks down the center of the nose, to keep the face from flattening out or appearing flat.

Where, in the past, it was thought necessary to use extreme highlight and shadow contrasts, this no longer is true; and television make-up has become very simple. There is no bugaboo about make-up for television.

Television reproduction is not as sharp as panchromatic film reproduction or Technicolor. It is softer on the television screen. Therefore, laugh-lines which are corrected by highlighting and shading in Technicolor and panchromatic do not need the attention in television.

Cheeks cannot be rouged as we do in panchromatic or Technicolor, because it appears white or light.

Where formerly use was made of purples, grays, blues and greens, television make-up has now resolved itself to a natural make-up. As stated before, the perfect make-up is a suntan for both men and women. Therefore, during summer months, when the actress or actor may have a natural suntan, no make-up is needed other than lips and eye shadow and mascara, the latter brown or black. Where a natural suntan is present, there is no need for the use of highlights, since natural highlights are then present and serve the same purpose.

Queen for a Day

August 24, 1955

Mr. Perc Westmore
House of Westmore
6638 Sunset Boulevard
Hollywood, California

Dear Perc:

I know that over twenty-five hundred Queens for a Day will add their voices to mine when I say I feel that the Westmores are unsurpassed in the art of making women beautiful. Your theories and techniques, developed over many years in the beauty field, have a basic simplicity which reveal an unparalleled sense of style, of enduring loveliness -- the ability to use simple things to obtain astonishing effects.

I would like my personal thanks to the Westmores to be a part of this book and I would like to include my congratulations to every woman who will read this book and, I know, profit by its instructions. You've given out a great many beauty and glamour "secrets" on our show over the years, but here, for the first time, is the complete story.

Your book will do much to make my daily wish come true.... May it help every woman to be a Queen every day.

Cheerfully,

Jack Bailey

RAYMOND R. MORGAN COMPANY, 6263 HOLLYWOOD BLVD., HOLLYWOOD 28, CALIFORNIA HOLLYWOOD 3-7144

Art Linkletter

July 13, 1955

Perc Westmore has been giving beauty advice on my "HOUSE PARTY" show for ten years, and has finally gotten around to putting his expert information between covers. I know that this "Beauty Book" will become the modern woman's encyclopedia on the art of make-up. Certainly, no one is better qualified to have written it.

Art Linkletter

APPENDIX B

Fifty Beauty Questions and Answers

Q How can I make my eyes appear much larger than they actually are?
A See Chapter Eight, Eyes and Eyebrows.

Q Is short or long hair appropriate for a full, long face and a large bone structure?
A See Chapter Ten.

Q How does one eliminate a mustache?
A See Chapter Nine, How to Remove Facial Hair.

Q How can I wear my hair? My head is quite wide at the top with my face coming to a point at the chin.
A See Chapter Ten.

Q How should a woman apply lipstick if she has large lips and prominent teeth?
A See Chapter Eight, Your Mouth, the Most Mobile Feature.

Q I have unruly eyebrows. The hairs tend to stand up. Creaming and brushing aren't much help and to eliminate this hair would cause my eyebrows to be too thin.
A Mustache wax should hold down an unruly eyebrow perfectly. Just ask for the colorless kind at your department or drug store.

Q The left side of my chin hangs down slightly lower than the right side. What can I do to correct this?
A See Chapter Five and Chapter Eight, Using Base for Feature Miracles.

Q I have very dark hair and very white skin so that my side-burns and the general hairline stand out. I'm very self-conscious of this.
A To have such a startling contrast between skin and hair should be very beautiful. However, if your side-burns are too dark and grow too far forward, they can be removed. See Chapter Nine, How to Remove Facial Hair. Remove the hair a little unevenly, to give a natural appearance.

Q What style would become a person with a high forehead and a slightly long nose?
A See Chapter Ten, Hair for Feature Correction; Chapter Four, Using Eyebrows for Feature Correction.

Q I am a mature woman and wear glasses. My problem is, is there some special make-up I should use to make the glasses less noticeable?
A Choose your eyeglass frames to increase the beauty of your face. See Chapter Fourteen.

Q I am especially concerned with the small area on either side where the hair is usually parted. Here my hair is very thin and short so I am limited in my choice of hair-style.
A See Chapter Eleven, Parts of Beauty.

Q I have a round face. How should I wear my hair?
A See Chapter Ten.

Q My eyes are quite small and it looks as though I'm half-sleeping all the time.
A See Chapter Eight, Eyes and Eyebrows.

Q I have almond-shaped eyes and high cheekbones; also a round full face and a nose which is rather broad. I would like to know how to make up properly, since I have seen similar types in show business and know that they are made very attractive.
A See Chapter Eight, Using Base for Feature Miracles, Eyes and Eyebrows.

Q How can a person determine the shape of her face?
A See Chapter Three.

Q The veins in my cheeks were broken due to childbirth. Powder doesn't cover them, and when I wear rouge, they show up even worse.
A See the section on tinted base make-up, Chapter Eight; also Special Skin Problems, Chapter Nine.

Q I have big lips.
A See Chapter Eight, Your Mouth, the Most Mobile Feature.

Q What is the correct rouge placement to make my face appear not quite so round and broad?
A See Chapter Eight, Applying Your Rouge.

Q Is there a way to obliterate permanently those broken capillaries on the sides of the nose and face?
A We do not believe the broken capillaries can be removed, but they can be covered successfully. See the section on bases, Chapter Eight; and Chapter Nine, Special Skin Problems.

Q I would like to know the correct way of making pin-curls. When I finish one, the end hairs are usually sticking out the side.
A See Chapter Eleven, How to Custom-Set Your Hair-Style.

Q What is the correct hair-style for a thin face?
A See Chapter Ten.

Q I have a problem with my hair, so I would like to find a new style. My face is wide at the jaw and narrows at the forehead like an egg.
A See Chapter Eleven, Suggested Hair Styles for the Greatest Flattery to Your Face-Type.

Q How is it possible to minimize a large mouth, especially if the teeth are not even?
A See Chapter Eight, Your Mouth, the Most Mobile Feature.

Q I have had a problem with my hair for many years. I have a very high and rather rounded forehead, and the hair recedes at both part-lines. I am inclined to be heavy. I would like to wear my hair high for height and yet cover my forehead, using a style other than the upsweep as that adds years.
A See Chapter Ten, Hair for Feature Correction and Chapter Eight on bases for correcting the rounded forehead.

Q I have worn my hair the same way for years. How can I create a new and flattering hair-style?
A See Chapter Eleven, Figs. 291-302.

Q I want to know the "do's" and "don'ts" of make-up, hair-style and hats for people who wear glasses all day.
A See Chapters Three, Seven, Eight, Ten, and Fourteen.

Q I am rather small-featured with a round face and close, deep-set eyes. Glasses are a constant necessity. My hair grows out onto the forehead at the sides, making my low forehead narrow as well.
A See Chapter Eight, Eyes and Eyebrows; Chapter Ten and Chapter Fourteen.

Q What can one do to distract attention from eyes that are deep-set and appear small because they are so far back in the head?
A See Chapter Eight, Eyes and Eyebrows.

Q My daughter's forehead from the hairline to the eyebrows is only 2 inches wide. Her hair on the sides starts growing near the temples close to her eyes. What should she do?
A See Chapter Nine on removing hair from the face. Be sure to make the hairline a little uneven, as this gives it a more natural appearance.

Q I am 48, blonde, 5 feet 4 inches tall, and weigh 140 pounds. I have a low forehead and wore bangs in my youth. I'd like to cut a bang again but am undecided.
A A full, heavy bang should not be worn. See Chapters Ten and Eleven, Types of Bangs.

Q I would like to know how to decide the eyebrow line most attractive to me.
A See Chapter Eight, Eyes and Eyebrows.

Q Is there a good liquid powder which one can use which will last better than dry powders? I perspire very much.
A In the case of one who perspires a great deal or has an extremely oily skin, we suggest using a liquid tinted base containing lanolin or other oils. The oily base will absorb the perspiration, whereas a liquid powder tends to be drawn into the skin and does not hold well.

Q My problem is a heart-shaped face with a widow's peak.
A See Chapter Ten, The Hair Contour for You.

Q Can you suggest a style of hair for a woman of 50, tall, with a long face and high forehead? The hair is auburn and shoulder-length.
A See Chapter Ten, The Hair Contour for You; Chapter Eleven, Suggested Hair-Styles for the Greatest Flattery to Your Face-Type.

Q I would like some detailed information on proper selection of eyeglass frames.
A See Chapter Fourteen.

Q My eyes are rather pretty, but under them are very dark circles that detract from their appearance. How can I eliminate these circles?
A See Chapter Eight, Fig. 100, for corrective eye make-up.

Q Two years ago during a pregnancy my face started showing dark brown marks on the forehead and each cheek. How can I camouflage them?
A See Chapter Nine, Special Skin Problems and Birthmarks.

Q My problem is a cowlick.
A See Chapter Eleven, Parts of Beauty.

Q I am 41 years old and wear glasses. Should they be rimmed or partly rimmed for a short face?
A See Chapter Fourteen.

Q My greatest difficulty has been finding a suitable hair-style for my facial type. It is hard to say what facial type I have. It is square at the jawline and tapers at the eyebrow line into a smaller square at the hairline.
A See Chapters Three and Ten.

Q My hair, which was very dark brown in my younger days, has been dyed from the time gray started to show. The color looked very natural until about five years ago. Then the dark, almost black dye looked very artificial to me. I am now in my middle forties. The problem is really with my husband, since I would like to let the natural color come through; but whenever I mention it, my husband says he likes it dark.
A As we grow older, the skin coloring tends to change. The hair usually begins to change in color about this same time. It is Nature's way of softening the effect of the skin-color change. Dyeing the hair the same color that it was fifteen to twenty years before has a hardening effect on the features. If it is necessary to keep the hair dyed, it should be dyed to the same color tone as the original, but two to three shades lighter.

Q My face is full and round. How should I wear my hair?
A See Chapter Ten, The Hair Contour for You.

Q Is there any way of reducing the legs?
A See Chapter Twelve.

Q I have a small narrow face. I cut my hair short because I don't know how to comb it.
A See Chapter Ten, The Hair Contour for You.

Q What can I do about wrinkles around the eyes and forehead?
A See Chapter Eight on bases; Chapter Nine, Complexion Beautifiers, and You Can Build a Face.

Q How can I achieve a pretty mouth when I have a short upper lip and a full bottom one?
A See Chapter Eight, Your Mouth, the Most Mobile Feature.

Q Will you please explain the proper method of applying rouge?
A See the sections on Rouge in Chapter Eight.

Q What kind of hair-style would you recommend for someone with a long neck?
A See Chapter Ten, Hair for Feature Correction.

Q I have large features and a short neck. Should I wear my hair short or long, low or parted high?
A See Chapter Ten, Hair for Feature Correction.

Q I am over 50 and wear a hearing aid. What hair-style is best for me?
A See Chapter Three to determine your face-type. If your face is not too broad or round through the ear area, wear soft curls or waves over the ear, tapering to the nape of the neck. The hearing aid cord can be pinned under the hair. There are hearing aids now available which are camouflaged as earrings or other fashion accessories. One type is contained in an eyeglass frame.

APPENDIX C

Beauty Progress Chart

This chart is to help you check your progress in your march to beauty. To be most effective it must be answered thoughtfully. When, for example, you rate your progress on the subject of make-up, you must consider not only the extent of your increased skill but also the skill with which you have adapted this new beauty know-how to your particular needs. This means that you must have mastered all the steps of make-up. It also means that you know how and when to vary your make-up, how to dramatize your good features and minimize your poor ones. It means additionally that you have acquired the skill to make the magic of make-up do its full and most beautiful work on your behalf.

To help you rate yourself to best advantage, we have included herewith an explanation of the intent of each of the ten subheadings listed on the chart. Read these before checking your beauty progress.

Face: To achieve the highest possible score in this department you must have learned all the characteristics of your face-type and determined how to use your ever-increasing beauty skill to take full and breath-taking advantage of your particular face-type. In a word, if you give yourself a perfect score, it means you think you've done everything possible for your face. So—if your face looks about the same, you rate yourself accordingly—0; if it looks better than before—5; if there is a marked improvement—7; if it looks better than you ever thought possible—10. This same type of reasoning applies to your scoring in each of the remaining departments of the chart.

Make-Up: Before you rate yourself on this subject, remember that this covers such questions as: Have you mastered all the steps of make-up? Do you take all the time you need to apply your make-up skillfully? Do you vary your make-up to suit the occasion? Do you follow the principles of light and shadow in applying your make-up and, consequently, do you know how to accentuate your good features and minimize your poor ones?

Skin: The most important question here concerns whether or not your skin has shown a marked improvement. If your skin was perfectly clear at the outset, this department will test whether or not you used your new beauty knowledge to dramatize its fine color and its beautiful texture. It also is a test of whether or not you have remembered to follow your cleanse, lubricate and stimulate beauty routine each and every day.

Hair: This department is self-explanatory. All you have to do is look in the mirror and see if your hair is at its shiny, lustrous best. If it isn't, it's time to start studying anew the chapters on this subject.

Hands: Do you cream them after every washing? Do you give yourself a good and professional-looking manicure? Do you use them to feminine advantage? Do you protect them when doing housework, etc.? Don't overlook the dramatic and beauty value of hands.

Figure: Have you brought your figure into line? Have you exercised each and every day? Do you zealously diet and exercise to keep yourself trim and healthy as well as beautiful? (All of this, of course, is done only with your family physician's approval and consent.)

Added Skills: If you have learned one new beauty skill since starting this book, give yourself a score of 2. If, by the time of the second check, you have learned a second skill, give yourself a score of 4. If you have learned two additional skills, give yourself a score of 6. In a word, you get a score of 2 for each new beauty skill, and you give yourself credit for each skill you have learned from the time of your first progress check. This means that if, on the first check, you have learned one skill, your score is 2. If you do not learn a new skill by the time of the second check, your score remains 2. (You haven't lost the previous skill but you haven't learned any new ones.) Add two points for each new skill learned.

Beauty Bonuses: This means just what it says. Have you given yourself any beauty treats like extra facials, special tricks with make-up, special tricks with clothes or color to make you look your very best?

Beauty Setbacks: Briefly, have you lessened the number of times you let yourself slip back into the old helter-skelter beauty routines?

Beauty Budget: Do you refuse to treat yourself to loveliness by not taking enough time or by failing to budget for beauty? Worst of all, do you like the things that keep you from beauty more than you like being your most beautiful self? You do—if you fail to follow a strict beauty plan each and every day. Please, no excuses!

MY BEAUTY PROGRESS CHART

	Score	1st Week	2nd Week	3rd Week	1st Month	2nd Month	3rd Month	4th Month	5th Month	6th Month
I. FACE										
About the same	0									
Better than before	5									
Marked improvement	7									
The best possible	10									
II. MAKE-UP										
About the same	0									
Better than before	5									
Marked improvement	7									
Spectacular results	10									
III. SKIN										
About the same	0									
Better than usual	5									
Decided improvement	7									
Flawless	10									
IV. HAIR										
About the same	0									
Better than before	5									
Marked improvement	7									
Lustrous, healthy, well-groomed	10									
V. HANDS										
About the same	0									
Prettier than before	5									
Soft, lovely, well-groomed	10									
VI. FIGURE										
Not up to par	0									
Improving	5									
Substantially improved	7									
Perfectly proportioned	10									
VII. ADDED SKILLS										
None	0									
Each added skill, 2	2-10									
VIII. BEAUTY BONUSES										
None	0									
Some	5									
Lots	10									
IX. BEAUTY SET-BACKS										
Lots	0									
Some	5									
None	10									
X. BEAUTY BUDGET										
None	0									
Small	3									
Adequate	7									
Best possible	10									
MY TOTAL										

SCORING: Perfect score for each department is 10. Perfect score for entire test is 100. The closer you come to 100, the closer you come to perfection. At the end of the third and six month, take the Beauty Questionnaire on page 22 as a double check on your progress.

APPENDIX D

Daily Beauty Plan

IF YOU WORK OR GO TO SCHOOL

On arising:

Shower, apply after-bath lotion over entire body, or dusting powder—or both
Apply deodorant
Brush teeth
Cleanse face
Apply make-up
Apply hand cream
Check handbag for needed beauty accessories

Noontime:

Freshen make-up
Apply hand cream after washing

Before dinner or date:

Rest for ten minutes—even if it means putting your head on the desk and just relaxing completely
Cleanse face thoroughly
Brush teeth
Check deodorant
Apply fresh make-up
Apply hand cream

On retiring:

Cleanse face thoroughly
Apply rich emollient (unless you have an oily skin)
Apply hand cream
Apply pads of cotton, saturated with witch hazel, to rest the eyes
Take care of one special beauty problem, such as a facial
Do your exercises, unless you prefer to do them in the morning

IF YOU ARE A HOUSEWIFE

On arising:

Shower, apply all-over body lotion and/or dusting powder. If time is limited, do this after husband leaves for work

Apply baby oil or rich emollient to face, leave on until you go out to shop, etc. If you have an oily complexion, eliminate this step

Brush teeth

Apply deodorant

Apply hand cream and wear gloves while doing housework

Noontime, or thereabouts:

If you are going out socially or to shop, remove baby oil

Cleanse face thoroughly

Apply appropriate make-up

Apply hand cream

Do one special beauty problem some time during the day

Set hair

Before dinner:

Rest ten minutes—no matter what happens

Apply make-up

Shower (You're at home and can do this; the poor working girl can't)

Cleanse face thoroughly

Brush teeth

Apply make-up

Check deodorant

Apply hand cream

Before retiring:

Cleanse face thoroughly

Brush teeth

Since you applied your rich cream during the day, you need not do it now. Many husbands don't like to see their wives with cream on their face or their hair up in curlers, which is why we suggest taking care of these items during the day

Apply hand cream

Exercise—do this in the morning if your husband objects to your doing it before retiring or if your program makes it impossible to exercise at night

APPENDIX E

Beauty Ways and Means

Every well-groomed beauty has these modern beauty aids at hand:

AT HOME

For the face and complexion:
- Cleansing cream
- Soap
- Lubricating cream
- Skin-freshener and/or astringent
- Special preparations such as face packs, extra rich emollients, eye creams, wax or other treatments to remove facial hair

For make-up:
- Make-up base
- Powder
- Rouge, cream, liquid or dry
- Eyebrow pencil
- Eye shadow
- Mascara
- Eyebrow tweezer
- Eyelash curler
- Lipstick
- Lipstick brush
- Powder brush

For the body:
- Body lotion
- Dusting powder
- Deodorant
- Perfume or cologne
- Manicure and pedicure kit
- Shaving kit or depilatory
- Pumice stone
- Bonus: bubble bath

For the hair:
- Combs
- Stiff brush
- Shampoo
- Special rinses (optional)
- Hair tint or bleach (optional)
- Cutting scissors
- Hair pins, bobby pins, hair-setting clips
- Bonus: hand dryer

For your clothes:
- Spot remover
- Dress shields
- Clothes brush
- Shoe-cleaning kit

For your teeth:
- Toothbrush
- Toothpaste or powder
- Mouthwash

AT THE OFFICE

For after-five and daily pick-me-ups:

- Cleansing cream
- Make-up kit
- Hand lotion
- Manicure repair kit
- Small mirror
- Soap
- Deodorant
- Perfume or cologne
- Brush
- Comb
- Toothbrush and powder
- Hair pins, bobby pins
- Needles, thread, pins
- Brush for clothes, shoes
- Tissues, cotton squares
- First aid kit

IN THE PURSE

- Compact with powder
- Lipstick with brush
- Tissues
- Sewing kit
- Small flaçon of cologne or perfume

INDEX

BEAUTY ℞

FOR ______________________________

RECOMMENDATIONS TO ACHIEVE YOUR MOST GLAMOUROUS SELF

The Westmore Individual Analysis Chart

Face-Type ______________________________

Nose ______________________________

Mouth ______________________________

Set of Eyes ______________________________

Color of Eyes ______________________________

Hair-Type ______________________________

Color of Hair ______________________________

Color of Skin ______________________________

Complexion ______________________________

Undertone ______________________________

Highlight	***Shadow***
☐ Under Eyes	☐ Sides of Nose
☐ Temples	☐ Tip of Nose
☐ Cheeks	☐ Jowls
☐ Bridge of Nose	☐ Jawbone
☐ Chin	☐ Under Chin
☐ Jawbone	☐ Tip of Chin

Special Remarks ______________________________

____

____

____

____

Recommended by ______________________________

CPSIA information can be obtained
at www.ICGtesting.com
Printed in the USA
LVHW020850110621
689949LV00005B/48